AIR COMMANDOS
against
Japan

Architects of the Air Commandos: John Alison, Orde Wingate, and Phil Cochran

AIR COMMANDOS against Japan

Allied Special Operations in World War II Burma

WILLIAM T. Y'BLOOD

NAVAL INSTITUTE PRESS
Annapolis, Maryland

Naval Institute Press
291 Wood Road
Annapolis, MD 21402

Library of Congress Cataloging-in-Publication Data
Y'Blood, William T., 1937–2006
  Air commandos against Japan : Allied special operations in World War II Burma /
William T. Y'Blood.
    p. cm.
  Includes bibliographical references and index.
  ISBN 978-1-59114-993-4 (alk. paper)
  1. United States. Army Air Forces. Air Commando Group, 1st. 2. United States.
Army Air Forces. Air Commando Group, 2nd. 3. United States. Army Air Forces.
Air Commando Group, 3rd. 4. World War, 1939–1945—Aerial operations,
American. 5. World War, 1939–1945—Campaigns—Burma. 6. World War,
1939–1945—Regimental histories—United States. 7. World War, 1939–1945—
Commando operations—Burma. 8. Special forces (Military science)—United
States—History. I. Title.
  D790.254.Y35 2008
  940.54'867309591—dc22
                              2008023338

Printed in the United States of America on acid-free paper

14 13 12 11 10 09 08   9 8 7 6 5 4 3 2
First printing

Contents

Preface

Before the Japanese attack on Pearl Harbor, American war planners considered campaigns against the three Axis partners and assigned defeating Germany the highest priority. As the Axis' aggression grew these plans merged into the Rainbow series for war against a coalition of enemies. The United States would defend the Western hemisphere and fight Japan, while Britain and France battled Germany and Italy. After the fall of France in May 1940, the United States planned to join Britain in defeating Germany while containing Japan. Once Germany was beaten the Allies would direct their attention against Japan. Although never formally ratified, the defeat of Germany first became the unofficial policy of the Allies during World War II.

Regarded as a backwater by many, the China–Burma–India (CBI) theater was vitally important to the Allies because it tied down 1 million Japanese troops to ensure China's isolation. Had Japan prevailed over the British in India and Burma, those Japanese forces might have been redeployed to fight elsewhere in the Pacific. By 1943 the Japanese controlled northern and central Burma, cutting Chiang Kai-shek's Nationalist Chinese forces and Maj. Gen. Claire Chennault's 1st American Volunteer Group, the "Flying Tigers," off from their supplies coming through Indian ports. Meanwhile, an airlift known as the "Hump Route" was begun in late 1942 to fly supplies from Ledo in Assam, five hundred miles over the Himalayas.

In December 1942 the Allies launched an offensive in Burma (the Arakan campaign), but it was beaten back. Outnumbered and outgunned, the British could not hope to match the Japanese in conventional warfare. Moreover, the jungle terrain and adverse weather also favored the Japanese. Enter Britain's legendary but quirky Brigadier General Orde C. Wingate, an expert in irregular warfare. Wingate developed the concept of Long-Range Penetration Groups

(LRPGs) to disrupt the enemy's lines of communication. Such groups, he suggested, offered a "greater opportunity of mystifying and misleading the enemy than any other form of warfare; and should be used as an essential part of a plan of conquest to create a situation leading to the advance of the Allies' main forces."[1] Wingate had organized the 77th Indian Brigade, a three-thousand-man force of British, Gurkha, and Burmese troops called Chindits (a corruption of *chinthe*) after the mythical creatures who guarded Burma's Buddhist temples. On February 12, 1943, Wingate launched Operation Longcloth, the objective of which was to penetrate Japanese lines.

Transported by air two hundred miles behind the Japanese, this raiding group wreaked havoc with its hit-and-run tactics, sabotaging transportation, especially cutting the Mandalay–Myitkyina railway line, and otherwise disrupting Japanese lines of communication. But British air resources came up short and failed to provide the support needed, including supplies, reinforcements, and medical evacuation. As a result, nearly 800 members of Wingate's force were killed, and of the 2,200 who came back to India, only 600 returned to combat duty. Nonetheless, the operation marked the first instance of taking the fight to the Japanese, and it, thereby, boosted British morale.

Prime Minister Winston Churchill, an admirer of Wingate's tactics, invited Wingate to outline his plans to Allied political and military leaders meeting in August 1943 at the Quadrant Conference in Quebec. Among those present at the briefings were President Franklin D. Roosevelt, Gen. George C. Marshall, and Gen. Henry H. "Hap" Arnold, commanding general of the U.S. Army Air Forces (USAAF). Arnold did not have to be convinced that Wingate needed American air support. He believed in air power's potential to support guerilla warfare and had coined the term "air commandos." Arnold offered to provide Wingate with many more aircraft than the Briton could have imagined.

Called to the Pentagon for reassignment, Lt. Col. John R. Alison and Lt. Col. Philip G. Cochran expected to go to "where the action was"—Europe. But Arnold had other plans for them. He recruited the two hotshot fighter pilots to organize, train, equip, and command the composite air force that would support Wingate. When Cochran and Alison first arrived in India in November 1943, their mission, called Project 9, presumably had top priority. Arnold told them only to be creative. "To hell with the paperwork," Arnold said. "Go out and fight."[2] On top of everything, Cochran and Alison had to complete their mission within six months so as to avoid operations during Burma's rainy season, which lasted from May to October. Thus, the Japanese would not have time to counterattack before the monsoons inundated the combatants.

Sixty-four years later Maj. Gen. Johnny Alison, USAF (Ret.), recalled with amazement how he and Cochran created the 1st Air Commandos. At first, many supply and personnel officers simply refused to cooperate, telling Alison, "Everybody has a number-one priority." Only after the he and Cochran obtained letters signed by Arnold himself did the two airmen get their equipment, including a variety of aircraft for their composite air force—fighters, bombers, transports, gliders, and even experimental helicopters. In all they assembled an air commando force of more than five hundred men and some 350 aircraft. There were no manuals on how to establish air commandos, but Alison knew he would succeed. As a member of Chennault's Flying Tigers, Alison had flown over the Japanese lines many times.

The Chindits doubted the Americans' ability to deliver, but lacking an alternative, they adopted a wait-and-see attitude. The British and Americans trained together and devised a masterful plan to invade Burma called Operation Thursday. On the night of March 5, 1944, using C-47s towing some eighty gliders, the 1st Air Commandos delivered 539 troops and about 66,000 pounds of supplies 250 miles behind Japanese lines. During the following week, additional transports flown by the Troop Carrier Command and the Royal Air Force (RAF) airlifted some 9,000 more troops and 500,000 pounds of supplies. These included some 3,000 American troops commanded by Brig. Gen. Frank D. Merrill, Merrill's Marauders, under Lt. Gen. Joseph "Vinegar Joe" Stilwell.

Even after Wingate was killed in a plane crash on March 24, Stilwell was able to advance. Operation Thursday resulted in relatively light casualties for the Allies. Only five Allied aircraft were lost in 1,500 fighter sorties, and one bomber went down in 500 sorties. Liaison aircraft evacuated 2,200 soldiers without a single combat loss. Japan's Fifteenth Army, consisting of 100,000 troops, counterattacked across the Chindwin River and reached Imphal, India before being driven back. By July 1944 the Allies' stiff resistance, heavy casualties, and the onset of the monsoons forced the Japanese to retreat.

Although the air commandos were primarily involved in air transport, they were also instrumental in defeating Japanese air assets. They owned Burma's skies and were the first in the USAAF to use aerial rockets. In a March 1944 message Gen. George Stratemeyer congratulated the 1st Air Commando Group (1st ACG) for having "obliterated nearly one-fifth of the known Japanese air force in Burma."[3] In just four months the air commandos destroyed ninety Japanese planes for the loss of four fighters, mounting attacks on bridges, rail facilities, and targets of opportunity.

Operation Thursday proved so successful that Arnold directed forming the 2nd Air Commando Group and 3rd Air Commando Group. News of the operation prompted Gen. Dwight D. Eisenhower, who was engaged in the final planning for the D-day invasion, to summon Alison to England so that he could learn about Arnold's experience in the use of gliders.

Thereafter, the Allies mounted more offensives in Burma, fought through the monsoons, and drove the Japanese to Mandalay, which fell on March 29, 1945. The air commandos were used throughout Burma, and some units fought on in the Philippines and in Thailand, carrying out the Don Muang raid. Several military leaders, who had doubted that the commandos would succeed, reversed themselves and tried to incorporate the air commandos into their commands.

Ironically, the air commandos were in great demand when Allied fortunes were down. But as the war turned in the Allies' favor, the demand for the air commandos' specialization dissipated.

William T. "Tom" Y'Blood completed this history shortly before his death in November 2006. He was a dedicated historian and meticulous researcher of many military history topics, including the World War II air commandos. While he focused on the three main characters—Wingate, Alison, and Cochran—he also accorded appropriate recognition to a great many other air commandos.

Tom certainly intended to acknowledge all of the individuals who helped him in the research and writing of this book. The best we can do in that regard is to mention his colleagues at the Air Force Historical Studies Office at Bolling Air Force Base, Washington, D.C. (Priscilla Jones, Yvonne Kinkaid, Roger Miller, George Watson, Richard Wolf, and Herman Wolk); the staff at the Air Force Historical Research Agency at Maxwell Air Force Base, Alabama (Joseph Caver and Archie Difante); and the history staff at the Air Force Special Operations Command, Hurlburt Field, Florida (Herbert A. Mason Jr. and Cindy Scharf).

JACOB NEUFELD
FORMER DIRECTOR, AIR FORCE
HISTORICAL STUDIES OFFICE

Note: "My husband died in November 2006 just after completing the manuscript for this book. It would not have been published without the dedication and hard work of his friend and colleague, Jack Neufeld, who took the rough draft and crafted it into a fine book. Thank you so much, Jack." Carolyn Y'Blood

Acronyms

ACG	Air Commando Group
ACSEA	Air Command South East Asia
ADS	Airdrome Squadron
AF	Air Force
AFB	Air Force Base
AFHRA	Air Force Historical Research Agency
AFHSO	Air Force Historical Studies Office
ASC	Air Service Command
ATC	Air Transport Command
BG	Bombardment Group
CBI	China–Burma–India
CCG	Combat Cargo Group
CCS	Combined Chiefs of Staff
CinC	commander in chief (used as shorthand for the commander of a joint force, not the president of the United States)
DSO	Distinguished Service Order
EAC	Eastern Air Command
ETO	European theater of operations
FEAF	Far East Air Force
FS	Fighter Squadron/Fighter Section (used in Notes and Bibliography only)
G-3	operations officer
HF	high frequency
HQ	Headquarters (sometimes abbreviated in records as Hqs)
IBS	India–Burma sector
IBT	India–Burma theater
IP	initial point

JAAF	Japanese Army Air Force
JCS	Joint Chiefs of Staff
JICA	Joint Intelligence Collection Agency
JPS	Joint Planning Staff
LRP	Long-rang penetration
LRPGs	Long-Range Penetration Groups
LS	Liaison Squadron
NAAF	Northwest African Air Forces
NATC	Northwest African Training Command
NCAC	Northern Combat Area Command
POM	Preparation for Overseas Movement
POW	Prisoner of war
RAF	Royal Air Force
RCAF	Royal Canadian Air Force
SEA	Southeast Asia
SEAC	Southeast Asia Command
SQ	Squadron (sometimes abbreviated in records as Sq.)
SWPA	Southwest Pacific Area
TAC	Tactical Air Command
TAF	Tactical Air Force
TCC	Troop Carrier Command
TCS	Troop Carrier Squadron/Troop Carrier Section
USAAF	U.S. Army Air Forces
USAF	U.S. Air Force
VCP	visual control party
VHF	Very High Frequency
WAC	Women's Army Corps
ZI	Zone of Interior

PART ONE

Any Place...
1st Air Commando Group

Chapter 1

"The Man" and the Men

For what seemed the thousandth time, the slight, prematurely balding U.S. Army Air Forces officer striding toward the imposing bulk of the recently completed Pentagon wondered why he had been ordered so urgently to report to USAAF headquarters. Lt. Col. John R. Alison was unaware that his old friend, Lt. Col. Philip G. Cochran, was at this time wondering the same thing about himself. What would draw these two men together and lead to the creation of one of the most unique organizations in U.S. Air Force history did not spring from a USAAF need. Rather, it originated with the British and, more specifically, one officer, Orde C. Wingate. Yet the organization that was formed to support Wingate—the Air Commandos—might never have been born but for the vision of an exceptional American officer, Gen. Henry H. "Hap" Arnold, the commanding general of the USAAF.[1]

Wingate was one of those eccentric, extraordinary individuals who seem to turn up regularly in British history. He was not particularly impressive physically except for icy blue eyes that could bore a hole through a person. "The laser beam of his daemonic stare" is how one author described this feature of Wingate.[2] Although often somewhat unkempt in appearance, he also exhibited a certain stiffness. A man of extravagant mood swings who to some even appeared insane, Wingate could at one moment be ecstatic, wherein all he ever wanted or needed was at hand, and at the next moment he could be wallowing in the depths of despair and wondering why his God had forsaken him.[3] Prone to mumbling, Wingate was given to long, rambling monologues replete with, to many listeners, mind-numbingly obscure references. He did not suffer fools gladly and did not hesitate to criticize anyone who disagreed with him or did not measure up to his standards. Naturally, his eccentricities and combative nature made him unpopular with many of his contemporaries. Yet for all his bizarre behavior, Wingate had an innate ability to persuade. It was a strength that carried him far.

Orde Wingate came naturally to the military profession. He was born in India, where his father had been a colonel in the British army. An uncle had served as governor general of the Sudan, following Maj. Gen. (later Field Marshal) Horatio Herbert, Lord Kitchener. A distant cousin, to Wingate's dismay, was T. E. Lawrence—"Lawrence of Arabia." Wingate believed Lawrence had been a poor soldier and, perhaps worse in Wingate's estimation, one who had taken too much pleasure in his cult status.[4] But Wingate never really became part of the British military establishment. He was both a zealot and pro-Zionist, traits not popular in the British army of the time. Serving in Palestine as an intelligence officer in 1938, Wingate organized formations of Jewish settlers leavened with a small number of British soldiers to combat increasingly aggressive raids by Fascist-funded Arabs against Jewish kibbutzim and the important oil pipelines threading through the region. These Special Night Squads were spectacularly successful and earned Wingate a Distinguished Service Order (DSO). They also earned him a swift boot out of Palestine because of his increasingly indiscreet support of the Jews. Thereafter, his passport was stamped, "The bearer of this passport should not be allowed to enter Palestine."[5]

Thus, when World War II started Wingate was languishing in England, not quite a pariah but an officer whom British leaders wished to keep under tight control. His expertise in irregular warfare, however, once again became invaluable when Italy attacked Ethiopia (then more commonly known as Abysinia) in 1940. The Italians vastly outnumbered the British in the region by 10 to 1 (400,000 to 40,000 men), and normal methods of combat would not work against these numbers. The British High Command sent Wingate to Abyssinia to establish an irregular force. Utilizing a group of only about 3,000 Abyssinian and Sudanese regulars, Abyssinian guerrillas, and a handful of British troops, Major (later Lieutenant Colonel) Wingate's Gideon Force routed 36,000 Italians and restored the Abyssinian leader, Haile Selassie, to his throne.

The campaign in Abyssinia and his usual quarrels with superiors and other officers, though, almost cost Wingate his life. He returned to Cairo in June 1941 considerably fatigued from the stress of the campaign and suffering from cerebral malaria. To combat the disease, he was taking great overdoses of Atabrine. (The Egyptian doctor who prescribed the medicine did not inform Wingate that it was a strong depressant, particularly if too much of the drug was taken.) A month after arriving in Cairo, fighting the malaria and the effects of excess amounts of Atabrine, but also depressed and seething with resentment over real and imagined affronts, Wingate attempted to cut his throat. His life was saved by an officer in an adjoining room who heard him crash to the floor. Wingate's suicide attempt left him with a scar extending from ear to ear, a rasping voice, and an odd mannerism. Forever afterward, when Wingate turned his head, he had to turn his shoulders also.[6] It appeared that his military career was over, but, perhaps in keeping with his deeply held religious beliefs, a "guardian angel" appeared in the form of General Sir Archibald Wavell, the commander in chief of the British forces in India since mid-1941.

Wavell knew Wingate from duty in Palestine and from when he had commanded British troops in Abyssinia. He had been impressed with Wingate's efforts in both places. Now, in early 1942, the Far East was ablaze as the seemingly unstoppable Japanese forces seized more and more territory. Faced with a rapidly deteriorating situation in Burma as the Japanese pressed toward the border with India, Wavell decided that the situation required unorthodox measures. The general sent for Wingate in the hope that the younger man could devise plans to stop or slow the Japanese advance in Burma. After arriving in India in mid-March 1942, now-Colonel Wingate threw himself into the task with his customary zeal. Promoted to brigadier in June and with the assistance of Major Michael Calvert, another young officer also versed in irregular warfare, Wingate soon envisioned a long-range penetration (LRP) force operating behind enemy lines. Although he was not alone in conceiving this idea, Wingate was able to capture the imagination of the public and of some of the military in a way others could not. Such a force would be lightly armed but highly mobile. Unlike most others who studied LRP operations, Wingate realized from the beginning that aircraft would be vital to the success of his force's operations. Because of the nature of LRP operations, aircraft would be used both for logistical support and for fire support in lieu of artillery. It was this realization of the importance of aircraft that led to the formation of the Air Commandos.

After obtaining Wavell's approval, Wingate assembled the 77th Indian Infantry Brigade, consisting of British and Gurkha troops, plus some Burmese. The men Wingate gathered were men who were available at the time; they were neither handpicked nor even particularly well trained. The formations that made up the brigade bore such prosaic designations as 142nd Commando Company or 3/2 Gurkha Rifles. Wingate had in mind a more colorful name. A conversation with a Burmese officer provided the name, though not quite accurately. The officer mentioned a "*chinthe*," the half-lion, half-bird stone creature that guards Burmese temples. Wingate misunderstood the pronunciation, hearing it instead as "chindit." Nonetheless, the name Chindit stuck to become one of the more famous appellations in military history.[7]

Wingate's first LRP expedition, Operation Longcloth, began in mid-February 1943. Initially, the Chindits were intended to be used against Japanese lines of communications and in conjunction with an amphibious landing in Arakan,

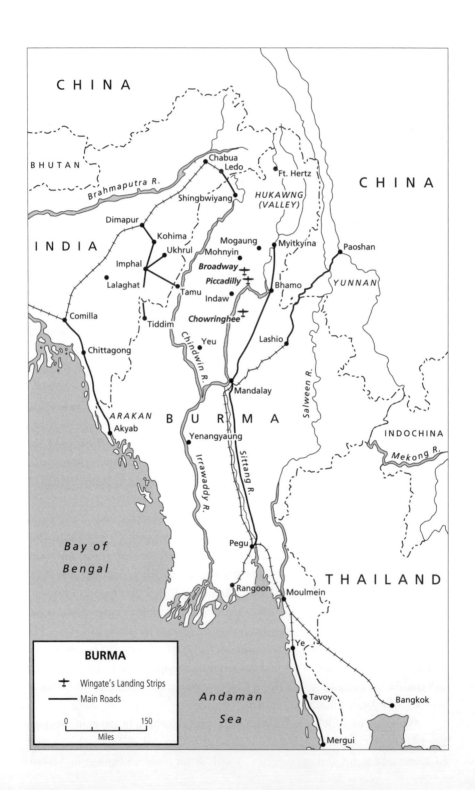

CHINA

BHUTAN

Brahmaputra R.

Chabua
Ledo
Ft. Hertz

Shingbwiyang

HUKAWNG
(VALLEY)

CHINA

Dimapur

INDIA

Kohima

Ukhrul

Mogaung
Mohnyin

Myitkyina

Paoshan

Imphal

Broadway

Lalaghat

Piccadilly

Tamu

Indaw

Bhamo

YUNNAN

Comilla

Tiddim

Chowringhee

Yeu

Lashio

Chindwin R.

Chittagong

ARAKAN

Akyab

BURMA

Mandalay

Yenangyaung

Salween R.

INDOCHINA

Mekong R.

Irrawaddy R.

Sittang R.

Bay of
Bengal

Pegu

THAILAND

Rangoon

Moulmein

Ye

Andaman
Sea

Tavoy

Bangkok

Mergui

BURMA

✦ Wingate's Landing Strips

▬ Main Roads

0   150
Miles

Burma, by a larger British force. When this operation was canceled, Wavell decided to use the Chindits independently in northern Burma. They were to destroy enemy supply depots, cut the railway line between Mandalay and Myit-kyina, and in general create as much havoc as possible. Royal Air Force aircraft would keep Wingate's force supplied. Still, with no major conventional operation to coincide with their actions, the Chindits were on their own.

The first elements of Wingate's force began crossing the Chindwin River late on February 13. At this time the river, which lies about 20 miles inside Burma from the India border, was the front line. Operations over the next eight weeks took a fearful toll. Some 3,000 men began the trek; just 2,200 returned to India, most in late April and early May. Only a handful of the wounded could be airlifted out; the rest had to be left behind. Few of the unevacuated injured survived. Having to leave so many of their comrades behind had a devastating impact on the morale of Wingate's men and left a lasting memory with Wingate himself. Many of the returnees were emaciated. The tortuous march of between 750 and 1,000 miles through dense, inhospitable jungle and across roaring rivers, and the sharp, close-in clashes with the enemy sapped their strength. Of those who came back, many had contracted beriberi and malaria; some were starving. During the last weeks of the operation, despite the tremendous efforts of the RAF, food had become pitifully meager. The Chindits were incapable of further action and would remain so for some time. Of the 2,200 men who came back to India, only about 600 would return to active duty. Yet, operating with what was an inadequate number of aircraft, Wingate had demonstrated the future of jungle warfare.[8]

Wingate's men inflicted some damage on the Japanese and gained valuable information about the enemy and the terrain. Of no less importance, the quality of the British and Indian troops was tested in the crucible of the Burmese jungle. However, because the operation had no follow-up, the Japanese repaired the damage quickly. Made more aware of their vulnerability in northern Burma, the Japanese moved to strengthen their forces in the area. If Longcloth had not made as much of a military impact as had been desired, it certainly had a great impact on morale, both military and civilian, for the ensuing publicity portrayed Longcloth as much more successful than it actually was. Of course Wingate, as the operation's commander, also benefited from the publicity. One of those whose morale rose considerably upon hearing of the operation was British Prime Minister Winston Churchill.

Churchill, who could be brutal in his treatment of military commanders, had a soft spot in his heart for those he viewed as daring or unconventional. His romantic notions were sometimes shattered or, fortunately more often, turned by his senior military advisers toward more realistic avenues. Wingate appealed to Churchill's capricious nature as one of those iconoclasts who often seized his interest. In fact, Churchill toyed for a time with the idea of making Wingate commander of the entire army in India.[9] Desperately seeking some ray of sunshine to break through the darkness of defeat shrouding Burma and the Far East, Churchill delighted in the good publicity concerning Longcloth, and he summoned Wingate to London.

The prime minister was about to attend the Quadrant Conference in Quebec with President Franklin D. Roosevelt. Like most of these wartime conferences, Quadrant, held from August 17 to 24, 1943, dealt with many subjects, chief among them the European theater.[10] Other operations, like those in the China–Burma–India (CBI) theater, had to be considered, however. Unlike talks involving the Pacific, which was an American ocean and which the British usually regarded as their ally's preserve, those regarding the CBI invariably entailed differing viewpoints. In the CBI, the plans of the United States, Britain, and China were a Gordian knot of conflicting interests.

At the Trident Conference three months earlier, the American and British contingents had debated a number of objectives for the CBI, such as enlarging the air route to China, including placing more USAAF units in the theater; limiting offensive operations in Burma during 1943 until after the rainy season; starting an all-out offensive to push the Japanese from Burma after the 1944 monsoon ended in November; and interdicting Japanese sea routes in the theater.[11] These discourses resulted in tentative decisions only, and it was left to Quadrant to finalize them.

Churchill knew that the CBI would be discussed at Quadrant, and he believed that a talk with Wingate could help him prepare for the conference. Their first meeting was short because Wingate arrived on August 4, the day before Churchill sailed for Quebec aboard the *Queen Mary*, which had been pressed into service as a fast troopship. Churchill heard enough from Wingate, however, to impulsively invite him to join the British entourage to Quadrant. In Quebec, Wingate could present his ideas to the Combined Chiefs of Staff (CCS). Still wearing the stained jungle battle dress he had left India in, Wingate joined Churchill's party.

On the 8th, Wingate met with the British chiefs of staff to discuss forthcoming operations in Burma and to present his case for LRP operations. His presentation was well received for, as Roosevelt biographer Eric Larrabee noted, Wingate "was trading in that most attractive and elusive of military commodities, the lure of a conspicuous victory that did not require lavish resources."[12] The chiefs of staff directed Wingate to proffer his proposals in a formal memorandum.[13] Upon his arrival in Quebec on the 10th, Wingate submitted to the British chiefs of staff a memorandum titled "Forces of Long-Range Penetration: Future Development and Employment in Burma," which outlined his views on proposed operations in Burma. In this brief paper of only five pages and a pair of single-page annexes, Wingate described the principles of long-range penetration, how Long-Range Penetration Groups would be used, and the forces required for LRPG operations. LRPGs were used, he wrote, to secure two main objectives: to disrupt the enemy's communications and rear area installations, and to "drive home" the strategic air offensive. Such groups offered "greater opportunity of mystifying and misleading the enemy than any other form of warfare." LRPGs "should be used," Wingate continued, "as an essential part of a plan of conquest to create a situation leading to the advance of our main forces."[14]

As to the employment of the LRPGs, Wingate initially proposed using three brigades: one from China against the Mandalay–Lashio–Mandalay–Bhamo line of communications, a second from India against the Shwebo–Myitkina railway, and a third operating from the Chin Hills against the Kalewa–Kalemyo line of communications. All three operations would occur simultaneously, and the LRPGs would be effective for approximately three months before they would require replacements and replenishment. Wingate also believed that an offensive in the Arakan to coincide with the LRPG operations would be advantageous to the success of both operations.[15]

He went on to discuss what he viewed as the tasks of the main forces following the disruption of the enemy's "interior economy" by his groups. The Chinese forces were to occupy Bhamo and Lashio. Troops of the IV Corps were to occupy the Katha–Indaw airfield and Pinebu to the west. Finally, the Chinese–American force would advance from Ledo to Mytikina, taking care not to develop a threat to Myitkina before the LRPGs were operating in the area so that a certain amount of panic could be generated among the enemy.[16]

Because of the monsoon's effect on operations, timing was extremely critical. If the attacks could be launched just prior to the onset of the monsoon, the Japanese might not have enough time to recover and counterattack before the monsoon struck and put everything underwater. Wingate gauged February 15 to be the suitable date for his LRPGs to begin crossing the "three Rubicons" of the Salween River, the Chindwin River, and the Myittha River.[17]

Wingate also correctly foresaw a Japanese counteroffensive, which he believed was most likely in the IV Corps area in front of Imphal, India. If the Japanese did attack, a pair of LRPGs would be available if they were not yet committed elsewhere. This, however, would naturally cause the main plan to be modified.[18]

In his memorandum Wingate noted that the British were then forming two small LRPGs in India. These two units needed to be enlarged and reorganized, and four more LRPGs needed to be created before the monsoons began in May. At least two additional groups could be raised during the rainy season. Each group would consist of eight columns of between 400 and 500 men per column. Given these numbers, it was obvious such a force would not be small. From the 3,000 men he had used in Longcloth, Wingate now envisioned a force of 26,383 personnel.[19] Although he still planned an overland campaign using mules and a few jeeps, Wingate realized that air support was essential to the success of his LRPGs. He insisted that RAF personnel be attached to each column to direct aircraft for supply drops and for close support.

Wingate requested a relatively modest twelve to twenty DC-3s (C-47s) to drop supplies. He was a bit more desirous of bombers, soliciting one bomber squadron per LRPG. If all eight groups were raised, the number of bombers requested would have totaled between 96 and 160 aircraft. Interestingly, he also discerned the importance of a recent development, the helicopter. Wingate saw the helicopter as the most suitable type of aircraft for use in the closely restricted spaces of the jungle. He did not, however, mention gliders.[20]

Hoping to stimulate Roosevelt's interest in the CBI theater, Churchill introduced Wingate to the president. This meeting was not particularly successful, for Roosevelt was not taken with the dour Briton. Discussions Wingate had with two of Roosevelt's top military advisers on August 17, however, had a more salutary effect. Both Gen. George C. Marshall, the Army chief of staff, and Hap Arnold, the commanding general of the AAF, listened closely to Wingate. His proposals for offensive LRPG operations proved quite persuasive. Marshall, in fact, suggested using American troops for one of the LRPG columns. His interest in this matter led to the establishment of a unit known as Galahad, which later became better known as Merrill's Marauders.[21]

Wingate also piqued Arnold's interest, for the American already had an idea that fit neatly with Wingate's concepts. In May 1942 Maj. Gen. George C. Kenney, then commanding the Fourth Air Force, wrote Arnold proposing an "Air Blitz Unit." This unit would consist of a P-39 squadron, another squadron of B-25s, two transport squadrons, an airdrome defense unit, and an aircraft warning unit. Its total complement would be 503 men. Kenney saw the unit as ideal for North Africa or the Middle East.[22]

Arnold was interested in Kenney's proposal, replying, "The necessity for offensive air forces which are capable of advancing by 'fire and movement' has long presented a problem to me." He went on to say that logistics and the concurrent problem of keeping up with rapidly advancing forces caused great concern. Although concurring with Kenney on the desirability of an Air Blitz

Unit, Arnold had to reject it because it was impossible at that time to divert the necessary forces to man the unit. He went on to say, however, that he was of the opinion that "with certain organization changes, we will have a special section who can handle such matters soon."[23]

A few days later, Brig. Gen. L. S. Kuter, in a memo to the commanding general of the Eighth Air Force that was then headquartered at Bolling Field in Washington D.C., noted that Arnold had written on Kenney's letter that "the Washington air representative of our Commando Division on General Spaats' [*sic*] staff will get busy on this right away.[24] The "Commando Division" apparently disappeared into bureaucratic limbo, for the term never appeared again, but the comment planted the seeds of a special USAAF commando unit.

Although he had read Wingate's memo, Arnold pressed him on what aircraft he needed. In his presentation, Wingate had mentioned light planes only obliquely, stating a need for a light transport—preferably helicopters—capable of landing and taking off in restricted spaces.[25] Now, reflecting on those men who had had to be left behind during Longcloth, Wingate requested light planes to fly out the wounded. Arnold's reply stunned Wingate. Two hundred? Three hundred? The numbers flowed from Arnold. Unaccustomed to such largess in the British army, Wingate was wary. Arnold assured him that he was very serious. Surprised but relieved, Wingate left the meeting with renewed hope for the success of his LRPGs in Burma.[26]

Meanwhile, the CCS and their planners wrestled with finalizing a plan for the defeat of Japan. The Americans still placed a high priority on keeping China in the war, a priority with which the British were not in full accord. Both countries held distinctly different views about China. At the Casablanca Conference in January 1943, Adm. Ernest J. King, the U.S. chief of naval operations, stated that "the key to our successful attack on the Japanese homeland is the geographical position and the manpower of China."[27] The United States thus wished to strengthen China. The British, on the other hand, still desirous of regaining and preserving control of their lost colonies in the Far East, were far more interested in the security of India and Burma and viewed a strong China as a probable threat to British colonialism.[28] Churchill, too, was not particularly thrilled about the possibility of getting bogged down in ground fighting in the Burmese jungle. Despite the fact that it really led nowhere, a thrust through Sumatra appealed more to Churchill's combative spirit. These significantly differing viewpoints colored both countries' strategic thinking concerning the Far East throughout the war.

The United States also intended to base B-29s in China, but the Americans were dissatisfied with what they perceived as British reluctance, despite supposed keen interest in that area, to commit to full-scale operations in Burma, operations the Americans considered essential for success in the CBI. Following Trident, the Americans decided to use Quadrant to pin down the British as to what they were actually willing to supply for a Burma campaign.

A major player in the evolution of CBI operations was Chiang Kai-shek. The Generalissimo, unfortunately, proved more adept at promising to take action against the Japanese than in actually carrying out his promise. Although his influence on CBI policy slowly waned following the Sextant Conference in Cairo in late 1943, Chiang Kai-shek retained enough influence to give both American and British planners severe indigestion as they struggled to formulate a coherent strategic policy for the CBI.

This strategic policy included the creation of a new command for Southeast Asia. The conduct of the war in Burma had troubled Churchill for some time prior to the conference. He was well aware that the Americans were dissatisfied with the progress of operations in the CBI. Perceiving Wavell to be a defeatist, the prime minister appointed him viceroy of India, a civilian post, following the Trident meetings. General Sir Claude Auchinleck became commander in chief for India. But Auchinleck would not have free rein in India and Burma. His job was limited to coordinating the defense of India proper and to the discipline, administration, and training of the Indian army and British forces in India.[29]

Churchill had in mind a supreme commander, à la MacArthur in the Southwest Pacific, to exercise command in East Asia, which, presumably, would include China. Following the MacArthur model, the CCS would exercise general authority over grand strategy for the theater, but the British chiefs of staff would have jurisdiction over matters involving operational strategy. The British chiefs would also issue all instructions to the supreme commander. This official, who would be independent of and equal to Auchinleck, was to prosecute the war with "utmost vigor." In turn, he would have a deputy supreme commander, a naval commander, an army commander, and two air commanders. Of the air commanders, one would be responsible for offensive air operations, and the other would handle air transport operations, primarily the routes across the Himalayas to China that were known as the Hump.[30]

The Americans were not enamored of a command encompassing China, especially one led by a Briton. They pointed out that creating such an organization would encounter serious problems because a supreme commander already existed for China in the person of Chiang Kai-shek. Jealous of his prerogatives and suspicious of British motives, the Generalissimo would be a formidable foe to the formation of the command. Also, one MacArthur was already more than enough for the U.S. Joint Chiefs of Staff to contemplate. They much preferred a command along the lines of Eisenhower in the Mediterranean, wherein the supreme commander was directly under the CCS. This was in keeping with U.S. policy that did not "permit direct subordination to the British chiefs of staff of any command which embraced U.S. means for supporting China."[31]

Faced with this opposition, Churchill clarified the supreme commander's authority and the area to be included in the new command. He eliminated China and selected an eastern boundary that ran along the Burma and Indochina borders with China, down the coasts of Indochina, Thailand, and Malaya to Sumatra, and thence followed an indirect path to longitude 110 degrees east. India would not be part of this command. The previous map shows the revised borders. Instead of being an East Asia command, it would now be known as the Southeast Asia Command (SEAC).[32]

After a few false starts the British nominated Vice Adm. Lord Louis Mountbatten as supreme commander of SEAC. Mountbatten certainly had the right connections, being a great-grandson of Queen Victoria and a cousin to King George VI, the reigning British monarch. He was also the uncle of Philip Mountbatten, who would become Queen Elizabeth II's consort following the war. Unlike Wingate, the handsome and dashing Admiral Mountbatten, with a reputation as a playboy, cut a debonair figure in his tailored uniforms replete with many ribbons. Like Wingate, however, Mountbatten appealed to Churchill's sense of adventure. Early in the war, Mountbatten commanded the 5th Destroyer Flotilla, with the destroyer HMS *Kelly* as his flagship. His tour on the *Kelly* was relatively brief and relatively unsuccessful, as his ship was sunk from underneath him, but his exploits drew tremendous publicity.

Looking for someone with panache and daring, Churchill had appointed Mountbatten chief of combined operations in April 1942. In this capacity, Mountbatten planned the famed, and disastrous, Dieppe raid in August 1942 and numerous other forays by the renowned British Commandos. He also was responsible for the development of the Mulberries, the artificial ports later used during the Normandy invasion. In the late summer of 1943, Churchill again called on the forty-three-year-old Mountbatten to apply his formidable and innovative abilities to bring order to the chaos that was the CBI. Mountbatten's appointment as supreme commander of SEAC and his elevation to admiral were announced on August 24, 1943.[33] Two days later, Mountbatten was in Washington for further discussions on the CBI. He took this opportunity to see Arnold and to find out if the American had been joking when he offered Wingate several hundred light planes. To Mountbatten's delight, Arnold reaffirmed that the planes would be made available. On the 28th, Mountbatten wrote Arnold, "I was most impressed with the way [at Quadrant] you solved the problem of evacuating

Wingate's wounded by providing special aircraft with low landing speed. Many men will owe their lives to you in the coming months in Burma."[34]

Upon his return to Washington, D.C., after Quadrant, Arnold quickly set about to establish an organization to support Wingate and began seeking a man to lead the promised unit. He directed his staff to submit names of promising candidates. Five names appeared on the list of candidates, but the list was swiftly pared to just two lieutenant colonels—Cochran and Alison. Cochran was suggested by Brig. Gen. Hoyt S. Vandenberg, a deputy chief of staff of the Air Staff. Vandenberg, who had served in North Africa, was familiar with Cochran's accomplishments in that theater. Alison, most likely, was Arnold's own choice. The general knew the junior officer from his series of adventures in the Soviet Union, Iraq, and China.

Both candidates were aggressive and successful fighter pilots, but their personalities differed markedly. An effervescent and gregarious Pennsylvanian of Irish descent, Cochran exuded an air of pugnacious confidence. Although completely serious about flying, he did not take his job seriously. He always found something regarding it to make a joke about. His favorite name for almost everyone was "Sport." For Wingate, though, Cochran applied a different name. He called him "The Man."[35]

In contrast to the ebullient Cochran, Alison was a quiet, self-effacing Southerner from Florida. His quiet demeanor earned him the nickname "Father Alison." Although he was not a voluble man, especially compared to the irrepressible Cochran, when Alison spoke, everyone listened. Alison knew what he was talking about, and he usually had the solution to any problem already mapped out in his mind. He knew aircraft, and he knew how to use them most effectively.

The two men had known each other from their aviation cadet days in 1936, where Cochran had been a few months ahead of Alison in flying school. Their friendship continued when both were assigned to the 8th Pursuit Group at Langley Field, Virginia. When the group moved to Mitchel Field, New York, in November 1940, Cochran and Alison went also.

At Mitchel, the two men made lasting impressions on a couple of disparate individuals. Cochran had known Milton Caniff at Ohio State University. Since then, Caniff had become a well-known cartoonist and was drawing the comic strip *Terry and the Pirates*. An avid aviation enthusiast, Caniff, who later created another memorable strip, *Steve Canyon*, wanted to add more aviation sequences to his strip, particularly ones involving the U.S. Army Air Corps. He went to Mitchel Field to gather data for *Terry and the Pirates* and to absorb what the Air Corps was then doing. Knowing Cochran, he naturally gravitated to his friend for advice.

The cartoonist, always seeking new characters for his strip, saw one ready-made in Cochran. It was easy to get a name for this character. His first name was a play on words on both Cochran's given name and his personality—"Flip." For a last name, Caniff used a nickname that Cochran received years before—"Corkin." Thus, Flip Corkin was born into *Terry and the Pirates* to live a long life in the strip.[36]

Meanwhile, Alison drew the attention of former Air Corps officer Claire Chennault, who had become the aviation advisor to Chiang Kai-shek. The Chinese desperately needed modern combat aircraft, and Chennault and several Chinese officials traveled to the United States to purchase them. One of the aircraft they were interested in was the P-40. Alison drew the task of demonstrating the plane to the Chinese. In early 1941 Alison flew a P-40 from Mitchel to Bolling Field in Washington, D.C., for the demonstration. Awaiting him were Chennault, two or three Chinese officials, and a couple of representatives from Curtiss-Wright, the builder of the airplane.

It was a windy, bitterly cold day at Bolling. Alison could feel the skeptical stares of the Curtiss-Wright representatives, who were probably wondering how this slight-appearing flier could possibly show off their plane. Alison, however, was conversant with all of the P-40's capabilities. In addition his fighter was very light. It was not weighed down with armor plating or bulletproof fuel tanks, items that were added later to make the P-40 combat-ready but that also made it much heavier. Alison put on a dazzling display of aerobatics that brought broad smiles to the faces of the factory representatives and caused the Chinese to go into paroxysms of delight. One of the Chinese rushed up to Chennault. "I am convinced. What we need is 100 of those," he exclaimed, pointing at the P-40. "No, General," Chennault replied. "What you need is 100 of those," stepping over to Alison and tapping him on his chest.[37] Alison and Chennault would meet again.

In mid-January 1941, two months after it arrived at Mitchel, the 8th Pursuit Group provided a cadre of officers and enlisted men to activate two new pursuit squadrons, the 33rd and the 57th. Alison and Cochran were part of the cadre for the 57th. Cochran became the 65th Pursuit Squadron's initial commander, while Alison became the squadron's operations officer. Upon the death of the 66th Pursuit Squadron's commander in a flying accident, Alison also assumed command of that squadron. His tenure, however, was short. In March 1941 General Arnold ordered Alison, along with the squadron's maintenance officer, Hubert "Hub" Zemke, to England to help the RAF break in its newly acquired P-40s.[38] After spending some time getting the RAF pilots acquainted with their new planes, Alison received new orders in July to go to the Soviet Union to assist the Russians with the P-40s they would receive under Lend-Lease.[39]

Alison traveled to the Soviet Union with Harry Hopkins, President Roosevelt's special envoy and confidant. Hopkins, who did not mind imbibing once in awhile, attempted several times while en route to the USSR to get Alison to join him in a drink. Though not a teetotaler, Alison usually preferred a soft drink. After his third failure at enticing Alison to take a drink, Hopkins looked at him with a twinkle in his eye and said, "You know, I don't really care whether you drink or not, but please don't look so damned superior."[40]

Hopkins gained a measure of satisfaction after his party reached Archangel. The Russians hosted a formal party to honor him. Like most Russian parties, this one involved many toasts of vodka. According to Alison, they were even toasting seagulls after a time. Somehow, Alison had been able to fill his glass with water, thus avoiding the effects of the liquor. He could escape the consequences for only so long, however.

Soon, the host of the party proposed a toast to the "American flyer who has come so far from his home to help us in the struggle against the common enemy."[41] His glass refilled with the potent Russian vodka, Alison downed his drink in one gulp. Tears welled in his eyes as he sat down and put his face in a napkin. Across the table, an amused Hopkins chortled, "Well, Alison, that shows a definite lack of character."[42]

The first shipment of forty-eight aircraft, along with Zemke, did not arrive in the Soviet Union until October. Until the P-40s arrived, Alison served as assistant military attaché for air at the American embassy in Moscow. This was a frustrating job because the Russians would not allow Alison to see anything of military importance. Finally, the P-40s arrived, and he was able to return to his first love, flying.

Russian engineers, with the assistance of three RAF mechanics who accompanied the aircraft, assembled the P-40s at Archangel, where they had been unloaded. Alison and Zemke then test-flew every one of the planes. The assembly and testing of the aircraft were not without problems, the major one being a lack of technical orders detailing how to assemble the planes. Although promised the documents before leaving the United States, the two men never saw them. So they and their mechanics assembled the P-40s through trial and error. Only after Alison left Russia in January 1942 did the manuals finally arrive.[43]

With their job finished and with the bitter Russian winter settling in to prevent the assembly of more aircraft, Zemke was ordered back to the United States. Alison, however, was directed to stay on in Moscow as air attaché. Unable to accomplish much because of the intransigence of the Soviets, Alison again felt frustrated and sought to be relieved of the job and reassigned to a fighter unit. Luckily, Lt. Col. Townsend E. Griffiss had come to Moscow as General

Marshall's personal representative to find out why the Soviets were not supplying data to the Americans. Griffiss soon surmised that the Soviets, with an almost pathological distrust of their putative ally, were not going to be open about the release of information from their side.

When Griffiss prepared to return to Washington, Alison, desperate to get into a fighting organization, approached the colonel about taking him back to the United States. Griffiss was amenable to this, stating that as Marshall's representative, he could bring Alison back despite a lack of War Department orders. In early January 1942, Griffiss and Alison left Kuibyshev, where the embassy staff had moved when the Germans reached the outskirts of Moscow, to fly to London by way of Tehran. When they arrived in Tehran, Griffiss thought it best for Alison to stay for a couple of weeks, while he went ahead to London. From London Griffiss could use a transatlantic phone to talk directly to Marshall about Alison.

Not wanting to sit idly by while awaiting orders, Alison decided to visit Basra, Iraq, where American engineers were building facilities for the shipment of Lend-Lease supplies through the Persian Gulf to the Soviet Union. Colonel Griffiss saw Alison off by train before proceeding himself by plane to London. Once again he assured the younger officer that his orders would soon be on their way. Alison never received them. Spitfires misidentified Griffiss' plane as it approached England and shot it down. All aboard were killed.[44]

While waiting for the orders that would never arrive, Alison reported to the Army engineer's headquarters. They were thrilled to see him, because they were then receiving A-20s for shipment to the Soviet Union and had only a small advance force of about nine people to prepare the planes. Alison had hardly seen an A-20, much less flown one, but he quickly found himself in charge of the program and of test-flying each of the light bombers. He also had to demonstrate these to the Russian pilots before they flew them to their country. B-25s began to pass through Basra beginning March 12, 1942, and Alison found himself again test-flying an aircraft he had never flown before. Because the Basra airfield was too crowded, Alison shifted the B-25 assembly program first to Shaibah, a few miles northwest of Basra, and then to Tehran, where there were better facilities for bomber assembly.

Alison eventually learned what had happened to Griffiss and wrote to General Arnold personally requesting new orders, particularly requesting a combat assignment. Every few weeks Alison would pen another letter to Arnold reiterating his request. When officers from USAAF headquarters passed through Basra or Tehran, they made it a point to tell him that Arnold did know where he was. Finally, in June 1942 Alison received orders directing him to report to the

Tenth Air Force in India. Alison had requested an assignment under Chennault in China, but at least the Tenth was a move in the right direction.[45]

Alison did not stay long in India. When a pilot scheduled to lead a flight of P-40s to China had a contretemps with some military policemen and could not make the flight, Alison replaced him. Upon Alison's arrival in China on July 21, Chennault made him deputy commander of the 75th Fighter Squadron. The squadron was part of the 23rd Fighter Group, which had just been activated from the remnants of the American Volunteer Group, the Flying Tigers.

Alison experienced a great deal of action as deputy commander and, later, commander of the 75th Squadron. He learned combat flying the hard way; he was shot down on one of his first missions. Early on July 30, several Japanese bombers made a night attack on the 75th's field at Hengyang. In the first successful night interception by the Fourteenth Air Force, Alison destroyed two Japanese bombers. A gunner in one of Alison's victims, however, managed to inflict mortal wounds to the American's P-40. Alison knew he had been hit, but his engine kept running, and the propeller kept ticking over, so it appeared that nothing important had been touched. Then, as Alison scanned his instruments, he saw he had no oil pressure, which demanded a speedy return to base.

As Alison neared the field, flames suddenly spurted from his engine. He dove for the airfield, but he was going too fast to land, and he knew he could not circle back for another try. A river lay a couple of miles from the field, and he planted his flaming P-40 into it. The water swiftly extinguished the fire with an audible sizzle, and the fighter sank slowly from sight. Cut and bruised but otherwise uninjured, Alison swam to shore. His wounds treated, he returned to duty a couple of days later. Even his fighter returned to duty. Salvagers pulled the P-40 from the river, and, checked over and reassembled, it flew again a month later. Alison received the Distinguished Service Cross for this mission.[46]

The salvaging of the fighter was typical for Chennault's Fourteenth Air Force. China lay at the end of a long logistics trail. Not considered an important theater, at least from the air standpoint, equipment was always in short supply in the Far East. Thus, the salvaging and cannibalization of aircraft and other equipment were common. The ability to make do with what was at hand would be a feature of Air Commando operations as well.

Alison flew air-to-air and ground attack missions regularly for almost a year. He also became one of the first Americans to fly an A6M Zero ("Zeke") fighter. The Chinese had captured one of these remarkable aircraft, and Alison flew it from Linchow to Kweilin on November 30, 1942. Although he considered the enemy plane a "beautiful flying machine" and appreciated its outstanding maneuverability, he did not like its light construction and light armament. He felt the P-40 was a better combat aircraft in terms of its abilities to inflict damage as well as absorb it.[47] The day following his Zero flight, Alison became the 75th's new commander. In late April 1943 Alison, then a lieutenant colonel, received orders back to the United States to become the commander of the 367th Fighter Group, which was forming at Hamilton Army Air Field, California. He did not leave immediately because he wanted to break in his replacement and perhaps shoot down a few more enemy aircraft. This decision almost cost Alison his life. During his last mission in China on May 31, 1943, he narrowly escaped being shot down a second time. An enemy fighter caught him from behind and blasted off most of his P-40's rudder, leaving only a few shreds of the rudder and the vertical stabilizer. A spent armor-piercing shell lodged in the back of his seat right between his shoulder blades. Using the skills built up over the years of flying fighters, and a lot of luck, Alison brought his P-40 back safely, landing with two flat tires.[48] Alison decided it was time to go home. During his China tour, he was credited with shooting down six Japanese planes and bagging one more on the ground.

A few weeks after Alison reported to Hamilton, western movie star Andy Devine and his wife invited him and an old friend, Maj. Arvid Olson, to spend a weekend in Malibu.[49] The two officers and their hosts were just starting to relax and enjoy themselves when the phone rang. It was Fourth Air Force headquarters. Alison's weekend of rest and relaxation came to a quick end. Told to report immediately to General Arnold in Washington, Alison asked if he had time to go back to Hamilton to pick up some clothes. Told there was no time, he then asked what he was to do with his car, in which he and Olson had driven from Hamilton. The reply was succinct: "Leave it. Your plane takes off at 11 PM." With not much more than the clothes on his back and the few items he had packed for the weekend, Alison found himself winging eastward in a DC-3. So on a steamy day in late August 1943 Alison headed straight from the airport to the Pentagon, wondering at the purpose of this meeting. About the same time, Alison's old friend, Phil Cochran, was also speculating about the purpose of his call to Washington.[50]

After Alison went to England in March 1941, Cochran remained at Mitchel and was then stationed at both Groton and Hartford, Connecticut. Over the next year he worked tirelessly to whip his squadron into combat shape. It was said that Cochran's squadron seldom lost a battle against its arch rivals, the 64th Pursuit Squadron, because one of his female acquaintances (and he was reputed to have many) lived near the 64th's field. Whenever the 64th took off to engage the 65th in a "battle," she was quickly on the phone to let Cochran know their numbers. Usually, Cochran's men were already in the air waiting when their rivals arrived.[51] Cochran would not take the 65th into combat, however. When the squadron was deployed overseas in July 1942, he was ill and unable to go with his unit. He remained in the United States to train more pilots, all the while badgering personnel officers in Washington to get him into a combat unit.

Finally, in the autumn of 1942 Cochran received orders to participate in Operation Torch, the invasion of North Africa. Because of the relatively untrained status of most of the USAAF fliers at that time, invasion planners calculated heavy aircraft and pilot attrition rates during Torch. Thus, a plan to supply two months' replacements was implemented for the operation. Instead of leading a squadron into combat, Cochran found himself in charge of training replacements for the 33rd Fighter Group—thirty-four pilots and their P-40Fs. Herding a bunch of replacements was not to Cochran's liking, but it was better than nothing, and, as events unfolded, he made the best of the situation.[52]

The P-40Fs shipped out on the British escort carrier *Archer*. She was constructed on a merchant vessel hull, was rather slow, and had a shorter flight deck than later classes of escort carriers. The USAAF planes would have to be catapulted off, a first for the pilots. Cochran drilled his pilots relentlessly during the voyage to North Africa on the proper catapult technique, even though all he himself knew about the subject was contained in a brief pamphlet he had been given prior to embarking and from a telephone conversation with a Navy officer.

Although the American fliers and the British sailors got along well with each other, the trip was not comfortable. Rough weather caused the top-heavy *Archer* to roll and bob unpleasantly, causing much seasickness and some minor accidents. Cochran had more than his share of the latter. Before reaching North Africa, he received a good wallop on his head when he hit a bomb shackle on one of the planes, a pair of black eyes from walking into a steel door, and lost the caps on two of his front teeth that had been damaged in an earlier accident when he hit his head a second time. Cochran remained snaggletoothed until he returned to the United States.

The *Archer*, part of a follow-on convoy, catapulted off the P-40s on November 14, a week after the invasion. Despite their lack of instruction, most of the green fliers, one of whom was only three weeks out of flight school, launched successfully from the tiny flattop. Two planes were lost, however. One just dribbled off the end of the flight deck when the catapult malfunctioned, but its pilot was rescued. A second spun in immediately after takeoff, killing the pilot.

Cochran's fledglings landed at Rabat, northeast of Casablanca, where he quickly instituted a stiff training program. In addition to the training, patrols were also flown in the vicinity. Because they had no official designation, Cochran named his charges the Joker Squadron. Although he was an outstanding instructor, Cochran had not come to North Africa to train pilots, and he soon became restless and looked eastward to the front lines.

The official records are unclear on whether Cochran was ordered to Thelepte, Tunisia, where two of the 33rd's squadrons were located, or whether he just wandered there, saw the situation, declared himself commanding officer based on his date of rank, and then was left in charge because of his fait accompli. The 33rd's history states, "It [was] characteristic of Cochran, that he took off from Rabat in French Morocco without definite orders and kept on flying east until he couldn't go any farther. That was Thelepte. There he proceeded to learn the lay of the land, the terrain, the disposition of forces, and led reconnaissance missions before anything could be said by those higher up, and then it was too late to change things, because it was obvious that what he was doing was of tremendous importance in that sector."[53]

Another source recounts, "Eventually Cochran and seven other pilots were ordered to fly to Oujda [in northeast French Morocco], where the P-40s were to be taken from them and sent on to the Tunisian front. The upshot was that Cochran arrived at Thelepte to take command, as ranking officer, of two halves of two squadrons of the 33rd which had proceeded to that most forward of all American airdromes."[54]

Many years later Cochran recalled that he had been ordered to lead six replacement pilots and their planes to Thelepte, give the squadron commander the planes and pilots, then return to Casablanca. When his little party reached Algiers, he was told to wait for further instructions because the replacements might be returned to Casablanca. This did not sound right to Cochran, who suspected that things were not going well at the front. A chance meeting with one of the Thelepte pilots who described the fighting up at the front confirmed his suspicions. Cochran decided to press on. As he commented, "I really think that I didn't disobey an order, because I could rationalize that I hadn't gotten it, and I got out of Algiers pretty fast before they could catch me."[55]

Cochran found the fighter unit at Thelepte in pretty bad shape. It had suffered a number of losses, primarily during strafing attacks on enemy positions, and the men were living under primitive conditions. Initially in pup tents, the squadron was dug into caves in ravines around the field after Cochran's arrival. Also, the field was under daily attack by the Germans, and aircraft maintenance was difficult because of the numerous enemy attacks and lack of supplies. The men eventually did learn how to live and operate under these conditions.

Recalling this time in later years, Cochran remarked with some amusement, "Anybody who was in a fighter squadron that had houses that they lived in, had actual mess halls, and all that sort of nonsense, were a bunch of sissies. . . . Our attitude was that we were the roughest, and we were the toughest."[56]

For some time Cochran and his men ran an almost guerrilla-style war. Communications with higher headquarters were often nonexistent or else so poor that the Thelepte airmen could freelance. Realizing both the capabilities and limitations of the P-40, Cochran soon had his fliers attacking ground targets and also staying generally below 10,000 feet. At that altitude, the U.S. fighter could usually hold its own against the superior German fighters. Above 10,000 feet that superiority could prove deadly to the Americans. One of the U.S. squadron's pilots who did enjoy great success against enemy fighters, however, was Capt. Levi R. Chase Jr., who shot down ten planes. Later, as a lieutenant colonel, Chase would become an important personality with the 2nd Air Commando Group in the CBI, where he bagged two more aircraft.

Air-to-air combat was not the Thelepte pilots' forte, however. Day after day Cochran sent his planes out to search for the enemy and to do as much damage as possible. In late December 1942 he added a new wrinkle to his unit's repertoire of tactics. He began loading his P-40s with 500-pound bombs and using them against bridges, buildings, railroad tracks, armored vehicles, troop concentrations, and other targets. It took a while for the fliers to learn how to drop the bombs accurately, but when they did, they became very proficient at their task. After the 33rd's commander Lt. Col. William W. Momyer (later a USAF four-star general) arrived to take charge, Cochran became the group's operations officer. Although no longer running things, he continued to be instrumental in orchestrating the group's missions.

Cochran himself carried out one of the more interesting attacks by the Thelepte-based airmen. Intelligence reports indicated that a major enemy headquarters was located at Kairouan, Tunisia, in the Hotel Splendide. Cochran made a one-man attack on the hotel. Accounts differ as to whether he hit the hotel or an adjacent building, but he certainly stirred up a hornet's nest.[57] Enemy flak holed his P-40, and a patrolling FW-190 severely beat up his plane before Cochran was able to chase off the enemy.

Meanwhile, the Germans retaliated vigorously against Thelpte, pounding it often. It was a nerve-wracking experience for the Americans. These raids whittled down the number of aircraft available for use, and replacements were slow in arriving. The constant operations and attacks, a lack of supplies, poor food, and poor sanitary and living conditions took their toll on the 33rd's men physically and mentally. Before they were finally relieved in early February, all, including Cochran, were on the ragged edge of endurance.

When the 33rd returned to combat in mid-March, Cochran was not with the group. Like most of the other men in the unit, he had been fatigued and drained from the constant operations. He personally had flown sixty-one missions and had shot down two enemy aircraft. His expertise as an instructor, though, was a more valuable commodity at that time than his skill in combat. Brig. Gen. John K. Cannon, commander of the newly established Northwest African Training Command (NATC), directed Cochran to work with a brand-new outfit that had just arrived in the theater. It was the 99th Fighter Squadron, an all-black unit. For the next two months Cochran readied these fliers for combat.[58]

In May 1943 Cochran returned to the United States with a Silver Star, a Distinguished Flying Cross with two clusters, and other decorations pinned to his uniform. He had instructions from Cannon and Lt. Gen. Carl A. Spaatz, commander of the Northwest African Air Forces (NAAF), to tell the Air Staff in the Pentagon how the lack of training in many of the units sent to North Africa was alarmingly affecting the efficiency of air operations. Cochran was glad to be going home because he hoped he would receive command of one of the new P-47 groups then forming.

After delivering his talk on the North African air operations to a roomful of staff officers and other interested individuals in Washington, D.C., on June 3, Cochran waited for his new assignment. The P-47 Thunderbolts appeared, and Cochran was given the job of whipping several new P-47 groups into combat shape. The pilots were all very raw, but they took to his combat-proven techniques like drowning men to life jackets. They devoured every bit of expertise he could impart. Unfortunately for Cochran, his time flying the big "Jug" was brief.

In late August he received a telegram ordering him to report to General Arnold. Cochran's first thought was, "My God, now what have I done?"[59] Cochran, like Alison, found himself trudging toward the Pentagon in the stifling summertime heat of Washington. What the general would tell them would greatly shock them both.

Chapter 2

Project 9

Upon his arrival in Washington, D.C., Cochran first saw General Vandenberg, who he knew had submitted his name to Arnold for a project that remained a mystery to the candidate himself. Cochran was not happy about being called to the Pentagon, for he had just received orders to England. That was where the action was, Cochran believed. When Vandenberg was noncommittal and vague about the project, Cochran grew wary and decided not to accept the job.

After he was ushered into Arnold's office, Cochran thought that he should be candid with the man he believed to be "right next to God." Cochran stated firmly, "I don't want any part of it."[1] Arnold may have been startled by Cochran's frankness, but he did not let it show. Instead, he asked the young officer to give him some reasons for his opinion. Not a man to mince words, Cochran replied that he now had a great deal of combat experience, experience that would be useful in Europe, where he was presently slated to go. He did not want to be sent to "some doggone offshoot, side-alley fight over in some jungle in Burma that doesn't mean a damn thing."[2]

By then General Arnold's patience was wearing thin. He halted Cochran's discourse with, "I don't know what kind of Air Force office I'm running here when guys come in and tell me that they are not going to do something!"[3] Cochran immediately quieted, and the meeting continued in a more restrained tone. Still trying to get out of the project, which Arnold had still not fully explained, Cochran mentioned Alison, whom he praised highly and who, he assured the general, was really the man for the job. Arnold, whose nickname "Hap" belied a steely inner strength, was not about to let Cochran off the hook. Not unkindly, but letting Cochran know that he would make the proper decision, Arnold told him to "get out of here" and that he would soon know what his future assignment would be.[4]

Arnold saw Alison next and was offered complaints similar to those from Cochran. Alison, having just received command of a fighter group destined for Europe, did not take well to the idea that a great opportunity to participate in what most USAAF fighter pilots believed to be the big show would be lost. Again, Arnold had to calm one of his fliers. He told Alison to come back the following day.

As directed, the next day, August 30, two rather depressed men met in Arnold's outer office and commiserated with each other over what the fates appeared to be doing to them. Both were still determined to get out of whatever job the general was offering. Soon, they were called into Arnold's office. In addition to Arnold, Vandenberg and Maj. Gen. Barney M. Giles, chief of Air Staff, were present.[5]

"Boys, I've got a big job for you," Arnold greeted Cochran and Alison.[6]

"That's fine, General," the pair replied cautiously.

Arnold told them about Wingate, whom neither had ever heard of, and what the British officer had done in Burma with his LRPGs. Continuing, Arnold described the Quadrant Conference and his talks with Wingate about the composition of an air unit to support the ground troops of the LRPGs.

Although Cochran was normally the loquacious one, it was Alison who interrupted Arnold with, "General, what are you going to give us to do this with?"

"I'm going to give you some L-5s [small liaison aircraft]," Arnold replied.

There was a brief pause, then Alison spoke again. "General, I'm a fighter pilot," he said. "I have a fighter group at Hamilton, and in a few months I'm going to be taking it to England, and I expect to see some pretty exciting warfare. I've spent my career in the service learning to be a fighter pilot. I've had one year of combat experience. I like the business, and I believe that I can be of value to the Air Corps. If all you're going to give me is some L-5s, you don't need me, and I don't want the job."

Cochran jumped into the silence that ensued. "General, he doesn't exactly mean that," Cochran said.

"Yes, I do mean it," Alison shot back.

"Now, wait a minute, boys," Arnold said soothingly. "Here's what I really want you to do." Leaning back in his chair, he quietly but forcefully outlined his plan. Since returning from Quebec, Arnold had mulled over what would be needed to support Wingate. The light planes were only a starting point. Arnold had a much larger force in mind. As he discussed his vision of the project, Cochran and Alison quickly sensed their leader's enthusiasm for this project. The "military entrepreneur" in Arnold, as Alison later described this aspect of Arnold's personality, impressed the pair greatly.[7]

What Arnold wanted was not just to support Wingate, but to spearhead the operation. As he said, "The next time [Wingate] goes in, I don't want him to walk. I want him to go by air. I want to demonstrate that we can use ships in the air just like we use ships on the sea. I want to stage an aerial invasion of Burma."[8] Although he never actually stated it, both Cochran and Alison believed the general meant, "Go over and steal the show."[9] Arnold then threw in a clinching argument, knowing that it would appeal to the creativity and resourcefulness of the two young officers. They would be given virtual carte blanche, a No. 1 priority, to obtain anything they needed to organize a force. If Vandenberg and Giles winced at Arnold's munificence, they uttered not a word. In fact, neither spoke during the entire meeting.

By this time, Cochran and Alison had become fully absorbed in the concept the general was espousing. When Arnold asked which of them wanted the assignment, they replied almost in unison, "Can we both go?" Arnold chuckled his agreement. As to who would command the force, Arnold, believing Alison to be the ranking officer, named him commander. Alison protested, saying that his friend was senior by a few months. Arnold brushed off the protestations with, "Oh well, make it a co-command."[10]

As was predictable, such an arrangement proved unworkable. Within a month the pair settled on a normal chain of command with Cochran as commander and Alison as deputy commander. Nevertheless, the two men thought so much alike and respected each other so much that at times they did operate, unofficially, as co-commanders, each making decisions for and about the force as needed.[11]

Arnold stated that the project they were undertaking, which was initially designated Project 9, was top secret and that Cochran and Alison could not tell anyone what they were about. He repeated, however, that they would be given a No. 1 priority to obtain men and equipment. Time was of the essence, Arnold emphasized, because Cochran and Alison would be expected to take just a few months to train and equip an entirely new kind of organization, move it to India, establish bases, and then lead the new organization into combat. Arnold closed the meeting with an airy, "To hell with the paperwork. Go out and fight."[12] Some months later Arnold conceded that these words may have been a personal whim because he knew a solid organizational structure was a prerequisite for modern war. He had every confidence, though, that Cochran and Alison would succeed at whatever task was given them.[13]

Though both had gone into the meeting wanting desperately to get out of the assignment, Cochran and Alison left it eager to take on Arnold's challenge. They quickly set up shop in the Hay-Adams, a Washington hotel, and began assembling their unique organization.[14] They had no table of organization, equipment prescribing numbers, or specialties of personnel and equipment. Project 9's structure would have to be built from scratch. Making the force the right size was especially important. If it was too small, it would be unable to perform its mission; if it was too large, it would be unwieldy and, again, unable to perform its mission.

The mission, as Arnold saw it in a September 13 memorandum for General Marshall, was fourfold:

1. Facilitate the forward movement of the Wingate columns.
2. Facilitate the supply and evacuation of the columns.
3. Provide a small air covering and striking force.
4. Acquire air experience under the conditions expected to be encountered.[15]

From this somewhat amorphous mission statement a recognizable entity coalesced, but before they could finalize any kind of structure for their force, Cochran and Alison realized they must talk to Wingate. After all, they would be supporting him, and they needed to know how he viewed their role. Cochran flew to London, while Alison, a better administrator than his friend, stayed in Washington to contact people and obtain equipment.

Cochran's trip began on an almost farcical note.[16] Upon his arrival at Mountbatten's headquarters, Cochran was ushered into a conference involving a number of British naval officers, including Mountbatten. Cochran was introduced, and the meeting began. Every now and then one of the conferees would look at him. He would smile or nod, and they would smile or nod back and resume their discussions. The session was almost over before Cochran and Mountbatten realized that the American was in the wrong meeting. This one had been concerned with SEAC shipping matters.

An amused Mountbatten invited Cochran home for lunch to make up for the misunderstanding. Cochran found himself in the company of several senior British officials and the Soviet ambassador to Great Britain. Following lunch Mountbatten sent Cochran to the War Office to see Wingate. The tiny, grim office where Cochran met Wingate was in stark contrast to the enjoyable luncheon surroundings.

This first meeting of the two men proved unpleasant for both. Cochran attempted to explain to the general that he had all kinds of aircraft to support the LRPGs, but it seemed to him that Wingate was not interested in what he had to offer. Rather, it appeared that Wingate was putting down the American and that he considered the offer standard American "hot air." Although irritated, Cochran persisted in trying to find out what Wingate planned.

He received a typical Wingate peroration. Instead of a one-word or a one-sentence reply to Cochran's questions about long-range penetration, Wingate launched into long monologues on not just LRP, but also on the effect of rainfall on Burmese monasteries, his battles with British officials in India, and bits and pieces of history having no relation to the topic being discussed. Wingate's raspy voice and mumbling speech also made it difficult for Cochran to understand what he was saying. Cochran "sat there wondering what it was all about."[17]

The meeting finally ended. It had not been an auspicious beginning to an undertaking that would require the pair to work closely together. Animosity crackled between them. Nevertheless, they decided to meet again the following morning, although both probably were not looking forward to it.

Remarkably, the next meeting, if it did not mark the complete resolution of all personal differences between them, saw Cochran and Wingate come to an agreement on how the Americans could help Wingate's LRPGs. Again, Wingate delivered a lengthy discourse on a variety of subjects, but as he talked, a lightbulb went on in Cochran's mind. Too, Cochran was now more familiar with Wingate's speech pattern, and he could follow more closely what the general was saying.

What caught Cochran's attention was Wingate's description of how he had used radios in both Abyssinia and Burma to control his columns as they moved forward. "I began to realize," Cochran commented later, "that what he was doing on the ground was what we did in the air, and how we vectored aircraft, and how we sent them out and followed them and brought them back."[18]

With this as a starting point the two men saw that they could work together to conduct operations behind enemy lines. Cochran asked Wingate what sort of air support he wanted. As he had done at the Quadrant Conference in Quebec, Wingate emphasized the need for light planes to evacuate the wounded. He also stated that transports would be valuable to move heavier cargo. Cochran said that he could supply a fighter force to attack the enemy when the Japanese threatened the LRPG columns. "What about bombers?" Cochran queried. The RAF would supply those, came the reply.

Cochran wondered what kind of timetable they were looking at. Wingate's response was not reassuring. He planned to attack in early February, after the monsoon season had ended in Burma. That was five months away. Cochran promised, nonetheless, that his planes would be ready. The meeting finally broke up, and the two parted. Each still had reservations about the other, but each realized that they could work together and that what they could accomplish cooperatively would be a milestone in tactical operations.

If the relationship between Cochran and Wingate had gotten off to a prickly start, the one between Cochran and Mountbatten went swimmingly. Mountbatten had been so taken with the airman that he invited Cochran to stay with him and his wife while he was in London.[19] The SEAC commander even offered the American the use of his car. This proved useful on Cochran's last day in London. An old polo injury had flared up in Mountbatten's hand. Cochran drove him home to pick up clothes and then to the hospital for treatment. The admiral was hospitalized for several days, unable to see visitors.

Following his recovery Mountbatten wrote Arnold on September 10 about several matters pertaining to the establishment of the SEAC. The admiral also wrote enthusiastically about Cochran. He added, "If the other officer [Alison] you have chosen is as good we shall certainly be in clover."[20]

En route back to Washington, Cochran's flight was delayed in Iceland by weather. While waiting in the officer's mess for the weather to clear, Cochran noticed a great hubbub. When he inquired what was going on, he was told that General Arnold was there and that he and the noted Arctic aviator Bernt Balchen, who was then in the USAAF, were going to give a briefing to all the stranded passengers.

In the briefing room Cochran sat across from Arnold, figuring he had nothing important to report to his superior. He did notice that every once in a while Arnold peered quizzically in his direction. Finally, an aide came over and told Cochran that the general wanted to see him.

"Cochran, what are you doing here?" Arnold asked.[21]

Cochran replied that he had been to England to see Wingate. This appeared to startle Arnold, for it had been hardly a week since he had appointed Cochran and Alison to the Project 9 job. He appeared pleased, though, that his choice was showing great initiative. Arnold mentioned that he had just been in England, also. "It's too bad you didn't get to see Mountbatten," he continued. "I would have wanted you to see him, but he is in the hospital."

Resisting a smile, Cochran declared, "Yes, General, I know; I took him." He then described to the flabbergasted Arnold, who had been unable to see Mountbatten, how he had come to drive the admiral to the hospital. An impressed Arnold laughed and said, "You'll do." He then asked if the young officer wanted to fly back to Washington with him. Cochran declined, believing that it would probably take "forever" to return while Arnold stopped at other bases.

Upon his return to Washington Cochran rushed to meet Alison and, based on his talks with Wingate, discuss what they needed in the way of equipment and men. The trip back from London had given Cochran time to reflect on what kind of force would be most useful to Wingate. Given Arnold's unspoken command to "steal the show" and what he had gleaned from his visit, Cochran began to visualize a much larger, much more combat-capable force than what light planes and cargo aircraft would afford. In the back of his mind also lurked the half-serious thought that if they kept enlarging the force, perhaps Arnold would become disgusted and they would not be sent to Burma.[22] He also came to the con-clusion that Wingate could exploit a so far little-used type of aircraft—gliders.

Meanwhile, Alison, in an example of how he and Cochran seemed to oper-ate on the same wavelength, had reached the same conclusion concerning gliders. Also, while Cochran was in London, Alison had obtained an office in the Penta-gon. The two now met there to flesh out their organization. Because they were virtually inventing their force as they went along, the number of planes, person-nel, and a multitude of other items had to be carefully, but speedily, calculated. From the beginning, they knew their force was a single-purpose organization that would operate for only three to six months and would have a minimum of personnel and equipment.[23]

Their first consideration for aircraft was, naturally, light planes for the evac-uation of wounded. Two types stood out, the L-1 Vigilant and the L-5 Sentinel, both built by Stinson and, later, Vultee.[24] Powered by a 295-horsepower radial engine, the two-seater L-1 had outstanding short takeoff and landing charac-teristics. Well suited for operations from unprepared airstrips, it could take off in less than 250 feet and land in less than 150 feet. It could also be used as an ambulance plane.

The L-5 was newer and smaller than the L-1 but also a two-seater. Powered by a 185-horsepower radial engine, it was marginally faster than the older plane. Because of the smaller engine, however, it needed a longer takeoff roll. The Sen-tinel could also be fitted with a stretcher for medical evacuation.

Next to be considered was a transport to haul Wingate's heavier equipment, as well as evacuate wounded. There really was no other choice than the ubiq-uitous Douglas C-47 Skytrain, known more commonly today as the "Gooney Bird." This outstanding aircraft, which soldiered on in various air forces well into the last part of the twentieth century, could carry six thousand pounds of cargo or twenty-seven fully armed troops or twenty-one paratroops or up to eighteen stretchers.

Whereas the L-1s or L-5s could fill the low end of the transport spectrum and the C-47 filled the high end, Cochran believed he needed another aircraft type to bridge the gap between the two types of planes. On his way back from Lon-don, his plane had stopped in Gander, Newfoundland, where Cochran noticed a muscular-looking aircraft parked on the ramp. When he asked what it was, he was told it was a Noorduyn Norseman, used since 1935 by Canadian bush pilots flying in the interior of the country. It was powered by a 550-horsepower radial engine and could carry eight people or an equivalent load of cargo. Cochran remembered that plane and decided it would be perfect for his purposes. As it turned out, the USAAF had recently begun purchasing the aircraft, which the service had designated the UC-64A.

Because Wingate had stated that the RAF would supply the bombers when Cochran's and Alison's unit reached India, the two Americans did not list any of these types of aircraft for their organization. Cochran, however, had promised Wingate fighter support, and he and Alison initially chose P-38s. These twin-engine aircraft had long range, good firepower, and, given the terrain and distances involved, the safety of a second engine.[25] This request was denied, however, and they settled on an aircraft with which Cochran was familiar, the P-47 Thunderbolt. In any event, the P-47s did not materialize either, and another fighter, the North American P-51A Mustang, had to be procured. An early version of what became one of the classic aircraft of World War II, the P-51A was powered by an Allison 1,300-horsepower inline engine, was armed with four .50-caliber machine guns, and could carry either two 500-pound bombs or two 150-gallon drop tanks.

The gliders that Cochran and Alison decided Wingate needed were of two types. The first, and most important, type was the Waco CG-4A. This fabric-covered wood and metal design could carry fifteen fully armed troops, including two pilots, or more than 3,800 pounds of cargo. Its unique upward-hinged nose provided easy access to the cargo compartment for jeeps, 75-mm howitzers, or other bulky items. The second glider chosen was the Aeronca TG-5. This small, three-place training glider saw little use with the unit.

Finally, Cochran and Alison decided that they needed an even more unusual mode of conveyance than gliders. Igor Sikorsky had only recently shown that the helicopter was a practical and useful flying machine, not just an interesting toy. His XR-4 had been demonstrated to government and military officials in 1942, and a production contract had been signed. Thirty XR-4s were ordered initially. The first three were designated YR-4As, and the remainder YR-4Bs. These aircraft were two-seaters and were powered by a 180-horsepower radial engine. Given the novelty of helicopters at that time, their performance was not the best. These early helicopters had a maximum speed of only 75 mph, a service ceiling of eight thousand feet, and a range of 130 miles; nevertheless, their unique capabilities would be useful in the Burmese jungles.

Large items such as aircraft were not the only equipment Cochran and Alison sought. Uniforms, small arms, medical supplies, and numerous other articles were added to their shopping list. Realizing that the standard USAAF uniform was not practical for jungle use, the two Project 9 leaders obtained the distinctive U.S. paratrooper jacket and trousers. With its many large pockets, this garment could hold a variety of objects such as first aid kits, extra ammunition, and food that would be handy in the jungle. For shoes, Cochran and Alison somehow arranged to get U.S. Marine Corps jungle boots.

Cognizant that their men would very likely be in close contact with the enemy on the ground, Cochran and Alison sought more and different weapons than was normal for a USAF unit of comparable size. Paratroop and jungle knives became standard issue. Waving their No. 1 priority wherever they went, they acquired some of the first M1A1 .30-caliber folding stock carbines made. All of the men, not just officers, were required to carry a pistol. Cochran also attempted to get Thompson M1 submachine guns for everyone, though it is doubtful that the unit actually received them all.[26]

Cochran and Alison probably went a bit overboard in their quest for equipment. If one or two items were sufficient, three or four were even better. One of the few instances in which they did try to cut back concerned typewriters. Cochran, a firm believer in fighting not writing, saw little use for the twenty-four typewriters his staff said were normal for an organization of Project 9's size. He pared that number to three, but eighteen typewriters were sneaked back onto the equipment list. "That was the only equipment they ever got by me," he later lamented.[27]

Armed with the following shopping list, the two men met with General Arnold on September 13, 1943:

- Thirteen C-47s
- Twelve UC-64As
- One hundred CG-4s [The TG-5s were not mentioned.]
- One hundred L-1s/L-5s
- Six YR-4s
- Thirty P-47s

Additionally, 87 officers and 436 enlisted men were requested to man the force.[28]

Arnold scanned the list then gave it to his staff for comment. No serious concerns were voiced, and that same day, Arnold forwarded the request to Marshall for his approval. This was received swiftly, and Cochran and Alison's "Air Task Force," as Arnold then described it, was in business.[29]

On October 4, 1943, the War Department directed the first personnel allotment for the manning of a "Provisional Air Commando Force." This allotment consisted of 87 officers, 75 flight officers, and 361 enlisted men, the same number of people that Cochran and Alison had requested the month before.[30] Almost three months later, on December 20, the War Department increased the strength of the Air Commandos to 127 officers, 60 warrant officers (the position of flight officer being eliminated), and 353 enlisted men, a gain of 17 men.[31] Following its arrival in India and the addition of men from other units, the Air Commandos still numbered less than 1,000 men. Yet these few hundred were to do the work of what was normally accomplished by more than twice that many men.[32]

Obtaining the best equipment was one thing; obtaining topflight personnel was another. From the outset both Cochran and Alison realized that they would need the best men available and that getting them would require a call for volunteers. Cochran later wrote that "no limitations were placed in the selection of personnel. The personnel were chosen by their eagerness to fight and on their ability to make maximum use of the equipment at their disposal. As nearly as possible an attempt was made to obtain specialists in each field to head each department of the unit. These people were picked with consideration for their personalities as well as consideration for their technical abilities. Personnel were volunteers and leaders were chosen as nearly as possible from officers who had seen combat duty."[33] Cochran and Alison relied on personal knowledge or friendships with individuals to recruit men they knew would be good leaders of the various sections of their growing force.

To help with the growing administrative workload, Maj. Samson Smith joined as executive officer. Former Flying Tiger Maj. Arvid E. Olson came on as operations officer, and Capt. Charles L. Engelhardt, an old squash partner of Cochran's, became administrative assistant. Later brought on as officers were Capt. Robert E. Moist as adjutant, Maj. Richard W. Boebel and Capt. Temple C. Moore as intelligence officers, and Royal Army Captain K. Richmond as liaison with Wingate's headquarters.[34]

Heading the fighter force was Maj. (later Lt. Col.) Grant Mahony, a friend of Alison's. A veteran of the disastrous early days in the Philippines and Java, Mahony had shot down four Japanese planes and had three more probables. He had also flown in China. Mahony's deputy was Maj. Robert T. Smith, an American Volunteer Group ace credited with 8.73 planes. Following the Air Commandos' arrival in India, Smith became a lieutenant colonel and commander of the bomber section and was replaced by Maj. Robert L. Petit, who had seen action on Guadalcanal.

The transport force consisted of three sections. The C-47 section was commanded by Maj. William T. Cherry Jr., with Capt. Jacob P. Sartz as his deputy.

Cherry had been the pilot of the plane in which Eddie Rickenbacker was riding when it went down in the Pacific, leading to a rather celebrated stay on rafts for weeks before their rescue. In command of the gliders was Capt. William H. Taylor Jr., with 1st Lt. Vincent J. Rose as deputy. The UC-64A section was led by Lt. Col. Clinton B. Gaty, assisted by Capt. Edward Wagner.

The light plane force was led by Maj. Andrew P. Rebori, who had been recommended by Taylor. Not a highly skilled pilot, Rebori nevertheless possessed boundless energy, a loud, boisterous voice, and natural leadership. Four "squadrons" of light planes and helicopters commanded by Capt. Everett F. Smith (also the section deputy), Capt. Wilbur H. Edwards, Capt. William W. Arnold, and 1st Lt. William C. Lehecka operated under Rebori.

Other important members to the staff included Maj. Edwin B. White (supply); Capt. John H. Jennette (engineering); Maj. Ernest C. Bonham (communications); Maj. Robert C. Page (medical); 1st Lt. Charles L. Russhon (photo), who joined in India; and 1st Lt. Patrick H. Casey (900th Airborne Engineer Company, Aviation), whose unit was also added to the force in India.[35]

Alison recalled years later that when he and Cochran began drawing up the plans for their organization they thought, "This will be easy."[36] It did not turn out quite that way. Because of the secrecy surrounding their project, they soon found that just because they wanted something, not everyone was going to hand it over to them without question. "You can't have it," a supply or personnel officer would often tell them.[37]

"We need it."

"What are you going to use it for?"

"We can't tell you."

This last statement was often greeted with gales of laughter, laughter that only grew louder when Cochran or Alison said, "Well, this is Project 9, and it has an A No. 1 Priority, given it by General Arnold."

"He gives everybody an A No. 1 Priority," came the reply.

If persuasion did not work and their requests did become stalemated, Cochran and Alison then resorted to typing a letter, having Arnold or Giles sign it, then taking this back to the reluctant party. This usually worked, and their organization grew. One particularly complicated issue, however, concerned the helicopters. The first YR-4s, of which there were only a handful, were still undergoing service testing at Wright Field, Ohio. Naturally, Materiel Command was not keen on letting an almost completely untested vehicle be sent into combat. The command was not sure helicopters could stand the stress of combat operations; they were not even sure they were safe to fly.

Talking with the helicopter project officer, Cochran told him that they needed the YR-4s and that they were going to get them. "It will have to be over my dead body," the project officer retorted.

"Well, so be it," the stubborn Cochran answered. "It is going to be over your dead body."[38]

There the matter stood, with Materiel Command refusing to turn over the helicopters and Cochran refusing to take "No" for an answer. Some movement was made in late October when Cochran arranged for the training of eight pilots in YR-4 maintenance and flight and for the training of a warrant officer in YR-4 maintenance.[39] On October 22 the Requirements Division at USAAF Headquarters asked the Allocations and Programs Division to initiate action to obtain the helicopters for Project 9. In turn, the latter division forwarded the request to the Munitions Assignment Committee (Air) for approval.[40]

Prior to the committee's decision, however, Cochran left the United States for India to make preparations for the arrival of his troops. Before he left Cochran told Alison, who remained behind to supervise the movement overseas and to gather last-minute equipment, "John, don't come unless you bring those helicopters with you!"[41]

To Alison's dismay, Materiel Command continued to rebuff the requests for the helicopters. Finally, on November 10, after much discussion, the committee's chairman, Brig. Gen. Eugene L. Eubank, directed Materiel Command to release the helicopters for use in Burma. Shortly thereafter four, and then six, of these precious aircraft were turned over to Alison.[42]

Meanwhile, the men newly recruited to lead the various sections of the Project 9 unit scattered across the country on recruiting trips of their own. Because of the overall force's small size, the men they picked to fill out the sections would have to be able to do a variety of tasks. Noted as a very aggressive fighter pilot, Mahony picked out a number of like-minded individuals for his section. Among these were 1st Lt. Paul G. Forcey, who had served in the Royal Canadian Air Force (RCAF) in Europe and Africa, and Capt. John A. Kelting, who had received the Silver Star and Purple Heart for combat in the Pacific.[43]

Captain Sartz proved so adept at getting volunteers that when he arrived at one field, the commanding officer refused to let him interview anyone and made it quite clear that Sartz's presence was unwelcome.[44] Several of the transport pilots had already served with distinction, including Capt. Richard E. Cole, who had been Doolittle's copilot on the Tokyo raid. First Lt. John K. "Buddy" Lewis held another distinction: He had been an All-Star third baseman for the Washington Senators.[45]

Enlisted men made up the bulk of Major Rebori's Light Plane Section. Most were sergeants, and more than 50 percent of these were college graduates. One had been with the Polish air force, another with the Chinese air force. Although many, for various reasons, had washed out of flight school, this did not prevent Rebori's enlisted men from later becoming excellent, indeed daring, pilots. They had also been chosen as much for their mechanical abilities as for their flying skills. This was in keeping with Cochran's determination that his men would have to master many different jobs.[46]

Perhaps the most energetic of the section leaders was Captain Taylor. On September 25, two days after being selected for the Project 9 unit himself, Taylor was at Bowman Field in Louisville, Kentucky, to recruit personnel. To ensure that he would get only the most enthusiastic individuals for his section, Taylor told potential volunteers that they should be "prepared for long, tough work" and to "entertain absolutely no consideration of gain in any form in recompense for their duty."[47] Over the next couple of days he personally selected seventy-five glider pilots and fifteen glider mechanics. He also obtained the services of another four mechanics from Sheppard Field, Texas. A quick stop at Maxton Field, North Carolina, netted six additional glider mechanics. All of these men were directed to report immediately to Seymour Johnson Field, in Goldsboro, North Carolina. There, the glider training began in earnest.

One of the men Taylor recruited was probably the best-known person in the force, Flight Officer John L. Coogan. Moviegoers knew him better as Jackie Coogan, the film star. He had been a glider instructor before joining the Air Commandos, and Alison considered him a first-class pilot, though a "little irregular and brash."[48] The ex-husband of the reigning sex symbol of the day, Betty Grable, the balding Coogan was a multifaceted individual, being an excellent musician, an amusing raconteur, and an outstanding swimmer. In addition to piloting a glider, Coogan also served as an assistant operations officer for ground operations and was in charge of the rope crew inspecting all tow ropes.[49]

It was at Goldsboro that Capt. Weldon O. Murphy, one of the unit's medical officers, cast a perceptive eye at the growing conglomeration of Air Commandos. He wrote, "More deeply impressed than these physical elements was the character, as I saw it, of the various groups assembled. The quiet, self-assured arrogance of the fighter pilot; verbose, reckless demeanor of the glider pilot; sallow, resentful indifference of the C-64 pilot; questionable enthusiasm of the helicopter pilot; the reassuring stability of transport pilots; the efficient, regulation-offending activity of ground personnel. Common to the entire group was a great enthusiasm; overwhelming eagerness to be about the business of performing what had been told them was a dangerous mission."[50]

Cochran and Alison had hoped that they could get their entire force assembled at Seymour Johnson, where they could train together. This proved impossible. It did not help that the force's movement date was shifted forward from December 15 to November 1, which left hardly one month to accomplish substantive training. Too, some members were just arriving at Seymour Johnson as others were starting their trek to India. Nonetheless, most of the men were instructed in the use of small arms, such as the M1A1 carbine and the M1 submachine gun.[51]

Driven by the realization that they had little time to whip their men into shape, Captain Taylor and Major Rebori were especially active in making use of what time they did have. Hour after hour Rebori made his men practice short-field takeoffs and landings and flying just off the deck. To make sure they got the idea, he made them land between ropes that had been placed across the runway. Soon they were making takeoffs and landings in less than 600 feet.[52]

Rebori also devised a rack that could be mounted under each wing of his light planes. Special "parapacks" weighing up to one hundred pounds for the L-1 and seventy-five pounds for the L-5 could then be attached to the racks for the airdropping of supplies to ground troops. In addition, a wedge-shaped trough was designed for installation in the rear cockpit. Supplies loaded in this trough could be delivered by the simple expedient of banking the airplane sharply.[53]

Major Taylor, meanwhile, kept busy traveling around the country acquiring the latest equipment for his gliders, some of which was still being tested. He obtained brand-new automatic tow devices that used a gyroscope and were sort of a poor man's autopilot, the latest aerial pickup (or "snatch") equipment, the newest arresting chutes for his gliders, and more items to ensure that his men would have the best equipment to take into combat. Unfortunately, much of this materiel would not be received until the unit was overseas.[54]

Despite the lack of equipment for training, Taylor drove himself and his men relentlessly day and night. His section had only ten CG-4As assigned to it, and of these, just three could be kept in flying condition. Thus, most of the training had to be done on the small training gliders, the TG-5 and the Frankfort TG-1, a two-place craft. Only twenty-five men received pickup experience in the big glider, but all pilots did do at least two snatches in the TG-5. Each pilot logged a meager five hours' flight time before shipping overseas.

Much of the tow work was done by Rebori's L-1s. A couple of C-47s were borrowed from the 436th Troop Carrier Squadron and the 439th TCS to give the glider pilots some experience with the aircraft they would operate in combat. Two of the C-47 pilots, 2nd Lt. Patrick J. Driscoll and 2nd Lt. Vincent L. Ulery, proved to be so accomplished that they were asked to join the project. It appears that the two C-47s were primarily used to perform standard tow plane–glider takeoffs. Not until October 28, when the men were beginning to leave for India, was a C-47 obtained for pickup practice. Practice with the C-47s, unfortunately, lasted only about a week before being terminated because of the movement overseas. The light plane pickup operations were also discontinued on November 5.[55]

In the brief amount of time he had for training, Taylor focused on using the automatic tow device, the double tow, and flying in the low tow position. The double tow, where a C-47 pulled two gliders on unequal lengths of towline, caused some controversy when it was employed during the lift of Wingate's troops into Burma. Taylor, however, believed that this method was the most efficient use of the transport–glider combination, no small consideration bearing in mind the small size of the force. He also preferred to use a low tow position for the gliders.

Taylor gave five reasons for using this position. First, the automatic tow mechanism required it. Second, it was much easier for the glider pilot to see his tug by looking up than by looking down, where the tow plane could be obscured against the ground. Third, flame from a C-47's exhaust stacks, which would give a relative position of glider to tug, was easier to see from below at night. Fourth, there was less drag in the low position than in the high. Finally, with glider pilots looking up, they were less likely to see ground fire aimed at them and, thus, less likely to attempt evasive action that could prove disastrous.[56]

Given the harsh pace of training, accidents were bound to occur. One pilot was killed in a TG-1 during a snatch session at Wright Field. Several others were injured when they undershot their landing grounds. Three premature releases resulted in no injuries and minor damage to the gliders. On one of his visits to Goldsboro, North Carolina, Cochran, perhaps reflecting on these accidents, ruminated, "People that fly airplanes are fool enough, but anyone that gets into one of these gliders is a damn fool."[57] Nevertheless, both he and Alison flew in the gliders to get a feel for how they worked.

On September 17 General Arnold wrote Maj. Gen. George Stratemeyer, commanding general, USAAF, India–Burma Sector (IBS), CBI, notifying him that the "1st Air Commando Force" would be activated in the theater. Although hearkening back to the exchange of letters between Arnold and Kenney, this seems to be the first appearance of the name Air Commando. Arnold told Stratemeyer that the force would be assigned to Lt. Gen. Joseph Stilwell, commanding general, U.S. Army Forces, CBI, for administration and supply, but would operate under Mountbatten's control. He directed Stratemeyer to provide the force with all necessary supplies. Arnold ended his letter, "It must be understood that the 1st Air Commando Force is set up for operations under the CinC, South-East

Asia and, more directly, with Brigadier Windgate's [sic] LRP groups. . . . This is the first time that such a composite unit has been organized and as we will all watch its progress closely, everything you can do to help pave its way will be appreciated."[58]

A little over a week later, beginning September 29, a flurry of messages passed between Washington and India concerning Project 9. The most important of these related to the substitution of P-51As for P-47s. Stratemeyer agreed to the substitution, provided the fighters came with the project and did not have to be filled out of theater stocks. Arnold replied on October 2 that thirty Mustangs would be shipped to arrive by December 1.[59]

Another important topic discussed by Stratemeyer and the Air Staff in Washington pertained to the addition of an airborne engineer company to the Air Commandos. Cochran and Alison had discussed this matter at great length with the Air Staff, but the request had been turned down when Stratemeyer indicated that he could not grant a priority to an engineer company for movement to India. He did, however, offer to assign the 900th Airborne Engineer Company, Aviation to the project. At this time the 900th was the only such unit in the CBI. Its addition to Project 9 proved prescient, for the company provided major assistance to the force prior to and during Operation Thursday.[60]

On October 28 the first man left Goldsboro for India. The trickle soon swelled to a flood as men received their orders overseas. Morale was high, and most men were looking forward to the experience and perhaps seeing some combat. When questioned by those wondering about their priority status, the general attitude seemed to be, "Blow it out! I'm from Project 9!"[61] Their exuberance occasionally got out of hand. One of the first group of light plane pilots were issued loaded small arms in addition to the rest of their equipment. While waiting in the Goldsboro railroad station for the train to take them to Miami, a few of the pilots decided to test their small arms prowess on various fixtures in the station. The following groups were not issued ammunition.[62]

Because of the urgency of the move, all men traveled by air. The scheduled route was Miami–Trinidad–Georgetown, British Guiana [now Guyana]–Belem and Natal, Brazil–Ascension–Accra, Gold Coast [now Ghana]–Khartoum, Sudan–Aden, South Arabia [now Yemen]–Masirah Island–Karachi. All aircraft assigned to this move navigated this general route. The unit's C-47s, which usually flew the route in formations of five, were the only aircraft of the force to fly to India. The rest were either deck-loaded on escort carriers or crated for shipment.

Leaving Alison behind to supervise last-minute details, Cochran, accompanied by Major Page, the senior medical officer, and others, left Washington on

November 1. On the 3rd, they boarded an Air Transport Command (ATC) C-54 for the flight to Karachi. Except for a five-day delay in Natal because of engine problems, the flight was uneventful. Cochran and his party arrived in Karachi on November 13.[63] By mid-December, the remainder of the force had gathered in India. Assembling and testing the aircraft, and checking over all of the equipment would be tedious and time-consuming, but the men of Project 9 were ready to show the world what they could do.

Chapter 3

A Cacophony of Plans

As Cochran and Alison assembled the Air Commandos, Mountbatten and Wingate were hard at work organizing their own forces. Mountbatten had been given one of the most convoluted command arrangements of the war. This was recognized by everyone from the start. When Marshall radioed Stilwell about the new SEAC chief and the various command relationships, he commented, "This is of course an abnormal arrangement but everything connected with this theater has of necessity been set up frankly on such a basis."[1] Mountbatten's relations with the highest ranking American in the CBI, Lieutenant General Stilwell, were especially complex. In his afterwar report, Mountbatten described Stilwell's various responsibilities:

> As Deputy Supreme Allied Commander, Lt. General Stilwell's allegiance was to me; and in my absence from the theater he was directly responsible, through the British Chiefs of Staff, to the Combined Chiefs of Staff. As Chief of Staff to the Supreme Commander of the China theater, his allegiance was to the Generalissimo. He therefore had to consider China policy and interests, although these sometimes conflicted with the requirements of South-East Asia strategy—particularly since the Generalissimo and the armed forces of China were independent of the Combined Chiefs of Staff. Thirdly, as U.S. Commanding General, CBI, Lt. Gen. Stilwell was responsible to the U.S. Joint Chiefs of Staff (JCS): reporting to, and receiving administrative orders directly from, the War Department at Washington. As I had operational control of forces in Southeast Asia, and the Generalissimo had operational control of forces in the China theater, when opposite arguments were submitted about the employment of all resources in SEAC in order to aid China, Lieut. General Stilwell had either to remain silent or oppose the policy of one or other of his superiors.[2]

Mountbatten had another, not always subtle, problem concerning Stilwell. The American was a rabid Anglophobe. Stilwell continually belittled the efforts of his allies, not always without cause. Nonetheless, his attitude, which permeated his staff, too often created rancor where none should have existed.

Stilwell gained additional responsibilities when he assumed operational command of the northeastern Burma front, which received the designation Northern Combat Area Command (NCAC). Although Mountbatten had overall command of Chinese forces in SEAC, Chiang Kai-shek insisted that they had to come under Stilwell's direct command. In part because of his Anglophobia, Stilwell did not want to operate under the command of SEAC's land forces CinC, Gen. George Giffard, but did agree to place himself and his NCAC troops temporarily under the operational control of a British officer he did like, Lt. Gen. William J. Slim, commander of the British Fourteenth Army, which was established in mid-October. This complex and serpentine arrangement proved generally adequate.[3]

SEAC headquarters became fully operational on November 16, 1943. Prior to this Mountbatten appointed three CinCs for his naval, land, and air components. They were Admiral Sir James Somerville, General Giffard, and Air Chief Marshal Sir Richard Peirse. Unlike the commands of his fellow CinCs, which were composed primarily of British Commonwealth units, Peirse's Air Command South East Asia (ACSEA) was truly a combined force. Although Commonwealth air units always outnumbered their American counterparts overall, U.S. squadrons were not a tiny minority, and American units actually predominated in air transport. Eventually, more than 60,000 USAAF personnel served in the CBI.[4]

While Mountbatten's appointment was well received by most Americans, the choice of Peirse was not a particularly felicitous one. Many U.S. airmen viewed Peirse as lackadaisical and unaggressive. In June 1944 SEAC Deputy Chief of Staff Maj. Gen. Albert C. Wedemeyer wrote about Peirse to Brigadier General Kuter, who was then the assistant chief of Air Staff for plans at USAAF headquarters. In this letter, Wedemeyer stated, "Hap [Arnold] told me that Peirse was a non-entity and I can tell you that in almost a year's contact with him, I have never known him to contribute a constructive idea."[5]

Wedemeyer's remarks were seconded after the war by then–Lt. Gen. Charles B. Stone III, who served as Stratemeyer's chief of staff, and by then–Maj. Gen. Howard C. Davidson, the wartime commander of the Tenth Air Force. Both men remarked also about what they perceived as a general lack of aggressiveness by the British in India. This view was widely held by the Americans in both India and the United States, whose impatience to get going with a job sometimes tended to cloud their acumen.[6]

Despite the misgivings of many senior U.S. officers in the CBI, Peirse remained in command of ACSEA until November 1944. It was then, however, that his personal life brought him down. His affair with Lady Auchinleck had been known for some time, but Mountbatten had more of a rapport with Peirse than with Somerville or Giffard, who were much older, and he hesitated to remove the air chief. Negative reports from American sources, though, reached the British chiefs of staff, and they decided Peirse must be replaced. He left quietly for England and an early retirement in late November 1944. Accompanying him home was Lady Auchinleck, whom he later married.[7]

When Mountbatten assumed SEAC command, the air units were operating under separate command arrangements even though both the USAAF and Commonwealth air forces were performing essentially the same functions. Thus, Stratemeyer, who held overall command of the USAAF forces in the IBS and was the senior U.S. airman in the area, took his orders from Stilwell, not Peirse. Stratemeyer had direct control of the Tenth Air Force (though Stilwell held operational control) and of the CBI Air Service Command (ASC). Stratemeyer was also responsible for several other functions, including the supply and maintenance of Chennault's Fourteenth Air Force in China, the air defense of the vital Hump route from India to China, the coordination of ATC activities in the theater, and assisting Stilwell in air matters.[8]

Stratemeyer's role in the CBI required him to make greater use of his political, rather than operational, skills. Arnold realized this, and on August 28, 1943, Arnold wrote Stratemeyer, "This new command setup and your relationships with Generals [*sic*] Stilwell, Mountbatten, and Chennault are somewhat complicated and will have to be worked out to a great extent among yourselves. . . . The success of this complicated command setup depends in a great measure on personalities. If a true spirit of cooperation is engendered throughout this command, it will work. If the reverse is true, it is doomed to failure."[9]

The Americans believed that Stratemeyer should be Mountbatten's air commander in chief. After all, it appeared at the time that the USAAF was more active against the enemy in the CBI than the RAF was. Nevertheless, the British wished to retain control of the top positions in what was essentially a British, although combined, command, and Stratemeyer became Peirse's deputy.

Settling on how to blend USAAF and RAF units into a cohesive organization took weeks of meetings and discussions. For the Americans there were never any doubts that Mountbatten could not be allowed to control ATC operations, nor could he control the Fourteenth Air Force's training and supply units in India. By late November, though, a workable plan was hammered out between the interested parties. Air Chief Marshal Peirse was given unified control of the Tenth Air Force and the RAF's Bengal Command. These forces were then merged into an organization subordinate to ACSEA. This new unit was designated Eastern Air Command (EAC). Stratemeyer assumed command of EAC on December 15, 1943. While not holding the highest position in ACSEA, he effectively controlled all combat units.[10]

Other important decisions followed. Because both the USAAF and the RAF had bombers, fighters, and transports assigned, Stratemeyer and Peirse realized that EAC had to be further divided along functional lines. A Strategic Force consisting of heavy and medium bombers was established under General Davidson, the Tenth Air Force commander. A Third Tactical Air Force (TAF), consisting of USAAF and RAF fighters and fighter-bombers, came under Air Marshal Sir John E. A. Baldwin of Bengal Command. Brig. Gen. William D. Old was named commander of Troop Carrier Command (TCC), which was made up of USAAF and RAF troop carrier units. Finally, a photo reconnaissance force was established. Under this new organization, the operational and administrative integrity of the USAAF groups and the RAF wings would be retained, but the operational staffs of the four new commands would be integrated. Such integration began as soon as EAC became operational. It was under this command setup that the Air Commandos operated.[11]

While the command arrangements for the CBI air units were being hashed out, planning for the 1944 Burma campaigning season and how the Chindits would fit into the overall strategy was well under way. General Auchinleck's India Command staff were heavily involved until Mountbatten's own staff arrived. Before the opening of the Quadrant Conference, Auchinleck had sent a progress report on planned operations from India. General Sir Alan Brooke, chief of the Imperial general staff, introduced this report on the first day of the conference. It was very pessimistic.

Transportation of supplies and lines of communications in India were the general's main concerns. Although approximately 4,300 tons a day of supplies had been projected as required for proposed operations from Ledo, Imphal, and Yunnan, 3,400 tons a day was the theoretical maximum for delivery over the existing lines of communication. Nonetheless, 3,400 was believed adequate for the northern Burma operations. With the launch of Project 9 and the expansion of Wingate's LRPGs, however, deliveries could not meet even the reduced tonnage figures. Auchinleck believed that canceling either the Ledo advance or the Imphal advance, or even both, would reduce requirements enough that the airlift of supplies across the Hump to China would not suffer. The Americans continued to give the Hump route and operations like Wingate's the highest priority because they appeared to offer the best way to keep China in the war.

Auchinleck believed that proposed operations farther south would provide better results than those in northern Burma. He focused on two operations: Bullfrog was an attack on Akyab Island and Ramree Island; Cudgel was an advance south into Arakan. Auchinleck did concede, though, that if these two operations were canceled, priority should then be given to constructing airfields in eastern Bengal.[12]

He concluded:

> Fully appreciate anxiety which exists to start large-scale offensive operations against Burma this coming winter. The course of planning for even the limited operations intended in Northern Burma has brought me to the conclusion that best military course would be to avoid such operations and to concentrate on supply to China by air, at the same time increasing and conserving strength of India and preparing resources for large scale amphibious operations against Malaya next winter. Preparation for these would enable us to bring training of troops to high standard. If they were definitely decided on for 1944–1945 it would be desirable to divert resources earmarked for Akyab to taking the Andamans in the late spring of 1944. We are urgently examining the possibilities of this and will signal results to you.[13]

A small committee was swiftly formed to study Auchinleck's message. This group concluded that either the Ledo or Imphal operations would have to be canceled. Since logistical support to China still was a cornerstone of U.S. policy in the Far East, and the Ledo operation was intended to support construction of the Ledo Road to China, the Americans leaned toward this operation. Realizing, however, that any curtailment of operations in 1943–44 would have a great impact on CBI strategy, the committee asked General Auchinleck to analyze the situation further and to present any new findings to the CCS before Quadrant concluded. The committee assumed that northern Burma operations would continue to receive the highest priority and that the United States would supply the personnel and equipment to enable the lines of communication to operate more efficiently. Given these assumptions, the committee believed that the Ledo and Imphal operations could both begin about February 15, 1944.[14]

On August 23, the penultimate day of the Quadrant Conference, the British presented a summary of messages they had received from Auchinleck in which he updated his views on operations in Burma in light of the assistance offered by the United States. The general remained pessimistic about the proposed operations. He estimated that even with the proffered assistance, his supply situation would still have a shortfall of 102,000 tons on March 1, 1944. Such a deficiency would have to be shouldered by the Ledo operation or shared between the Ledo and Imphal operations.

Additionally, Auchinleck remained skeptical about Wingate's LRPGs and particularly with the junior officer's request to establish a force headquarters to organize and train the new unit. Auchinleck saw this as an attempt by Wingate to set off on his own and not have to answer to higher headquarters. The field marshal also did not believe that Wingate's LRPGs would help at Ledo, stating that "the extensive use of LRPGs in the manner proposed by Brig. Wingate will not alleviate the position since the LRPGs must be followed up by our main forces to hold the ground gained, and the capacity of the L. of C. [lines of communication] will not be sufficient for the purpose."[15]

The British chiefs of staff believed that there were only three possibilities for action in northern Burma during the 1943–44 dry season. The first, and the one which they favored, was to exert the main effort into land and air operations designed to establish land communications with China and to improve and secure the Hump route. This, however, could be done only at the expense of the airlift. A second possibility was to give priority to the China air route. If this was done, sufficient transportation capacity would not then be available to initiate operations in northern Burma. The last possibility was to adopt a longer-term policy and put the main effort into developing the Assam lines of communication so as to make the Hump route secure by the 1944–45 dry season. This would require curtailing land operations and accepting a lower delivery rate to China in the meantime.[16] Following a discussion of the official British presentation at the Quadrant Conference, the CCS agreed that "the main effort should be put into offensive operations, with the object of establishing land communications with China and improving and securing the air route."[17]

Although both sides were in agreement regarding northern Burma, other operations in the area continued to generate much discussion but little resolution. In the CCS's final report to Roosevelt and Churchill, they stated rather vaguely that Project 9 and the LRPs were intended "to continue preparations for an amphibious operation in the spring of 1944. Pending a decision on the particular operation, the scale of these preparations [would] be of the order of those contemplated at Trident for the capture of Akyab and Ramree."[18] The Combined Chiefs also directed that further studies be made of operations against Sumatra, Bangkok, Singapore, and southward from northern Burma. The U.S. Joint

Chiefs put some pressure on their British counterparts to identify the "amphibious operation" as the capture of Akyab and Ramree. The Americans seriously believed the enemy in Akyab could flank the operations in northern Burma and that an assault could forestall this and draw the Japanese away from northern Burma. The British thought that Akyab's capture would not play much of a part in northern Burma either way.[19]

Like Trident before it, the Quadrant Conference did not resolve all the strategic problems that had been brought to it. It did, however, result in the selection of a supreme commander for southeast Asia and in agreements for offensive operations in northern Burma. These operations were to include the extensive use of Wingate's LRPGs. The target date for these operations was delayed from November 1943 to mid-February 1944. The British chiefs of staff disregarded Auchinleck's concerns about the LRPGs, stating that it would be up to Mountbatten to decide who should have operational control of the group. On August 26, following the Quadrant Conference, British chiefs directed Auchinleck to begin planning for the use of LRPGs. Auchinleck's planners and Wingate's staff had just a bit over six months to draw up and execute these plans.[20]

One of the early plans to emerge from Quadrant for operations in northern Burma envisioned two possibilities. The first had two LRPGs moving into the Mansi–Katha area and followed by a light division. At the same time another LRPG would cross the Chindwin to raid the Yeu–Shwebo area while the remainder of IV Corps would advance to the line of the Chindwin. The second plan, and the one favored by the British, reversed the first by sending one LRPG to Mansi–Katha and two LRPGs and a light division against Yeu–Shwebo. In either case, air supply was vital. Already fighting a battle to keep transports flying the Hump, Stilwell warned his superiors at the Pentagon that "longing eyes" were already being directed at ATC aircraft. Stilwell believed that the British, and even some of his own commanders, tended to ask for more air supply than they really needed. How much air transport was actually required by units remained a concern throughout the whole of the Burma campaign.[21]

In early September Auchinleck's staff floated a proposal to bypass Burma in favor of an attack on Sumatra and Malaysia. Since this was against the wishes of the CCS, this proposal sank quickly, but the idea would resurface later. Nonetheless, it reinforced the impression among the Americans, particularly Stilwell, that the British really were not interested in major operations in Burma. Auchinleck's staff then recommended (among other movements) that the British IV Corps, located along the central Burma border, begin a gradual movement toward the Chindwin in January 1944, with "minor activity" (evidently Wingate's operations) occurring only up until February. Another LRP operation would begin an advance from Homalin, on the Chindwin east of Imphal, toward Katha in mid-January.[22]

A refinement of these initial studies was contained in Joint Planning Staff (JPS) Paper No. 107, "Operations in Northern Burma—1944. Course 'B,'" which was issued on September 25. This paper was not a full-fledged study, but rather a brief overview of the strategic situation in eastern India and Burma with possible courses of action outlined to conform with the objective of "the capture of Upper Burma in order to improve the Air Route and establish overland communications with China" as agreed to by the CCS at Quadrant.[23] This JPS Paper was similar to the operations Wingate proposed at Quadrant. It consisted of (a) the capture and retention by British airborne forces of the Katha–Indaw area of Burma,[24] with these forces to be supplied by air during the monsoon; (b) the capture and retention of Myitkyina by combined Chinese and American forces from Ledo; (c) the capture and retention of the Bhamo–Lashio area by Chinese forces from Yunnan; and (d) the advance of the main forces to the above objectives being preceded and assisted by LRP forces.[25]

These northern Burma operations were not to take place in a vacuum. The planners also considered several other major operations to coincide with those in the north. Bullfrog was the attack on Akyab and Ramree; Cudgel was the advance south into Arakan; Culverin, also known as First Culverin, was an amphibious assault on northern Sumatra; and Buccaneer was, in the eyes of the British at the least, perhaps the most doable of these four operations with the available forces because it was an invasion of the Andaman Islands. None of these proposed offensives survived the planning stages.

Regarding the Katha–Indaw operation, the planners visualized using either Wingate's force, parachute troops, or a combination of both. Perhaps still skeptical about the usefulness of the LRPGs, the planners preferred to use paratroopers to capture the Indaw airfields. In addition to problems associated with where to drop these men, however, the 50th Indian Parachute Brigade was still being formed, and it would be some time before it was available. Still, a combination of units was seen as the best solution to the capture of the airfields. The joint planners also noted that Wingate's LRPGs would be supported by an "American Air Task Force" (i.e., the Air Commandos), with this force arriving by December 25, 1943. Because supply for this operation would be entirely by air, the JPS believed that both Katha and Indaw could not be held permanently against a probable Japanese buildup. They therefore suggested holding only Indaw and keeping just a small detachment at Katha.[26]

General Auchinleck's staff, when they reviewed JPS No. 107, did not agree with the proposal to use paratroops and the LRPGs jointly against Indaw. They felt that the function of the LRPGs was more "to draw off forces from the objective than to deliver the assault."[27] Too, they noted that these groups needed time to concentrate their forces in order to obtain the best results. To this end, Auchinleck's staff preferred an assault on the Indaw airfield by paratroops alone, with the LRPGs kept to their "true diversionary role." This problem, the staff concluded, required further study.[28]

The authors of JPS No. 107 believed also that the movement of one of Wingate's brigades to Yunnan, China, at Paoshan would be of material assistance to a successful outcome to the operations in northern Burma. This movement, however, would require the use of one air transport squadron exclusively. More cargo aircraft were needed to fly in reinforcements to Indaw. These tasks and other commitments led the planners to settle on a requirement of twenty-three air transport squadrons by April 1, 1944. At this time, and for the foreseeable future, only five squadrons were available. Where to get the additional squadrons was a quandary.[29]

For this reason, the British chiefs of staff saw the plan as unworkable. They also believed that Auchinleck had proposed a much larger operation than they had envisioned. Auchinleck was told to rethink the plan. Interestingly, the authors of JPS No. 107 believed that horses and mules could not be airlifted to either Paoshan or Indaw—an assessment with which Auchinleck's staff agreed—or that aircraft based in India could support the brigade operating from Paoshan.[30] Cochran's arrival, and his belief that animals could be airlifted, would cause some serious rethinking of air transport requirements and usage.

One week later, on October 2, the JPS issued its Paper No. 109, which focused more on the transport needs for the Indaw operation. It had become apparent that an LRPG operation from Paoshan was unlikely and that the Americans would not maintain it if launched. This meant, however, that instead of supplying two Chindit brigades, the transport force would now maintain three brigades. In addition to this new commitment, the planners had to deal with several revised requirements. They were directed to include an engineer battalion for airfield development and to increase tonnage for unit equipment and the number of Jeeps for the forces. Despite this growth JPS estimated that the aircraft assigned to Chindit support could take greater loads per sortie. Using the higher estimate, the planners believed an assault force would need only between fifteen and twenty squadrons, or a total of 373 to 508 aircraft.[31]

Although this revised estimate reduced the number of transport squadrons required, the planners still faced a probable shortage of cargo aircraft. Despite this concern JPS still believed that using a parachute force to take Indaw was the most desirable option. They hoped that this tactic would force the enemy to dissipate its strength in static defense of other important areas, thus reducing an enemy buildup against Indaw. Chindit operations were not ignored, either, as JPS forecast that the LRPGs would begin their operations on February 15, with the main attack on Indaw taking place one month later. It was obvious, however, that India Command still viewed the Chindits with jaundiced eyes, seeing Wingate's force as capable of little more than diversionary tactics. The main thrust against Katha–Indaw would thus be borne by other, more regular forces.[32]

Based on the new requirements for the operation and the possibility of shortages of transport aircraft, JPS considered the following modifications to their earlier scheme:

- Increase the period over which the landing force would fly in.
- Reduce the size of the landing force.
- Increase the period over which airfield construction equipment would fly in.
- Reduce or dispense with the RAF fighter force to be located at Indaw for air defense.
- Reduce the stocking tonnage and/or increase the period for stockage buildup.[33]

After examining the alternatives to the original plans for the Indaw course of action, the JPS recommended extending the period in which the landing force would be flown in from one week to two weeks, advancing the date on which the engineer stores would be delivered, flying out the parachute force, and stationing four fighter squadrons at Indaw only during the dry months.[34]

The Americans were not particularly impressed by the British plans. In a message to Stilwell, Col. Frank D. Merrill, who was Stilwell's operations officer (G-3), reported from New Delhi, "It does not represent a very substantial contribution by the British towards the conquest of North Burma."[35]

As high command worked on its strategy for operations in the CBI, Wingate arrived in India prepared to show everyone just what his LRPGs, assisted by the Air Commandos, could do. He had remained in London for only a short time after meeting with Cochran before proceeding to India. During that time he picked an old friend of his, Derek Tulloch, to be his staff brigadier general responsible for plans and operations. Wingate, newly promoted to major general, and Tulloch arrived in Karachi on September 16, 1943. While en route, though, Wingate made a disastrous decision that almost brought his plans for LRP operations to an end before they even started.

During a brief stop at the Castel Benito airfield near Tripoli, Libya, Wingate became very thirsty. Instead of waiting to be served a drink, he impetuously seized a flower vase from which the flowers had been removed but in which the water still remained. He quickly downed the entire contents. Without considering what he had drunk, Wingate reboarded the airplane to continue his trip. Unknown to him, the water contained typhoid bacteria that began infiltrating his system.[36]

From Karachi Wingate traveled first to Agra, about 115 miles southeast of Delhi, to check on the training camps that had been set up in that area for his forces. He then went to Delhi to meet with Auchinleck's staff to discuss plans for the use of his troops in Burma. As had happened many times previously, Wingate encountered hostility—not to say actual hatred—from those who disliked him or distrusted his motives. Too often, Wingate's meetings with the JPS degenerated into shouting matches as staff officers brought out every conceivable obstacle to place in the path of his plans. Wingate then would threaten to play his trump card—a direct channel to Churchill via Mountbatten.[37]

It is not known if Wingate ever actually used this card, but it had the desired effect of temporarily quashing opposition. It also served to heighten the animosity of those who disliked him. Unfortunately, Wingate's combative attitude, and what he apparently considered his moral superiority to almost everyone else, also alienated some of those who wanted to be his supporters. It would only be a matter of time before his enemies would seek a reckoning.

Such hostility toward Wingate was shown publicly when he sought office space in the India Command headquarters. Although many lower-ranking officers were afforded well-appointed offices, the India Command staff just could not seem to find space for Wingate. Neither could they provide him a car nor a stenographer, both of which should have been automatic assignments given Wingate's rank. He finally broke through this bureaucratic barrier and was consigned a small office and a few clerical personnel. But while Wingate labored in his office, his staff was relegated to a corridor where they had to work amid the hubbub of passersby and native vendors hawking their wares.[38]

As was typical for Wingate, however, he threw himself wholeheartedly into planning for the Burma operations and gathering troops for the undertaking. The most notable acquisition for Wingate was the 70th Division, a veteran unit that had fought at Tobruk. Wingate, however, intended to break up the division and form the remnants into three new brigades. Auchinleck, who was very fond of the division, and many others were aghast at this idea. They believed that a perfectly good division, which would be of greater value as part of a major offensive in Arakan, was being destroyed to no purpose. The 82nd West African

Division, which was soon to arrive in the theater, was thought to be a better choice because it had been trained in jungle fighting and relied little on motorized transport.[39]

These complaints and arguments failed. The 70th was dissolved and reformed into three independent brigades, the 14th, 16th, and 23rd. The 14th Brigade was commanded by Brigadier Thomas Brodie, and the 16th was led by Brigadier Bernard E. Fergusson. As it turned out, the 23rd Brigade would not be available to Wingate for the upcoming operation. A major Japanese offensive into India forced the brigade's use in the defense of Kohima. Several other brigades, however, rounded out Wingate's Special Force, which was the settled-on name for the LRPGs and which totaled nearly 23,000 men, a far cry from the 3,000 men employed in Longcloth. For security purposes Special Force was designated the 3rd Indian Division.[40]

Reconstituted following the first Wingate expedition, the 77th Indian Infantry Brigade was again made available to Wingate for LRP operations. The unit's commander was now-Brigadier Michael Calvert, who had gained Wingate's attention prior to Longcloth. Brigadier William D. A. Lentaigne's 111th Indian Infantry Brigade had been undergoing LRP training since April. A latecomer to Special Force was the 3rd (West African) Brigade, which was under the command of Brigadier A. H. Gillmore and which did not arrive in India until late November. The contribution of the U.S. military to the Special Force's ground troops was the prosaically designated 5307th Composite Unit (Provisional). The American unit's code name was Galahad, but it later gained immortality as Merrill's Marauders. Galahad, as Stilwell and most of its men preferred to call it, was General Marshall's contribution to ground operations in the CBI. It did not remain long under Wingate, arriving in December and being transferred to Stilwell's control in January 1944.[41]

A tireless Wingate traveled back and forth ceaselessly between his training camps in Delhi and other places to cajole, threaten, harangue, and sermonize his officers and men, and senior officials as well, regarding the importance of the task his force would be undertaking. Time was short. The end of the monsoon season and the consequent start of ground campaigning was not many months distant. Getting his men ready and supplied for combat was Wingate's first priority, and woe be to anyone who came between him and his priority. The constant travel, though, sapped Wingate's energy and left him vulnerable to the insidious infiltration of the typhoid bacteria he had imbibed in Libya. At last, on October 5, his health broke.

It was an inauspicious time for this to happen because Admiral Mountbatten was to arrive two days later to assume his duties as SEAC commander.

Major General Orde C. Wingate, the leader of the Chindits. (U.S. Army Air Forces archives)

The Combined Chiefs of Staff in Quebec for the Sextant Conference. At far left is Vice Admiral Lord Louis Mountbatten. Gen. Henry H. "Hap" Arnold is fifth from the right, and Gen. George C. Marshall is at the far right. (U.S. Army)

John Alison, the 1st ACG's "co-commander." (U.S. Army Air Forces archives)

Lt. Col. Grant Mahony, leader of the 1st ACG's fighter section. (U.S. Army Air Forces archives)

Lt. Col. Robert T. Smith, in front of his personal B-25. (U.S. Army Air Forces archives)

Phil Cochran, commander of the 1st Air Commando Group. (U.S. Army Air Forces archives)

Maj. William T. Cherry Jr., commander of the 1st ACG C-47 section. (U.S. Army Air Forces archives)

The 1st ACG glider section leaders, Capt. William H. Taylor Jr. and 1st Lt. Vincent J. Rose. (U.S. Army Air Forces archives)

Flight Officer Jackie Coogan inspects the vital tow rope fittings before a training exercise. (U.S. Army Air Forces archives)

Led by Barbie III, a group of *Air Commando B-25s pose for a photograph. The white tape on Barbie III was for controlling corrosion around the nose armor plating and was painted over later.* (U.S. Army Air Forces archives)

Cochran greets Mountbatten and Wingate following their arrival for the January 10 night exercise. (U.S. Army Air Forces archives)

Mountbatten, Wingate, and Alison discuss the night's work. (U.S. Army Air Forces archives)

Prelude to near disaster: Mountbatten taxies for takeoff while Cochran waves to onlookers. (U.S. Army Air Forces archives)

An L-5 in typical surroundings: Parapacks containing various supplies are being prepared for dropping to columns operating behind enemy lines. Two parapacks have already been hung on the plane. (U.S. Army Air Forces archives)

Using ink-stained bedsheets, Cochran briefs his men on landing sites as Taylor watches. Broadway is on the left, and Piccadilly is on the right. (U.S. Army Air Forces archives)

Chindits puzzle over photos. First Lt. Charles L. "Rush" Russhon is at the far left, and Cochran has his back to the camera. Alison and Lt. Col. Walter Scott hold the photos, while Air Marshal Sir John Baldwin, Brigadier Michael Calvert, Wingate, and Brigadier Derek Tulloch consider the ramifications. (U.S. Army Air Forces archives)

Wingate scans the skies anxiously as Lt. Col. Clinton B. Gaty waits with a "biscuit gun" to signal another glider to land at Chowringhee. (U.S. Army Air Forces archives)

Air Commando P-51As are lined up neatly prior to another mission. (U.S. Army Air Forces archives)

First Lt. Carter Harman (standing left) flew the first helicopter rescue mission in history. Other members of the helicopter unit include 1st Lt. Frank M. Turney (standing right), Sgt. Alexander Zalman, Sgt. Warren C. MacArtney, SSgt. John A. Manter, and Sgt. James D. Phelan. (U.S. Army Air Forces archives)

Chinese troops board a 319th Troop Carrier Squadron C-47 during Operation Grubworm, December 10, 1944. (U.S. Army Air Forces archives)

B-25s of the Night Intruder Section line the side of the runway at Chittagong between missions. (U.S. Army Air Forces archives)

After being damaged by flak, this L-5 required a good number of patches at Asansol, March 17, 1945. (U.S. Army Air Forces archives)

1st ACG P-47s are lined up awaiting another mission. (Courtesy of Dr. C. W. Getz)

319th Troop Carrier Squadron C-47s crowd the strip at Nyangu after Meiktila was closed because of enemy attacks, March 16, 1945. (U.S. Army Air Forces archives)

At rigid attention, a Gurkha paratrooper leaps into the air from an Air Commando C-47 over Elephant Point. (U.S. Army Air Forces archives)

Wingate had to meet his superior to inform him of the status of the plans. On the 7th, Wingate rose from his sick bed to go to the airfield where an official party had gathered to welcome the SEAC commander. Wingate was conspicuously shunned by those in the welcome party. Just as conspicuously, Mountbatten noticed Wingate standing apart from the crowd and came over to see him. Although he wished to schedule an immediate appointment with the Special Force leader, Mountbatten quickly realized how sick Wingate was. Wingate confirmed his illness and remarked that he was going to the hospital, but he first had wanted to tell the admiral that planning was well under way and that Mountbatten would be briefed as soon as possible.

Following this short meeting, Wingate entered the hospital. His delay in seeking medical help and a series of misdiagnoses by the doctors almost resulted in his death. Wingate remained in the hospital for almost a month, chafing at his inability to do serious planning and railing at the doctors for their incompetence. Fortunately, during this period Wingate was well-served by a pair of subordinates.

Major General G. W. Symes had commanded the 70th Division, and its breakup had been a traumatic blow to him. Made deputy commander of Special Force even though he was much senior to Wingate, Symes nevertheless controlled his personal feelings concerning this experience and gave Wingate his loyalty and, more importantly, his outstanding administrative abilities. The other subordinate was Wingate's longtime friend, Derek Tulloch. Although not particularly good at administration, Tulloch oversaw an outstanding staff. Tulloch was probably Wingate's one true confidant, and because of this close relationship, Tulloch really acted as Special Force's chief of staff. Tulloch and Symes, and their staffs, kept Wingate's plans on course, and on October 25, they opened Special Force's headquarters at Gwalior, India.[42]

Wingate left the hospital in November, but he required several more weeks of convalescence, most of which were taken at either Field Marshal Lord Wavell's or Admiral Mountbatten's residences. During this period Wingate received several messages from Prime Minister Churchill expressing concern over Wingate's illness and wishing him a speedy recovery. It is not known if Wingate actually used these missives to further his purposes, but the knowledge throughout India Command that the prime minister was writing to Wingate personally undoubtedly produced the desired effect for Wingate.[43]

As Wingate fretted and seethed at his enforced confinement, Cochran and the first members of his unit arrived in India. Upon his arrival in India on November 13, Cochran discovered that Wingate was seriously ill. When the American finally saw "The Man," he found Wingate morose and depressed. As Cochran related later, "He looked terrible. He looked atrocious. He frightened me."[44] Wingate stated that American and British high-level strategists at the Sextant Conference had said that the resources to mount the offensive could not now be provided. Something had to be scaled back, and that something was Wingate's operation. Wingate realized this setback would tremendously please some individuals in India Command, and this was a realization that infuriated and depressed him further.[45]

Some years later Cochran recalled that "it seemed that this special Project 9, being what other people laughingly called 'Tragedy 9,' was destined for many barriers. It seemed that things were just getting in our way to stop us. I remember feeling that if Wingate didn't pull out of this illness that he was in, if he weren't to be there, all our efforts were going to go for naught. We would just be assimilated into the theater, and that would be the end of Project 9, because he was the key."[46]

A few days after this first meeting, Cochran and his operations officer Arvid Olson, returned to see Wingate. This time, Wingate went into more detail about his plans. Using a large map spread out on the floor, Wingate described for the Americans how he intended to use his LRPGs. Pointing to various sections of the map, Wingate ticked off the movements of his brigades. One would move east from India into Burma. A second would advance from the north, paving the way for Stilwell's Chinese troops. The third brigade would come from China and head west across the Salween River. All three columns would walk in from their jump-off points and would meet at a point in northern Burma.

It was the third brigade that had created the problem that was so alarming to the strategists. Wingate's force would have to be flown over the Hump to Paoshan in the Yunnan province. This meant that many aircraft would have to be taken off that critical transport route in order to fly the three thousand men of the brigade into China. With Stilwell, Chennault, the Chinese, and the British all demanding air transport for their own operations, it became an easy matter to deny Wingate the use of the cargo planes needed for the Chindit operations.

As he bent over the map, Cochran felt that it was time to broach the subject of gliders to Wingate. He asked Wingate how long it would take for his troops to move through the jungle. When Wingate replied that it would take one month, Cochran said that he could fly the same distance in a little over one hour. Not yet discerning what Cochran was leading up to, the Special Force commander responded with a bland, "I suppose so."

The increasingly exuberant Cochran then blurted out to the senior British officer that because he was already flying in Wingate's equipment, soldiers could be flown in as well. Using gliders, the soldiers and their equipment could be placed just where they needed to be, which would save time and spare the soldiers a debilitating trek before they even met the enemy. Wingate's fertile mind quickly grasped the prospects offered by the gliders. He realized that using them would eliminate the need for aircraft to be taken off the Hump route, and he soon became very animated over these new possibilities.

Wingate told Cochran that he must represent the Special Force commander at a meeting of senior SEAC officials. Calling in a stenographer, Wingate outlined his revised views on the upcoming operation that would use gliders. He then had these notes quickly typed into a letter that he gave to Cochran. Wingate directed the American to present the letter to Mountbatten and to be prepared to strongly defend it at the meeting. Cochran and Olson rushed to the meeting, which, according to both Thomas and Cochran, was attended by Auchinleck, Stilwell, Chennault, and Stratemeyer.

At this rather gloomy conference, Mountbatten read Wingate's letter to the others. In it, Wingate dispensed with any need for extra air transport. Cochran's force would be enough to establish the LRPGs behind enemy lines. Such an abrupt change in plans piqued the interest of those attending the meeting, and they peppered Cochran with numerous questions, which he fielded adroitly. After some discussion Wingate's operation was back on. Alison commented later that Cochran's presentation of Wingate's revised plans was a tonic to Mountbatten. Alison reported that the SEAC commander told Cochran, "You are the first ray of sunshine we have seen in this theater in a long, long time."[47]

Although Thomas' account makes for entertaining reading and does contain some kernels of truth, it is quite inaccurate on major points. Immediately following the Quadrant Conference decision makers' conclusion, the British chiefs of staff directed that until Mountbatten established his headquarters and took up the baton of command, General Auchinleck was to proceed with preliminary planning for the operation that had been decided upon at the conference. Included in these plans was the establishment of an LRP headquarters and associated units.

The British chiefs, using Wingate's August 10 memorandum as the basis for the formation of the LRPGs, saw Wingate's men assisting a main operation by "disrupting enemy communications, finding targets for tactical air forces and creating such widespread confusion behind the enemy's forward areas that there would be a progressive weakening and misdirection of his main forces."[48] Until Wingate's arrival, Auchinleck's staff oversaw the formation of the 3rd Indian Division.

Regarding the use of gliders, it was common knowledge to the planning staffs, and most likely Wingate, by late September 1943 that the Americans were bringing with them a number of gliders. However, Wingate still intended to

march his troops in with mules carrying the heavy equipment. The Air Commandos would supply his men by air, primarily by parachute, though airstrips would
be carved out off the jungle for use by C-47s bringing in other supplies.

In *Back to Mandalay*, Lowell Thomas makes it appear that the Special Force
commander knew nothing about gliders until Cochran's mention of them set off
the proverbial light bulb in his head. Even though Wingate was a ground officer
and was not particularly well versed in aerial operations, he could not have been
unaware of the value of gliders. The invasion of Sicily in July, where gliders had
played an important role, surely did not escape the attention of either Wingate
or the JPS staff. Wingate was also most likely familiar with JPS No. 107, the India
Command paper issued on September 25, 1943. In fact, the authors of this paper
mention that Wingate's recommendations on the employment of his LRPGs had
been taken into account in the report.[49]

Chapter 4

Strangers in a Strange Land

When he arrived in India on November 13, Cochran was still unsure of just how his unit was to be used to support Wingate's LRPGs. For the moment, however, Cochran had more important matters to occupy him. He had to find bases where his men could train and facilities to assemble his aircraft. He selected Karachi, on India's west coast, as the place to assemble his aircraft, except for the gliders and C-47s. The C-47s had flown to India and just needed inspections. The gliders would be assembled on the opposite side of India at Barrackpore Field, north of Calcutta. Looming over the field at Karachi was a huge hangar originally built to house dirigibles. The local authorities gave permission to use the hangar for the erection of aircraft. The shelter afforded by the immense structure proved invaluable when rains swept through the area, and slowed down or halted outside work. Most of the L-1s and L-5s were erected inside the hangar by the light plane pilots. After assembling their aircraft, the pilots then flight-tested their own work.[1]

When he arrived at Barrackpore, Captain Taylor discovered that the CBI ASC could not spare people to erect the gliders. So he divided his men into several groups to facilitate the assembly of the gliders. He had an uncrating crew, a rope crew to check the condition of the tow ropes, a carpentry section, four assembly teams, an aircraft inspector, and a dispatcher and a load check group. Because his unit's tools had not yet arrived, Taylor obtained from the 28th Air Depot all of the necessary tools for the erection of the gliders. The assembly of the gliders initially took place alongside a taxi strip, but when space in a hangar was obtained, construction was moved there.[2]

The first test flight of one of the newly assembled CG-4As occurred on December 14, and by the 18th, all thirty of the first shipment of gliders had been erected. Most of the test flights were accomplished with the assistance of a Troop Carrier Command (TCC) C-47 that had been obtained from a transport unit based in Assam. Even as these events were taking place, Taylor was sending men and a few gliders to Ondal and Panagarh, both of which are about eighty miles northwest of Calcutta, to prepare those fields for further training by the unit. Taylor also had to send several men to Karachi in late December to assemble some gliders mistakenly sent there. Men from the fighter section and headquarters pitched in to help erect the wayward craft. Those CG-4As rejoined the Glider Section at Lalitpur in early January. Taylor's men eventually assembled a hundred CG-4As and twenty-five TG-5s. By then, ASC had made available enough personnel that the command took over the assembly of the final fifty gliders.[3]

Taylor also decided to make some administrative changes to his unit in order to meet additional operational requirements thrust upon the Air Commandos, and to keep his glider assembly line operating smoothly. He divided the Glider Section into a headquarters flight and three operational flights. All of the operational flights were capable of carrying out independent operations. These flights rotated between Ondal, Panagarh, and Calcutta for training, ferry missions, and glider assembly.[4]

While the assembly of the gliders proceeded fairly well, that of the Mustangs encountered serious problems. The first shipment of P-51As had been deck-loaded on an escort carrier and had been subjected to the elements during the voyage. When soldiers unloaded these fighters at Karachi in mid-December, they discovered that severe saltwater corrosion had damaged them. A second shipment of fighters arrived in no better shape even though they were shipped crated. The cargo vessel on which the second allotment of Mustangs came ran into a typhoon. In addition to saltwater corrosion, these planes had suffered dents and gashes from being pounded against the crates during the storm. No P-51A spares were available in-theater, and Stratemeyer radioed Arnold twice, on December 17 and 22, to send more Mustangs by priority shipments.[5]

As the assembly of light planes and gliders continued, the Project 9 unit received a new designation, the 5318th Provisional Air Unit. The unit activated on November 29, 1943, under this new appellation. It is doubtful if most of the men took notice of their unit's new designation. The name Project 9 continued to be used regularly.[6]

Meanwhile, Alison, having completed his job in the United States, had arrived in Delhi. On the 24th, he and Cochran flew to Calcutta with several other officers to observe the assembly of the gliders. The party then flew to Lalaghat and Hailakandi, south of Silchar in the Surma Valley of Assam. These two airfields, which were about nine miles apart, would serve as the Air Commando's forward bases. The countryside around these fields consisted primarily of flat paddy or rice fields surrounded by low hills. Numerous hillocks ranging from five to fifty feet high and covered with trees and underbrush dotted the flatland. Fol-

lowing a survey of Lalaghat, Captain Taylor declared that it would be suitable for
the tow planes and gliders, provided the landing strip was lengthened. By March,
when Wingate forayed into Burma, the Lalaghat strip was 6,300 feet long.[7]

Taylor, who was ill with malaria he had contracted while stationed in Panama, remained at Lalaghat while Cochran and the others inspected Hailakandi.
The 4,500-foot-long field at Hailakandi was located on a former tea plantation
and would need a great deal of work, but it would be satisfactory for operations.
Cochran planned to use Hailakandi as his headquarters and as the base for the
fighters, bombers, and light planes. Cochran named Colonel Gaty as commander
at Lalaghat.[8]

Both Cochran and Taylor gave pep talks to the glider personnel in Calcutta
on the 28th. Taylor reminded his men that good relationships with the British
and the Indians was essential to the success of their mission. In particular, he
told them to show some discretion "in regard to such matters as money, America, and Texas."[9] Cochran continued in the same vein, telling the glider crews that
actions spoke louder than words and implying that they would be seeing a lot of
action. He also mentioned that there were many "potentates" in India Command
who seriously doubted the Americans' abilities.[10]

Regarding the latter point, although Cochran and Alison insisted years later
that they received all the support they required from both the senior American
and British staffs in the CBI, resentment smoldered at many staff levels toward
the Air Commandos. In a report to General Arnold, Alison stated, "High RAF
offices [had] from the first doubted our capabilities."[11] He mentioned, however,
that Mountbatten strongly condemned this attitude.

Much of this animosity was really directed at Wingate, and the airmen were
simply caught in the crossfire. But Cochran's force was also a target of envy
because it had up-to-date equipment that was still in short supply for many CBI
units. Alison later commented, "We made some people mad, and we're sorry
about that, but it couldn't be helped."[12] There was also the uncertainty of many
senior staff officers about the unknown, the untested, and the unusual. The Air
Commandos were just not the USAAF organization to which they were accustomed. Arnold received appeals to abandon this experiment even before the unit
had settled into the CBI.

There was also the misperception that the Air Commandos were Wingate's
"private air force," a misperception that some authors have clung to in recent
years.[13] Even one who should have known better, General Slim, who was the
commanding general of the British Fourteenth Army and Wingate's superior,
made this error. In his memoirs, Slim mentioned that Special Force had "the
unique luxury of its own air force."[14]

Actually, not only were the Air Commandos not Wingate's private air force, they were not the only USAAF units deeply involved in Operation Thursday. Wingate quickly realized that he needed more air transport than what Cochran's force could supply if his operation was to succeed. This transport could only come from General Old's TCC. Though Wingate made his decision in December to use TCC aircraft, it was not until a January 4 dinner meeting that Wingate informed Old of this. To write that Old was astonished by Wingate's remark is an understatement.[15]

The following day, Old's staff began planning for TCC's part in Operation Thursday. The TCC had come into existence on December 15, and its headquarters was established at Comilla in southeast India near the Ganges River on January 2. Thus, there was uncertainty about how many aircraft would actually be available from the RAF and USAAF. Old's force comprised four RAF and four USAAF transport squadrons. The four American squadrons were the 1st Troop Carrier Squadron (TCS), the 2nd TCS, the 27th TCS, and the 315th TCS. Organized from cadres of the 1st and 2nd squadrons, the 315th moved to Sylhet in Assam, on January 12. Sylhet would be TCC's primary operating base for the upcoming venture. The 27th TCS, newly arrived from the United States, was also ordered forward to Sylhet. Although all four RAF squadrons participated in Operation Thursday, only the 27th and 315th squadrons were available for use in the operation; the other two USAAF units were fully committed to other supply missions. Nevertheless, Old's staff believed that TCC would be able to handle the added demands of Wingate's operation.[16]

On the 8th, Old personally flew Tulloch over areas bordering the Chindwin. Poor weather hindered visibility and not much could be seen, but Old did note that the terrain was very wild, with high jungle ridges. Over the next few weeks, Tulloch and other Chindit officers would make more flights over the assault area, flying with both the Air Commandos and the troop carriers.[17]

Meanwhile, flight training for the Air Commando glider and transport pilots had begun in earnest at Panagarh and Ondal on December 30. This initial training involved night landings in fully loaded gliders. The tow planes would approach the landing zone at an altitude of 200 feet and a speed of 110 mph. When the gliders received a light signal when they were 4,660 feet from the midpoint of a cross marked out with five flare pots, the glider pilots would release their tow rope. The glider pilots then made a standard rate glide of 70 mph to landing. From landings, the training swiftly evolved into night pickups.[18]

On January 2, 1944, following initial dry runs at Ondal, the first night snatches were made at Panagarh. Taylor described the pickup technique and apparatus in his after-action report as follows:

Night pickup is easily effected when proper alignment of the four red lights in the system is achieved; the three rear red lights upon the same horizontal plane, and the first red light in the same longitudinal plane with the center red light in the horizontal plane. During the properly flown pickup the airplane assumes an angle of convergence with the ground of 13 degrees, and at the actual moment of the pickup the pilot is 38.6 feet above the ground. The airplane propellers have a clearance of four feet over the upright poles suspending the loop. The lighting system employs four separately connected 12-volt batteries capable of continuous use for six hours.

Angle irons with base assemblies for the leap[?] support poles were driven in 28 feet apart. These poles, which were of steel tubing, are 24 feet in height and designated by a white light on the top of each. Three hundred feet to the front of the pickup assembly is a red light upon the ground, while 535 feet to the rear is another red light extended from a pole, which is 19 feet in height. Five hundred feet to the rear, further, or a total of 535 feet to the rear of the pickup assembly, are two red lights 38 feet apart. The left hand pole of the pickup assembly is set off 19 feet to the left of the longitudinal axis, which compensates for the pickup mechanism which protrudes from the left hand side of the tow plane.[19]

The intense training pace, coupled with the night operations, led to accidents. Fortunately, although several gliders were lost, there were no serious injuries. A more serious loss was a C-47 that crashed on New Year's Eve because someone had forgotten to remove the elevator control locks. No one was hurt in this accident, but it left the unit with only twelve transports. Stratemeyer radioed Arnold to rush a C-47 replacement to India.[20]

During the last stages of this training, Taylor, still ill with malaria, was ordered to bed by Major Page, the unit's chief flight surgeon. While Taylor convalesced, Cochran oversaw the glider training. Meanwhile, Wingate, now up and about and his usual irascible self, was whipping his troops into shape near Gwalior, about 180 miles south–southeast of Delhi in central India. Wingate's brigades had completed their unit training by Christmas, but much more individual training had yet to be accomplished. Too, there was still the matter of integrating the Americans into Wingate's scheme of operations. The Special Force leader decided to hold some combined exercises in early January.[21]

Taylor was back on his feet within a few days, and Cochran returned to Delhi to discuss with Wingate plans for the combined exercises. Before leaving Calcutta, Cochran told his glider commander that he would notify Taylor when the date for the maneuvers had been determined. In the meantime the P-51s, C-47s, and light planes began moving to the exercise area.[22] Six Mustangs flew from a three-thousand-foot strip carved out of a golf course at Nowgong, located about 110 miles southeast of Special Force headquarters at Gwalior; the C-47s operated out of Lalitpur, which was about 70 miles southwest of Nowgong and 110 miles south of Gwalior; and the L-1s and L-5s were attached to the ground units participating in the maneuvers.

Before the maneuvers started, Cochran gave a talk to Wingate's officers. Usually, Wingate seized center stage, but this time he was content to sip tea as Cochran spoke expansively of what his unit consisted of and how it would be able to do almost anything for the Chindits. Brigadier Fergusson, commander of the 16th Brigade, recalled blushing at Cochran's audaciousness.[23] Others were not quite sure what to make of the brash, somewhat sloppily dressed American. Many looked at each other with a resigned, "Yeah, sure . . ."[24]

Fergusson thought he saw Wingate's eyes twinkling as Cochran spoke. Another Chindit believed that Wingate was uneasily eyeing the doorways as if Wingate was expecting his men to suddenly bolt the room in disgust and dis-belief.[25] Even after they pressed Cochran on the matter of their control of the planes over the targets and received his affirmative reply, they remained skepti-cal because the RAF would not agree to such an arrangement. Still, Cochran's breezy good humor and apparent desire to help them in any way impressed them. "Look," one Chindit exclaimed, "even if nine-tenths of what this chap says is bullshit, we'll get twice what the RAF are giving us."[26]

Comments like that and Wingate's concluding statement that Cochran's "planes are our artillery. They will bomb and destroy the targets you produce," were bound to rile the RAF personnel who would be accompanying each Chindit column. The Commonwealth crews had responsibilities for arranging airdrop zones and performing the essential task of controlling air strikes and talking planes onto targets. Though the term had not yet entered common usage, these RAF men were for all intents "forward air controllers."[27]

Mostly pilots, the LRPG officers listening to Cochran knew the jungle and what aircraft could and could not do. They realized that Cochran had not guar-anteed that his force would destroy everything in front of the columns, but only that they would try anything for the Chindits. It was Wingate who had virtually guaranteed success. As usual, his rhetoric cast its spell over most of his audience. When one of the RAF officers attempted to explain the differences between air and artillery support and the pluses and minuses of both, he was jeered as being jealous of the Americans. No admirer of Wingate, the flier thought the Special Force commander was, if not ignorant, rather naive about air warfare.[28]

One of the few British officers still reserving judgment on the Air Commandos was Bernard Fergusson. Following the meeting the 16th Brigade leader told Cochran that he was skeptical of Cochran's claims, particularly those pertaining to the light planes. Would the Air Commando leader, Fergusson asked, be willing to put his planes and pilots to a test using some short and rough landing strips that Fergusson's men would carve out of the jungle? Cochran jumped at the opportunity, and the two men began planning for the test. It came much sooner than they expected.[29]

Before then Wingate kept Cochran's men busy. The fighters flew missions in support of the ground troops, often using only map coordinates to designate targets. It was during this period that the P-51s demonstrated their ability to use depth charges to dislodge enemy troops ensconced in pillboxes. To test the concussion effect of the depth charges during training flights, live sheep and goats were placed in dummy pillboxes. The Mustangs then dropped 350-pound depth charges in dive-bombing attacks on the ersatz fortifications. Afterwards, it was noted that although the depth charges had stripped the trees of foliage, the "sheep were still bleating healthily."[30]

Training flights by the C-47s in India consisted of making low-level night supply drops to elements of the 3rd Indian Division and Galahad, which was still under Wingate's command. These missions were hazardous because even though the terrain was relatively level, it was punctuated by many buttes and hills that rose steeply into the air. Also, dense scrub growth in the drop zones necessitated the use of flares, lights, smoke or brush fires for the identification of the drop zones. This, in itself, provided valuable training in light of the conditions encountered during Operation Thursday.[31]

But it was the light planes and their pilots—the ones Fergusson was skeptical about—that the Chindits grew to love and respect. Exercises involving the light planes quickly revealed the importance of these aircraft. Major Rebori's pilots developed new techniques in food and supply dropping, and they became particularly skilled in using the newly installed bomb racks on the wings of the planes. Dropping "agents" behind enemy lines was also practiced. Wingate's men and some of the light plane pilots, however, were concerned about the vulnerability of the little aircraft. To assuage their fears, Lieutenant Forcey, one of the Mustang pilots, took an L-5 up in a mock dogfight against Major Petit, who was flying a P-51. A marvelous pilot, Forcey utilized the L-5's slower speed and smaller turning radius to continually outmaneuver Petit in his Mustang.[32]

One incident during the maneuvers served more than any other to cement the respect and affection of the Chindits for the light plane pilots. Although it was unplanned, the event served as Fergusson's test of the American airmen.

Two L-5s, piloted by Captain Smith and Sgt. (later Flight Officer) Robert Chambers, arrived at Fergusson's headquarters to begin the planned test when word arrived that a muleskinner had been kicked in the groin by his mule. Severely injured, the muleskinner needed immediate hospitalization.

A clearing not much longer than four hundred feet was then being prepared. According to the flight manuals an L-5 required more than twice that distance for takeoff. Nevertheless, Smith decided to give the rough strip a try. Carrying Fergusson as a passenger, Smith took off for the clearing. Shortly, Fergusson and Smith were over the spot where fifty men could be seen feverishly working on the strip. Circling once, Smith then turned to Fergusson and asked him if he wanted to land. The brigadier nodded, but not too confidently. Smith was too high on the first pass, but he planted his L-5 right at the end of the tiny, rutted strip the next time.

When the L-5 shuddered to a stop, it was immediately surrounded by fifty excited soldiers who were all anxious to see what the L-5 could do. The injured man, who was in considerable pain, took Fergusson's place in the rear seat. Fergusson remained behind to be picked up later. Smith taxied to the edge of the clearing, went to full power, and putted down the strip. (An L-5 just didn't roar like a P-51 or P-47!) As he lifted into the air, a resounding cheer came from the soldiers. In less than half an hour, the injured man was in the hospital. The Chindits, recalling how they had had to leave too many wounded men behind during Wingate's first expedition, were overjoyed. An American had put his own life on the line to save a Briton. Morale soared; now the wounded would not be left behind, and the Air Commandos had shown how air evacuation could be done. The light planes and their pilots had passed Fergusson's test.[33]

It was apparent to all during these exercises that Special Force would benefit if Cochran's unit had greater firepower. Although the British had promised bomber support to Wingate, the RAF disclosed that it would be unable to do so because of difficulties with its VHF radios and commitments elsewhere. Wingate subsequently turned to Cochran for help in obtaining bombers. Cochran had already been considering the possibility of obtaining bombers. He, Alison, and Gaty met with Stratemeyer on November 24 to discuss what Project 9 was all about. At that meeting, Gaty stated that both the B-25G and H models of the American bombers were available in large numbers. For the present, Stratemeyer did nothing, but when it was announced that the RAF was not going to supply bombers, on January 7, 1944, the general radioed Washington for twelve B-25H Mitchells and six crews to arrive not later than February 15. He stated that the other six crews would be formed from Project 9 personnel. Stratemeyer was emphatic that "close assault type aircraft [were] necessary for the support and success of the Wingate columns and that the Baker Two Five How [was] best suited for this task."[34] B-25Hs carried only one pilot in its crew of five. A flying arsenal, the H was armed with a lightweight 75-mm cannon and four .50-cal. guns in the nose, four .50-cal. guns in blister packs on each side of the nose, two guns each in the dorsal and tail turrets, and two guns in the waist positions. It could also carry three thousand pounds of bombs and up to eight 5-inch rockets under the wings.

Arnold agreed to the twelve B-25s but he did not approve the assignment of six crews. As a result Cochran had to scrounge for additional personnel to man the bombers. He obtained these crews from the 341st Bomb Group that had a surplus of personnel, and on February 10, 1944, the B-25 section was officially assigned to the Air Commandos.[35] Cochran looked to his fighter section for a man to lead the bombers. He selected Major Smith, the fighter section's deputy commander. "Tadpole" Smith had flown with the Flying Tigers and had been credited with ten victories. A fighter pilot to the core, Smith was not pleased with being sent to bombers, but when promised he could still fly P-51s, Smith turned to his new task with zeal. He quickly had his new charges flying their twin-engine mounts like fighters and performing daring tasks. As soon as the Mitchells arrived, Smith's unit had the five white diagonal stripes that denoted the Air Commando planes painted on their fuselages.[36]

When Cochran left Calcutta, he told Taylor that Taylor would be notified when to have his gliders at Lalitpur for maneuvers. Subsequently, Wingate and Cochran set the date for the glider participation as January 8, which would be the date when the gliders would be used to land four hundred Special Force troops. Cochran's cable to Taylor specifying the 8th was delayed, however, and Taylor did not receive it until the day before the exercise was to begin. A mad scramble ensued, as Taylor and his men hastily readied their gliders, made arrangements for tow planes, and held cursory briefings. Leaving just three glider pilots in Calcutta to handle administrative duties, Taylor was able to move eighteen CG-4As from Ondal and Panagarh. Another six gliders flew in from Karachi.

It was drizzling when Taylor arrived at Lalitpur. To his dismay, he was told that the maneuvers would begin in thirty minutes. Taylor protested vehemently to Cochran, arguing that none of his men had seen the landing zone and that the low clouds and rain would complicate what was already a difficult, even dangerous, situation. Cochran attempted to talk Wingate into delaying this portion of the maneuvers, but the general remained obdurate. For all Wingate knew the conditions for the exercise might be similar to what would be encountered when his men entered combat.

No, he said, the exercise was on. Wingate then drove off to the landing zone, where he would observe the exercise from the ground.

From a small map of the area, Taylor drew a crude sketch of the landing zone to brief his pilots. Cochran, who had seen the zone from the air, decided to fly with Taylor in the lead glider. The first two gliders were pathfinders that were pulled in a double tow. Taylor's CG-4A carried Scots of the Black Watch. They would provide an initial defense of the landing zone. The other lead glider carried radio equipment to guide the following aircraft in and markers to outline the zone. Thirty minutes after the two pathfinders took off, the main force of eighteen gliders carrying four hundred more soldiers was pulled aloft by Captain Cherry's C-47s.

In the rain and mist Taylor had a hard time picking out the clearing in which he was to land. Suddenly, Cochran yelled that he saw the landing zone. He pointed it out to Taylor, who cut his glider away from the tug. Taylor was too high to make the shallow, slow, straight-in approach he had taught his pilots to use. Instead, he had to make a steep, fast, twisting approach. His glider plopped into the sticky mud and came to a quick stop. The Scots poured out of the glider to take up defensive positions. A short distance away, the second glider shuddered to a halt, and its crew began laying out the landing markers.

Cochran saw a figure running and stumbling across the muddy field. It was Wingate, who was as excited as Cochran had ever seen him. Pounding the American on his back, Wingate yelled, "Phil, you've done it! . . . You brought these gliders in and landed the troops!"[37] A bit nonplused, Cochran agreed. He then went off to check on arrangements for the arrival of the main force while the animated Wingate continued to chatter excitedly to his staff.

On schedule, half an hour later, the main force arrived to disgorge its load of troops. Four of the eighteen gliders would not release from their tow planes and returned to Lalitpur, but the rest landed safely, with only a few incurring minor damage. The soldiers of the Black Watch raced from their gliders into the brush surrounding the field. Nearby, troops of Wingate's brigade lay in wait as "defenders." They had not been told how the attackers would arrive, and the glider assault surprised them. The two units then engaged in a brief mock battle.

Wingate was so taken with the success of the glider assault that he decided to participate in a snatch of the gliders for return to Lalitpur. Taylor and Cochran teamed again to fly Wingate's glider. Special Force came close to losing its commander on the ensuing snatch. The C-47 was approaching to make the snatch when Taylor glanced back to see if everyone was ready. To his horror, Wingate had unbuckled his seat belt and was leaning out the glider's open door. "Tell the RAF," he was yelling to one of his officers, "that I not only have seen it, I have done it."[38]

At the last minute Wingate was steered back to his seat. Oblivious to all the commotion, the Chindit leader pulled a book from his pack and began reading. A furious Taylor was restrained by Cochran from showing Wingate a few of the more unusual aerial maneuvers that a glider could do. When he landed at Lalit-pur, a still steaming Taylor guided his glider to a stop so skillfully that he pulled up next to Wingate's car, again impressing the Special Force leader. Meanwhile, all but three of the gliders were brought out before darkness fell. The remaining craft were snatched the following day.[39]

Because Wingate placed great store in mules as pack animals for his force, Taylor and his men spent much of their time devising a method of transporting the animals in the gliders. Doping the mules had been seriously considered until the enormity of trying to dope hundreds of mules was brought to the airmen's attention, not to mention the ramifications of having to deal with groggy or unconscious mules after landing. The mules were finally given the benefit of the doubt that they would behave themselves. In the gliders designated to carry these animals, coconut matting was placed on the floors as reinforcement, and bamboo stalls were built to hold three animals. The mules were hobbled, and their heads were tied down to keep their long ears out of the control cables. A sort of sling was constructed by tying ropes from the mules' pack saddles up to the glider's corner longerons and down to the corner tie-down rings.[40]

Flying Officer Allen Hall Jr. made the first mule flight during the January 8 exercise. He carried three mules, each weighing about seven hundred pounds. Though a muleskinner was also carried and instructed to shoot the animals if they became unruly, the mules did not seem to mind flying at all. Cochran reported later that the mules appeared to take naturally to flying; when the glider banked, the mules banked also. After the glider landed in the exercise area and its nose came up, the mules "walked out in good spirits."[41]

The daylight exercise was followed on the 10th by a night dress rehearsal of the tactics to be used in the upcoming operation. The Scotsmen would again be the invaders, and the West Africans would be the defenders. This exercise was so important that Mountbatten came down from Delhi to observe it. The affable Mountbatten usually enjoyed talking to the troops, and this site visit was no exception. Cochran assembled his men on the Lalitpur airstrip to hear the SEAC commander. It turned out to be a memorable occasion, but not for Mountbat-ten's formidable oratory skills.

Because the admiral would be speaking at the field, Cochran ordered that no engines be run up during the speech. Cochran also ordered that everyone possible attend. He believed he had taken every precaution to ensure that Mountbat-ten's talk would be successful, but Cochran forgot one thing. Not everyone was present. Tadpole Smith was out flying his Mustang when Mountbatten arrived.

When Smith came back over the field, he was unaware that it was the SEAC commander standing on the hood of a jeep talking to the crowd.

Believing the individual on the jeep was Cochran, Smith decided to have a little fun. Mountbatten was midway through his talk when there was a tremendous roar. Smith's P-51 flashed by just a few feet over the admiral's head, almost blowing off his hat. The unflappable Mountbatten just stood there waiting for the racket to die down and then resumed his speech as if nothing had happened. A mortified Cochran felt like crawling into a hole. Cochran later apologized to the SEAC commander, who shrugged the incident off with the remark that he should not have been speaking right on the airstrip anyway. Mountbatten assigned more blame to his aide for getting him into this situation than to Smith or Cochran. Smith apparently escaped with little more than a tongue-lashing from Cochran.[42]

That evening Mountbatten and Wingate drove to the landing area, while Cochran flew there in an L-5. Although the rain had stopped, clouds scudded across the sky, intermittently revealing and then concealing a pale half moon. It would be very dark at the landing zone. Right on schedule, the two pathfinder gliders set down in the clearing. Men of the Black Watch ran out of one to set up defensive positions, while Taylor and 2nd Lt. Neal J. Blush set up a diamond pattern of lights to guide in the main force of twenty-two gliders. Two of the CG-4As on a double tow did not reach the landing zone, having suffered tow rope problems. They cut loose from their tug and landed safely in rice paddies. The other twenty gliders swept in silently, landing and disgorging their passengers in efficient order.

Flight Officer Nesbit L. Martin was given the chore of bringing in some animals. Instead of mules, he carried three bullocks, each weighing about nine hundred pounds. Like their predecessors, these big animals apparently did not mind flying and remained docile throughout their ride.[43]

The West African defenders were not caught unawares this time. They were ready to meet the Black Watch, and the mock battle quickly turned into a real donnybrook. Until the exercise umpires finally called off the battle, it was one of the scrappiest melees going. Fortunately, except for a few broken bones, cuts, black eyes, and bruises, no serious damage was inflicted to either side.[44]

Initially, Mountbatten did not believe that all of the gliders, minus the two that cast off early, had made it safely into the clearing. He wandered throughout the landing zone counting each glider individually before he concluded that all had arrived. By this time the glidermen had erected their pickup assemblies for the C-47 snatches, and the first gliders, which carried not entirely simulated casualties, were being snatched out. Ecstatic over the success of the exercise, Wingate gushed, "This is what I've prayed for."[45]

Mountbatten, catching his subordinate's excitement, bounced up and down and shook hands with anyone in reach. Whether he was in awe or fright at the sight of the big gliders rushing in for landings and then being pulled back into the air, Mountbatten's favorite phrase appeared to be "Jesus Christ."[46]

Despite his excitement and enthusiasm over this showing by the Air Commandos, Wingate remained his irascible self. Encountering some medical personnel trying to catch some sleep in one of the gliders following a full day's and night's work, Wingate kicked them awake. "That is a hell of a place to sleep, and get the hell off [the field]," he roared. The Air Commandos quickly scrambled out of his way.[47] Taylor, after preparing one of the damaged gliders for removal the next morning, also fell asleep on the field. He woke early the next morning to find a jackal wondering hungrily if he was dead or alive.[48]

Mountbatten, Wingate, and Cochran huddled in the darkness following the exercise. The trio agreed to alter the plan for the Burma operation by spearheading it with gliders and then bringing in aviation engineers to prepare airstrips. The final stage would be bringing more personnel, supplies, and heavy equipment with TCC planes. Taylor was called over and asked when he and his men could be at Lalaghat.

By February 1, Taylor replied.

"You be damn sure you're there!" they rejoined.[49]

The next morning Mountbatten returned to Delhi. He noticed that Cochran had brought in an L-5. A light plane pilot at one time himself, Mountbatten could not resist asking the American if he could fly the little craft back to Delhi. Ever accommodating, Cochran said yes, and the pair hopped in. Mountbatten took the controls in the front seat, and Cochran sat behind. It was not long before Cochran realized he had made a serious mistake in allowing the admiral to fly.

Mountbatten lost control of the L-5 on his first takeoff attempt and ground-looped it—fortunately with only minor damage to a wingtip. Half crouched over the front seat, Cochran guided Mountbatten through the next, successful though wobbly takeoff. It took a bit over an hour for the flight to Delhi, and every now and then the SEAC commander would look back at Cochran to nod and grin. Cochran would smile back, but he would wonder at the same time what the landing would be like. At last Mountbatten made his approach. His landing, on two wheels (a "two-pointer") and nose down, was not good. For a moment Cochran feared that they were going to flip over, but the plane's tail came down, and it rolled to a safe stop. Mountbatten apologized profusely for his poor showing, revealing that he had not flown in seven years.[50]

A few days later Mountbatten wrote Cochran to congratulate him and his men on the success of the maneuvers. He also apologized for his troubles in

piloting the L-5. "I am sorry," he wrote. "I nearly wrecked your L-5 by manipu-
lating the brakes so badly and hope I did not frighten you too much!"[51]

By this time Cochran's men were using the designation that Arnold had
first applied in September 1943—1st Air Commando Force—more often than
the duller-sounding but still official 5318th Provisional Air Unit. On January 21,
1944, Alison wrote to Arnold requesting that the unit be redesignated the "First
Air Commando Force Special." Alison pointed out that his command was a
special, not a provisional, unit and that the 5318th Provisional designation was
"seriously limiting us in administration of our force and throws an extra burden
on the theater."[52] It was not until late March, however, after Operation Thursday, that the unit finally received the designation 1st Air Commando Group (1st
ACG).[53] The name Air Commando greatly pleased Mountbatten. In his letter to
Cochran, the admiral said, "As you may know, the name 'Commando' has a very
special significance for me and I was delighted to find that the high traditions of
this name were being more than carried on by your party."[54]

Following the success of the exercise, events took on even more urgency
because Operation Thursday was set to start in less than two months. On February 1 Wingate held a map exercise at Imphal that was attended by many Special
Force, Air Commando, and TCC officers. Wingate spread a map scaled one inch
to one mile on the floor and had all present remove their shoes so that they could
walk on it as Wingate lectured.[55] Even at this late date, with the LRP operation
just a month away, many senior officials in the theater remained dubious of the
entire affair. EAC Vice Commander Air Vice Marshal T. M. Williams told Old
that he had "expected" (perhaps "hoped" is more what he intended to say) TCC
to reject Wingate's increasing demands for air supply, which would then have
forced the operation to be canceled or, at least, considerably altered.[56]

While the undercurrent of opposition surged along, the Air Commandos
were placed under 3rd TAF's operational control on January 13. The Air Commandos remained under USAAF control for administrative matters, however.
This operational control was reconfirmed on February 4, when Slim and Stratemeyer issued their combined Operation Instruction No. 4 that detailed various
aspects of the forthcoming Special Force operation.[57] Three days later Cochran
and Alison met with Old and his staff to coordinate operations in the impending invasion. Old read some amendments to the Fourteenth Army's directive to
Wingate. This directive gave command of the Air Commandos to the 3rd TAC.
Despite assurances that there were no "sinister implications" in the directive,
Cochran protested and the matter was dropped for the moment.[58]

Old quickly realized that his troop carriers were being asked to take on
more responsibilities for supplying and transporting Special Force. During one
meeting, Tulloch stated that Old's planes might have to supply two, instead of

one, brigades for Wingate's northern force. Because the British supply dumps were far removed from the staging area, the supply missions would involve round-trip flights of more than 740 miles. These would be flown over very bad terrain and with bad weather en route a high probability. The costs in aircraft, engine maintenance, and crew availability were exceedingly high. Old could not believe any experienced airman would have agreed to the air supply requirements that Tulloch outlined. The general told Tulloch to borrow food from American supply dumps nearer the staging areas. Tulloch blandly suggested that Old could perhaps arrange the loan, which was an idea the TCC leader immediately turned down.[59]

The next day, at another meeting with General Slim and the Special Force staff, Old was told that the operation was now a bit tenuous. Still, if it did go off as planned, the troop carriers would have to supply five more brigades at the same time that they were supplying two of Wingate's brigades as they were being relieved. The amorphous state of plans at this rather late stage bothered Old considerably, especially when Wingate confirmed a few days later that details of the operation still had not been decided.[60]

Wingate, who already had three C-47s assigned to his force, wanted five more for training LRP brigades. These aircraft would be used between February 1 and March 10. The transfer of matériel would place a greater strain on the transport squadrons that were already heavily engaged in Hump operations and in supplying the Fourteenth Army. After considerable discussion regarding the extra C-47s, the request was canceled. Wingate's continual requests for more aircraft and supplies, however, irritated Old, who had enough problems trying to keep his regular cargo runs operating with increasingly overworked crews and planes. Commenting on these tribulations, Old wrote in his diary, "Our experience with the Wingate forces . . . are in the parable of the camel in the Arab's tent."[61]

Wingate did obtain the temporary use of a B-25 to survey the general territory through which his men would be moving. On several occasions, Old piloted the B-25 himself. To throw off the Japanese as to its intentions, the B-25 usually carried bombs that were dropped in widely separated areas. The Chindit leader still remained concerned about tipping off the enemy about the operation. He refused to allow reconnaissance flights over the clearings selected for the landings, even though the clearings lay along the normal flight paths of bombers and fighters attacking targets farther east. While Old respected Wingate's authority to restrict this reconnaissance, he did not agree with it.

Old worried that because the landings were to take place at night, the clearings might be unrecognizable to the transport and glider crews. Photos could only show so much. How would moonlight shadows affect the appearance of the clearings? Would the crews be able to pick them out? It was Old's responsibility to see that the transport phase went off without a hitch, and Old decided that he must personally see what the moonlight's effect would be.

On February 7, which was a night when the moon was in a phase similar to what it would be on the night chosen for the assault, Old flew a C-47 over the clearings. He found that the ground features would be recognizable to his pilots from photo study alone. To ensure that the enemy did not become suspicious about the C-47's activities, Old's plane carried a small number of 100-pound bombs. Just shoved out the aircraft's cargo door, the bombs were dropped on a convoy moving along a road, headlights blazing. Old's flight had repercussions. He had made no attempt to conceal the flight, but Wingate was furious when he heard about it. Thereafter, Wingate was quite circumspect in his dealings with TCC concerning landing zones. As a result planning suffered during the last important days prior to the assault.[62]

In the meantime extra commitments continued to cascade upon Old's transports. The troop carriers were deluged with requests for additional supply missions from the Fourteenth Army, from Special Force, from the Air Commandos, and from organizations throughout the CBI theater. Day after day, plans developed under great pressure had to be scrapped and recalculated as new commitments were dumped into the TCS unit's laps. On top of all these commitments, both the 27th and 315th TCSs discontinued their air supply missions to concentrate on night flying training. Then, Old was not particularly happy to be notified that his planes would also be used to tow Air Commando gliders during the assault.

An additional problem confronting the general was that the day he was to begin dropping supplies to the Chindits kept creeping forward. Initially set as February 25, the initial delivery date had been moved to the 10th and subsequently brought forward to the 6th. Old was unsure that the supplies to be dropped would even make it to Sylhet, which was his primary operating base, by the 6th. Also, the Japanese offensive in the Arakan area had siphoned off more U.S. aircraft because they were needed to keep the beleaguered defenders supplied. In a transport-starved theater, just where to get the aircraft for all the planned missions was a problem that was never satisfactorily resolved.[63]

Meanwhile, as Old and Wingate's representatives negotiated supply requirements, the Air Commandos began moving supplies and equipment forward by air, train, and barge. The unit was able to move a great deal of supplies quickly by using its own C-47s, but other equipment had to be transported by rail or water. Barges were the slowest, but train transport provided the most interesting and frustrating stories. Cochran's men soon discovered that they would have to use some innovative techniques to move via the railroads.

Bureaucratic inertia and the inefficiency of theater supply organizations sometimes forced the Air Commandos to resort to other means of obtaining transport for their supplies. This often meant the midnight requisitioning of box-cars in Calcutta. But there were other problems to overcome. Guards had to be placed alongside supplies because other Allied units and Indian military units and rail yard staff proved quite adept at midnight requisitioning themselves. Too, a standard rail gauge did not exist in India. Transferring equipment from a train on one gauge to a train on another was time-consuming. Then, train crews often decided to stop on their own in order to brew some tea or to discuss affairs of the day. Nevertheless, over the next few weeks, supplies and equipment wended their way to Hailakandi and Lalaghat.[64] Neither Hailakandi nor Lalaghat were really ready for full-scale operations. Both fields were hardly more than emergency strips scraped out of rice paddies. Lalaghat in particular needed a great deal of work. To help get the fields in shape, the 900th Airborne Engineer Aviation Company was attached to the 5318th, which was a logical decision because the use of this company by the Air Commandos had already been discussed back in September. The 900th had been building airstrips along the Ledo Road in northeastern India and northern Burma. Its removal from this job prompted a stern query from Stilwell, who wondered if the USAAF was disclaiming its responsibility for airfield construction in the combat zone. Stilwell also stated that he should have been notified before the reassignment of the 900th was made.[65]

The engineers' primary purpose was to construct airfields behind enemy lines, but when they arrived at Lalaghat on February 3—a month after the first Air Commandos moved in—the men of the 900th were quickly assigned the task of whipping the field into shape.[66] The camp sites at both fields had been built by the British, and it consisted primarily of split bamboo huts known as *bashas*. These could not be called first-rate accommodations, but they could be erected quickly. While Casey's men focused on the airstrips, Cochran's men did much of the other work. Cochran was not a man to pull rank, and he made sure that officers and men worked and ate together. The work was demanding and dirty, and a man's appearance was of less importance than what he had accomplished each day. A prominent visitor to Lalaghat the day Operation Thursday was launched was not impressed with Cochran's men, however.

Brigadier General Old, the TCC leader, was appalled at what he saw. He wrote in his diary:

> Upon arrival at Lalaghat around noon 5 March, CG's first impression of station was definitely bad. Col. Cochran's men were nothing more or less than a mob. No two wore the same uniform, almost all were growing beards. Many appeared idle. Officers and men messed together and

shared the same latrines. Sanitation was bad. Directed Flight Surgeon report to me. He did not. Salutes were absolutely unknown. Spoke to Col. Cochran about this. He admitted the conditions and only excuse was that the men were "too busy." They appeared to be busy at bunk fatigue. CG TCC ordered a cleanup of men, which was done, but nothing like discipline could be established in the press of other matters.[67]

In response to the general's order, Cochran wrote one of the more memorable directives of the war:

To: All Personnel and Attached Organizations.
Look, Sports, the beards and attempts at beards are not appreciated by visitors.

Since we can't explain to all strangers that the fuzz is a gag or "something I always wanted to do" affair, we must avoid their reporting that we are unshaven (regulations say you must shave) by appearing like Saturday night in Jersey whenever possible.

Work comes before shaving. You will never be criticized for being unkempt if you are so damn busy you can't take time to doll up. But be clean while you can.

Ain't it awful?[68]

Lieutenant Casey's men were given another important task also. Tamu, a village in the Kabaw Valley on the India–Burma border, was chosen to be the advanced base whence Thursday would be launched. The village was only about 100 miles from the landing grounds in Burma. More important than bringing the assault force closer to the target, however, Tamu's value lay in the fact that it was beyond the Chin Hills. This range of mountains, which were between the two Air Commando fields and the proposed landing grounds, rose in places to over seven thousand feet. From Tamu it would be much easier for the C-47s to pull the gliders by double tow as Cochran proposed. Otherwise, the transports and gliders would face the daunting task of having to fly a much greater distance (approximately 270 miles from Lalaghat to Piccadilly) at a much higher altitude (at least eight thousand feet to clear the Chin Hills).[69]

Like the Air Commando fields at Hailakandi and Lalaghat, the one at Tamu needed a lot of work. Almost as soon as he arrived at Lalaghat, Casey was ordered to send a detachment to Tamu to prepare its strip. The engineers labored at improving the field for more than two weeks. Their efforts came to naught when the Japanese began an invasion of India.

For some time the British, including Wingate, were sure the Japanese were preparing to launch a major offensive toward Imphal and Kohima. Ironically, this offensive had its origin in Wingate's first foray into Burma one year earlier. Following that operation, the Japanese realized that enemy movement across the Chindwin and deep into their territory was easier than they had envisioned. Fifteenth Army commander Lt. Gen. Mutaguchi Renya felt that in order to keep the enemy at bay, he must take more positive actions. He asked General Kawabe Masakazu, the Burma Area Army commander, for permission to begin planning an offensive into India.[70]

Planning for an offensive toward Imphal and Kohima began in June 1943, just as Longcloth petered out. This offensive was designated U-GO (the "C Operation"). Not until January 7, 1944, however, did Kawabe issue the orders putting U-GO into motion. Indeed, it became a race between the Allies and the Japanese as to who would attack first. U-GO was to begin around March 7, 1944, almost simultaneously with Wingate's movement into Burma. One month before U-GO started, another operation, HA-GO (the "Z Operation"), would jump off in Arakan. HA-GO, though, was nothing more than a sideshow for the Japanese, an operation designed only to draw British attention and reserves away from the main attack toward Imphal.

As it transpired, even though the fighting in Arakan was heavy and at times leaned toward the Japanese, HA-GO was a failure. Few British reserves were drawn to Arakan, and the Japanese suffered heavy losses. Although HA-GO may have been planned as a sideshow, both Slim and Mountbatten felt it was a turning point in the Burma campaign because it showed that a British force could, at last, hold against and then decisively defeat a major Japanese attack. The effect on morale was tremendous. Also, Commonwealth troops were not the only forces used in Arakan. USAAF troop carrier aircraft were pulled off other missions to keep the ground troops supplied. These aircraft were a major factor in ensuring the defeat of the Japanese. Though few in number, Air Commando liaison pilots also played a vital role in Arakan.[71]

Meanwhile, in the north, because of the mountainous terrain and dense jungle, British forces were spread thinly along the Burma border. The 20th Indian Division screened the Tamu area but did not completely control it. For some weeks Japanese patrols operated very close to Tamu. An all-weather road leading out of Tamu and running almost directly to Imphal was believed to be a primary objective of the Japanese. The British commanders intended to hold the Imphal Plain, but not necessarily outlying positions in the Kabaw Valley like Tamu. The 20th was directed to remain near Tamu until the enemy's intentions were established; then it was to withdraw to a spot known as the Shenam Saddle that was northwest of the village, where the 20th was to fight to the last man.

Wingate was unaware of these plans, but he was concerned about Tamu. He had forecast a Japanese offensive toward the Imphal Plain for some time, and he was sure that an attack was imminent. On February 8, Wingate directed Old to begin preparing alternate plans in case Tamu did become untenable. Almost two weeks later, on the 21st, Tulloch announced that Tamu was definitely too dangerous to upgrade. On the 25th, Cochran reported that Japanese reconnaissance planes had been over Hailakandi. A disgusted Old recorded in his diary, "The work improving Tamu landing grounds now goes for nothing and the airborne engineers must be brought out."[72]

With the engineers returned to Lalaghat, only the light planes would use the Tamu airfield for the time being. The village did in fact fall to the Japanese on March 22. And although the engineers ceased work at Tamu, they had more than enough duties at Lalaghat and Hailakandi to keep them busy.[73]

Another unit newly assigned to the Air Commandos was also busy. Because of the importance of the impending operation, the Tenth Air Force assigned a small photographic unit to the Air Commandos to record their activities. This unit initially consisted of 1st Lieutenant Russhon and three enlisted men. The unit grew on February 15 when Capt. Edward C. Collins arrived to take command along with two more officers and four additional enlisted men. The unit was designated Detachment 3, Tenth USAAF Combat Camera Unit.[74]

Collins and four of the enlisted men remained only until Operation Thursday was launched. They were then reassigned to the Matterhorn Project to record B-29 activities. Russhon was eventually permanently assigned to the Air Commandos, where he had become a favorite. Oddly, Russhon was not originally a cameraman. In fact, he had been a sound technician for one of the radio networks and for a movie studio. It was as a sound man that he had come to India, but his equipment had been ruined during shipment, and he switched to taking pictures instead of recording.[75]

The photo unit soon gained an importance in the Air Commandos that far exceeded its size. Film developing required hyposulfite, which was referred to as "hypo." Somehow, the Air Commandos had acquired 15,000 pounds of this material. This amount of solution was enough to supply all the photo units in the CBI for a year. There was no way the Air Commandos could use all that hypo. Or was there? Russhon and his men knew what happened when hypo and water were combined; the resulting chemical reaction quickly chilled the water. It was not long before the hypo was being used for a much more important task (at least to the men) than developing pictures. The Air Commandos soon were drinking hypo-chilled, and very tasty, beer.[76]

With the addition of the aviation engineers and the photo unit, the Air Commandos were ready for Operation Thursday. Even before that operation took place, however, the Americans had already entered battle.

Chapter 5

First Blood

The fields and facilities at Lalaghat and Hailakandi were not completed when Cochran sent his men into action. The first two missions on February 3 and 4, 1944, were just warm-ups—photo reconnaissance only. They served, however, to acclimate the pilots to the areas over which they would be operating. Finally, on the 5th, twelve Mustangs, each carrying two 500-pound bombs, accompanied by four other P-51s providing cover, bombed the rail junction at Wuntho, southwest of Indaw. Several fires were started, and a number of boxcars were destroyed. The attackers then turned south to take a look at the enemy airfield at Shewbo. No planes were sighted, but antiaircraft fire slightly damaged two fighters. By 1:00 PM all the Air Commando planes had returned to Hailakandi, and the group successfully completed its first mission under fire.[1]

For the remainder of February, the Mustangs, joined by the Mitchells on the 12th, were out almost daily attacking airfields, railroad yards, river traffic, bridges, and storage areas. They ranged across Burma from Homalin, which was just across the Chindwin, to Mandalay in central Burma, and almost everywhere in between. Cochran insisted that his pilots learn the area thoroughly, particularly the section south of the landing zones from where it was expected that most of the opposition would come.[2]

Two missions were flown on the 12th. The second was a one-bomber show with a sextet of fighters providing cover. Tadpole Smith flew the B-25. After bombing a couple of rail bridges and a roadbed, Smith took time to place a 75-mm shell into a building, blowing off its roof. Somewhat embarrassed, he later confessed that he had really been aiming at tracks and switches several hundred yards in front of the building.[3]

Two days later the Air Commandos almost lost their leader. Cochran was heading a dive-bombing attack north of Mandalay when ten Oscars of the 50th Sentai jumped his thirteen P-51s. With an altitude and speed advantage, the Japanese caught the Americans in a bad position. In the ensuing fight, 1st Lt. Carl

Hartzer Jr. was killed when his aircraft exploded. Capt. Donald V. Miller bailed out safely from his stricken craft and became a prisoner of war (POW). In return the Americans claimed three Oscars as damaged. During the fight, Major Smith, flying a P-51, thought Cochran had been shot down and radioed the base with this report. Cochran, hearing his bomber leader, quickly straightened out Smith, shouting over the radio, "The hell I am!"[4]

This close call, however, resulted in Wingate going up the chain of command to get orders restricting Cochran, as well as Alison and Olson, from flying missions over Burma. The trio knew too much about the impending LRPG

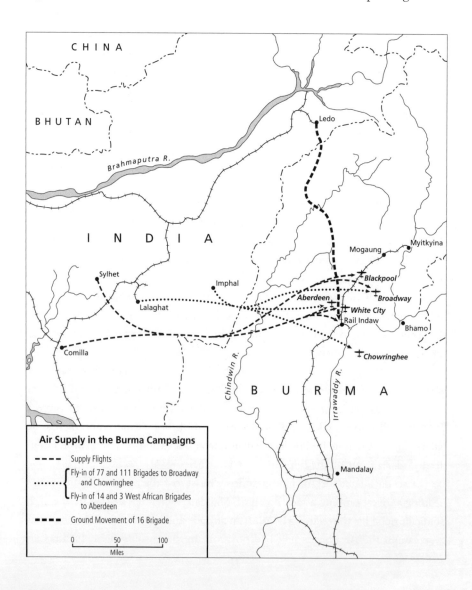

Air Supply in the Burma Campaigns

- – – – Supply Flights

⎧ Fly-in of 77 and 111 Brigades to Broadway
· · · · · · ·⎨   and Chowringhee
⎩ Fly-in of 14 and 3 West African Brigades
      to Aberdeen

– ▪ – ▪ Ground Movement of 16 Brigade

0   50   100
Miles

operations to chance their capture. The American officers were not happy about this restriction, but they understood the reason.[5]

Cochran and Alison knew their small force could not completely isolate the battlefield, but they could certainly make it more difficult for the enemy to concentrate their forces against the landing grounds. To confuse the Japanese, many attacks were made north of the landing grounds, particularly against the supply lines of the 15th Division and the 31st Division, then preparing for the offensive against Imphal. The airfield at Shwebo, the closest strip to the assault area, also received much attention. The P-51s and the B-25s usually carried 500-pound general-purpose bombs on their missions, but they occasionally also used 325-pound Navy depth charges (an idea of Major Petit, who had seen the blast effectiveness of these weapons on Guadalcanal), incendiaries, and 100-pound fragmentation clusters. On February 21, the Air Commandos dropped 1,000-pound bombs, becoming the first Mustang unit to use the large bombs in combat. They made most attacks at low level, which was an exceedingly dangerous tactic. Ground fire holed several planes, and on March 4, one of the group's B-25s was shot down during an attack on a river steamer. There were no survivors.[6]

The assault force did not see all the action. The light planes soon proved themselves to be significant factors to not just Chindits, but in operations through-out the CBI. Major Rebori's light plane unit consisted of 120 enlisted men and six officers. Rebori split his organization into four "squadrons" of approximately 33 men each. A squadron had four elements of four aircraft each, with another two aircraft held in reserve. Except for the officers, every pilot was a sergeant who was also a trained mechanic. In addition to their flying duties, the sergeants were responsible for maintaining their own aircraft.[7]

Instead of functioning as a single unit, the light plane unit was parceled out to different areas where they would operate with separate brigades. B Squadron was sent to Ledo. Its primary mission was to assist in the medical evacuation of Stilwell's Chinese–American forces in northern Burma. (The American portion of Stilwell's combat troops consisted primarily of the three thousand men of Galahad.) A Squadron, assigned to work with Fergusson's 16th Brigade, made its base at Taro, which is approximately seventy miles south-southeast of Ledo on the Chindwin. Not long before, Japanese troops had infested the area, but under pressure from one of Stilwell's Chinese regiments, the Japanese withdrew on January 30. Upon arrival at Taro, the Air Commandos set up a complete radio station to serve not just themselves, but the British as well.[8]

Because of its distance from Indaw—some 360 miles in a straight line—the 16th Brigade had to begin its movement from Ledo on February 5, one month before Operation Thursday began. The terrain the brigade had to traverse just to reach the Chindwin, its true jump-off point, was harsh and unforgiving. Mountains rising to 8,500 feet had slopes so steep that it took hours just to climb a few hundred feet. Much of the area was unexplored and unmapped. Rain was constant, and men and mules slipped off muddy trails and fell to their deaths while the columns trudged on. Reaching the top of a peak was not the end of the Chindits' torment, for they then had to descend the slippery slopes and stumble forward to scale yet another towering height. In such terrain, air supply was crucial.

Near Lulum Nok, about sixty miles south of Ledo, the brigade received its first supply drops. Fergusson established radio contact with the A Squadron planes. There were enough clear areas that the L-5s could drop messages and also snatch them from a wire strung between two poles. One of the first messages Fergusson received was from Rebori. Printed at the top of the message was:

REBORI FIELD, TARO
The only United Nations Airfield beyond the Chindwin[9]

The work was not without its dangers. On the 10th, two L-5s had a midair collision near Ledo. Both pilots, SSgt. Ngon T. Tom and SSgt. William H. Neff, were killed. They would not be the only pilots of the light plane unit to lose their lives.[10]

The light planes were not the only aircraft assigned to support Fergusson's brigade. C-47s of the 27th TCS and the 315th TCS began supply drops to the columns on February 10. In this role these squadrons generally flew five sorties a day, dropping up to five thousand pounds of supplies per sortie. These missions, however, severely strained the TCC's resources, which were also being directed toward gearing up for Operation Thursday. Fortunately, some C-46s from the ATC were made available temporarily to assist in regular supply operations.[11]

C Squadron was initially stationed at Tamu, where Casey's engineers were working.[12] The squadron's mission was to provide medical evacuation for Indian Army units in the area. Additionally, following the invasion, it was to find and evacuate any glider passengers forced down along the Chindwin. After the engineers left, C Squadron remained at Tamu until it flew into Broadway, Burma, to begin operating with its brigade.[13]

Meanwhile, D Squadron had been sent to Ramu in Arakan, far afield of the Air Commandos' intended area of operations. Ramu was about ten miles east of Cox's Bazar, a field which would play an important role in later Air Commando operations. On February 4, Commonwealth and Japanese forces joined battle when General Kawabe launched HA-GO. Two days later, as they groped through dense mist and fog, the leading Japanese formation bumped into, and eventually overran, the 7th Indian Division's headquarters. This headquarters lay just a couple of miles north of the XV Corps' logistics base (or administrative area) at Sinzweya. Forever afterwards, this area would be known as the "Admin Box," and the ensuing fight would be dubbed the "Battle of the Box."[14]

The Admin Box itself was about one square mile of flat, open terrain surrounded by hills and jungle. Because it had been the main supply area, it was densely stocked with all kinds of supply dumps. With all this congestion, the Japanese always found some target to hit. Commonwealth troops occupied some of the hills at the Box's edges, but the defenders could not cover all the highlands, which enabled the enemy to place observers and artillery on select hilltops. Yet even with this tremendous advantage, the Japanese could not prevail.[15]

Many times previously when the Japanese had attacked their Commonwealth foes, the Allied forces had retreated, sometimes in panic. Not this time.

General Slim, through intensive training and a charismatic personality, had imbued his troops with renewed fighting vigor, and they were not going to be pushed around. And, unlike most of the earlier battles, while the Japanese still fought a ground-based, horizontal battle, Slim's men fought vertically, being well supplied and supported from the air. Though surrounded at the Box, the Commonwealth men knew they could rely on the USAAF and RAF transport crews to keep flying in supplies and that the light planes (two Fox Moths and some aircraft from the Air Commandos D Squadron) would be available to evacuate casualties and bring in reinforcements. So instead of panicking, the XV Corps troops stayed in their cramped Box and made it into a bristling pincushion studded with tanks, artillery, and machine guns.

D Squadron's flying sergeants were quickly in the thick of the action. Between February 10 and March 6, they evacuated more than seven hundred wounded or sick soldiers from the Box to a field near Ramu. From there, larger aircraft flew the casualties to hospitals in the rear. Because only one or two men could be taken out at a time, the pilots flew six to eight missions a day into the Box, most often under fire. The squadron's one-day evacuation record was seventy-three men flown out. The L-5s also brought in fresh soldiers to take the places of those evacuated. Despite having to operate under primitive conditions and enduring heavy enemy fire whenever they flew into the Box, D Squadron lost only one L-5, and that was due to engine failure. The light plane unit also lost one pilot, SSgt. Walter R. Waugh Jr., who was injured but lived. The squadron's exploits, and those of their RAF comrades, were deeply appreciated by those who fought in the Box, and also by senior officers. One report reads effusively, "Their [the light plane pilots] performance was unquestionably the greatest flying feat of the campaign."[16] Air Marshal Baldwin, the 3rd TAF's commander, was so impressed that he made a visit to Ramu to personally congratulate the light plane pilots.[17]

Meanwhile, the transport and glider force, in addition to hauling supplies and erecting gliders, was undergoing intensive training for the upcoming Operation Thursday. Because it was planned for the operation to begin at night, most of the training was done at night. Bullocks and mules were carried in gliders to get them accustomed to flying, night snatches were accomplished, and night double-tows were made. It was while doing the latter that tragedy struck the Air Commandos and the Chindits.

On the night of February 15, 1st Lt. Kenneth L. Wells was piloting a CG-4 in the long-tow position. Accompanying him were his copilot, Flight Officer Bishop Parrott, crew chief Cpl. Robert D. Kinney, and four Chindits. Something happened and Wells' glider slid into the glider of 1st Lt. Donald E. Seese. There was a "crunch" as the two gliders tangled, then Wells' craft fell out of control. All aboard were killed when the CG-4 smashed into the ground. Fortunately, Seese, with considerable help from his copilot, Flight Officer Troy C. Shaw, brought his own glider back safely despite losing much of the trailing edge of his right wing.[18]

With less than a month to go before Operation Thursday launched, this tragedy could have had a serious effect on the morale of both the Air Commandos and the Chindits had it not been for Lieutenant Colonel D. C. Herring, who was the commanding officer of the Chindits killed in the accident. After receiving a note from Taylor expressing concern that the Chindits might have reservations about flying again in gliders, Herring talked with his men. He then wrote Taylor that as far as his men were concerned, "Please be assured that we will go with your boys any place, any time, anywhere."[19] Later, the 1st Air Commando Group adopted the phrase as its motto, and the phrase has been a part of USAF special operations lore ever since.[20]

The first combat glider mission was flown on February 28. Flight Officer John H. Price Jr. and Flight Officer John E. Gotham piloted a glider carrying a sixteen-man Chindit patrol. The patrol's mission was to conduct a diversionary action near Minsin on the east bank of the Chindwin and to destroy a nearby radio station. The ground was rougher than it appeared from the air. Upon landing, the glider hit a trench and lost its landing gear and suffered a crumpled wing. Price was slightly injured, as were three Chindits. Nonetheless, the patrol continued its mission successfully before heading north to join the 16th Brigade. Price, Gotham, and the three injured Chindits, who could all walk, were directed to head back to Lalaghat.

The trek back took fifteen days and covered about 130 miles, but all five men made it home safely. At one point they had to swim several miles down the swift and turbulent Chindwin to evade patrolling Japanese. They quickly learned to eat off the land, which was a valuable lesson in itself, and avoided all native villages, unsure of what kind of reception they would receive.[21]

The day after the first glider mission, February 29, a second mission was flown to help Fergusson's brigade cross the Chindwin. Because of dense jungle and heavy bamboo growth, which deflected its march, the brigade reached the river about five miles downstream of its intended crossing point. Unfortunately, this also put the Chindits just five miles from a Japanese garrison at Singkaling Hkamti. Although the enemy would not be able to stop the crossing, they could make it very bloody.

Fergusson decided to have a couple of patrols flown in to block the only track into Singkaling Hkamti and to set up an ambush in case the Japanese did decide to see what was happening. A Squadron flew one patrol onto a sandbank ten miles downstream of the village to catch the Japanese if they did come out. Indeed, they did emerge later to their regret. A second patrol was delivered onto a sandbank directly across the river from where the crossing was to be made. This patrol then booby-trapped the track into Singkaling Hkamti, effectively isolating the garrison and at the same time providing warning of enemy movement toward the river.

Some days earlier, Fergusson had transmitted warning orders to Lalaghat, informing the base that he would need river-crossing equipment and asking that gliders be loaded with this matériel. He also made arrangements that the gliders would be flown in when the code word "trip" was given. Early on the 29th, Fergusson sent the code word. But the gliders did not show up as expected. Fergusson became worried and angry because crossing the Chindwin would not be easy without the equipment he had ordered.

Then, about an hour before dusk, he heard the drone of planes. Two C-47s roared slowly overhead, each towing a glider. The planes made a leisurely circle and came back at a lower altitude. The first glider was cut loose over the opposite bank of the river. It drifted down, almost seeming to hover, then touched down in a cloud of dust on the sandbank. A group of Chindits swiftly manhandled the craft out of the way so that the second CG-4 could land. As soon as both gliders were on the ground, they were unloaded. Their cargo included six outboard motors, six folding boats, bamboo poles, paddles, and gasoline. Fergusson's men immediately set about erecting the boats so that the brigade could begin crossing the river.

It had been planned that after the gliders were unloaded, the C-47s would snatch them and return to Lalaghat. In anticipation of this, the Chindits raised two poles with the glider tow ropes extended between them. Meanwhile, the glider pilots sat in their cockpits awaiting the snatch. Suddenly, the C-47 pilots circling overhead saw an unknown pair of planes in the distance. In enemy territory and aware of their vulnerability, the Americans beat a hasty retreat to Lalaghat.

The aircraft the C-47 pilots had seen were not Japanese, however, but Air Commando planes from Taro. Unaware of the excitement they had caused, the light plane pilots proceeded to shovel out loads of boots, clothing, and rope. Since this equipment was dropped without parachutes, the loads picked up speed as they plummeted earthward. The glider pilots, still in their cockpits, were suddenly confronted with the thud and crack of bundles hitting all about them. Fortunately, no damage was done to men or gliders, and the two gliders were retrieved the following day. After reaching Lalaghat, one of the CG-4 pilots discovered that this mission could have had a different ending. When he inspected the tow rope after landing, he found that the rope had been slowly unraveling in flight, and only one strand of the rope was left![22]

Now with folding boats powered by outboard motors, Fergusson's men were able to cross the Chindwin faster and more easily. Throughout the night the boats putted back and forth carrying men and equipment. The following day, March 1, Wingate flew in to see how things were going. Clint Gaty brought the Chindit leader in a UC-64, along with Cochran, Wingate aide Captain George Borrow, and four war correspondents. While Fergusson was happy to see Wingate and the other officers, he was less than pleased by the presence of the reporters. Previously, Fergusson had asked Wingate to bring in a couple of desperately needed officers.

Wingate brushed off the matter, but Gaty volunteered to fly back to Imphal the next morning to pick up the officers. Additionally, Gaty asked Fergusson if any of his men cared to make the trip. One of the muleskinners was chosen. Fergusson later recorded that Gaty had even allowed the Chindit to fly the plane, and that when the man returned, he was so ecstatic that he had a smile that lasted almost a month.[23]

Wingate stayed overnight at the crossing site to discuss the upcoming operation with Fergusson. Though Wingate was generally pleased with the 16th Brigade's progress, he was worried that the crossing was behind schedule. In less than a week Operation Thursday would open with the glider fly-in. Fergusson's men had to make the best possible time toward Indaw. The brigade commander replied that it probably would not be able to reach the area until March 20.

Wingate agreed that it would take the brigade that long to make Indaw, but he urged Fergusson to press on as quickly as possible. Then, Wingate was in his plane and headed back to his headquarters to make his final plans for the airborne assault.[24]

The Special Force leader's visit was not a respite for Fergusson's men, for several columns were already on the move when Wingate arrived. As soon as Wingate left, Fergusson had the rest of his troops slogging toward what would be their final destination, the stronghold that became known as "Aberdeen." And as they had already been doing, the Air Commando and TCC fliers were present to keep the Chindit columns supplied.

February had been a busy month for the Air Commando P-51s and B-25s. At the end of the month they tallied three Oscars damaged, two river vessels set afire, fourteen probable barracks burned, four locomotives and sixty-three rail cars and other rolling stock destroyed, another six locomotives damaged, three large trucks destroyed and a steamroller damaged, an oil storage tank burned, and a radio station destroyed.[25] But as busy as it had been for the fighters and bombers, the rest of Cochran's force had perhaps been busier.

With Operation Thursday's starting date approaching rapidly, the glider and transport sections, as well as General Old's TCC crews, were working at a feverish pitch to get ready. Wingate, as was his wont, was everywhere, overseeing all aspects of these preparations. Such activities did not always sit well with other commanders. On February 20 Wingate briefed the TCC crews at Sylhet. To Old's disgust, the Special Force leader presented himself as an expert on supply dropping. Compounding this affront to the TCC commander, Wingate offered the crews his own manuals as the way things should be done. Furthermore, in a talk to all USAAF personnel at Sylhet that evening, Wingate not only bitterly criticized the Fourteenth Army, he also revealed confidential information on basic strategy and the plans for his upcoming operation. Old felt that Wingate had been extremely indiscreet in his talk and had come close to compromising the operation.[26]

Meanwhile, the TCC leader was becoming increasingly concerned about Cochran's plan to use C-47s towing two gliders each. Despite Cochran's strong position that the transports could easily perform a double tow, Old remained dubious. He asked for a service test of the idea. Only on the day of the invasion did the general learn that such a test had been conducted only two days earlier and that the test had yielded questionable results.[27] A major reason for these results could be traced to Wingate's supply section. According to the CG-4A flight manual, the gliders' maximum useful load was 3,750 pounds. During training, the Chindits, who saw only area capacity, not weight, as the loading criteria, insisted on increasing the loads by 250 pounds to 4,000. Cochran, after consulting glider unit leader Taylor, agreed. Still, Wingate's officers pushed for additional weight, asking for 4,500-pound loads. Although concerned, Cochran reluctantly consented. A further complication was that the Chindits charged with loading the gliders ignored suggestions by the Air Commandos and loaded the CG-4s without regard to center-of-gravity factors. Now officially overweight by several hundred pounds, the CG-4s would gain even more poundage, albeit surreptitiously. This creep in glider weight, plus the center-of-gravity problems, had serious ramifications during the initial fly-in.[28]

Weight was also a concern for the C-47 tow planes. Although it had been planned that the tugs would also carry one thousand pounds of cargo to be dropped when the gliders were released, the tests had shown that it would be difficult for the C-47s to gain enough altitude to cross the mountains while pulling two gliders. Instead, Cochran decided to use ten of his UC-64s to carry this cargo for free drops. To his dismay, Old apparently did not learn of this change until after the fact.[29]

By late February Old had grown weary of Wingate's expanding supply requests. He had also become exasperated by what he viewed as a bit too much independence on Cochran's part. Many complaints about Cochran's attitude stud Old's diary, particularly in the entries made during the two weeks prior to the invasion, when proceedings were getting more hectic. Old was also disturbed about what he saw as a lack of firm decision making by both Wingate and Cochran.[30]

Cochran was firm on one thing. He would be responsible for all glider operations, although transport operations would remain under Old's control. With only thirteen C-47s but twenty-six pilots experienced in double tow, Cochran requested that TCC provide thirteen more planes to operate as tugs and another twenty-six pilots from the 27th and 315th Squadrons to act as copilots for the Air Commandos. Old was willing to supply the planes, but he was worried about the morale of his pilots being subordinated to Cochran's men. Eventually, though, Old did provide the copilots.[31]

In a February 29 operations order, Old directed that the Air Commandos furnish twelve C-47s, that the 27th and 315th TCSs each supply twelve aircraft, and that the three RAF transport squadrons (the 62nd, 117th, and 194th) provide another forty C-47s. Seven aircraft from the 31st Squadron would serve as a reserve force. Additionally, Tulihal and Hailakandi in India were designated as the RAF bases for the operation, and Sylhet and Lalaghat were made the USAAF fields. Specific numbers of sorties were established for the first week. All aircraft dispatched from Lalaghat on D-day and D+4-day, which were the days when gliders were used, would be controlled by Cochran. Old would control all other aircraft.[32]

To facilitate loading, pens numbered 1 to 40 were constructed around the Lalaghat runways. Men, equipment, and animals were divided into six-thousand-pound loads and assigned to the pens. Each pen also contained a loading ramp for the animals. Cochran and Alison planned that the 27th and 315th squadrons would arrive each afternoon at Lalaghat for the night's operation. Upon landing, each C-47 would taxi to a predesignated pen where loading would begin immediately. While loading was under way, the aircraft would be serviced. It was an efficient and time-saving procedure.

The planners specified the particular routes the C-47s would fly to and from the landing sites. Specific altitudes were also mandated: Eight thousand feet was the minimum safe altitude over the mountains for outbound aircraft; nine thousand feet was the specified altitude for returning aircraft. As it turned out, with the heavy loads some aircraft carried and the double tows of other C-47s, even these relatively low altitudes proved daunting for aircraft and crews.[33]

Concerned about casualties during the operation, Cochran directed that at least six gliders be converted into ambulance ships. Two gliders were converted into ambulances by adding three cases of medical supplies into each of the CG-4s and by mounting a litter that could be used as an operating table. In case of an accident, this equipment could be moved to another glider or a ground site. Four more gliders had six litters each mounted, which made them able to evacuate six litter and six ambulatory patients. An Air Commando doctor was to fly in each of the hospital gliders. The Chindits also had twelve doctors going in on the landings.[34]

On the evening of March 4 it seemed that the Air Commandos and Chindits were as ready as they would ever be. Yet Cochran had a nagging feeling about the affair. Over the protests of the Air Commandos and even some of his own officers, Wingate had forbidden any reconnaissance flights over Broadway and Piccadilly. Cochran believed this to be a serious mistake, but he would try to follow Wingate's orders. Still, Cochran would have liked to get one final look at those grounds.

Chapter 6

Into the Darkness

L alaghat, and every other field sending aircraft for Operation Thursday for that matter, was a beehive of activity on the morning of March 5. A constant roar permeated the air as plane after plane landed or took off. Some transports taxied to the sides of the runway where tow ropes had been strung in long rows to be connected to plane and glider. Other C-47s taxied to designated pens where equipment was being muscled into position for loading. On almost every road leading to the runway, British and Indian soldiers and their mules clustered while waiting for orders to board gliders or planes. The men checked and rechecked their equipment. Away from the airstrip hubbub, flying personnel were briefed on the mission. Large maps drawn on bedsheets that showed the landing areas were studied carefully by the men.

Slim, Stratemeyer, Baldwin, and Old had flown in to Lalaghat to watch the show. The only major commander not present was Mountbatten himself. He had suffered an eye injury in a jeep accident a few days earlier and had not yet recovered.

Ironically, the atmosphere at Lalaghat was both tense and relaxed. Many men were tense in anticipation of what lay ahead. Just as many were relaxed for the same reason because now they could get on with the task they had trained so hard to accomplish. Cochran and Alison seemed to be everywhere as they made last-minute inspections. Both men had planned to fly a glider into one of the clearings, where they would assume command. Not happy about the possibility of losing both his air commanders, Wingate ordered Cochran to remain at Lalaghat. Cochran tried in vain to change Wingate's mind. For once, the soft-spoken Alison outtalked his friend, and Wingate chose him to command the force at Piccadilly. Olson, the group's executive officer, would command Broadway.[1]

Several days earlier, Russhon had gone to Cochran to ask about photographing the clearings. Russhon wanted to get some last-minute pictures for the photographic record he and his team had been compiling about the operation.

He also believed that taking the pictures was a reasonable precaution against receiving a nasty surprise when the troops actually flew in. Cochran reminded the photographer that Wingate expressly forbade aircraft from flying over the landing sites. Still, Russhon thought the colonel was not enthusiastic about leaving Broadway and Piccadilly unobserved.[2]

Russhon approached Cochran again the following day. This time the Air Commando leader was amenable to the proposal. The concern over the landing grounds that had been nagging at Cochran for some days now caused him to defy Wingate's orders. He told Russhon to fly over the clearings in the late morning or early afternoon of D-day and see what things were like there. The photographer raced to the airstrip to find Maj. Robert Smith. The bomber leader listened quietly to Russhon then told him to climb into Smith's B-25. Smith would fly the mission himself. Shortly before noon, the B-25 roared off the field and headed for Broadway. Almost two hours later the clearing came into view. Everything seemed normal as Russhon snapped away with a handheld camera. Smith then turned south for Piccadilly.

Whereas Broadway had looked fine, something appeared to be wrong at Piccadilly. As Smith and Russhon neared that clearing, both men could see numerous parallel streaks stretching across the open field. On closer inspection, the pair saw that the streaks were actually teak logs that had been pulled into the clearing and effectively blocked the site from glider landings. Only one small area seemed usable, but freshly turned dirt was spotted. The logs had not been there a few weeks earlier, and Russhon also wondered if the fresh dirt concealed mines. He was so astonished at the sight that he forgot to take photos. Smith circled over Piccadilly once more so that Russhon could get his pictures then sped for home.

Time was of the essence. The B-25 was under strict radio silence, and it would be between 4:00 and 5:00 PM before Smith and Russhon could get back to Hailakandi, where Russhon's photo lab was located. The takeoffs for the operation were set to begin at 5 PM, just before sundown, from Lalaghat, twelve miles from Hailakandi. Russhon was out of the plane and running for his photo lab before the B-25's propellers had stopped turning. At the lab, Russhon turned his photos over to 1st Lt. Irving A. Greenspan and his three enlisted assistants for developing and printing.

The four men turned to work with careful haste. The darkroom was a crude structure of bamboo. It was not light tight, and extreme caution was necessary to minimize light streaks. Water for fixing and washing the prints had to be carried from a well some distance away. No drying facilities were available, so Greenspan used desk blotters to blot and dry each negative and print. Working under these adverse conditions, the men made some thirty 20- x 24-inch enlargements.[3]

While Greenspan and his men were developing the pictures, Russhon had been trying to telephone Cochran. He could not reach either Cochran or Alison, however, and he despaired that he would not get the information to them in time. Because Lalaghat was so crowded, Russhon could not use a large plane like Smith's B-25 to fly there. Russhon had just commandeered a jeep to make the frantic twelve-mile drive to Lalaghat when fortune smiled on him. A USAAF colonel, having become lost on the way to Lalaghat, landed his fighter at Haila-kandi to ask for directions. Russhon ran to the plane to assist the colonel and to also ask him to deliver the precious photos to Cochran. The pilot consented and was soon on his way.

Russhon was headed back to his jeep when a second bit of luck came his way. This time it was in the form of an Air Commando sergeant and his L-5. The little plane had hardly stopped when Russhon was beating on its door and asking the pilot to fly him to Lalaghat. Agreement was swiftly reached, and the L-5 putted off for Lalaghat. It was not as fast as a fighter, but it was at least heading in the right direction.

As soon as he reached Lalaghat Russhon began searching for Cochran and Alison. He found them puzzling over the photos. The photographer quickly told his story. Now fully alarmed, Cochran and Alison took the photos to Wingate. At first the Chindit leader was irate, berating Russhon for disobeying orders. Cochran finally broke into Wingate's tirade by saying that he had felt a hunch. This seemed to mollify Wingate, for he quickly calmed down and even managed a small smile.

Wingate called a conference of his brigade commanders to decide what to do. Slim, Stratemeyer, and Baldwin also joined the group. Initially, it was thought that Japanese agents had found out about the operation or, at least, about Pic-cadilly. Could the other landing zones now be ambushes? Someone remembered that a photograph of the Piccadilly site had appeared in *Life* following Wingate's first foray into Burma. Perhaps the enemy, knowing that an Allied offensive was imminent, was just taking a routine precaution to block potential landing sites. (As it turned out, Burmese loggers, not the Japanese, had dragged the trees into the clearing to dry.) Using Chowringhee in place of Piccadilly was considered but "Mad Mike" Calvert, the 77th Brigade commander, did not believe that was wise since his force would be split between two widely spaced points separated by the Irrawaddy River. He thought this would be an invitation to disaster, as did Lieutenant Colonel Walter Scott, whose 1st Battalion, The King's Regiment was to be first in. Cochran and Baldwin also agreed, saying that changing the landing site would require too much rebriefing.[4]

There were other important points to consider. After weeks of intense training, the Chindits and Air Commandos were at their peak. Any delay would take the edge off their preparations. Also, if Operation Thursday was delayed, it would be a month before the moon would again be in the right phase. This would result in the operation being one month closer to the start of the monsoon season, which was not an appetizing thought. There was one other major consideration: The operation was already under way. Even as the senior officers were in conference, Fergusson's brigade was moving toward the landing area. To stop the advance would effectively end the participation of Fergusson's troops in Operation Thursday because they could not remain behind enemy lines by themselves for another month.

What happened next has been controversial ever since. Wingate supporters state that he alone made the decision to go ahead with the landings but to use just Broadway. Wingate critics disagree, claiming that Slim, as Army commander, had to make the final decision. It was more likely a meeting of minds among those present—Wingate, Slim, Baldwin (who was in charge of the air elements), and, not the least, Calvert, whose brigade would lead the operation. Whoever ultimately made the decision—and in the end it does not really matter who that was—gave the fateful words to continue Operation Thursday.[5]

With the matter resolved, controlled chaos took over as flight plans were revised and loading manifests were adjusted to account for the elimination of the twenty gliders scheduled to land at Piccadilly from that night's launch. Unfortunately, this haste resulted in carelessness in reloading. Equipment was just piled in the gliders and stowed wherever it would fit, creating weight and center-of-gravity problems that would only become apparent later. Cochran and Alison rushed over to their men to quickly rebrief them. Clambering atop the hood of a jeep, Cochran told his men, "Say, fellers, we've got a better place to go!"[6] He then showed the glider and transport crews their new assignments. The briefing ended quickly, and the men ran to their aircraft.

Alison was now out of a job, for he had been scheduled to lead the mission into Piccadilly. Not willing to be left out of the operation at this late hour and willing to serve under Olson at Broadway, he took the spot of another glider pilot. The Air Commando glider leader, Taylor, who had been scheduled for Piccadilly also, bumped the pilot who was to fly the first glider into Broadway.

The ground trembled with the roar of C-47 engines as the planes waddled into position for the final checks prior to takeoff. At 6:12 PM, just seventy-two minutes late, Bill Cherry took off, towing two gliders behind. These were the first of eight gliders carrying the advance party that was to reconnoiter the land-ing site and prepare the ground for the arrival of the main force. At five to ten minute intervals, the rest of the Broadway force followed.

It quickly became obvious to the tow pilots that something was wrong. Continuous high power was needed in the climb, and even then the aircraft were climbing at only 150 feet per minute. Not until later did it become known that most of the gliders had been dangerously overloaded by their passengers. In some cases the glider loads reached 5,500 pounds, which was nearly 2,000 pounds more than what the CG-4 flight manual recommended as a maximum safe load. Like soldiers everywhere, Wingate's men did not trust that supplies would reach them any time soon, so the Chindits had loaded their gliders with more ammunition, food, and other supplies.

The tow ships climbed laboriously to eight thousand feet, an altitude that gave them just five hundred feet to spare over the highest peaks of the Chin Hills. Some gliders did not make it that far. Men on the ground at Lalaghat soon saw red flares in the distance, which indicated that some of the CG-4s had been cut loose from their tows. Ten gliders were released before reaching enemy ter-ritory. Two of these separations were caused by electrical problems in the tow planes, necessitating a return to the Lalaghat area; two more were the result of higher than anticipated fuel consumption. Those two gliders were cut loose near Imphal. Fortunately, no casualties resulted from these misadventures, but needed supplies were lost.[7]

Further losses were sustained as the remaining tugs and gliders struggled on toward Broadway. Prior to reaching the Chindwin, a bright full moon shone directly into the faces of the pilots. Then a haze enveloped the aircraft, and it became difficult for the glider pilots to see their tugs. This problem was exacer-bated when all lights on the C-47s were turned off. In the turbulent air, with just the blue exhaust flames of the C-47 engines dimly observed in the gloom, pilots began to overcontrol their gliders. The gliders surged forward and then recoiled, placing great strain on the tow ropes. Inevitably, some ropes failed. Nine more gliders fell away between the Chindwin and the Irrawaddy.

Two of these came off the same tow. One carried Lieutenant Colonel Olson, who was to have taken charge at Broadway. This glider was also one of the two radio ships destined for the landing site. Olson's pilot turned back toward the Chindwin and was able to make a relatively smooth landing near the river. Although suffering a foot injury that caused him to fashion a jury-rigged crutch, Olson led his party back to safety within a few days.[8]

The second glider almost suffered a disastrous fate when the broken tow rope whipped back over its wing and cut into the fabric and caused the pilot to lose control momentarily. Fortunately, the pilot was able to recover and make a safe landing in a rice paddy. As the seventeen men, including Air Commando intelligence officer Major Boebel, scrambled from their glider, rifle and machine-gun fire met them. They had landed almost on top of 31st Division headquarters. As the commandos lay low in the shadows, it became evident that the Japanese were just shooting in the direction of the sound of the crash. Nevertheless, the men decided to get out of the area as fast as possible. It took almost a week for the party, traveling mostly at night, to reach safety.

On their fourth night one of those incidents that reveals the heroism that often dwells in the unlikeliest of men occurred. The group had reached the Chindwin, which they were going to have to swim. But of the seventeen men, eight could not swim. The swimmers took off their trousers, tied knots in them, and blew them up like balloons. Along with a few life preservers, the trousers were used to help float the nonswimmers across the swift-running river. A Japanese patrol was known to be nearby, so there was to be no talking during the crossing. One of the nonswimmers was a small, thin glider mechanic who also wore thick glasses. Although he did not appear tough enough for an arduous jungle campaign, Cpl. Estil I. Nienaber had pleaded to go on the mission and was finally allowed to go. He had held his own during the jungle trek, but he was going to be pulled across the Chindwin. About halfway across Nienaber lost his grip on his swimming partner, and the current ripped him away. He could have cried for help, but even at the cost of his life, Nienaber obeyed orders to remain quiet. He disappeared into the blackness and drowned. Eventually, with the help of Burmese villagers and a Chindit patrol, Boebel's party reached friendly lines.[9]

Other downed parties had varying degrees of luck. An ambulance glider carrying Captain Murphy, an Air Commando medical officer, and a load of Gurkhas landed near the enemy airfield at Katha. Unperturbed, the men climbed nonchalantly from their glider, formed into a column, and marched away into the jungle in the bright moonlight. Hardly a shot was fired at them. Instead of heading back to India, this group marched toward Broadway, reaching there on the 13th. Another glider landed near the 15th Division headquarters. Most of these men escaped into the jungle, but the pilot, blinded in the crash, was captured. He refused to give his captors any information, but the Japanese were able to study the crashed aircraft and made some shrewd observations. They were already fairly sure that Wingate would be involved in new operations into Burma, and this was confirmed by interrogations of other Chindits and Air Commandos who were captured when their gliders landed near the 31st Division headquarters and a regimental headquarters in the Paungbyin area. These scattered and inadvertent landings confused the Japanese, however, and they were unsure of where the main airborne landings had been made and in what strength. The Japanese remained in the dark on these matters for several days.[10]

While some Japanese officers considered the airborne invasion serious enough to recommend that U-Go, the invasion of India, be postponed, others remained sanguine; none more so than the Fifteenth Army commander General Mutaguchi. When the 5th Hikoshidan leader, Maj. Gen. Tazoe Noboru, warned Mutaguchi of the dangers of enemy units running wild behind the lines, Mutaguchi dismissed such threats. Considering the Chindits little more than a minor diversion, Mutaguchi told Tazoe that he would be in Imphal before the Chindits could cause major damage, and then he would destroy them. Although Tazoe continued to press the issue, pointing out what the enemy had accomplished with aerial resupply in Arakan and declaring that this could happen now on a greater scale, Mutaguchi refused to accept Tazoe's entreaties. The Fifteenth Army leader believed that whatever units there were in the areas of the landings were capable of handling the Chindits. After all, Mutaguchi told Tazoe, the Chindits were just mice in a bag.[11]

Mutaguchi assigned several battalions to counter the threat. The Burma Area Army leadership, while agreeing with Mutaguchi that U-Go should proceed, took the airborne landings more seriously. In mid-March, well after the landings, the Burma Area Army sent the 24th Independent Mixed Brigade from Moulmein and a number of 2nd Division units from the Bassein area to reinforce the Fifteenth Army against the Chindits. This slow buildup of forces against the Chindit strongholds would not prove very effective, however.[12] It was fortunate for the Chindits that the Japanese were confused by the inadvertent glider landings and that the enemy commanders were more interested in their offensive against Imphal than in what they perceived to be hardly more than nuisance raids, for the Broadway landings came close to disaster.

Shortly before 10 PM, Cherry arrived over Broadway with his two gliders still safely in tow. The clearing was plainly visible in the moonlight—a pale island in an ocean of blackness. Taylor cut loose from the C-47 and found himself plunging almost straight down. Only with great effort could he get the glider's nose to come up. Taylor could not figure out what was wrong. Another problem cropped up as he tried to slow his aircraft to its normal landing speed of about sixty miles per hour. The glider would not slow, its airspeed remained ninety miles per hour. Still, under these circumstances, Taylor's landing was better than most that evening.[13]

At the last moment, as he passed through shadows cast by the trees surrounding the clearing, Taylor momentarily lost his feel for his aircraft's attitude. Then he saw a large white patch in front of him. Hauling back on the controls with all his strength, he hopped his glider over what was a large and deep elephant watering hole. With a thud and the sound of ripping fabric as a wheel tore off, his glider slewed to a stop.

Two more gliders arrived, the air flowing over their wings whistling eerily in the darkness. One was flown by Blush, and the second, piloted by Alison, was carrying Scott. Their landings were also signaled by crunching and snapping sounds as they, too, crashed. As Scott and his men spread out to set up a perimeter defense, Alison and Taylor were left wondering what was causing the crashes. They soon had their answer. The landing ground was not as smooth as it had appeared to be on the reconnaissance photos. Large ruts made by logs dragged across the field were hidden under the tall grass. Some logs still remained, presenting hazards to the landing gliders. Here and there, large, deep elephant and buffalo water holes lay in wait to ensnare unlucky gliders. Two large trees, inexplicably unnoticed in the photos, towered right in the middle of the clearing.

When it became obvious that Olson was not going to arrive, Alison quickly took charge. He, Taylor, Blush, and Russhon, who had landed in a fourth glider, scurried about to set up beacons to guide the rest of the CG-4s. The regular lights had been lost, along with all aboard, when the glider carrying the equipment crashed into the jungle. The quartet were able to set out smoke pots as a temporary expedient. They had to relocate the smoke pots continually, however, because most of the arriving CG-4s cracked up upon landing, blocking the landing areas. It was exhausting work, and the Chindits pitched in to help. The sound of gliders smashing into each other was an unforgettable booming drum-like sound that was accompanied by a sharper snapping noise as glider frames twisted and broke.

Seese flew in Calvert and his team. Just prior to touching down, Seese saw Taylor's glider looming dead ahead. Yanking back on his control column, Seese managed to jump the other glider and land safely. The CG-4 carrying Casey, the 900th Engineer's commander, slammed into the trees, killing all aboard. The glider carrying the all-important radio equipment also crashed, and the equipment was damaged. With Olson's radio glider missing, this was a serious complication. Wingate and Cochran needed the latest information from Broadway, but despite the feverish efforts of the Air Commandos, the radio remained silent. More men were killed or wounded as the remaining gliders came in higher and faster than had been anticipated and crashed. It was some time before the Air Commandos realized that too-heavy and out-of-balance loads were the cause of most of the landing problems.

The hardworking radio crew finally got their equipment operating, albeit fitfully. Alison, assessing the chaotic conditions, directed them to send out the code word "soyalink." Chosen because it was the name of a meat substitute the British soldiers detested, soyalink meant that conditions at the landing zone were unfavorable and no further gliders should be dispatched. Alison intended to expand on that message, but before he could do so, the radio died again.

Wingate finally received the message at 2:27 AM, but only after it had passed through a couple of other communications links. Both he and Cochran were horrified. What was happening at Broadway? Was the landing zone under attack? The anguish of the unknown weighed heavily upon them. Wingate wrote later, "At the conclusion of the first night's operations there was little cause for optimism with regard to the future."[14] Old, who had never been enthusiastic about Operation Thursday, was even more critical, complaining in his diary, "It was on the whole a poor show."[15]

Before he received the disturbing message from Broadway, Cochran had dispatched a second wave of gliders. Because of the difficulties encountered by the first wave of gliders in double tow, Old directed his aircraft to tow only single gliders on the second mission. Cochran soon followed suit. Cochran was able to recall all but one tow and glider from the later group. In hindsight this unrecalled glider provided one amusing moment in a night of less-than-humorous events, and as it turned out, the glider's cargo also played a major role in the eventual success of the operation.

With the landings finally apparently halted, Alison and the others, completely worn out from running all over the field, prepared to get some rest. Suddenly, the sound of a motor cut through the air. The men thought at first that it was a Japanese plane, but then they recognized the sound of C-47 engines. Calvert tried to get a flare to warn off the incoming aircraft, but could not find one. Attempts to douse the smoke pots were just as unsuccessful. Those on the ground could tell by the sound of the C-47's engines that it was turning away and had evidently released its tow. Then they heard the eerie whistling of the glider approaching. Fearing the worst, Alison and Calvert awaited the inevitable crash.

The sound of the glider hitting trees was terrifying. "Oh my God!" Calvert muttered. Alison could say nothing. More men had been killed or wounded and more needed supplies had been lost, they thought. Discouragement began to set in, as can happen in the blackness of night when everything seems to be going wrong. Finally, Calvert said, "Let's go to bed. It always looks better in the daytime."[16]

Fate has a funny way of managing things, however, and the situation was not as dire as it seemed. Amazingly, the men and much of the equipment in the crashed glider survived. When the CG-4 crashed, it passed between two huge trees and had its wings ripped off. The fuselage careened on and was brought to an abrupt halt by the rough ground. The sudden stop broke the moorings of the bulldozer the glider was carrying, and the dozer surged forward toward the pilots. Flight Officer Gene A. Kelly, well aware of the consequences of this occurrence, had rigged the dozer's moorings to the corner braces of the glider's hinged nose. Now, as the dozer shot forward, it broke the braces, unhinging the nose. The nose swung upward with Kelly and his copilot, Sgt. Joseph A. DeSalvo, still strapped in their seats. The dozer shot forward some ten yards in front of the glider to land on its side. After the dozer passed, the glider's nose fell back down. "I planned it that way," an unflappable Kelly observed. Except for a broken thumb, he and DeSalvo were none the worse for wear.[17]

When daylight finally came, Alison and Calvert surveyed the landing ground. Of the fifty-four gliders dispatched for Broadway and not recalled, thirty-seven reached the objective. Two of these crashed into the jungle, killing most aboard. The remaining thirty-five gliders landed in the clearing, but most became wrecks themselves.[18] Smashed gliders littered the field. As the two men gloomily assessed the situation, they were startled by the sound of an engine coming from where the last glider had gone into the trees. A bulldozer, driven by 2nd Lt. Robert Brackett, the 900th Engineer's second in command, emerged from the undergrowth. With Brackett's appearance, things began to look a little brighter. Three small bulldozers were available, but the commander of the engineers had been killed. Alison turned to Brackett. He did not appear too impressive to Alison, but first impressions can be misleading. He turned out to be a tiger.

Alison asked the young man, "Do you think you can make an airstrip here?"

Brackett shook his head ruefully but said, "Yes, I think we can."

"Well, how long is it going to take you?"

Taking a measured look at the littered field, Brackett answered, "Well, if I have it done late this afternoon, will that be soon enough?"

Laughing, Alison told him to go to work.[19]

Brackett gathered the nine surviving engineers and a number of Chindit volunteers and began clearing a strip. Dynamite blasted trees out of the way; the bulldozers and men with shovels filled in holes and leveled a usable strip. Calvert was worried about his wounded. They needed hospitalization, and their presence limited what actions he could take in securing the surrounding area. At 6:30 AM Calvert reestablished communications with Wingate. The brigade commander requested that light planes with fighter escort be sent immediately to evacuate thirty casualties and to bring in replacement radio equipment. He reported thirty men killed. (A subsequent count revealed twenty-four fatalities, all but four of which were the result of crashes into the jungle.) Radio contact was again lost, leaving Wingate still unsure of the situation at Broadway. Nevertheless, light aircraft were dispatched. One L-1 took off from Tamu carrying the radio equipment. After delivering the radios, this aircraft brought out the first two wounded soldiers. All the available L-1s and L-5s at Taro followed shortly thereafter to evacuate the remaining wounded.

One part of the operation was apparently thrown together at the last minute and entailed using the group's UC-64s to drop supplies, and it was a disaster. Ten UC-64s were loaded with various supplies to deliver to Broadway. The planes were poorly equipped for night flying, and just two of them reached Broadway. The supplies they dropped were damaged or scattered all over when they hit the ground. Little could be used by the Chindits. Three of the UC-64s were lost—luckily without casualties—when they got lost on their way back to base.[20]

Finally, around 10:00 AM, Wingate received the heartening words "pork sausage." Unlike soyalink, pork sausage meant all was well at Broadway, and the field would be ready to receive C-47s by nightfall. The glider loads that could not be flown in on D-day were quickly reloaded on the transports. Old flew the first C-47 into Broadway on the evening of March 6. Sixty-two C-47 sorties carrying 77th Brigade reinforcements went in that night. For once the general was pleased with the way the Air Commandos handled things, particularly praising Alison for his traffic control at Broadway. Except for a minor collision between two taxiing RAF C-47s, operations went smoothly. Troops were unloaded, and the wounded and glider pilots were loaded with commendable speed; the aircraft averaged just twenty minutes on the ground. The two damaged transports were flown out later.[21]

With things now looking up at Broadway, Wingate began planning to open a second field at Chowringhee. This site was located about sixty miles south of Broadway and twenty miles southeast of Katha across the Irrawaddy. A small number of gliders would be dispatched there to prepare a field for the arrival of Brigadier Lentaigne's 111th Brigade. As the first C-47s were en route to Broadway, twelve gliders in single tow were launched for Chowringhee. All except one landed safely. Unfortunately, the one that crashed was the glider carrying engineering equipment, including the only bulldozer slated for the new field. All three Air Commandos aboard were killed, and the dozer was destroyed. This was a serious handicap, for it made grading a usable strip difficult.

Cochran immediately sent a C-47 to Calcutta to pick up a spare dozer. The new dozer arrived that evening and was transferred to a waiting glider that was shortly on its way to Chowringhee. In the meantime, Alison had sent one of his machines to the new field. The delay in getting the Chowringhee landing field open resulted in many of the transports slated for there being switched to Broadway. But shortly before midnight word came that the second field was ready to accept C-47s.

Six transports departed for Chowringhee at midnight, followed by additional waves at twenty minute intervals. After twenty-four planes had taken off, the disturbing news came that only 2,700 feet of lighted runway was available. Because it was believed that C-47s needed at least 4,000 feet of runway for safe operations, a recall message was sent to the transports. The first seven planes did not receive this message and continued on. Old again led the transports and did not receive the recall, but he landed without difficulty. He did, however, have some choice words for his favorite targets, the Air Commandos. He claimed that they had shown no flight discipline at Chowringhee, twice cutting his plane out of the landing pattern. The decision to recall the transports had been wise, however. There was not yet enough room on the ground to maneuver the C-47s.[22]

As work continued to expand Chowringhee, March 8 turned out to be a red-letter day for the Air Commandos. To keep the Japanese away from the vulnerable landing zones, the Fighter Section pounced on the enemy airfields at Anisakan, Shwebo, and Onbauk. The attacks temporarily halted Japanese interference with the Chindit operations at Broadway and Chowringhee.

As it transpired, Chowringhee was not operational for very long anyway. Wingate had already decided, during a conference on the 7th, to fly the maximum number of sorties into Broadway. He flew into Broadway that evening to observe the activities there and stayed overnight. The next evening, he flew to Chowringhee, returning to Lalaghat a few hours later. After inspecting the second field, Wingate decided that Chowringhee was too exposed to enemy attacks from both the ground and the air. Since the Japanese had not yet discovered Broadway, Wingate would use that field as the main hub for his operations.

Also influencing his decision to abandon the second field was that most of the 111th Brigade had flown into Chowringhee by the time of his visit, and its columns were pushing toward the Irrawaddy. To assist the brigade in crossing the river, four gliders were towed to a sandbar along the riverbank on March 11. The gliders carried boats, outboard motors, and other river-crossing equipment. That evening, two of the gliders were snatched out, with one carrying some Burmese prisoners. Meanwhile, the rest of the brigade was ordered to fly into Broadway and join up later.[23]

It was good that Wingate was concerned about Chowringhee because the Japanese had found it. The last loads of Chindits were flown in on the 9th, and the Air Commandos sent C-47s from Broadway to snatch undamaged gliders and equipment from Chowringhee. Six gliders were brought out that evening.

Early the next morning, after demolishing the field, the last Chindits moved out. A few hours after the last men disappeared into the jungle, enemy planes bombed and strafed the field. The Japanese returned the following day to waste more bombs on the deserted strip.[24]

While Chowringhee was used only briefly, Broadway (so far unnoticed by the enemy) had become a beehive of activity. Air Vice Marshal Baldwin wrote Stratemeyer, "Nobody has seen a transport operation until he has stood at Broadway under the light of a Burma full moon and watched Dakotas coming in and taking off in opposite directions on a single strip all night long at the rate of one landing and one takeoff every three minutes."[25]

Following the chaotic activities of the first night, operations at Broadway had settled into a regular, if furious, routine. For all this activity there were no accidents except for the C-47s taxi mishap until a Bomber Section B-25 crash-landed on March 8 after an engine failed during a mission. Fortunately, there were no injuries, and the wreck did not obstruct operations.[26]

One of the damaged C-47s was repaired and flown out on March 9, but the other plane remained grounded awaiting parts. A section of the stranded plane's leading edge had been bashed in almost to the main spar, and an aileron had been crushed. Alison believed that just a little sheet metal work and a new aileron would make it flyable again. He requested that the RAF send parts to effect a repair. Instead, he got a repair crew that would only estimate the damage. Alison hit the ceiling. He did not want a large target sitting in the open. Further requests for parts were ignored, and he finally told the sergeant in charge of the RAF crew that he would fly it out as is. The sergeant was aghast, sputtering that he could not let Alison take the plane in that state. Alison reminded the man that he outranked him and that Alison would accept responsibility. Still grumbling, the sergeant backed down.

Russhon decided he would accompany Alison even though Alison told Russhon that he had never flown a C-47 before. The photographer shrugged that off, replying, "Let's go." Alison took off and got the gear up easily because he read a large placard in the cockpit telling how to raise the gear. The flight to Lalaghat went smoothly. Even with just one aileron, the C-47 was a docile beast. The only concern Alison had about the flight arose when he arrived at Lalaghat. He could not read the landing gear hydraulic pressure gauge very well because it was located on the other side of the cockpit. While circling the field, he contacted a C-47 pilot in the tower and told him what he was doing. The pilot told him that he had done the right things, and Alison brought the plane down with ease. A laconic Old recorded in his diary, "Landing okay."[27]

Alison turned the plane over to the Air Commando mechanics to repair. Before giving it back to the British, they apparently made sure that some needed spare parts made their way onto a few of the Air Commando C-47s.[28]

By March 11 (D+6), Operation Thursday was completed. Because little information had been received concerning conditions at a proposed landing site known as Templecombe, Wingate directed that Dah Force be moved to Broadway instead. Thursday had been a remarkable operation and, despite the glider losses suffered the first night, a highly successful one. In addition to the fourteen Air Commando C-47s, two TCC squadrons and four RAF C-47 squadrons had been used. These units flew 660 C-47 and 74 glider sorties. According to figures compiled by Special Force, 7,023 men had been flown into Broadway, and another 2,029 had been delivered to Chowringhee through March 11. In addition, 175 ponies, 1,183 mules, and 509,083 pounds of supplies had been delivered to the two fields.[29]

Recognition over the success of Thursday was quick in arriving. Wingate wrote Cochran, "Please convey to all ranks under your command my thanks and appreciation for their devoted service in support of Thursday. In particular the courage and skill of the glider pilots should be praised as the foundations of the success gained. The continuous and unflagging operations of fighters and bombers is also one of the major factors in what has been achieved."[30]

Mounbatten passed on a message he had received from Churchill in which the prime minister said, "I reported to the president your airborne attack to which he has replied as follows—'I am thrilled by the news of mobile column success under Wingate. If you wire him please give him my hearty good wishes. May the good work go on. This makes an epic achievement for the airborne troops, not forgetting the mules.'"[31]

Broadway escaped the attention of the Japanese until March 13. Cochran had sent four fighters under Mahony to the field the day before for defense of the field and to provide close support to the Chindits fighting nearby. To Cochran's displeasure, the British had also dispatched several Spitfires there without telling him. A radar set also became operational that morning to provide early warning capability. It was limited in its coverage primarily because of nearby hills, a limitation that soon became painfully obvious.

When the Japanese finally attacked Broadway on March 13, they were met by the Spitfires and antiaircraft fire and suffered the loss of three planes and damage to six more. The enemy was not about to let Broadway escape unscathed, however. They returned in force on the afternoon of March 16. After four days of supporting the Chindits, Mahony was about to lead his men back to Haila-kandi when warnings were received that an enemy force was approaching and only twenty-eight miles away. He immediately ran to his fighter yelling, "Come on, guys, let's go!" First Lt. Hubert Krug had thought that getting to a dugout was a better idea, but he raced to his plane anyway. The first three American pilots roared off safely, but the last thing Krug remembered was placing his hand on the throttle. When he came to, his plane was on fire, but the engine was still running and pulling the Mustang around in a big circle.

The fire was eating into the right side of the cockpit, and Krug was attempting to shield his face from the flames with his right hand while trying to open the canopy with his left hand. It was probably just a few seconds before he got the canopy open, but it seemed like forever to Krug. Then he could not move. "Oh, yeah, my safety belt," he thought. He snapped it open and rolled out of the burning plane.

When he hit the ground and tried to run, he could not. He suddenly realized he still had his parachute strapped on. As he unstrapped it, he noticed that his hand was bloody and that skin was hanging off it in strips. In shock but not hurting, Krug stumbled to a dugout, where Capt. Cortez F. Enloe, an Air Commando doctor, gave Krug a shot of morphine and some grapefruit juice. A C-47 evacuated Krug back to India that evening.[32]

Now fully aware of Broadway, the Japanese sent twelve Oscars against it on March 17. They caught the defenders unaware and shot down one Spitfire and destroyed three others on the ground. With only a couple of fighters left operational, the Spitfires were pulled out. On the 18th the enemy returned again and burned the radar set. An RAF unit was already en route to Broadway before this happened, and its arrival on March 19 was most welcome.[33]

Although the fighters were withdrawn, Broadway remained an important base for the Air Commandos' light planes. The Japanese offensive toward Imphal had forced the evacuation of Tamu, where many of the smaller planes had been stationed, and they had moved to Broadway. There, the L-1s and L-5s were much closer to the action and were available to deliver supplies and evacuate the wounded that much more quickly. While at Broadway, one pilot was killed and one was wounded by strafing. Several aircraft were damaged, as well.[34]

Two events of importance to the Air Commandos occurred during this period. The first was that they finally shed their provisional status and became an officially designated group. The unit was constituted as the 1st Air Commando Group on March 25 and activated four days later. Its provisional designation had indicated its temporary status to perform a specific task, in this case the support of the Chindits. As such, however, the Air Commandos' logistical support was subject to the whims and vagaries of senior commanders, which were not always in the Air Commandos' favor, especially when requests for men and supplies clashed with the needs of already established units. By using their access to Arnold, Cochran and Alison could often circumvent this problem, but it was not an efficient way to operate. But now they would be recognized as a "proper" unit and be in the pipeline to receive logistical support.[35]

Unfortunately, the second significant event had serious negative ramifications for the light planes. A small strip, called Dixie, was built just inside Burma. A and B squadrons moved to the new field to be nearer to the columns they were supporting. The two units had been at Dixie for but a day when reports of enemy troops approaching were received. The strip was hastily evacuated—too hastily, as it turned out. Code books and other communications and intelligence information were left behind. Also, word of the evacuation was not spread, and a pair of light plane pilots landed at the abandoned field. Luckily, the Japanese had not yet reached Dixie, and the two men escaped.

Although the Japanese apparently did not capture any secret material, this close call was something that could not be tolerated. As commander of the Light Plane Section, Rebori was ultimately responsible for the actions of his men. And like the manager of a losing sports team, it is the manager who usually gets fired, not the players. So it was with Rebori. Cochran relieved Rebori, who was already ill with malaria, and replaced him with Gaty. Additionally, Cochran decided to end the four squadron setup and instead placed them into a single unit. Gaty remained the Light Plane Section leader until he became commander of the 1st ACG, at which time Major Boebel assumed command of the light planes.[36]

Because of the unwelcome attention of the Air Commandos and other Tenth Air Force fighter units, the Japanese never again mounted an air attack on Broadway following March 18. They did, however, attempt a ground assault on the stronghold in late March. On March 26 a Chindit floater column ambushed an enemy force of some 150 men and killed 31. The following day other Japanese troops succeeded in breaching the Broadway perimeter. Although they slashed the fabric of a few light planes (easily repairable) and did deny use of the strip by C-47s, this success was temporary. Garrison troops evicted the attackers by April 1, inflicting 150 casualties. The Japanese withdrew and never again threatened Broadway. By that time other fields had been opened, and Broadway had assumed more of a secondary role. It was finally closed down on the morning of May 13 after the men and equipment were ferried to the new fields or evacuated back to India.[37]

The Air Commandos, in the meantime, had been kept busy supporting the Chindits with air attacks, supply drops, and the evacuation of wounded. It should be noted that because the group had only fourteen C-47s, much of the heavy lifting was done by Old's TCC planes. The gliders continued to be used in the establishment of new fields, but their numbers had been whittled down considerably since March 5. Typical of this attrition was a mission on the night of March 19/20. That evening five gliders landed a small force of sappers known as Bladet Force near Tigyaing in the Meza Valley about eighteen miles southwest of Chowringhee. A sixth glider had been intended to land, but it received a red light from the ground before it was released and was brought back to base. The gliders that landed were burned, and their pilots fought alongside Bladet Force as it operated against enemy lines of communication in the Kawlin–Wuntho area. After about ten days the pilots were evacuated back to Broadway by light planes.[38]

The Chindits needed all the support they could get from the Air Commandos, for the Japanese had finally realized the danger of having large armed columns operating behind their lines while they were moving against Imphal and Kohima. Such danger was reinforced when Fergusson's 16th Brigade discovered a major supply dump and destroyed it, thus depriving the Japanese of much-needed supplies for their offensive. Then on March 16, Calvert established a road- and rail block near Mawlu, which lay about twenty miles north of Indaw. This block later received the name White City for the many supply parachutes that festooned the trees and lay upon the ground. White City would play a major role in Chindit activities for many weeks.

Another stronghold that soon drew the enemy's attention was Aberdeen, which was about fifteen miles west of Mawlu, near the village of Mahnton. Almost completely surrounded by low hills, Aberdeen would be the 16th Brigade's stronghold. The brigade had finally arrived on March 19, following its grueling and debilitating march from Ledo. Wingate visited Calvert at White City on March 20 and then flew to Mahnton the next day. After consulting with Fergusson, Wingate decided to establish Aberdeen as the base for the 16th and 111th brigade's operations as well as a reception center for the landing of the 14th Brigade.[39]

At first light on March 22 six gliders carrying two bulldozers and other engineering equipment flew in to Aberdeen to prepare a C-47 strip. The American engineers swiftly completed this job, and the fly-in of the 14th Brigade and a garrison force from the 3rd West African Brigade began the next day.[40]

But as Aberdeen was being developed, tragedy struck both the Chindits and the Air Commandos. Following his visit to Aberdeen on the 21st and subsequent visits to his other strongholds, Wingate returned to Broadway on March 23, where he stayed overnight. The following afternoon Cochran sent a B-25 to pick him up and return him to his headquarters. After picking up a couple of war correspondents, Wingate left Broadway for Imphal.[41] The B-25 stopped at Imphal for a short time, where Wingate met with Air Vice Marshal S. F. Vincent, commander of 221 Group. The next leg of the trip to India ended in disaster, as Wingate's B-25 crashed into a jungle-covered mountain and all aboard were killed.

White City was a hot spot for the Chindits for some time. It became the locus of Japanese attention, particularly by the 24th Independent Mixed Brigade. In the process, this enemy force was cut up severely, and playing a major role in the defeat of the enemy were the Air Commandos. Though they had already been busy attacking other targets, March 18 marked the opening of the Air Commandos' activities in direct support of the Chindits. The first mission, however, was not successful. Six B-25s and a like number of P-51s were scheduled to support Calvert's brigade at Mawlu. Upon arriving over the target the pilots were unable to contact the troops, and smoke shells that were fired appeared to land in friendly territory, so no attacks were made. Later missions would be much more satisfactory.[42]

The Air Commandos and Chindits developed a control system that the Chindits preferred to the one used by the RAF. The RAF insisted on detailed indications of target locations so that its pilots could be carefully briefed prior to takeoff. Ground-to-air communications or changes in targets while airborne were not favored. The Americans, on the other hand, preferred to talk directly with a controller on the ground and to combine this up-to-the-minute information with the use of smoke to mark targets. If a target was not exactly where the American pilots had been told it would be before they took off, it did not matter. They would usually find it. This system proved much more flexible, which appealed to the Chindits as being "infinitely" more effective.[43]

The Chindits had no illusions that air attacks were more accurate than artillery, but the morale effect of bombing on friendly and enemy troops was considerable. Nonetheless, the mutual confidence that grew between the Chindits and the Air Commandos was such that air strikes were often called in and flown within yards of friendly lines.[44] An innovation introduced by the Air Commandos during this period contributed to the accuracy of the air attacks. Fergusson's men had discovered a large gasoline dump south of Indaw. The dump was out of range of their mortars, so the brigade air liaison officer asked the Americans to help put the dump out of business. With the liaison officer as a passenger, Gaty personally flew an L-5 to reconnoiter the area. The two men returned on April 9, this time bringing with them six Mitchells and eight Mustangs. After Gaty marked the target with smoke grenades thrown from the L-5, the bombers and fighters proceeded to beat up the dump with bombs, depth charges, and machine-gun fire. The numerous fires left burning marked a successful attack.[45]

A second such mission was flown on April 21 at Indaw. After an L-5 marked targets along a road north of Indaw, six B-25s dropped incendiaries and 500-pounders on the markers, starting many fires. In the meantime, eight Mustangs bombed a bivouac area with 500-pound incendiaries, again leaving numerous fires burning.[46]

Not to be left out of this excitement, the C-47 crews began carrying British mortar shells, fragmentation clusters, and incendiaries, heaving these explosives from their planes when flying over enemy territory. As one pilot commented, "We may not have done any damage, but I'll bet we scared the hell out of them."[47]

The Air Commandos also employed an unusual tactic sparingly, perhaps only once. This involved the cutting of telephone and telegraph lines by trailing a line from a P-51. This ingenious device consisted of a 150-foot length of 3/4-inch line secured to bomb racks on both wings. On this line was a sliding metal ring to which was attached a 150- to 200-foot 5/16-inch steel cable. At the end of this cable were mounted a series of three or four weights totaling 12 to 15 pounds. If needed, the entire device could be released from the bomb racks. For takeoff the cables were strung out behind the fighter in a similar fashion to the C-47/glider tow ropes. The only recorded use of this device occurred on March 20, when a P-51 was sent to cut wires north of Mawlu. The cable broke, so the pilot resorted to cutting the wires with his wings! He did this five times along the railroad tracks near Mawlu, then repeated the process three more times along the Indaw–Banmauk road. Just what condition the fighter returned in was not reported.[48]

Chapter 7

Into the Light

While Thursday and the Chindit's succeeding operations had been the primary reason for the Air Commandos' existence, this did not preclude them from operating afield of Wingate's troops. This was especially true of the fighters and bombers, which were often not needed for close support of the columns and could thus attack other targets. Of particular importance were the enemy airfields. The Japanese had moved many of their aircraft forward to support the offensive against Imphal. It was imperative for the Allies to gain air superiority over the Japanese lest the enemy's aircraft be used with devastating effect against Allied ground forces. Air Commando aircraft would play a major role in achieving that superiority.

In March 1944 the Japanese still had a potent air force of approximately 270 aircraft in Burma. The Japanese Army Air Force's (JAAF) main fields were in the Rangoon area at Mingaladon, Hmawbi, Zayatkwin, and Hlegu. The 5th Hikoshidan was headquartered at Rangoon and controlled several *sentais* (groups or air regiments) equipped with Oscars, Ki-46 Dinahs, Ki-21 Sallys, and Ki-49 Helens. Other important bases were located in the Meiktila region (Aungban and Heho) and the Mandalay area (Anisakan, Monywa, Shwebo, and Onbauk). Airfields farther forward included Indaw and Bhamo. These latter fields lay close to Broadway and Chowringhee.[1]

The need to gain air superiority did not negate the obligation to weaken the enemy in other ways. Numerous targets presented themselves for the Air Commandos' attention. One such target was the town of Wuntho, east of Indaw. The Japanese had a number of supply installations there, and it was also the site of a major railroad marshaling yard, and 1st ACG planes visited it many times. The Air Commandos had first bombed the Wuntho rail yard on February 5. The enemy would regularly rebuild their warehouses following a raid, and just as regularly, the Americans would return to knock them down again. On March 13 and 14 B-25s and fighters made especially strong attacks that left the entire town burning. The March 13 attack was notable in that it was the first extensive use of rockets by the Mustangs.[2]

The 1st ACG was a pioneer in the USAAF in the use of aerial rockets. The service had developed a 4.5-inch projectile, and the rocket had worked well in tests. A more grueling combat test was needed, however. Because one of Cochran's instructions had been to develop new forms of combat operations and tactics, it was natural that his group be given the task of trying out these new weapons. One of the rocket project officers, Maj. Frank Fazio, was sent from the United States along with one thousand rockets to assist the Air Commandos with the new rockets. The combat test was almost stillborn when the rockets were delivered to the Fourteenth Air Force instead of the Air Commandos. Probably unsure of what to do with these weapons, the Fourteenth's head of logistics was easily induced to return them in exchange for three bottles of Scotch.[3]

Fazio's first task was to determine how to mount the rockets on the P-51s. The rockets were encased in tubes similar to the bazookas used by the infantry. The recommended place to mount these tubes was on the Mustang's bomb racks. Mahony was absolutely against this because his planes nearly always carried bombs, drop tanks, or both. A rocket installation would interfere with these normal loads, and changing back and forth between bombs and rockets would be too time-consuming. After consulting with the Fighter Section's armament officer, 1st Lt. Andrew Postlewait, and obtaining the assistance of a couple of enlisted men to fabricate and install the device, Fazio created an attachment that was located nearly two feet outboard of the bomb racks. Though this was not supposed to be possible according to the manuals, the attachment worked.[4]

Carried in a triangular arrangement of three tubes under each wing, the 4.5-inch rockets soon became standard armament on the group's Mustangs. When fired, the rockets would go in almost any direction and were thus not great for pinpoint accuracy, but they were devastating against buildings and other large targets. The pilots also liked to use them against locomotives, usually firing all six rockets at the same time. If a rocket hit, the explosion would tear the locomotive's boiler to pieces, and steam and smoke would shoot hundreds of feet into the air, which was always a gratifying sight to the pilots.[5]

Meanwhile, two days before the landings at Broadway, twelve Air Commando P-51s carrying bombs attacked the Shwebo airfield north of Mandalay to open the campaign to obtain air superiority. Since no enemy aircraft were on the ground, the Air Commandos took their time bombing and strafing buildings and antiaircraft positions. A few hours later four B-25s also bombed and strafed the field and the neighboring town.[6]

On the morning of March 7, ten B-25s and a like number of P-51s raided the Bhamo II airstrip southeast of Broadway. They cratered the strip for most of its length but, once again, found no enemy aircraft. Later that afternoon Mahony and Capt. Mack Mitchell made an armed reconnaissance of the fields at Mandalay, Heho, and Anisakan. As they neared the latter Mahony saw six Oscars that appeared to be freshly painted in a dark green color and with yellow wingtips and cowling fronts that were taking off from the field. Four had already gotten airborne and were stacked up to about two thousand feet. The fifth plane was just leaving the ground, and the last one was at the end of the strip preparing for takeoff. Mahony and Mitchell immediately attacked, but the guns on one of the Mustangs jammed after just a couple of shots. Fortunately, this did not prove disastrous, as the enemy pilots were more intent on escaping and rapidly disappeared to the east. The Air Commandos claimed damage to one of the fighters.[7]

The Japanese may have escaped with little harm that day, but they had no such luck on the next. An early morning mission by nine B-25s and sixteen P-51s to the Indaw and Katha strips was moderately successful. The usual tactics on these joint missions was for the P-51s to open an attack with 500- or 1,000-pound bombs. They would be followed by the B-25s dropping bombs, fragmentation clusters, or incendiaries, and then both types of planes would return to beat up the target with repeated strafing runs.[8] Although no enemy aircraft were found on this morning raid, the fields were well beaten up with 500- and 1,000-pound bombs. An afternoon visit to Anisakan, Shwebo, and Onbauk proved very profitable, however.

To support the offensive toward Imphal, which began on March 8, the 5th Hikoshidan moved its 62nd Sentai, 64th Sentai, and 204th Sentai from Mingaladon to the airfields in the Mandalay area that same morning. There was a mix-up when the 62nd Sentai arrived, as its bombers landed amid the already parked 64th Sentai's Oscars. The subsequent congestion caused the cancellation of an afternoon mission and a very strong reprimand to the 62nd's commander to get his planes to their proper field. As the two sentais were sorting out their problems, the 50th Sentai's Oscars arrived at Shwebo from Anisakan only to be informed of the cancellation of the mission and to return to Anisakan.[9]

As the Japanese were trying to sort out this mess, the Air Commandos put in an appearance. The engagement the previous day had whetted the ever-aggressive Mahony's appetite for combat, and sensing that more enemy aircraft could be found, he had requested another raid on the Mandalay fields. This time he led a force of twenty-two Mustangs carrying 500-pound bombs and belly tanks. When Mahony arrived over Anisakan, his mouth must have watered at seeing so many enemy aircraft caught on the ground. Leaving four planes as top cover, Mahony led the remainder of his flight group screaming down to savage the field.

Because the Japanese were unprepared and unable to take off, the Air Commandos raked the enemy planes unmercifully, returning again and again to strafe and bomb. Columns of smoke erupted one by one as the grounded fighters and bombers exploded and burned. Soon, a dirty pall cloaked the field. The strafers were well into their work when the top cover radioed of more fighters approaching. It was the 50th Sentai returning from the fiasco at Shwebo.

The two sides met in a furious but relatively brief battle in which Capt. Holly Keller claimed an Oscar destroyed. Another Oscar was claimed damaged. Sadly, Capt. Erle H. Schneider was lost when he apparently became fixated on an Oscar that was already on fire (possibly Keller's victim) and flew into the enemy plane.

Leaving Anisakan burning fiercely, Mahony led his fighters toward Shwebo and Onbauk. The Japanese were still unaware of the presence of enemy aircraft, for these fields were also covered with planes. Towering smoke pyres once again marked the destruction of parked aircraft. Several 64th Sentai Oscars did manage to get off the ground to engage the Americans. They probably got 1st Lt. Martin O'Berry, who was never seen again, but may have lost a pair to Capt. Lester Murray, who got credit for probables, and had one more plane damaged by 1st Lt. Robert Boyd.

The big scorer at Onbauk was Krug. He was not flying his usual plane that day. Not all of the Air Commando P-51s carried gun cameras, but the one Krug was piloting did. Krug and 1st Lt. Roland Lynn were headed back to Hailakandi when they flew over Onbauk. It had appeared to be deserted earlier, but now it appeared to be crawling with bombers. The Americans dropped down and proceeded to beat up the field. To Krug it seemed that everywhere he looked, there was another target in his gunsight. Upon his return to Hailakandi, Krug was about to claim six bombers destroyed—there had been so many targets that he had lost track of what he had shot at—when his crew chief came in holding the gun camera film canister. The film was quickly developed and revealed that Krug had actually destroyed five Helen bombers.[10]

Mahony radioed that a second strike was needed and requested the B-25s be armed for this mission. As soon as he returned Mahony had his fighters hastily rearmed, also. Five B-25s and fifteen P-51s were sent on the second raid. The afternoon was descending into evening, however, and smoke smudged the air, making it difficult to see the target. Some of the smoke undoubtedly came from Burmese loggers, who often burned slash and undergrowth to clear the areas around where they were logging. The resulting haze caused all but two of the fighters to miss Onbauk. The bombers did reach Shwebo, though, and started fires that caused two heavy explosions.

This last mission almost turned into disaster for the fighters. Darkness had fallen when they returned to Hailakandi, but the field had no lights An unnamed but innovative individual had the idea of pouring drums of gasoline into a drainage ditch that ran around the field and setting the gasoline on fire. This was quickly done, and the resulting blaze outlined the runway perfectly. All planes landed safely, but it had been a close call.

The raids on the Mandalay fields had been spectacularly successful. The Air Commandos claimed twenty-seven Oscars, six Dinahs (actually Helens), one Sally, and an unidentified twin-engine transport destroyed on the ground and one Oscar destroyed, two probables, and two damaged in the air. On the other hand, the Japanese recorded only six Helens and five Oscars destroyed on the ground at Onbauk and another five fighters lost at Anisakan. Two more fighters were shot down. The 64th Sentai at Shwebo recorded only an unspecified number of aircraft damaged. Whatever the actual results, the Air Commandos had delayed the JAAF's participation in the Imphal offensive by several days and had forced the 62nd Sentai to return to Malaya to be reequipped. Better still, the Japanese had been kept from attacking the Chindit landing zones until Wingate's men were already in place.[11]

Onbauk received further attention on March 9, when eighteen fighters strafed and bombed the field. The attackers noticed that the Japanese had tried to clean up the wreckage of the day before, but piles of debris and pieces of aircraft still littered the field. One camouflaged bomber hidden in a revetment was set on fire, and an Oscar was damaged.[12]

Praise for the missions came swiftly. Stratemeyer wrote on March 9, "Our admiration for your mission on Shwebo and Onbauk is unsurpassed. In one mission you have obliterated nearly one-fifth of the known Japanese Air Force in Burma. Heartiest congratulations to the First Air Commando Force."[13]

For the next few days the Air Commandos reconnoitered enemy airfields and found little activity. Several runs along the rivers were made, hunting for river steamers and other small vessels. One steamer was found south of Katha on the 10th and sunk. The rail yard at Hopin was struck the next day with good results.[14]

Then on the 12th, the Japanese struck back. That afternoon all three fighter sentais and a few bombers from the 8th Sentai went after the Allied airfields in the Silchar region, escorted by fighters from the 64th Sentai. Hailakandi lay along the enemy's path. British radar provided some warning of the incoming raid, and a squadron of Hurricanes rose to meet the Oscars. The Japanese claimed fourteen Hurricanes shot down, but, in fact, the Japanese just damaged two of the British planes. In any event, this fight did not turn back the attackers, who continued toward Hailakandi.

At the time most of the Air Commando fighters were out supporting the 111th Brigade's crossing of the Irrawaddy. Just a few P-51s were available to meet some eighteen raiders who were aiming at the Air Commando field. Four American fighters scrambled, but only two were able to make an intercept. First Lt. Neil Bollum and 1st Lt. Olin B. Carter had both been in the dispensary with dysentery (a common ailment among the Air Commandos) when the order to scramble came. Despite their illnesses, the two ran to their planes and took off. Neither man's plane was ready for combat; they had not been fueled, nor had they a complete load of ammunition. Carter's Mustang had an oxygen leak, as well, so he found himself at 24,000 feet without any oxygen.

The two fliers continued with the intercept despite these problems. When Carter reached the spot where the radar controllers said the Japanese were, he did not see anything. At this time in the war, however, radars were poor at indicating altitude, so Carter rolled onto his back and spotted the Japanese directly below him. Woozy from the lack of oxygen, he dove right through the formation without firing a shot. His pass still caused the Japanese to scatter momentarily, but they quickly regrouped.

Carter pulled up and ahead of the enemy and then whipped around to make a head-on pass. Still a bit oxygen-deprived, he did not hit anything as he zipped through the formation. Neither did the Japanese, who seemed to be content just to lob a few shells his way. With the adrenaline now rushing through him, Carter's next attacks were more focused.

He crept up behind an Oscar and fired several bursts. A large section of its wing near the wing root ripped off, and the Oscar began to smoke. The plane fell off to the right, gradually steepening its dive until it was going straight down. It finally disappeared into the haze. Another Oscar came under Carter's guns, and he blasted off a section of its stabilizer. The fighter flipped onto its back and fell away. Bollum had also been busy, damaging another Oscar before his guns jammed. Although Carter was credited with one probable and one damaged, he may have actually scored a victory because the 64th Sentai recorded the loss of one aircraft during this action.[15]

Meanwhile, the attacks on Broadway had shown the need to destroy the enemy's air units whenever and wherever possible. The Japanese airfields around Meiktila were bombed on March 19 by twelve Mustangs. Little was found at any of the fields except for one shiny twin-engine aircraft hidden in a revetment at Onbauk. A 500-pounder dropped on it but failed to explode. The rest of the fighters expended their bombs on buildings and antiaircraft positions at Meiktila.[16]

The airfields were kept under observation over the next couple of weeks, and an occasional enemy plane was caught on the ground but little real damage was usually done. An attack on Anisakan on April 3 by six P-51s was successful, with one fighter claimed destroyed and three others damaged. But this was merely a warm-up for what would come a day later.[17]

Allied intelligence learned that the Japanese were again moving aircraft north from Rangoon as plans were drafted to raid the Heho and Aungban fields. EAC directed the 3rd TAF to be ready to make such raids at a moments notice. At 4:00 AM on April 4 word was received that twenty-one aircraft were at Aungban and seventeen more on the ground at Heho. The P-38-equipped 459th Fighter Squadron was directed to attack Heho, and the 1st ACG was given Aungban. Just four hours later, the 1st ACG's Fighter Section launched nineteen Mustangs. As usual, Mahony led the mission.

As Mahony's flight group neared the target, Mahony sent two fighters to look over another nearby field. Finding nothing, they rejoined the others circling to the south. At this time one of the pilots experienced engine problems and returned to Hailakandi. The rest pressed on for Aungban. About an hour and a half before the Air Commandos arrived, the 459th had attacked Heho and destroyed and damaged a number of 8th Sentai bombers and also damaged some 50th Sentai Oscars. The Japanese had attempted unsuccessfully to intercept the Americans. Because of the destruction at Heho, the Japanese interceptors had been told to land at Aungban. Now, as the Air Commandos approached, that field was even more crowded.[18]

A few miles north of Aungban Mahony ordered the wing tanks dropped and took eleven planes down for the attack. Seven P-51s led by Forcey remained at ten thousand feet as top cover. The sudden appearance of the Mustangs was a complete shock to the Japanese. Planes were crowded together on the ground, some with cowlings off as mechanics worked on them. A few were taxiing to parking spots, and at least one was being towed.

Mahony led two other pilots against the antiaircraft positions ringing the field. When the Americans saw that these guns were not manned, they switched over to strafing the aircraft. Mahony bagged one bomber and two fighters with his guns and damaged another fighter with rockets in six passes. First Lt. William Gilhausen made five runs, destroying two Oscars by gunfire and a third with a rocket. The latter plane disintegrated when the rocket struck. Boyd followed the other two down on the gun positions but quickly changed to the aircraft massed below. An Oscar taxiing along the strip groundlooped and then burned when it was hit by Boyd's shells. Boyd also damaged two other fighters.

Aungban became chaotic as the Air Commandos zipped by just off the deck in pass after pass. As he climbed up to relieve the top cover, Boyd took the time to count the number of smoke columns rising from burning planes and came up with twelve separate plumes. A bit later, Petit counted at least twenty planes burning. Petit claimed three fighters destroyed, as did Bollum, who was flying Petit's wing. The two also shared another aircraft destroyed. First Lt. Younger Pitts made nine passes over the field, claiming three fighters and a bomber destroyed. An unusual sighting was made by 1st Lt. John Meyer on one of his five runs. He believed that an aircraft he had destroyed had an inline engine, which was not a common feature of JAAF aircraft in the CBI. This plane may actually have been a Kawasaki Ki-61 Tony that the 50th Sentai was evaluating at the time.[19]

Mahony ordered the first group of attackers to change places with Forcey's seven aircraft, which came down to inflict even more damage on the Japanese. Several enemy planes fell victim to the power of the new rockets, each one blowing up and flying to pieces when hit. Forcey also damaged an aircraft he identified as a Tony. Whether this was the same plane that Meyer saw or a different one is unknown. One of the unluckier pilots this day was 1st Lt. Robley Melton. Every time he lined up for a shot, another pilot cut in to blast his target.

The Japanese had called for help, but only four planes could get airborne from Heho. They did not seem that eager to mix it up with the Mustangs, however. Only one flier made a pass, and he was blasted off the tail of his quarry by Forcey. On the way home Carter remembered that he had seen a well-camouflaged Sally at Anisakan. Spotting it again he attacked and sent it up in flames. Behind them at Aungban, the Americans left four Sallys, nineteen Oscars, and one Tony destroyed, an Oscar and a Tony probably destroyed, and eight Oscars damaged. Enemy records of this encounter state that only about fifteen planes were destroyed or damaged. The Japanese also claimed one Mustang shot down. Actually, only one P-51 suffered minor damage from a single 7.7-mm round. The wide variance in claims just illustrates the difficulty in accurately assessing the actual damage incurred to an opposing force in a fast-moving aerial battle. And this dilemma applied to any air force in any theater.[20]

Whatever the true results were, they were devastating to the Japanese. Unlike the Allies, who could easily replace their aircraft and personnel, the Japanese were suffering losses that could not be sustained. For the Japanese, replacing aircraft was possible but increasingly difficult. The losses in aircrews were troublesome, however. Both the Japanese army and navy had started the war with small, well-trained air forces. As the war turned against it, though, many of Japan's veteran fliers were dead or wounded, and there were not enough trained personnel to replace them. The young Japanese airmen who now entered combat were too often cannon fodder to their better-trained and better-equipped adversaries. It was a downward spiral from which there was no recovery.

Airfield attacks were not the only missions flown by the 1st ACG. Bridges were also often-visited targets. These ranged from simple wooden structures over small streams to more elaborate ones such as the Meza railroad bridge. This bridge, northeast of the landing zones, was a 700-foot-long, three-span, truss-type structure mounted on strong concrete and brick abutments. Five short spans at each end led to the main bridge. Tenth Air Force attacks in the autumn of 1943 had dropped at least one span into the river. Japanese engineers, though, were consummate rebuilders, and they often had temporary repairs in place very quickly so that repeat raids had to be made. The Air Commandos first joined in attacks on the Meza bridge on February 12, when a B-25 blew the rails out of the roadbed leading to the bridge and also destroyed a temporary bridge there. The ACG fliers continued to bomb the bridge off and on, as did the other Allied units, but a few days before the group was pulled out of combat, a reconnaissance mission reported that the bridge was still intact, with nearly one hundred railcars parked at the Meza station.[21]

The Shweli highway bridge on the road from Bhamo to China also received much attention. Shweli was a very difficult target. It was a 250-foot-long suspension bridge towering 70 feet above the Shweli River. Its suspension cables were securely anchored in huge concrete blocks. Hits on the bridge itself would just make easily-patched holes in its flooring. Only a direct hit on the towers between which the cables ran would produce any measure of major damage from an air raid. No attacker had been able to score a hit on a tower until the Air Commandos got a chance.[22]

In early April the ACG Fighter Section received five P-51Bs as replacements. The B was a much improved version of the Mustang, with a more powerful engine driving a four-bladed propeller and a greater range and service ceiling. It was also significantly faster than its predecessor. The B's longer range enabled the 1st ACG to go after more distant targets, such as the Shweli bridge, which was 375 miles from Hailakandi. On April 20 Air Commando pilots got their first crack at the bridge when Petit and two other pilots took the brand-new P-51Bs against it. Their 1,000-pound bombs were just off target, and the bridge remained standing. Petit, accompanied by three other Air Commandos, returned the following day to score a brilliant success. Roaring in at just 1,200 feet, the quartet toggled off their 1,000-pounders. Petit's pair were right on target in striking the towers, which crumbled and sent the bridge span and its torn cables tumbling into the river.[23]

Attempts to destroy the Gokteik Viaduct were not as successful. This remarkable structure had been built by American engineers in 1900–1901. It spanned a 2,260-foot-wide gorge and was mounted on 320-foot-tall latticed steel piers rising from a natural bridge. The rock formation itself was 550 feet above a stream, making the overall height of the viaduct 870 feet. Earlier Tenth Air Force raids had only done minor damage to the viaduct. The Air Commandos' try at the Gokteik, which was heavily defended by many antiaircraft guns, on April 22 caused little damage, and no more attacks on it were mounted.[24]

Meanwhile, the 1st ACG was making aviation history elsewhere. Shortly after taking off from Aberdeen, an L-1 carrying three passengers, including two wounded, had engine failure and was forced down behind enemy lines about fifteen miles west of Mawlu. The pilot skillfully landed his plane on a road in an area devoid of enemy troops. There were indications, though, that the Japanese would soon become aware of the plane and come looking for the men. Rough terrain prevented a rescue attempt by a light plane, so Cochran decided to use one of his helicopters, which had not yet been tested under combat conditions.

Another light plane dropped a message to those on the ground. They were told to destroy the plane and then to head for higher ground nearby that would give them cover from prowling Japanese patrols. The party made it up a ridge, where they lived for the next four nights while being supplied with food and water dropped by the light planes.

Back at Lalaghat 1st Lt. Carter Harman was directed to bring his YR-4 helicopter forward. He left Lalaghat on April 21 and flew by stages to Jorhet, India. The next day he flew to Ledo and Taro. At Taro an L-5 gas tank was fitted to Harman's YR-4 for the long flight over the hills to Aberdeen. Harman arrived at the Chindit bastion on the afternoon of the 23rd and was immediately sent out to pick up the stranded men.

A note dropped to the party told them to head for a nearby rice paddy. As the men made their way toward the paddy, Harman flew his chopper to a small field several miles from the paddy that was used by the light planes. There, he awaited a signal that the party had arrived to be picked up. This signal was soon received when an L-5 slowly flew over the strip and waggled its wings. Harman made two trips to the paddy, bringing one wounded man back each time. The men were then transferred to an L-5 for further transport to Aberdeen.

Harman could make but two trips the first day because the oppressive heat had put too much strain on the YR-4's underpowered engine. He remained overnight and then brought the last two men out. On April 24, Harman flew back to Aberdeen, where he remained until May 4, flying four more missions, including the pickup of two more casualties. Because of enemy raids on Aberdeen that had destroyed all the aircraft there except for the helicopter, Harman was ordered back to Lalaghat. Fighting thunderstorms along the way, he returned home safely three days later.

Despite the unreliability and lack of power of the YR-4's engine, Harman had demonstrated the bright future that lay ahead for helicopters for rescue missions. Today, such missions are flown on a regular basis and are taken for granted, but Harman and his YR-4 had shown the way.[25]

The raids by Tenth Air Force on enemy airfields had reduced Japanese air operations temporarily, and the 1st ACG fighters and bombers spent much time bombing enemy supply installations and transportation routes. In addition to flights in support of the Chindits, the Air Commandos were racking up an impressive number of combat sorties and hours in the process.

Road reconnaissance missions were flown regularly in hopes of finding any kind of vehicle. When they were found the results were usually bad for the enemy. For example, a group of camouflaged trucks was found near Momauk on April 13 by a Mustang pilot. He proceeded to destroy at least three of the vehicles and got another one speeding along a nearby road. A few hours later two Mustangs strafed a convoy near Ye-U, damaging several trucks. On April 16, twenty fighters and nine bombers attacked the village of Mohnyin, which lay along the railroad track from Indaw to Myitkyina, with good results. For missions such as this incendiaries and fragmentation bombs proved more destructive against the lightly built and flammable native structures used by the Japanese for storage. Using this ordnance, B-25s completely burned out the village of Nalong on April 22, did the same to Nanyinbya the following day, and finished off Tali on the 27th.[26]

Enemy aircraft were again sighted on April 16, when two P-51s made an offensive reconnaissance of Shwebo and Anisakan. The Americans sighted three or four fighters and a two-seater biplane at Anisakan and attacked immediately. Little antiaircraft fire was met, so six passes were made, and two of the Oscars went up in flames.[27]

Most of the fighter combat against the JAAF involved airfield attacks. Aerial battles were not as common, but on April 17 the Air Commandos ran into a batch of Oscars east of Imphal. The Japanese had dispatched a major attack against British airfields in the Imphal area. While twenty Oscars of the 50th Sentai went after nearby fields, fifty Oscars from the 64th Sentai and the 204th Sentais escorted six Sallys of the 8th Sentai to Imphal. Defending Spitfires downed one enemy plane and damaged several more, but with so many Japanese attacking, the RAF radioed for help. Thirteen Mustangs were on their way to support the Chindits at Mawlu when they were told to intercept the enemy formation. After jettisoning their bombs, the fighters turned west and soon saw twelve Oscars flying at about 14,000 feet. The 64th Sentai pilots saw the Americans at the same time and began to climb. Passing underneath the Oscars, Mahony led his men around behind them and also began a climb.

The two forces met, with the Americans doing the most damage. Mahony picked out a target and closed to four hundred yards before opening fire. He continued firing as he crept to within two hundred yards. The Oscar broke down and away, giving Mahony a good deflection shot. His shells tore into the Oscar's fuselage, and the Japanese plane continued straight down into the ground. Meanwhile, Mahony's wingman, Mitchell, followed up by damaging two other Japanese fighters.

Gilhausen put in a long burst into another Oscar but had to break off his attack when he got into the other plane's prop wash. He was watching that plane disappear into the haze below when two more Japanese jumped him. Because he had to evade their passes and lost sight of his first victim, he could only claim one damaged.

Four Oscars bounced Forcey, who turned the tables on his attackers. He followed one down to five thousand feet and with his first burst, blew off the Oscar's canopy and started a small fire. After a second burst Forcey saw the pilot's head and arm drop over the side of the cockpit. Just before the Oscar spun in, Forcey passed just feet from it and saw blood splattered all over the cockpit. Just then another fighter closed on Forcey's tail, and he dove for the deck at full throttle with the enemy close behind. Forcey headed for a cliff and made a violent pull-up at the last moment. The enemy pilot attempted to do the same, but as he did, his wing ripped off and his plane smashed into the ground.[28]

May saw the 1st ACG's operations winding down, although it was hard to tell as the fighters and bombers continued to fly daily. But the monsoon season was about to begin, and when that happened, both Hailakandi and Lalaghat would be underwater and unusable. Too, the group was undergoing many personnel changes. Alison had gone back to Washington, D.C., in early April. Cochran had been held in the theater for awhile longer, but then turned command of the group over to Gaty. Olson, Mahony, Smith, and others also returned to the United States. The men who were left behind were tired, and many were ill. Dysentery and malaria were taking their toll, but the men still flew, still maintained the planes, still performed the everyday tasks required of combat units.

Three P-51s flew an armed reconnaissance of Shwebo and Anisakan on May 9. Nothing was seen at Shwebo, but an Oscar was found and burned at Anisakan. Another fighter was strafed without any observed results, and it was believed that it had already been wrecked.[29]

Several Oscars put in an appearance over Blackpool on May 16 and attempted to interfere with the Air Commandos supporting the Chindits. The Japanese pilots contented themselves with feinting at the B-25s, but four of them jumped a pair of Mustangs. In the brief action that followed, one of the Japanese planes was damaged and the Americans were forced to jettison their bombs.

The 1st ACG's last fighter missions before the group was pulled back to reorganize were flown on May 19. The day began in tragedy but ended in satisfaction and partial retribution for the Air Commandos. Gilhausen had taken off at 6:00 AM to reconnoiter enemy airfields. Forty-five minutes later he reported finding aircraft on the Kawlin West strip and burning two planes there, but he also said he had been hit. At the time he made this report, he was five miles west of Kawlin, and said he was going to try to put a few more miles between him and the Japanese field before bailing out. That was the last message received from him. Gilhausen was carried on the group's rolls as missing until the end of the war. It was revealed after the Japanese surrender that Gilhausen had bailed out successfully but had been captured. He was taken to Rangoon, where he eventually died from malnutrition. The Air Commandos had been noted for being somewhat casual in their dress, and Gilhausen was no exception. On his last mission he was wearing a T-shirt and slippers.[30]

An hour after Gilhausen took off seven more P-51s were airborne for Blackpool, where they were to bomb enemy positions. When they arrived over Blackpool the pilots spotted six Kawasaki Ki-48 Lilys flying at seven thousand feet. The bombers were escorted by fourteen Oscars, with one group of ten fighters about two thousand feet higher and to one side and the other four fighters on the other side. The Mustang pilots immediately salvoed their bombs on the enemy ground positions and turned to attack the bombers from the rear. The Lily pilots were very disciplined, keeping a tight formation throughout and letting their gunners handle the Mustangs. Six Oscars also remained with the bombers while the rest broke away to make individual runs on the P-51s.

While Mitchell led a flight against the Lilys, Carter took his men after the Oscars. First Lt. Jack Klarr was Carter's wingman. When the two Americans attacked, Carter went after one Oscar, and Klarr took on the wingman of Carter's target. It was a short fight. Klarr stitched his victim's fuselage thoroughly, and the Oscar fell off to one side with flames completely enveloping its undersides. Klarr did not see his target crash but was told by others that it did. That "was a big thrill for me," he recalled later.[31]

A second pass on the Oscars resulted in a victory with hardly a shot fired. Two were attacked, and one of the Japanese pilots attempted a split-S at too low an altitude when trying to escape and plowed into the ground. Melton was given credit for the demise of this plane. Another Oscar that was creeping up beneath the Mustangs was fended off and, when last seen, was diving toward the ground with its entire forward fuselage ablaze.

Mitchell and his flight, meanwhile, were raking over the Lilys. Mitchell destroyed one of the bombers with a burst into its right engine that set it afire.

Two other bombers were damaged. The Japanese headed south at high speed as the Mustangs reformed. At this time one of the Japanese fliers became temporarily confused, for he tried to join up with the Air Commandos before realizing his mistake and swiftly scuttling for home. In the last aerial combat for the 1st ACG Fighter Section, the Americans were credited with one Lily destroyed and two damaged and two Oscars destroyed and two damaged.[32]

Two more missions were flown on the 19th. One was an unsuccessful search for Gilhausen, and the second, and last, mission for the original Air Commando group was a dive-bombing mission by eight Mustangs in support of the Chindits at Blackpool. Shortly thereafter the 1st ACG abandoned Hailakandi and Lalaghat for the drier climes of Asansol.[33]

Cochran's 1st ACG established a fine record in its little more than four months of combat operations, a record for the later two Air Commando groups to aspire to. The 1st ACG Fighter Section had destroyed ninety Japanese aircraft in the air and on the ground against the loss of four fighters. One other fighter (Gilhausen's) was apparently lost to ground fire, and one had been destroyed at Broadway. Three more had been lost in accidents. One B-25 had been lost in combat, and four others were lost in accidents. Seven fighter pilots and two bomber crews were also casualties. A quick statistical rundown shows the Fighter Section flew 1,432 sorties on 230 missions for a total of 4,495.5 combat hours. These totals were accomplished with an average of 19.8 Mustangs in commission. The B-25 statistics were just as impressive: 422 sorties flown on 102 mission for a total of 1,274 hours. Records for the Transport and Light Plane sections are harder to total, but both compiled equally impressive records. One C-47 was lost when it ran into a water buffalo on takeoff, and seven UC-64s were lost. The Light Plane Section wrote off some forty aircraft. Five of the L-1 and L-5 pilots were killed. The greatest losses, of course, were suffered by the gliders. Fragile to begin with, the operations to which they were committed resulted in nearly a 90 percent loss rate because few were ever retrieved. Such losses also came with high casualties—ten glider pilots and four enlisted men killed.[34]

Most of the 1st ACG moved on May 20 to Asansol, which was an abandoned British base in northeast India. The light planes, still busy evacuating casualties and providing supplies to the Chindits, returned a bit later. At Asansol, with the same élan that characterized their operations from the beginning, the Air Commandos set about building what they stated was "one of the finest rear bases in the Theater."[35] But being stationed at a rear base was not the purpose for which the group had organized. Combat operations were their mission, and the 1st ACG would see combat again in a new and reinvigorated form.

Chapter 8

Rebirth

J ust what to do with the Air Commandos had long been a source of discussion within the CBI, even before they had arrived in the theater. There were some, notably SEAC air CinC Peirse, who had been against the Air Commando concept from the beginning. The critics' dislike may have been prompted more by their antipathy toward Wingate and anything associated with him, but, rightly or wrongly, they wished to see such an "irregular" organization disappear. This meant absorbing the Air Commandos back into standard military formations. And with the death of Wingate, that now seemed attainable.

Another who wished to see the Air Commandos absorbed into conventional units was Air Marshal Baldwin, the 3rd TAF leader. He made his feelings plain in a letter to Stratemeyer on March 24, 1944. Baldwin wanted a quick resolution to the matter, saying, "The longer this remains an independent outfit working with the Special Force, the harder it is going to be to get it away from Wingate."[1]

Baldwin was particularly incensed that, although Cochran was very cooperative, Wingate continually butted in on air operations and regarded the Air Commandos (in Baldwin's view) as his "private air force." In one instance, Baldwin related, this reached the point that Wingate forbade the Air Commandos from participating with other units in an operation that was designed to gain air superiority in the area near Broadway. This was totally unacceptable to the 3rd TAF commander, and he told Stratemeyer "how delighted I shall be if you can, at an early date, arrange for the absorption of No. 1 Air Commando Force."[2]

The British Air Ministry also voiced concern about the independence of the Air Commandos. "We cannot afford to lock up packets of air forces outside centralized control of TAF," the ministry wrote Peirse in mid-April, "when with careful planning of equipment and training we can guarantee LRPG's fuller measure of support from within TAF than could hope for from independent commandos."[3]

Stratemeyer had to tell Baldwin and Peirse that the Air Commandos would not be dissolved. He had recommended to Arnold on March 18 that such an action should take place as of May 1, 1944, and that then the components of the unit would be absorbed by other USAAF units in the theater. Because support of the LRPGs could just as easily come from regularly constituted organizations as from the Air Commandos, Stratemeyer reasoned, he could not justify using them for the exclusive support of Special Force. Stratemeyer initially recommended to Arnold that the TCC and the 3rd TAF take over the functions of the Air Commandos and that the American unit should be dissolved. He next proposed that the 1st ACG be made a wing that would then be inactivated and absorbed into the Tenth Air Force. Arnold turned down this idea because personnel would not be available for a wing. He did state that the 1st ACG could be maintained at its present strength and asked Stratemeyer if, given this, did the junior office still want to dissolve the group.[4]

Stratemeyer demurred, for he was not about to butt heads with Arnold. As the commanding general of the USAAF and a member of the Joint Chiefs of Staff, Arnold wielded considerable clout, and at the moment, he was very interested in establishing four more Air Commando groups and a like number of transport units known as Combat Cargo Groups (CCGs) for employment in the CBI. In fact in mid-March 1944, Arnold had already orally directed his Plans Division to take the first steps to organize, train, and dispatch these two organizations to the CBI. Finally, a message from Cochran to Arnold that passed through Stratemeyer's hands may have given Stratemeyer pause also. Cochran stated in it, "We would not have been able to do our job had our boss not set us up the way he did. . . . Freewheeling is wonderful. I am convinced after recent goings on that the line from the Almighty to us must be as direct as possible. George Washington said it."[5]

To clarify the situation and explain what he wanted from these new units, Arnold wrote a "Dear Dickie" letter to Mountbatten on March 24, 1944. Arnold told the SEAC leader that he was insisting on five principles that had to be followed for the employment of these units. These principles were:

1. They would be known as U.S. Army Air Forces Air Commando Unit No. _____.
2. Their operations would be directed by the senior U.S. Air Force Commander.
3. Orders and control would employ a U.S. chain of command.
4. The American integrity of the units was to be maintained.
5. The theater had to contribute to the support of their operations.

Additionally, Arnold requested that Alison and several other key Air Commando personnel be returned to the United States to assist him in organizing the four new units.[6]

Alison actually received two messages ordering him to report. The first, of course, was from Arnold, but the second was from Gen. Dwight D. Eisenhower, directing him to report to England without delay. Alison radioed Arnold for authorization to see Eisenhower. Permission came swiftly, and Alison left India for England almost immediately. Eisenhower, who was then in the final planning stages for the Normandy invasion, wanted to hear about the Air Commandos experiences with gliders because the aircraft would be used extensively in the invasion. Alison spent a couple of days discussing Operation Thursday with General Spaatz, who was commanding the U.S. strategic air forces in Europe, and General Vandenberg, who was deputy commander of the Allied Expeditionary Air Force, before returning to Washington, D.C.[7]

Alison arrived back in the United States in early April and reported to Arnold. The general was in an exuberant mood, having seen the publicity generated by Thursday. According to Alison, the general told him, "This has been such a success. I have given authorization to form four more Air Commando groups and the necessary transport. I have already implemented the organization of two of them."

"General, what are they going to do?" Alison replied.

"We are going to retake Burma from the air."

"Whose troops are we going to use?" a skeptical Alison asked.

Arnold said, "We are going to move the British Army into Burma."

This was too much for Alison, who blurted, "General, I don't think the British Army is going into Burma."[8]

Alison then told the USAAF leader that from what he had seen in India, the British were not expending a great deal of energy planning for large operations in Burma. Alison added that Cochran probably had a better feel for the situation because he had close relationships with Mountbatten and Wingate. Now angry and disturbed, Arnold ordered his staff to bring back Cochran as soon as possible. What Alison and Cochran could tell Arnold would certainly have an impact on what additional forces would be sent to the CBI, and the information they provided could play a decisive role in determining the number of Air Commando groups that would be formed. Stratemeyer, however, did not wish to release Cochran until the Air Commandos had been removed from combat, so it took a number of increasingly insistent messages from Washington before Cochran was pried loose. He finally arrived in the United States in late May.[9]

When he had spoken with both Alison and Cochran, Arnold pressed Mountbatten and Stratemeyer on their plans for the use of the Air Commandos in the overall operational strategy for the theater and their ability to support more Air Commando groups. Although Stratemeyer warned Arnold that Mountbatten and Peirse might be planning to pressure the USAAF leader to let them control the Air Commandos in a different manner than Arnold had insisted on, little other information reached Arnold concerning future plans. After a while, Arnold became impatient. It was becoming evident that, given the continual shortage of transports in the CBI, the British and, to a lesser extent, the senior American leaders in the theater were more interested in obtaining additional transports than in gaining more Air Commando groups.[10]

While Arnold awaited some indication of what Mountbatten and his subordinates intended to do in Burma, he directed Alison to prepare a plan to retake northern Burma utilizing the Air Commando and Combat Cargo units. On April 22 Alison submitted a broad overview for the employment of these forces. His one-page plan postulated the use of three Air Commando and four CCGs in the "vertical envelopment" of the enemy. The plan was dependent on knowing the exact number of troops to be maintained behind the lines, a figure that the SEAC commander was slow in presenting. Alison was well aware of this tendency of the British command, for he stated, "The success of this plan will depend on the willingness of the British Commanders in India to commit themselves to this operation, and this decision will be made or denied depending on the ability of the Air Commander to sell the planners on the advisability of putting troops down and maintaining them by air."[11]

Alison went on to describe the composition of the first three (and, as it turned out, only) Air Commando units. Unusually, the groups would consist of five P-51 squadrons and one B-25H squadron. He evidently figured that since they were familiar with the bombers, the 1st ACG would get the newly created B-25 section and an additional fighter squadron. Indeed, the 1st ACG initially had just one P-51 squadron, but a second was swiftly added when the B-25s did not materialize. Significantly, in light of what he had already told Arnold concerning the ennui surrounding the British in the CBI, Alison concluded, "The results to be obtained by employment of an Air Commando force in conjunction with Combat Cargo units is limited only by the imagination and driving force of the Commander."[12] Sadly, what was lacking in the senior leadership in the CBI was imagination and drive.

Nonetheless, movement was made on a reorganization of the EAC. Despite the misgivings by both the Americans and the British about an "integrated" organization such as the EAC, the command had worked. But as spring flowed into summer, both sides felt that it was time for a change. In one way this was the result of shifts in headquarters. Mountbatten left Delhi to set up his headquarters at Kandy on Ceylon (now Sri Lanka), which really was in his command area, unlike Delhi. Stratemeyer also moved the EAC headquarters to the Hastings jute mill north of Calcutta. These moves freed both leaders from the stifling closeness and lackadaisical atmosphere of Delhi, and allowed them to work more efficiently.

Following his move Stratemeyer directed his staff to come up with a plan to streamline the EAC and reduce its overhead. Stratemeyer also felt that a reorganization would result in a closer coordination between air and ground forces. The staff study met with the EAC leader's approval, and on June 20, 1944, the EAC was reorganized. Two weeks earlier the TCC had been disbanded, and its units were placed under the 3rd TAF's control.

The "new" EAC consisted of five components: the Strategic Air Force was composed of the 231 Bombardment Group (BG) and the 7th BG; Photographic Reconnaissance Force consisted of the 171 Wing and the 8th Photographic Group; the 3rd TAF kept the 221 Group, the 224 Group, the 12th BG, and the 3rd CCG (which was not yet in the theater); the Tenth Air Force was composed of the 80th Fighter Group, the 311th Fighter Bomber Group, and the 443rd Troop Carrier Group, plus the 11th Combat Cargo Squadron; and an Air Task Force made up of the 1st ACG and the 3rd CCG (pulling double duty, it seems). Numerous other supporting units were also assigned.[13]

It is doubtful if any of the Air Commandos were aware of the attempts to break up their unit. Even if they were, they were too busy training to worry about things they had no control over anyway. On August 9, 1944, USAAF Headquarters authorized Stratemeyer to activate a new 1st ACG utilizing the personnel of the original group and replacements as needed. The reconstituted group was to consist of a fighter squadron, a troop carrier squadron, three liaison squadrons, and a medical unit. Like the two Air Commando groups organized in the United States, the second version of the 1st ACG would reflect a more standard USAAF group structure than it had earlier.[14]

The omission of a second fighter squadron bothered Stratemeyer, and he radioed Arnold to amend the activation instructions to include the second squadron. Arnold was willing to activate it but worried that the theater had inadequate service units to accommodate an additional unit. Stratemeyer agreed that theater service facilities were spread thin, but added, "We feel that the necessity to fight this group properly outweighs the handicap of the additional strain of one fighter squadron on our service facilities. Our urgent recommendation for the additional fighter squadron stands."[15] A second squadron was quickly authorized.

Another organization type that was slow in reaching the 1st ACG was the airdrome squadron, or ADS. This unit, which handled maintenance and house-keeping chores for a squadron, was part of the other two Air Commando groups from the start, but such squadrons did not reach the 1st ACG until the fall, when three were assigned.[16]

The new 1st ACG was activated at Asansol on September 1, 1944, under the command of Gaty. The squadron commanders are listed in the accompanying table. Beginning the fall of 1944, the 1st ACG consisted of the 5th Fighter Squadron (Commando), equipped with twenty-five P-47D Thunderbolts; the 319th Troop Carrier Squadron (Commando)—the 319th TCS—with sixteen C-47s and thirty-two CG-4As; the 164th Liaison Squadron (LS), the 165th LS, and the 166th LS, each with thirty-two L-5s and four UC-64s; and the 285th Medical Dispensary, Aviation. The group's second fighter squadron, the 6th, was activated on September 30 and also had twenty-five Thunderbolts.

1st Air Commando Group, September 1944
    Col. Clinton B. Gaty
5th Fighter Squadron (Commando)
    Capt. Roland R. Lynn
6th Fighter Squadron (Commando)
    Capt. Olin B. Carter
319th Troop Carrier Squadron (Commando)
    Maj. Neil L. Holm
164th Liaison Squadron, Commando
    1st Lt. David C. Beasley
165th Liaison Squadron, Commando
    Capt. Vincent L. Ulery
166th Liaison Squadron, Commando
    1st Lt. Fred H. Van Wagner
72nd Airdrome Squadron
    Maj. Henry Barry (November 26, 1944)
309th Airdrome Squadron
    Capt. Ray E. Stewart (November 26, 1944)
326th Airdrome Squadron
    Maj. Peter Skalin (November 26, 1944)
285th Medical Dispensary, Aviation
    Maj. Donald C. Tulloch

The group was placed under the operational control of the Combat Cargo
Task Force, which was established on September 15. This organization, commanded by Brig. Gen. Frederick W. Evans, would control all phases of combat
cargo flying, including the delivery of supplies, the transport of ground or airborne troops, and the air evacuation of personnel.[17]

With the Air Commandos still intended to support LRPGs, Gaty had one
of his first meetings as commander of the reformed 1st ACG on September 3.
The purpose was to discuss training with Special Force. Although the Air Commandos would spend considerable time training with Special Force at Lalitpur
over the next few months, they would never again be used to support the Chindits. Because Mountbatten and Slim now placed less emphasis on LRP operations, the British commanders were planning to use the Chindits more as regular
infantry. Actually, the Chindits had already fought their last battle in August near
Mogaung. They had been bled dry, as had Merrill's Marauders, by foolish actions
on Stilwell's part. Incapable of further action, the Chindits were finally withdrawn. After a rest period, what was left of the Chindits went back into training
for battles that never came.[18]

Training for its own men consumed most of the 1st ACG's time in September. The war-weary P-51s were flown to Karachi and turned in, while new
P-47s arrived to be checked out. Brand-new C-64s and L-5s arrived in crates to
be assembled and test-flown. The L-1s they had also used had now gone out of
production and were in short supply in the theater. Stilwell wanted to place the
remaining planes into one formation, so the Air Commandos ferried their L-1s
to Ledo, where the planes became part of the 1st Liaison Group (Provisional).
Group headquarters also took possession of a B-25H to act as a liaison ship
and general hack aircraft. In addition to training, men of the group began with
enthusiasm to turn Asansol into something looking more like a base back home
than the somewhat shabby spot it had been. The underlying current running
through Asansol, though, was speculation over when the group would return to
combat. That time was fast approaching. The liaison squadrons had been the last
to return from combat in the spring, but they would be the first to begin operations in the fall.[19]

But as the group prepared to reenter combat, momentous changes were
occurring within the CBI. For many months the antagonism between Stilwell
and Chiang Kai-shek had been growing more pernicious. The American saw
the Generalissimo as corrupt and venal, militarily inept, and unwilling to fight.
Stilwell viewed the Chinese leader as not worth the effort the United States was
exerting to support him against the Japanese. Chiang, on the other hand, saw

Stilwell as one trying to usurp his power and as an individual incapable of grasping the broader aspects of diplomacy or Chinese politics.

A series of events in September brought the Stilwell–Chiang situation to a head. Earlier, the British had already been seeking Stilwell's removal, citing his prickly personality and the complicated and awkward command arrangements under which Stilwell operated. In June the Japanese had an offensive well under way in eastern China. The situation was looking grim for Chiang's troops and for the Fourteenth Air Force's bases located in eastern China. Marshall suggested that Stilwell give up his position as the SEAC deputy commander to Maj. Gen. Daniel I. Sultan and go to China to reinvigorate the Chinese.

Stilwell preferred that President Roosevelt write a "stiff" letter to Chiang stating the massive contributions in supplies and money that the United States had already given China and insisting that Chiang needed to act decisively. Stilwell also believed that the Nationalist troops stationed in northwest China just to keep an eye on the Chinese Communists there were needed to help stem the Japanese offensive. Roosevelt did write a blunt letter in which he recommended that the Generalissimo place Stilwell in charge of all Chinese and American forces in China. Such an option would be a bitter pill for Chiang to swallow, but he did reply that he agreed in principle, but political considerations could delay acting on this proposal. The U.S. president attempted to bring Chiang and Stilwell together by sending his personal representative, Brig. Gen. Patrick J. Hurley, to mediate the differences and to assure the Chinese leader of the United States' continued support.

Hurley's mission was doomed to failure. Following his arrival in early September, Hurley had several meetings with Chiang and came away from them feeling that the issue of Stilwell assuming command of the Chinese forces had been settled. His positive feelings were abruptly quashed within a few days. On September 15 Chiang informed Stilwell that he was going to withdraw his Yunnan Force (then under Stilwell's command) back across the Salween unless Stilwell resumed the offensive toward Bhamo within a week. Stilwell was quick to see this ultimatum as another instance of the usual foot-dragging and blackmail that he always ascribed to Chiang. He reported as much to Roosevelt.

After the president received Stilwell's message, Roosevelt responded with an ultimatum of his own. He wrote that placing Stilwell in command of the Chinese forces offered the greatest opportunity to defeat the Japanese. On the other hand Chiang could be jeopardizing his air supply route over the Hump by withdrawing his troops. Was the Generalissimo willing to accept the consequences of such an action?

Ironically, the man who delivered Roosevelt's message was not Hurley, but Stilwell. He handed it to Chiang on September 19 in Chungking as Hurley was preparing to meet the Generalissimo. The Chinese leader quickly excused himself, leaving the two Americans to ponder what to do next. They did not have long to wait. Chiang notified Hurley on September 23 that Stilwell had to go. He followed this two days later with a formal aide-mémoire calling for Stilwell's removal.

After long discussions with his Joint Chiefs of Staff, Roosevelt finally wrote Chiang on October 18 that Stilwell would be recalled. The president did state, however, that Stilwell had been operating under the directives of the CCS, Churchill, and himself. Nevertheless, Stilwell was to go.

A new command structure was also established with Stilwell's departure. The CBI theater was split in two. General Wedemeyer[20] was named commander, U.S. Forces, China Theater, and also chief of staff to Chiang, while Sultan became commander, U.S. Forces, India–Burma Theater. Sultan also became commander of the NCAC, which was the organization controlling American and Chinese forces in Burma. Finally, Lt. Gen. Raymond A. Wheeler, who had been Mountbatten's principal administrative officer, became the deputy Supreme Allied Commander on November 12. As Mountbatten pointed out later, Stilwell had to be succeeded by three lieutenant generals, of whom each had at least two entirely separate functions.[21]

The Air Commandos took little notice of these high-level maneuvers. They were too busy working. A detachment nicknamed the Boston Detachment was established in October to evacuate wounded from the Kabaw Valley south of Tamu in Burma. It was made up primarily of men and aircraft of the 165th LS and initially consisted of sixteen L-5s, three UC-64s, four RAF DH 82 Tiger Moths, and three CG-4As. The squadron moved first to Palel, India, but quickly realized that an evacuation strip was needed closer to the front lines. A further move was made to Tamu on October 18, where the squadron remained until November 4. At that time a new strip at Yazagyo (code-named Yell) at the southern end of the valley opened, and the squadron again moved forward.[22] The 319th TCS was also directed to rush a C-47 and a glider to Imphal to evacuate wounded from that area. The glider, with nine wounded aboard, was snatched on October 9, and the men were safely delivered to a hospital in the rear.[23]

The evacuation of wounded was helped immeasurably by a modification to the L-5s that made loading litters easier. Although the L-5s could already carry litters, it was a time-consuming effort to place a litter in a plane. Members of the liaison squadrons' engineering sections removed the rear seats from a couple of the planes and cut into the rear fuselages directly behind the cockpit so that a section of the fuselage hinged upwards. This modification proved so successful that more of the L-5s quickly underwent this surgery.[24]

The men at Yazagyo quickly found themselves in the thick of the action. Enemy ground troops were in the area, although none made any attempt to attack the strip. It was a different story in the air. Several earlier alerts had come to nothing, but on the morning of November 5 a lone Oscar jumped a Spitfire landing at Yazagyo. The enemy pilot did not get the Spitfire, but when he saw a B-25 parked alongside the strip, he fired an accurate burst into the bomber and destroyed it. He then made one more pass on the field, lightly damaging a pair of L-5s. There was no return fire because antiaircraft defenses had yet to be emplaced. This was swiftly remedied. The dangerousness of the area was emphasized three days later when a C-47 was shot down close to the field and several other transports were reported shot down nearby.[25]

As can be seen, the light plane operations were never easy. Just a couple of days after they arrived at Yazagyo, the men of the 165th LS found themselves short of gasoline, and all flying had to be curtailed. C-47s dropped an emergency supply of gasoline in two-gallon containers on the morning of November 7. These were scattered all over the field, and it took time to recover the cans. The cans were delivered to the L-5s, where the crews (after laboriously separating rusty water from the fuel) poured eighteen cans of fuel into each plane by hand.

This process took up most of the morning, but the light planes were back in the air that afternoon.

Yazagyo was a very dusty place, and when the aircraft returned they churned up so much dust that the late arrivals had to make several passes before landing. Once everyone was on the ground, there was a "general stampede" for the nearby river to wash away the layers of dust coating everyone.[26]

Though the little planes suffered no losses to enemy aircraft, the rather short and narrow strip carved out of the jungle was itself a factor in accidents. One particularly serious accident occurred on November 5 as night descended on Yazagyo. A 165th LS UC-64 pilot with passengers on board attempted to land in the growing darkness. His first try, with landing lights on, was unsuccessful. He turned his lights off on his second approach, perhaps thinking he could see out of his windshield better that way. He touched down fine but apparently lost his sense of direction on the unlighted strip and struck another UC-64 parked alongside the runway. The impact swung the landing plane around, which then plowed into a pair of Tiger Moths, starting a fire that consumed all three aircraft. Two passengers were killed, two more suffered critical burns, and the remaining two passengers and the pilot received minor burns. This incident ended tragically, but less severe takeoff and landing accidents on such rough and dusty fields were not uncommon.[27]

The 1st ACG's fighter squadrons entered combat not soon after the liaison squadrons did. Increased enemy air activity in the Rangoon area brought intense scrutiny by the EAC's intelligence officers. They estimated that some fifty-five single-engine Japanese fighters were based on the Rangoon fields, but they soon noted that this number had dropped while there was a corresponding increase in numbers of aircraft at Bangkok. This was interpreted to be the result of American activity toward the Philippines. Nevertheless, there were numerous targets still available at Rangoon, and Stratemeyer decided it was a good time to hit the enemy. A major effort, called Operation "L," was scheduled to begin October 17 but no later than the 19th, weather permitting, and it was to last for three days. In addition to the Rangoon strikes, a series of diversionary attacks were to be made on Japanese airfields in central Burma two days prior to the main operation. The diversionary attacks started on October 15, but weather did hamper operations, and the main effort did not commence until the 18th.[28]

In addition to an Air Commando composite squadron composed of its two fighter units, two USAAF squadrons with P-47s and P-38s, and four RAF squadrons flying Bristol Type 156 Beaufighters, DH 98 Mosquitoes, and Thunderbolts were tapped for the Rangoon operation. The twenty-four planes of the Air Commandos were placed under the operational control of the 3rd TAF and attached to the 224 Group at Cox's Bazar in Arakan. Maintenance personnel to tend the squadron's Thunderbolts were flown in by the 319th TCS's C-47s, and the P-47s arrived at Cox's Bazar on October 15 to prepare for the mission.[29]

Weather did delay the start of Operation "L," but the Allied formations took off finally for Rangoon early on October 18. Led by six Beaufighters of the 177 Squadron, the squadrons arrived over Rangoon at intervals of approximately forty minutes. The first four Allied units generally had little luck in their attacks, claiming just one Dinah damaged on the ground. The 58th Fighter Squadron did better, claiming two Oscars destroyed in the air and four destroyed on the ground.

The twenty-four 1st ACG Thunderbolts arrived over Mingaladon a few minutes before 11:00 AM and found eight Oscars airborne. The defenders were not particularly aggressive, generally making rather feeble passes on the attackers and breaking these off before they got too close. Captain Lynn, the 5th Fighter Squadron commander leading the mission, got involved in a tight, turning battle with one of the more aggressive enemy pilots and was able to pump enough shells into the Oscar to set it spinning wildly. The last Lynn saw of his adversary, the plane was still spinning as it fell through four thousand feet. Lynn received credit for a probable kill.[30]

In the meantime, the other Air Commandos were beating up Mingaladon quite badly. Many enemy aircraft had been unable to take off, and they were prime targets. Although the defenders put up some antiaircraft fire, it was sparse and inaccurate. The raid was over by 12:30 PM, and the attackers started back. On the way home 1st Lt. Everett L. Kelly, a 6th Fighter Squadron pilot, heard his wingman calling that an enemy fighter was on his tail and asking if Kelly could chase it off. Kelly and his wingman began a dive, and Kelly whipped his Mustang around to get a side shot on the pursuer. The Oscar shuddered and burst into flames. Kelly followed it down and saw the pilot bail out and land in the marshes. It was Kelly's first combat mission.[31]

The mission was not a stunning success, however, and one Beaufighter was lost. Nevertheless, the attackers left behind six enemy aircraft destroyed on the ground, three more destroyed in the air, one probably destroyed in the air, and another six planes damaged on the ground. Of these victories, the Air Commandos were credited with five.[32]

Twenty P-38s of the 459th Fighter Squadron returned to Mingaladon the following day but did not have any success. A final mission against the Rangoon airfields was flown by four squadrons, including the Air Commandos, on October 20. One of these squadrons, the 58th Fighter Squadron spent its time circling over the area and did not even attack. A pilot from the 459th shot down an Oscar, but honors again went to the Air Commandos, who bagged another fighter in the air and damaged three more on the ground. Second Lt. Marion C. Ball, on just his second combat mission, had become separated from his element leader as they flew through some clouds. When he emerged Ball found an Oscar just beneath him. The enemy pilot was caught unaware and died for his carelessness when Ball set his plane aflame.[33]

Second Lt. Lee "Moon" Mullins damaged an Oscar but came under machine-gun fire during his run across Mingaladon. The gun was mounted atop a hangar, and Mullins was flying so low that the gunners were firing down on him. A shell hit his windshield, broke the armored glass and dropped into his lap but, fortunately, did not injure him. When he got back to Cox's Bazar, Mullins hopped out of his plane to inspect the damage. As he looked at the cracked windshield, he began cursing the enemy, the damage, anything he could think of. Someone walked up behind him and asked what had happened. Mullins ignored the questioner, continuing to swear at full throttle. When he finally calmed down and turned to face the inquirer, an embarrassed Mullins discovered it was Stratemeyer, who had only been interested in the circumstances of the incident.[34]

With the three-day operation concluded, the EAC analyzed the results. It was not particularly happy with what it found. Although seventeen enemy aircraft were claimed destroyed in the air and on the ground, with two probables and another thirteen planes damaged against the loss of a single Beaufighter and minor damage to several others, the EAC had expected more. Except for the Air Commandos, most of the other participating units were cited for a lack of aggressiveness. The writer of the study had especially caustic comments for some of these units. For example, he described the leader of the 58th Fighter Squadron as having exercised poor judgment inasmuch as it appeared "that he preferred a totally abortive mission, to attacking the target with a smaller force" when he was in a position to make a very successful attack. The author recommended possible replacement of group, squadron, and flight leaders who showed a lack of aggressive spirit and the will to destroy the enemy.[35]

The 459th Fighter Squadron received similar chastisement. Even when the squadron had been in an excellent position to bounce the enemy, the report notes, the resulting attack had been lackluster, and only one Japanese plane had been shot down by the 459th. The writer believed this had been due to a "prolonged siesta on their back-sides during the past few months. It is recommended that adequate measures be instigated in order to show them the light."[36]

Only the Air Commandos received overall praise. "This unit conducted itself most admirably in carrying out their mission," the author said. "It was amazing to see a squadron composed of inexperienced pilots flying over unfamiliar territory, achieve success which was better than twice the combined efforts of other units participating."[37]

The EAC and the 3rd TAF decided a return to Rangoon was needed when they noted that the Japanese were moving aircraft back there following Operation "L". This time not only the airfields would be attacked, but other facilities as well, notably the Insein locomotive shops. It was hoped that these raids would finally succeed at making the airfields untenable for the Japanese aircraft. A new operation, named Eruption, was laid on for November 3 and 4. This was a very large operation that would include not only P-47s and P-38s, but B-24s and XX Bomber Command B-29s, as well. Allied intelligence personnel estimated that the Japanese now had more than sixty aircraft operational on the fields surrounding Rangoon. A sweep of the airfields was scheduled to open the action on the 3rd, followed by B-29s bombing the Mahlwagon marshaling yards, and finishing with a second sweep of the airfields by the Air Commandos.

Before moving forward to Cox's Bazar for the operation, the fighter pilots spent the first couple of days of November painting their Thunderbolts in SEAC's newly required markings. These markings consisted of dark blue bands on the wings, vertical and horizontal stabilizers, and forward portions of the cowlings. In addition, the five diagonal stripes (also blue) carried by the original group were painted on. Finally, the planes' markings identified them by squadron. The 5th Fighter Squadron's planes had their aircraft numbers painted under the cockpit, and the 6th Fighter Squadron's planes had their aircraft numbers in white on the tail band.[38]

On the morning of the 3rd, Lynn led twenty freshly painted 5th Fighter Squadron aircraft toward Rangoon, while now-Capt. Younger Pitts had seventeen 6th Fighter Squadron planes under his command. Mechanical problems forced the return of one 5th Fighter Squadron and two 6th Fighter Squadron planes. A third P-47 from the 6th crashed in shallow water shortly after takeoff when its engine failed, but its pilot was uninjured. The remaining thirty-three planes pressed on for Rangoon.

RAF Thunderbolts and USAAF P-38s opened the action with attacks against the Mingaladon, Zayatkwin, and Hmawbi airfields. A few Japanese aircraft were spotted airborne, but except for one brief encounter with three Oscars, no aerial combat ensued. Even fewer aircraft were seen on the ground, and no claims were made by the three squadrons attacking the airfields. Close on the heels of the fighters came forty-four B-29s to lay their bombs onto the marshaling yards in an extremely tight pattern. As the bombers were dropping their last bombs, the Air Commandos arrived for the final sweep of the airfields.

When the nineteen 5th Fighter Squadron planes arrived over Mingaladon at about 10:30 AM, they found numerous clouds obscuring the field. As eleven planes flew a high cover, the remaining eight went low to strafe. The clouds almost completely foiled the strafers. Three became lost in the clouds, another failed to find any targets, and the four that were left reported only one aircraft visible on the ground. No claims were made, and light flak slightly damaged one of the Thunderbolts.

The 6th Fighter Squadron's pilots had better luck. Leaving four planes as top cover, ten P-47s strafed Zayatkwin. No planes were seen, but a hangarette was burned, as were several other structures. As the planes swept over the field, an unusual "jet-like" explosion that sent debris soaring 150 feet into the air was noted. It was thought this might have been a land mine set off by the defenders in hopes of catching an attacker. The top cover spotted a couple of Oscars at 30,000 feet, well above the Americans, but these disappeared before they could be reached.

Meanwhile, the other Air Commandos headed for Hmawbi and ran into a pair of Oscars on the deck. These two planes proved too nimble to be shot

135

down, but they were holed by several Thunderbolts before escaping. Lt. Joe Setnor blew up a Sally on the ground, and another Sally and a Tony were claimed damaged. Flak was light but damaged two planes. Another burst shot away a fighter's rudder controls. By skillful flying, the pilot of the rudderless plane was able to bring his plane back to Cox's Bazar. He might have made a successful landing had his brakes not been disabled also. Unable to stop, he ran off the runway and smashed into a truck, unfortunately killing an Indian worker. The pilot walked away unhurt.[39]

The two squadrons returned to Asansol on November 5. The 5th Fighter Squadron remained only briefly at the home field, leaving for Fenny, about one hundred miles north of Cox's Bazar, three days later. Fenny was home to the 12th BG, a B-25 outfit, and the Air Commandos would be used to escort the bombers and fly independent sweeps. The men of the bomb group were delighted to see the P-47s and went out of their way to make the Air Commandos welcome and comfortable. Just two days after their arrival, the 5th flew its first mission from Fenny, a sweep of the airfields at Meiktila. The mission began poorly when one P-47's engine failed on takeoff, and the plane slammed into a revetment and burned. Luckily, the pilot escaped with minor injuries and was flying again at the end of the month. Nothing was found that day and little turned up over the next few missions.

An Oscar was burned on the ground at Nawnghkio on November 11, a Sally was destroyed at Laihka the following day, and another Oscar was damaged on the 19th at Hmawbi as the Air Commandos were flying an escort mission. During the November 12 mission, however, 2nd Lt. Hilton D. Weesner was hit by ground fire while strafing a Meiktila field and plowed into a hill. He was last seen slumped over in his cockpit as flames began to spread along the fuselage. Appearances can be deceiving, though. Weesner survived the crash, was taken prisoner, and was freed from a Rangoon POW camp in May 1945.[40]

Another 1st ACG pilot went down on November 22 during an attack on the Mu River Bridge bypass, an oft-visited target of the Air Commandos. As he pulled out of his run 2nd Lt. Walter C. Lair smelled gasoline fumes in his cockpit. He also noted that his fuel gauge was beginning to drop rapidly. About ten minutes later his engine stopped, and a switch to the auxiliary tank only worked momentarily. Lair picked out some firm ground to belly in on. He overshot the spot, however, and plowed through some trees, which sheared off both wings about four feet from the P-47's fuselage.

Just slightly bruised from this rough encounter, Lair was able to start walking west. He tried to avoid natives for some time, but growing weakness from lack of food finally forced him to seek help. Fortunately, the Karens he met were friendly, and they eventually took him to a British patrol. Lair was reunited with his buddies at Fenny in January after some 39 days in the jungle.[41]

While the 1st ACG's fighter pilots plied their trade, the liaison squadrons remained busy evacuating wounded soldiers, primarily those of the 11th Division in the Chindwin area and the 5th Division south of Tiddim. Eight evacuation strips were built specifically for this purpose, and many other airstrips near the front lines were also used for light plane evacuations. Most of the latter were hardly worth the designation of airstrip, being just a few hundred yards of somewhat level ground carved out of the jungle.

The little planes were not the only means of evacuating the wounded, however. The 1st ACG's gliders were used extensively in that role. Between November 11 and November 16, for example, the CG-4s delivered 127,330 pounds of supplies and brought out 208 casualties. These flights were not without danger. A glider pilot washed out his aircraft on the 12th when he stalled out on landing and ripped the tail off his glider. A short time later another pilot came in too fast and slammed into a pair of gliders that were parked off the end of the runway. Although all of the aircraft were destroyed, no one was seriously injured.[42]

The pilots of the 165th LS had been flying as many as twenty missions a day, and by mid-November both they and their planes were weary. Men and planes of the 166th LS began arriving on November 13, and that squadron took over operations on November 20. The 165th returned to Asansol to have its planes reconditioned and allow its men to get some rest. This change in squadrons did not mean any letdown in operations. Evacuation and supply missions continued without skipping a beat.[43]

Some very welcome additions to the 1st ACG arrived in late November when the airdrome squadrons joined the group. After sitting for some time awaiting orders, the 72nd Airdrome Squadron (ADS), the 309th ADS, and the 326th ADS had moved from their training bases to Camp Anza, Calif. The men tramped aboard the USS *General H. W. Butner*, which weighed anchor on October 2 for the journey to India. On November 23 the *H. W. Butner* docked at Bombay, whereupon ADS crews boarded a train for Asansol. It took three days to reach Asansol but when the squadrons reached the field, they were greeted warmly by the Air Commandos, who had been maintaining their own aircraft. The 326th ADS was assigned to work with the fighter squadrons, the 72nd assisted the 319th TCS, and the 309th went to the liaison squadrons. The 326th was first to begin work, being sent to Fenny to join the 6th Fighter Squadron, which was then based there. The yeoman work of all the airdrome squadrons was immediately apparent, as sortie and in-commission rates soared.[44]

December also saw a final reorganization of the EAC. Mountbatten wished to have two of the command's RAF groups released for use in support of the ground forces that would shortly be opening what was hoped would be the final offensive in Burma. Therefore, Stratemeyer inactivated the 3rd TAF as of November 21 and directed on December 1 that a reorganization take place on December 4. The EAC now consisted of the Tenth Air Force, the Strategic Air Force, the 221 Group, the 224 Group, the Combat Cargo Task Force (which included the Air Commandos, the 1st CCG, and the 4th CCG), the Photo Reconnaissance Force, and a Wing headquarters for the air defense of Calcutta and the B-29 bases nearby.[45]

In the meantime, the Japanese 11th Army in China had begun an offensive from Liuchow to the northwest toward Tushan. By the beginning of December the 11th Army neared Kweiyang. If the Japanese took this town, they could head toward either Chungking or Kunming. Chiang Kai-shek, who had threatened earlier to remove his troops and who had never been that enthusiastic about using his troops in Burma anyway, used this danger to recall a couple of his divisions. He demanded that two divisions and some of his other forces be flown back immediately.

Having arrived in China only on October 31, Wedemeyer was still getting his new command organized and was unsure of the abilities of the Chinese forces. Too, given the troubles between Stilwell and Chiang, Wedemeyer did not want to further strain relations between the United States and China. Thus, he decided that Chiang's demand must be met. Moreover, he requested that two CCGs be sent to China. This would be about half of the SEAC's transports.

While Mountbatten may have been sympathetic to Chiang's problems, he had problems and upcoming operations of his own to consider. The removal of the CCGs could very well result in the Fourteenth Army's operations grinding to a halt, for it relied heavily on air supply. Returning the Chinese divisions could have serious repercussions on operations in northern Burma and could conceivably delay the opening of the Burma Road to China. Mountbatten could not accept this and reported that to the British chiefs of staff. Following serious discussions the CCS decided that some of the aircraft could be sent to China, but the planes would only be on loan and they must be returned by March 1, 1945. They also agreed that the two Chinese divisions could be returned to China.[46]

Initially, Chiang had wanted the 22nd Division and the 38th Division, which he considered two of his best. These two units, however, were in action and Sultan asked if the 14th Division and the 50th Division, which were then in back areas, could be substituted. Chiang was unwilling to lose both of his top divisions, so Sultan suggested returning the 14th and one other division.

Chiang approved, and the 14th and 22nd Divisions were chosen. The 22nd became a relatively easy choice because it was much less involved in combat than was the 38th.[47]

With that settled the EAC directed the Tenth Air Force to handle the movement of the divisions. In turn, Davidson placed his deputy chief of staff, Col. S. D. Grubbs, in charge. It is unknown what wit first dubbed it so, but in a play on the colonel's name, the operation became known as Grubworm. The transport squadrons for the operation came from the Air Transport Command (ATC), the Tenth Air Force, the 1st ACG's 319th TCS, and the newly arrived 317th TCS of the 2nd ACG. The Air Commandos received short notice of their assignment but were in place at Myitkyina North on the evening of December 4. Little tentage and few cots were available for the men, so most settled for sleeping in the open on the ground.

The first flights were out of Myitkyina North, but four other fields were swiftly put to use. One of these, Nansin, had been finished only the day before Grubworm began and was still subjected to Japanese sniper and artillery fire, which slowed operations there somewhat. Capt. Archie L. McKay of the 319th flew the first mission. On this first day of Grubworm, sixteen C-47s of the 319th and ten of the 317th flew thirty-six sorties over the Hump to Chanyi, seventy miles northeast of Kunming.

With these first sorties under their belts, the Air Commandos and the other transport pilots began a remarkably efficient and speedy delivery of Chinese troops back to China. It was remarkable in that the Americans often did not know how many individuals or how much equipment was to be transported. It seemed that every day additional units were added to those selected to be flown back. The Tenth Air Force later reported that Grubworm appeared to be an operation to haul "an unknown amount of cargo, with an indefinite number of aircraft, to an undetermined number of bases."[48]

Grubworm was completed on January 5, 1945, despite weather over the Hump that often threatened to force the cancellation of missions. There was a momentary suspension of the operation between December 16 and December 22 when the ground situation seemed to be improving in China. This allowed the hardworking transport crews to get some needed rest and their aircraft to receive maintenance.

All of the horses and mules were hauled by the Air Commandos. Bamboo stalls were fitted into the C-47s, and their floors were covered to prevent damage. Because the flight crews could not then reach the cockpit through the cargo cabin, they had to enter through the baggage door in the forward fuselage. The animals proved surprisingly docile; only one acted up in any manner.

When Grubworm ended the two Air commando squadrons had flown 488 sorties, carrying 3,451 personnel and 488 animals. The ATC squadrons accounted for 597 sorties, and the Tenth Air Force units added another 243 sorties. A total of 25,095 Chinese troops were moved. In addition, forty-two jeeps, forty-eight 75-mm howitzers, forty-eight 4.2-in. mortars, and forty-eight antitank guns were transported. Grubworm was not a well-known operation compared with those mounted in Europe, but it was one of the major accomplishments of USAAF transport units in World War II.[49]

While the 319th had been participating in Grubworm, the other 1st ACG units had hardly been resting, and a new unit had been added to the group. This was the Night Intruder Section with B-25Hs. The attachment of this section is somewhat mysterious. It is not known what organization supplied the Mitchells —whether it was CBI Air Service Command or one of the bomb groups—and no orders can be found attaching the bombers to the 1st ACG. Nonetheless, the B-25s became very useful and welcome additions to the group. Capt. Edward Wagner, a UC-64 pilot during Operation Thursday, was named commander of the Night Intruder Section.[50]

The bombers flew their missions by the light of the moon, and when the moon waned, they would return to Asansol until the moon's next phase. Based at Chittagong in what is now Bangladesh for operations, the Night Intruders made their operational debut on November 25, when four B-25s went out to harass enemy supply lines and airfields. The Air Commandos became very adept at destroying locomotives with their 75-mm cannon, as well as trucks and railway rolling stock. Additionally, the Night Intruders provided valuable information for early morning fighter sweeps by observing road and rail traffic.[51]

Although Japanese antiaircraft fire was light at first, it picked up quickly as the B-25s became more destructive. Capt. Frank B. Merchant found out the hard way that this fire could be very accurate. On the night of December 29 Merchant and his crew were pulling off from strafing a train when a stream of tracers began tracking them. Merchant felt and heard a thud and saw the oil pressure jump on one of his engines. The top turret gunner called out that something had just gone past his leg.

Merchant began a climb. A quick check with his crew showed that everyone was okay, though one man had been hit in the back by a ricochet and been bruised. As the B-25 climbed through five thousand feet, the radio operator reported the left vertical stabilizer was getting coated with oil. Merchant continued to climb, hoping that both engines would keep purring, but he also told his crew to prepare to jettison the guns, ammunition, tools, and other loose equipment.

Suddenly, the left engine's oil pressure dropped to zero, followed shortly by its propeller beginning to run away. Merchant shut down the engine immediately and feathered the propeller. His crew began to toss equipment out, and most of it was jettisoned quickly. In the rear of the plane, though, there was a difference of opinion on what to save until the last—machine guns or tool boxes. The tail gunner wanted to wait until the last minute to throw his guns out, while the crew chief was loath to part with the tool boxes containing his carefully obtained tools. The pair finally came to an agreement under which the gunner was able to save some of the more irreplaceable gun parts, and the crew chief got to keep a few of his favorite pliers and wrenches.

When he was unable to transfer fuel from the left to right tanks, Merchant knew he was not going much farther. To make things worse, ground fog had covered most of the area, and it was out of the question to crash land. Then, a break in the fog showed trucks moving along a road, headlights blazing. Merchant ordered his crew out. He was the last to go. The Air Commandos had picked a good spot to bail out. The trucks they had seen were British, and most of the Americans had been picked up within a few hours. Only the radio operator decided to wait for daylight, wrapping himself in his chute and making himself comfortable. A few sprained ankles and minor cuts and bruises were all the crew suffered, and they were back flying a couple of weeks later.[52]

Meanwhile, the 6th Fighter Squadron replaced its sister squadron at Fenny on December 1. During its stay the 5th Squadron had compiled an outstanding record, flying 355 sorties on 51 missions. Although escorting the B-25s remained the primary mission, bridge busting had occupied a great deal of the 5th's time, as it would for the 6th also. The ACG fighters' attacks on these structures were generally accurate, but the industrious Japanese kept repairing the bridges, so the targets had to be revisited often. The Mu River bypass, dubbed "Old Faithful," was in particular attacked and reattacked. The Japanese, desperate to keep that vital rail line open, continued to repair it after every raid. Not until the advancing Fourteenth Army drove the Japanese back was that bridge finally removed from the target list.[53]

Other bridges were also sturdy. Such a structure was the bridge at Sinthegon, which had heavy concrete abutments. An attack on December 15 by eight planes dropping sixteen 500-pound bombs was unsuccessful. A return the next day by ten P-47s was equally ineffectual. Even after a third raid by ten aircraft on the December 20, the bridge remained serviceable.[54]

The 6th Fighter Squadron wasted no time getting started at Fenny, flying its first missions the morning after its arrival. Eleven Thunderbolts made a sweep of the Heho, Meiktila, and Kangaung airfields, while another eight aircraft escorted thirty-two Mitchells to Yamethin, south of Meiktila. Sadly, a pilot was lost on the fighter sweep. Finding nothing on the airfields, the Air Commandos began prowling for targets. Near Yanzingyi, 2nd Lt. Brents M. Lowry found a line of boxcars. As he strafed them, one erupted in a huge blast, and the explosion engulfed Lowry's plane. A pass over the area later revealed just small pieces of the P-47 scattered about.[55]

By this time Japanese aircraft had almost disappeared from the air. Every now and then, however, a few would put in an appearance. On December 13 the two Air Commando squadrons joined with the Thunderbolt-equipped 30 Squadron and 135 Squadron of the RAF to escort a dozen RAF B-24s on a mission to bomb bridges. As the mixed escort unit neared the target Pitts, the 6th Fighter Squadron's commander, sighted Oscars high and to the left of the formation. Klarr's flight was nearest the enemy, and Pitts told him, "Go get 'em!" Klarr pulled up and fired a burst at the enemy leader. The Oscar began to smoke, then rolled over and headed for the deck. Klarr's wingman, Lt. A. E. Haunt, fired at a second Oscar and blew off several pieces of it. Although Klarr believed he had scored a kill, he was credited only for a probable, and Haunt was given credit for one plane damaged.[56]

The two 1st ACG fighter squadrons again exchanged places on December 28, and as 1945 began, the Air Commandos and Slim's Fourteenth Army were ready and eager to carry the fight to the enemy. The final battle for Burma was about to commence.

Chapter 9

Mission Accomplished

For the Air Commandos 1945 opened almost literally with a bang. The last few days of 1944 had seen the pilots of the 5th Fighter Squadron attack the usual bridges and enemy positions along the Irrawaddy. Lynn, the squadron commander, had something more spectacular in mind, however. He had long believed that the 500-pound bombs the P-47s usually carried were too light to inflict serious damage to bridges. The Air Commandos had hung two 1,000-pounders on their Thunderbolts occasionally, but Lynn wanted to use three of these big bombs. He talked to Pitts, the 6th's commander, at Asansol and asked him if he thought the idea was feasible. Pitts thought so and agreed to make a test flight carrying the three bombs.

Klarr's P-47 was chosen for the test and was loaded with a 1,000-pounder under each wing and one under the fuselage. Pitts flew the test himself on December 30. After dropping full flaps and applying full power to the Jug, Pitts lumbered off the runway. The takeoff run took a bit more ground than normal, but plenty of runway remained. Pitts thought the fighter flew pretty well, although turns were somewhat sluggish. After becoming comfortable with his plane's handling characteristics, Pitts dropped the bombs in a standard glide-bombing run. The bombs came off smoothly, and Pitts radioed Lynn to go ahead and fly a mission.

Lynn was eager to go, and on the afternoon of January 1, he and Lt. Malcom Wilkins, the 5th's operations officer, each with three of the big bombs, staggered off from Fenny bound for Taungdwingyi and its important bridge. The bridge was sixty miles south of Meiktila, and it carried the main Mandalay–Rangoon rail line. This was a long mission—a round trip of seven hundred miles—and the planes had to climb to over 10,000 feet to clear the Chin Hills. Lynn attacked the bridge first, dropping his two wing bombs, then returning to drop his fuselage bomb. Wilkins followed, dropping all three of his bombs on his pass. Lynn scored a direct hit with one of his bombs and knocked out one of the bridge's spans. Lynn's other bombs were near-misses. Following the return to Fenny, a check of the fighters' fuel tanks showed they had about thirty minutes of fuel still available. Although the concept of hauling three 1,000-pounders was proven, the Air Commandos never flew another mission with them. Range was greatly reduced when carrying these weapons, and this was too valuable to waste.[1]

The ACG's 5th Fighter Squadron continued to attack bridges and rail facilities with success, but one of its more spectacular missions was flown on January 3, when thirteen aircraft defied heavy antiaircraft fire to bomb oil refineries at Yenangyaung. Dense columns of smoke soaring thousands of feet in the air attested to the accuracy of the bombing. An escort mission to Mandalay on January 13 was a bit more difficult. Second Lt. Earl Price was shot down but evaded capture and returned to the squadron in February.[2] Two days later eighteen P-47s hit the airfield at Heho. After bombing the runway the planes strafed hangarettes scattered about the field. As Lynn passed over a hangarette he had been strafing, he noticed white smoke coming from it. He circled the field to allow his flight to catch up and saw the white smoke had turned to a heavy black cloud. He thought little of it then, believing the enemy had probably stored fuel there.

The 5th Fighter Squadron was flying at a rapid pace, escorting B-24s to Mingaladon on January 16 and 12th BG Mitchells to Hsumhsai and Nawnghkio on January 17. The first mission was a milk run, but heavy antiaircraft fire greeted the Air Commandos on the second mission. This fire was accurate and holed six planes, one seriously, but no one was wounded, and all planes returned home.

It was a different story on January 18 when they returned to Heho. After safely escorting B-25s attacking the Heho and Aungban airfields, eighteen P-47s dropped down to strafe. Lynn led the attack again and set afire a hangarette. Making a second run he saw an Oscar surrounded by flames in the hangarette he had just strafed. His pass was similar to the one he had made on the 15th, and he saw the remains of a Lily in the hangarette he had hit on that raid. Upon his return to Fenny Lynn put in claims for a Lily destroyed and an Oscar probably destroyed.[3]

One Air Commando did not return from Heho. First Lt. Richard T. Gilmore's plane was struck by ground fire. He pulled up and bailed out. Others in his flight saw Gilmore land safely, and plans were dispatched to rescue him. Before he could be reached, however, he was captured. He suffered brutal treatment as a POW in Rangoon, and although he survived the war, his health had been ruined by this mistreatment.[4]

On the ground by mid-January, Slim was ready to unleash his troops on the enemy in an operation named Multivite. With typical English humor, the operation consisted of the following four phases, designated as vitamins:

1. Vitamin A—A concentration of IV Corps, less non-motorized elements, in the vicinity of Pauk;
2. Vitamin B—The securing of a bridgehead in the vicinity of Nyaungu by the 7th Division;
3. Vitamin C—A concentration of motorized elements of the IV Corps (the 17th Division, less one brigade) in the bridgehead, and:
4. Vitamin D—A rapid advance to Meiktila and the seizure and construction of an airfield there for use in a fly-in of a brigade group of the 17th Division.[5]

As can be seen by these phases, Meiktila, not the storied city of Mandalay, was Multivite's primary objective. An attack toward Mandalay would most likely just push back the Japanese, whereas Meiktila offered a great opportunity to trap, then annihilate, the enemy. Meiktila was also the site of several airfields and supply dumps, as well as a major rail and road junction. The British army commander proposed an attack by XXXIII Corps on Mandalay to hold the defenders in place while he secretly moved his IV Corps south to the area between Chauk and Pakokku. From there, the corps would head directly for Meiktila. Although Slim stated later that the choice of Pakokku probably came out of discussions with his staff, it may be that he remembered Wingate proposing back in March 1944 the possibility of using one of his Chindit brigades against Meiktila via Pakokku.[6]

In preparation for the attack toward Meiktila Air Vice Marshal Vincent, commander of the 221 Group, chaired a meeting at Fourteenth Army headquarters on January 26. Among those in attendance were planning officers from Fourteenth Army and the Combat Cargo Task Force, Colonel Gaty, and Col. Arthur R. DeBolt, the 2nd ACG's leader, and his operations officer, now–Lt. Col. Levi Chase. It was decided at this meeting that air operations for the IV Corps' drive on Meiktila would be handled almost entirely by the two Air Commando groups, with the exception of some fighters from the 221 Group for interceptor duty and some Combat Cargo Task Force aircraft. The Air Commandos would be responsible for close support, fighter cover, transport, and glider duties, with one 1st ACG liaison squadron for reconnaissance, artillery spotting, casualty evacuation, and liaison. Also, the fighter squadrons were to undertake tactical reconnaissance and photo reconnaissance missions as soon as possible.[7]

Following this meeting, Stratemeyer decided to combine the fighter and transport squadrons of the two Air Commando groups into a pair of provisional groups. The 1st Provisional Fighter Group, which also contained the B-25 Night Intruders, was commanded by Chase of the 2nd ACG. Major Neil I. Holm, the 319th TCS's leader, commanded the 1st Provisional Troop Carrier Group. A proposal by Maj. Vincent Ulery of the 165th LS to combine all of the liaison squadrons into one organization was denied, however. Probably, it was thought that the widespread operations of these squadrons would create more of an administrative headache than consolidating command was worth.[8]

Although Arnold had specified that the Air Commandos were to be under USAAF operational control always, Stratemeyer performed a bit of sleight of hand regarding who actually controlled their actions during Operation Multivite. Nominally, Combat Cargo Task Force headquarters held control over the two Air Commando groups. However, Col. Robert D. Gapen was detached to the 224 Group headquarters to be the Combat Cargo Task Force representative there, where he was to exercise operational control of the Air Commandos. Actually, the staff of the 224 Group ran the show in violation of Arnold's directive. Stratemeyer would state later, in commenting on a USAAF Evaluation Board report on air operations in the CBI that mentioned this arrangement, that the Air Commandos had remained in the U.S. chain of command, with the commanding general of Combat Cargo Task Force retaining operational control, and that Gapen's position was just to coordinate the Air Commando's operations with the No. 224's headquarters.[9]

Meanwhile, prior to the January 26 meeting, on January 14, the XXXIII Corps' 19th Indian Division crossed the barrier of the Irrawaddy north of Mandalay. Believing this to be the Fourteenth Army's main thrust, the Japanese rushed reserves to the bridgehead in a desperate attempt to wipe it out. For a month, from January 20 to February 20, heavy fighting raged, which cost the enemy dearly in losses that could not be sustained. While the Japanese were stubbornly resisting the XXXIII Corps' attacks, Slim's IV Corps prepared to swing around the Fourteenth Army's right flank to get behind the Japanese and cut them off. On the evening of February 14, the IV Corps' 7th Division crossed the Irrawaddy south of Pakokku. Embroiled in fighting with the XXXIII Corps near Mandalay, the Japanese were unable to bring up enough defenders to contain this new threat. On February 21 IV Corps broke through the Japanese lines and drove toward Meiktila.[10]

PART TWO

...Any Time...
2nd Air Commando Group

Col. Arthur R. DeBolt, commander of the 2nd ACG, stands in front of his personal aircraft, Stinky, with his armorer and crew chief. (U.S. Army Air Forces archives)

327th Airdrome Squadron personnel lay pierced steel planking for ramp parking at Cox's Bazar three days before the start of 2nd ACG combat operations. (U.S. Army Air Forces archives)

Sporting the group's "!" insignia, a CG-4A is towed from Kalaikunda to Sinthe.
(U.S. Army Air Forces archives)

Gurkhas board a 317th Troop Carrier Squadron C-47 for transport to Thabutkon.
(U.S. Army Air Forces archives)

A pair of P-51s takes off from Cox's Bazar on the 2nd ACG's first combat mission, February 14, 1945. (U.S. Army Air Forces archives)

2nd ACG L-5s were tossed around like toys when a tornado hit Kalaikunda on March 12, 1945. (U.S. Army Air Forces archives)

The fighter pilots gather on the night of March 14 for a briefing on the Don Muang raid. (U.S. Army Air Forces archives)

2nd ACG P-51s, carrying their distinctive lightning bolt insignia, on a pierced steel planking hardstand at Cox's Bazar. (Courtesy of the World War II Air Commando Association via Edward Young)

Gen. George Stratemeyer awards the Silver Star to Lt. Col. Levi R. Chase Jr. (U.S. Army Air Forces archives)

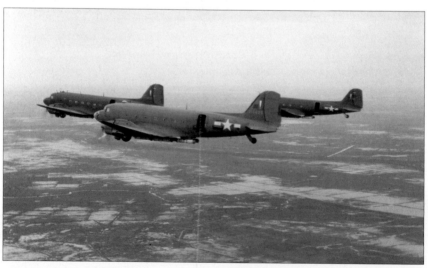

Carrying supply parapacks beneath their wings, a trio of 317th Troop Carrier Squadron C-47s near Rangoon. (U.S. Army Air Forces archives)

Chapter 10

And Then There Were Two

Ever since he had initiated the Air Commando concept back in September 1943, Arnold had followed the project's progress closely. The success of the 1st ACG during Operation Thursday had been deeply satisfying to him. In late March 1944 the general proposed expanding the concept. Along with new ACGs, Arnold planned to add transport groups, designated CCGs, to operate alongside the Air Commandos. He saw these two organizations as the solution to jungle warfare. By building on the "bold and unorthodox" operations pioneered by Cochran's force, he believed the Allies could overcome logistical handicaps they suffered in comparison to the lightly equipped Japanese troops.[1]

After discussing this proposal with Marshall, Arnold wrote Mountbatten:

> Let me say that I believe I am getting more returns from my Air Forces in your theater than in any other theater in the world save perhaps the United Kingdom and Australia. It is this factor which moves me to do what I now propose.
>
> First, I intend to organize four more Air Commando Units. These units in general will be organized along the general lines of Cochran's forces. I hope to have the first unit ready for your theater by July and I will endeavor to have organized and en route overseas one unit in each of the following three months. . . . In the employment of these units I must insist on the following principles:
> (1) They shall be known as U.S. Army Air Force Commando Unit No. _____.
> (2) Their operations be directed by the senior U.S. Air Force Commander.
> (3) Orders and control will employ a U.S. chain of command.
> (4) The American integrity of the units be maintained.
> (5) The Theater contribute to the support of their operations.[2]

Arnold went on to describe the organizing of a four-group Combat Cargo wing, with each CCG having one hundred C-47s. Like the new ACGs, Arnold intended to have one group in-theater by July and to have the others ready over the next three months. He emphasized to Mountbatten, however, that the formation of the units compelled him to pull aircraft and personnel from other units around the world and that, thus, circumstances demanded that some of these groups would probably go to the Pacific.[3]

On the same day that he wrote the SEAC commander, March 24, Arnold met with the CCS to discuss future plans for Southeast Asia and the Pacific. As in his letter to Mountbatten, Arnold described his plans to raise additional Air Commando groups and organize the new CCGs. In general, the CCS felt that these new units would make a great difference to the possibilities for operations in northern Burma.[4]

Pending a deeper study of the proposal, Marshall verbally approved Arnold's plan following the CCS meeting. This study was swiftly completed. Although Maj. Gen. Thomas T. Handy, the Army assistant chief of staff, noted that Arnold's idea was a "revolutionary conception in the utilization of air power," he also stated that to support the projected Air Commando force in Burma, several vital operations, including the Hump, Ledo Road construction, and support for the Fourteenth Air Force and the Yunnan (or Y) Force, would have to be slashed 50 percent. Nonetheless, Handy recommended approval of the new project. On April 9 Marshall officially authorized the establishment of the new ACGs and CCGs. Although the 1st ACG and 2nd ACG would operate under a Combat Cargo Task Force in the CBI, the Combat Cargo concept developed separately and will not be discussed further than it was in the preceding chapters.[5]

Even before receiving Marshall's final okay, Arnold's staff was hard at work finding the forces needed for the new units. It was initially estimated that each Air Commando group would consist of two fighter–reconnaissance squadrons with twenty-five P-51s each, two TCSs with sixteen C-47s and thirty-two gliders each, and three liaison squadrons with thirty-two L-5s and four UC-64s per squadron. A group headquarters, a tactical control detachment, and an aviation medical dispensary rounded out the combat portion of each group. Each group was to have 687 personnel, making a total of 2,748 men for all four groups. The 1st ACG, which was already in Burma, would be authorized to include an additional 147 men.[6]

Because it was intended that these new units would operate under difficult conditions and lack many of the essential services most other USAAF combat units normally enjoyed, a considerably larger air service organization was planned for the Air Commandos. Four augmented service groups with additional mobile repair sections, twelve augmented ADSs, an airborne engineer aviation battalion headquarters and service company, four airborne engineer aviation companies, and an air depot group that included two quartermaster truck companies and a military police company were attached. These service organizations added another 7,094 men to the ACGs. It was a far cry from what Cochran and Alison had at their disposal with Project 9.

As it turned out, changing requirements eventually meant that the last two Air Commando groups and their associated units were not established.[7]

Although readiness dates for all of the new groups were established early— July 15 for the 2nd ACG and continuing every thirty days for the other groups— where to get the personnel to man them was perplexing. As one officer wrote, "Where do we get the mechanics? This is a tough one. We have to start getting 640 a month by April 15 and the 3 months thereafter. You can tap Training Command, ATC or *anything* [emphasis in original]. What is the cost involved in doing this? Probably costs the VHB [B-29] program."[8] The B-29, of course, was one of the USAAF's highest priority programs at that time.

Speed was also essential if the readiness dates were to be met. The tentacles of the USAAF personnel octopus spread throughout the Western Hemisphere to obtain the men and equipment for establishing the new ACGs, which received the code name Project X. Although the 76th Tactical Reconnaissance Group, which was disbanding, provided an initial source of personnel, the Caribbean Defense Command proved to be the prime source of men for the new units, particularly for the fighter squadrons and the air depot and service groups. The 29th Fighter Squadron, the 31st Fighter Squadron, and the 52nd Fighter Squadron, which had been used in the air defense of the Panama Canal which were now being inactivated, supplied many of the pilots and maintenance personnel for the 2nd ACG's fighter squadrons.[9]

Obtaining personnel for the Air Commandos' TCSs required more effort. The Operations Division at USAAF Headquarters would not consent to using men returning from the Caribbean Defense Command after July 1 to fill Air Commando positions. Therefore, more personnel had to be obtained from units in the Zone of Interior, with a consequent reduction in staffing throughout the ZI. Initially, eight TCSs, two for each ACG, were needed. Because of overriding commitments elsewhere, primarily for the upcoming invasion of Europe, the number of squadrons for the Air Commandos was soon slashed in half.[10] Even though the number of squadrons and planes had been halved, there was still a need for experienced flight crews and mechanics. On April 15, 1944, the Air Transport Command was directed to provide 660 pilots, each of whom had at least one thousand hours of flying time and a minimum of one hundred hours on twin-engine aircraft. These men would serve as first pilots for the C-47s. In addition, the Air Transport Command was to transfer 660 experienced crew chiefs and another 660 experienced radio operators/mechanics. Finally, the Training Command was told to furnish 660 twin-engine pilots to serve as copilots.

Time was of the essence. The first group of these men were to report to Bowman Field, Kentucky, just five days later on April 20. By calling on the continental air forces and commands, eighty experienced multiengine pilots were obtained for this initial group. Another eighty-five pilots with minimal qualifications were assigned from the Training Command.[11]

Both the Air Transport Command and the Training Command were reluctant to supply the experienced crews for the remaining increments (some 495 first pilots), citing various commitments, including the very important B-29 program. A quick decision was needed, and General Giles, as chief of Air Staff, decided the B-29s had overriding priority. The Training Command and the continental air forces would furnish less-experienced multiengine pilots who had about six hundred hours each.[12]

While the bureaucratic fighting over resources was going on between USAAF headquarters, the Air Transport Command, and the Training Command, the 2nd ACG was born at Drew Army Air Field (AAF) in Tampa, Florida. The group was activated on April 22 under the temporary command of Capt. L. H. Crouch, pending the arrival of DeBolt as commanding officer. Prior to the war, DeBolt had served in Puerto Rico with the 36th Pursuit Group. More recently he had been at Mitchel Field with the I Fighter Command. DeBolt arrived at Drew AAF on May 1, and the remainder of his staff officers joined the group over the next month. Among these arrivals were Maj. Alfred J. "Jack" Ball Jr., executive officer; Capt. Edwin R. Kimbrough, group chaplain; Maj. T. Kevin Mallen, intelligence officer; and Lt. Col. Henry A. Crawford, group surgeon. DeBolt was familiar with most of those on his staff because many had served with him in Puerto Rico or at Mitchel Field. Also joining the staff as operations officer was Colonel Chase, who had flown with Cochran in North Africa and was a ten-plane ace. Chase would acquire more fame in Southeast Asia.[13]

Meanwhile, the other major portions of the new and expanded Air Commando units were also being formed. Both the 1st Fighter–Reconnaissance Squadron and the 2nd Fighter–Reconnaissance Squadron were activated on April 20 at Lakeland Army Air Base, Lakeland, Florida, where they were joined in May by the squadron headquarters staff. The fighter–reconnaissance designation lasted a little more than a month before being changed to Fighter Squadron, Commando, on June 6. By then the unit had received some rather tired P-51Cs for training. Anticipating an early departure for overseas because warning orders had been received, the two squadrons flew a tiring schedule. The 2nd Fighter Squadron, for example, averaged seventy-seven hours of flying a day during the last half of May.[14]

While most of the pilots in the two squadrons had no combat experience, there were a number who had seen action, primarily in China. The 2nd Fighter Squadron's commander, Maj. Roger C. Pryor, had notched five victories in China, as had the squadron's operations officer, Capt. William Grosvenor Jr. In the 1st Fighter Squadron Capt. Mathew M. Gordon Jr. had knocked down three Zeros and two bombers, while Capt. Donald S. Brookfield had gotten four enemy planes, and Capt. William B. Hawkins had bagged another three.[15]

On May 1 the 317th Troop Carrier Squadron, Commando was activated at Camp MacKall, in Hoffman, North Carolina. Training began almost immediately for the transport and glider crews. May saw the 317th fly several glider tow missions both day and night. Additionally, on May 13 six 317th C-47s, joined by several aircraft from the 3rd ACG's 318th TCS, participated in a joint paratroop dropping exercise.[16]

The final portions of the 2 ACG's flight echelon were the liaison squadrons. Oldest of all of these was the 127th LS. Initially designated the 127th Observation Squadron and allotted to the Kansas National Guard on July 30, 1940, it was ordered to active service on October 6, 1941. It went through a series of designation changes before becoming the 127th LS on April 2, 1943. On May 1, 1944, the squadron added Commando to its designation when it was assigned to the 2nd ACG.[17]

The next liaison squadron to be activated was the 155th. Activated at Aiken AAF, South Carolina, on January 10, 1944, the squadron's first couple of months was spent getting organized. Even as the squadron was still receiving men and aircraft, the 155th sent almost 150 men and half of its fifty aircraft on temporary duty to the Tennessee Maneuver Area in support of Second Army war games. The squadron was reunited at Aiken in late March and continued its training. Then, on May 1, the 155th LS added the coveted Commando to its designation.[18]

The last of the 2nd ACG's liaison squadrons, the 156th, was activated on February 10, 1944, at Statesboro AAF, Georgia, and swiftly embarked on an intensive training program. It was initially a replacement training unit charged with training liaison pilots for overseas duty; thus, its personnel status was unstable, as men transferred in and out of the unit. This all changed on May 1 when the 156th LS was assigned to the 2nd ACG. Squadron morale soared at this news and the probability of an overseas assignment. Overseas deployment was still several months away, however, and much more training would have to be endured.[19]

2nd Air Commando Group, May 1944
    Lt. Col. Arthur R. DeBolt
1st Fighter–Reconnaissance Squadron/1st Fighter
Squadron, Commando
    Maj. Paul B. Ash
    Maj. William E. Buxton (July 29, 1944)
2nd Fighter–Reconnaissance Squadron/2nd Fighter
Squadron, Commando
    Maj. Roger C. Pryor
317th Troop Carrier Squadron, Commando
    Maj. Arthur Kaufman
    Maj. Wirt E. Thompson (July 31, 1944)
127th Liaison Squadron, Commando
    Capt. John B. Noble
155th Liaison Squadron, Commando
    Capt. Robert E. Gross
    Capt. Jack S. Ziegler (May 10, 1944)
156th Liaison Squadron, Commando
    Capt. Leo J. Griffin
    Capt. Anthony J. Maurel (June 2, 1944)
327th Airdrome Squadron
    Capt. Tyler H. Slocumb
328th Airdrome Squadron
    Capt. John H. Goodwin
    Capt. George R. McKee Jr. (October 15, 1944)
340th Airdrome Squadron
    Capt. William L. Reynolds
    Capt. Frank J. Slater (September 23, 1944)
342nd Airdrome Squadron
    Maj. Ford R. Nelson
236th Medical Dispensary, Aviation (assigned June 21, 1944)
    Capt. Padie Richlin

Note: The dates in parentheses indicate when the officer began serving with the 2nd ACG.

In addition to the 236th Medical Dispensary, Aviation, which was assigned to the group on June 12, several other organizations made up the remainder of the 2nd ACG.[20] The war in the Pacific was a much more mobile war than the one in Europe. Distances were much greater when leapfrogging from island to island. This often meant that an air echelon's ground and service units were left behind. To provide for such situations, USAAF Headquarters created special maintenance units. The highly mobile ADSs could support one to three squadrons for seven to ten days on the ground by performing what was called "second echelon maintenance." Such maintenance included the servicing of aircraft and equipment, periodic inspections, and engine changes. ADSs were intended also to prepare not only advanced airfields, but fields behind enemy lines. Finally, these squadrons performed housekeeping functions for the units they supported. Four of these unique organizations were assigned to the 2nd ACG.[21]

The 327th ADS and the 328th ADS were activated on April 20 at Lakeland, while the 340th ADS and the 342nd ADS were activated on May 1 at, respectively, Aiken AAF and Camp MacKall. The 327th was assigned to work with the 2nd ACG headquarters and the 1st Fighter Squadron, and the 328th supported the 2nd Fighter Squadron. The 340th worked with the three liaison squadrons, and the 342nd supported the 317th TCS.[22]

Although USAAF Headquarters had originally specified readiness dates for the 2nd ACG's units as extending from June 1 to July 15, 1944, and planned that movement overseas would occur shortly afterwards, these plans soon changed.[23] Interest in the Air Commando concept was already beginning to wane in various headquarters, despite its success in Operation Thursday. There had been some resistance to the Air Commandos from the outset, primarily from "traditionalists" who could not conceive of a unit (or units) that was a bit out of the ordinary or outside the normal chain of command. Questions over who would control these units was really the key to this resistance, not how well they could perform nor the innovations they could bring to air warfare.

There was still a great deal of resistance following the 1st ACG's success in the CBI. Even as late as December 1944, as the 2nd ACG was arriving in India, Tenth Air Force commander General Davidson was considering breaking up the group into small detachments. Stratemeyer had to remind him that this was against Arnold's previous directives concerning the use of the group and recommended that Davidson rethink his plans for use of the Air Commandos.[24] Nevertheless, the group's squadrons were separated shortly after arrival and seldom operated together throughout the war.

Also bogging down the discussions on the use of the Air Commandos was the continual internecine feuding so prevalent in the CBI over who would control whatever assets that were sent. Finally, at least to Arnold, there appeared to be a lack of drive on the part of many senior leaders in the CBI to detail long-range plans that could be used to establish a firm basis on how to use the Air

Commandos. In letters to various commanders Arnold tried to wring out a decision from them by dangling the possibility that the CBI might get only a portion of the Air Commando and Combat Cargo units being formed. The commanders were informed that Kenney, who was now the Far East Air Force (FEAF) commander, might instead get the bulk of the units.[25]

Arnold's veiled threat, combined at last with plans for offensive operations in Burma, apparently helped break the logjam over the use of the new Air Commando units in the CBI. On June 25 Stilwell, in a letter written by Stratemeyer, requested the "firm" allocation of two ACGs and two CCGs by November 1. These four groups would be placed under a special task force. Stilwell went on to say, though, that the Air Commandos would most likely not be used to their full capabilities as envisioned by Arnold. Rather than being used for a massed airborne assault on Rangoon, they would be used to support Stilwell's ground advance in northern and central Burma. A ground pounder at heart and not the most air-minded of senior officers, Stilwell nevertheless wrote, "If you will secure for me one or more American Divisions, I will prove the value of the Air Commando units and I think I can make Buck Rogers ashamed of himself."[26]

Stilwell followed this letter with another on August 5 that provided more details on how he would use the Air Commandos. He realized that long approach marches in the jungle sapped the energy of ground troops. (This did not stop him, however, from virtually destroying both Merrill's Marauders and the Chindits by keeping them in combat long after they had reached their limits, thereby drawing the lifelong enmity of men from both organizations.) The use of air transport to move troops wherever they needed to go, or either dropping them by parachute or air-landing them on the objective, would avoid tiring the troops and keep them fit for battle. Stilwell still smarted from the fact that the 1st ACG had been assigned specifically for use with the Chindits and that it would continue to operate with the British in an advance toward Mandalay. To him, such operations were wastes of effort that frittered away the highly trained and specialized unit. Therefore, he wanted to make sure that a second ACG be assigned to him so, he seemed to be thinking, it would be used properly. He mentioned in his letter that he planned to use the group to help take Lashio. In any event, Stilwell was gone from the CBI before the 2nd ACG reached Burma, having been recalled at the insistence of Chiang Kai-shek.[27]

As discussions continued over where to send the new Air Commando units and how best to utilize them, the 2nd ACG kept busy readying itself for combat. The major portion of the group's training was conducted in the Gainesville, Florida, area. Initially based at Cross City, forty-five miles west of Gainesville, the fighter squadrons moved to Alachua AAF, Gainesville's former municipal airport, in late June. The 317th TCS, which moved much of the other squadrons' equipment in its C-47s, stayed at Alachua for a short time before switching to Dunnellon, about fifty miles southwest of Gainesville. Also based temporarily at Dunnellon before moving to Cross City were the three liaison squadrons. The ADSs moved with their flying units. It was in the triangle formed by these three fields that the group held most of its exercises.

A visitor of interest during this period was Major Rebori, late of the 1st ACG. Now assigned to USAAF Headquarters, Rebori gave several lectures to the group on his experiences in Burma and also oversaw some of the training of the liaison squadrons. An even more engrossing visitor, though, was Alison. He had also come down from Washington, D.C., to see how the group's training was progressing. While visiting old friends from China (Pryor, Grosvenor, and Capt. Robert L. Tempest), Alison was persuaded to speak to the men of the 2nd Fighter Squadron. Although he claimed he "talked too much," what he had to say about the operations of the 1st ACG kept everyone enthralled.[28]

There was some disappointment throughout the group when warning orders for overseas movement were rescinded, but this did not last long, as DeBolt kept the training going at a high pitch. A notable mission during this period was a joint interception by the ACG two fighter squadrons of a force of two hundred bombers making a mock attack on Tampa. Unfortunately, the intense tempo came with a cost. Several pilots were injured in various mishaps. The 2nd Fighter Squadron lost two pilots during practice dive-bombing missions. In each instance pieces of aircraft were seen coming off their P-51s. It was determined later that metal fatigue in the tail sections of the well-worn aircraft had caused the accidents, and no more dive-bombing was authorized until a fix could be accomplished. Another 2nd Fighter Squadron pilot died when he apparently became disoriented when caught in a thunderstorm and plowed into marshy ground at high speed. A 1st Fighter Squadron pilot was lost when he crashed into a tree during a simulated strafing attack. The other squadrons did not go unscathed, either. A pilot from the 155th LS was also killed on a training flight, and the 317th TCS lost a plane during a paratrooper dropping mission. All aboard the C-47 were killed when it spun in from low altitude.[29]

Following the conclusion of the field exercises, in which all elements of the 2nd ACG were finally brought together, the pace of training lessened. Many aircraft were turned over to other units, particularly the 3rd ACG, which was also training nearby. This left few planes with which to operate, but enough were available for cross-country flights across the United States. The slackening in training also enabled many men to receive some much-appreciated furloughs. Meanwhile, with other units moving into Gainesville to perform their field maneuvers, the 2nd ACG, except for the 317th, which flew to Camp MacKall to continue its training with paratroopers, returned to Drew Field temporarily before moving to Lakeland.

While the group settled back in at Lakeland, the CCS were meeting in Quebec for the Octagon Conference. As part of their strategic planning for the defeat of Germany and Japan, the Combined Chiefs finalized plans concerning the movement of the Air Commandos overseas. They directed that one group, the 2nd ACGs, be sent to the CBI and another, the 3rd ACG, be sent to the southwest Pacific. USAAF Headquarters immediately issued a warning order to the 2nd ACG and began final planning for the group's movement to the CBI. Arnold initially desired the 2nd ACG to be in-theater by October 15, but this proved unfeasible, and the group's arrival date was slipped to November 20.[30]

Receipt of the warning order on September 25 sent the 2nd ACG into a flurry of activity. Those men still on leave were hurriedly recalled, and final preparations were made for the move overseas. With most of the group's aircraft transferred, much of the men's time was taken up with obtaining new equipment and filling out a seemingly endless number of forms. A temporary diversion to these proceedings was a hurricane that lashed central Florida on October 19. Because it was believed the flimsy prefabricated buildings on base might not stand the winds, personnel were moved into sturdier structures in the town of Lakeland to wait out the storm. As it turned out, the hurricane caused little damage as it raced by, and the group was back finishing its preparations as soon as the storm passed.[31]

Finally, October 28 arrived, and the men boarded trains to begin a five-day journey across the United States to Camp Anza near Los Angeles. Newly promoted Colonel DeBolt and several other members of the 2nd ACG stayed behind until October 31, when they left for India by plane. Debolt and his contingent arrived in Karachi on November 10 and began arranging for the arrival of the rest of the group. Upon arrival the advance party learned that EAC had assigned Kalaikunda, which lies about eighty miles west of Calcutta, as the group's home. This field had been developed as a base for B-29s. Its primary purpose, though, had been for use by C-109s (B-24s modified as tankers) and C-46s for flights over the Hump to China. It had a fine concrete runway and plenty of ramp space, but its other facilities were still meager.[32]

Actually, the first elements of the 2nd ACG to arrive in the CBI belonged to the 317th TCS. The squadron had flown to Baer Field in Fort Wayne, Indiana, on September 29. Baer was the staging area for all TCSs, and it was here that the 317th received new aircraft. After checking out their new planes, the 317th's air echelon left Baer for Morrison Field near West Palm Beach, Florida, on October

16. It then flew by stages across the Atlantic and Africa, arriving in Karachi on the 26th. Moving to Sylhet, India, a few days later and then to Bikram, the squadron was immediately put to use dropping supplies to British and Indian troops fighting in the Chindwin Valley. Thus, the 317th became the first unit of the 2nd ACG to engage in combat operations.

Its first major operation, though, was Grubworm, the transfer of two Chinese divisions from the Burma front back to China. The 317th was alerted for this operation on December 2 and was officially assigned to it on the 4th. Eleven aircraft were available for Grubworm, taking off from Bikram that morning and arriving at Myitkyina North in the evening. With insufficient tents and cots to go around, most of the officers and men of the squadron camped out and slept in the open on the ground.

The next day began early, with the first C-47 taking off at 7:00 AM with a load of troops from the Chinese 14th Division. During the day the squadron sent ten planes to Chanyi, seventy miles northeast of Kunming. Sadly, only eight planes returned that evening. The wreckage of 1st Lt. William G. Clegg's plane was found on December 14. It had crashed into the first ridge of mountains between Myitkyina and China. All aboard had been killed.

Maj. Wirt E. Thompson and all on his aircraft just disappeared. His plane was not found until after the war. It had also crashed near the same ridge that had claimed Clegg's plane.[33]

Many in the 317th believed that these planes and crews had been lost because the briefings on Hump flying had been lackadaisical and that the briefers had indicated that it was possible to cross the Hump at 10,000 feet. Since many of the mountains along the route were above 14,000 feet, asking a pilot new to the route to find a 10,000 foot pass, particularly in poor weather, was asking too much of him. The squadron pilots also discovered that they could not climb high enough to clear the mountains while heading directly toward them from their Assam fields or Myitkyina. It was far better to gain altitude over the fields before setting out for the Hump. This was just one of the many lessons fliers in the CBI learned the hard way.[34]

On the other hand, the 319th TCS pilots, who were mostly CBI veterans, thought the briefings were as good as they were accustomed to. They told the newcomers that they never relied too much on the briefings anyway, but they studied their maps carefully and learned how to use them properly. Finally, they urged the new pilots on the Hump run to use particular caution on their first trips over unknown terrain.[35]

Hump missions were tiring for the 317th's pilots, particularly in the early days of Grubworm, because their planes were not fitted with oxygen. Most of their previous flying had not been above 8,000 feet where oxygen was not needed. Now flying above 14,000 feet regularly, the flight crews reported headaches, nausea, and fatigue. These problems disappeared after oxygen supplies were delivered to the Air Commandos. Weather, also, was always a factor when flying over the Himalayas. Missions had to be canceled or delayed many times when clouds, rain, and fog moved in over the mountains or closed the landing fields in China.[36]

The two TCS units stood down on December 9 when orders were received from Tenth Air Force to prepare their C-47s to carry animals. For the rest of the operation the Air Commandos transported all of the animals. Seats were removed from the aircraft, and stalls were constructed using bamboo. Tarpaulins were placed on the floor of a plane to prevent animal urine from seeping onto control cables. Over these were laid coco matting, and then two hundred pounds of hay was spread. The horses and mules were not drugged; still, they proved remarkably docile throughout the flights. Of the 1,595 animals the Air Commandos hauled, only one acted up. Luckily, the crew chief on that plane was a veterinarian in civilian life. He promptly got the horse to lie down, whereupon he sat on the animal's neck until the C-47 landed. Actually, many pilots preferred hauling animals to hauling the Chinese troops. The latter were more susceptible to airsickness than were the animals.[37]

Movement of the Chinese 14th Division was completed on December 16. For the next few days the transport units performed needed maintenance on their aircraft, which had been flying almost constantly. The respite also allowed the flight crews to get some needed rest. On December 22 Operation Grubworm restarted with the initial movement of the Chinese 22nd Division. This was a bigger unit than the 14th Division, and it tended to grow through the addition of previously unattached organizations. But by that time the transport crews were familiar with boarding techniques, particularly in the case of the animals, and there were few problems with this movement. Grubworm officially ended on January 5, 1945. It had been a highly successful operation, and the Air Commando squadrons had performed especially well.[38]

Back in the United States in the meantime, much of the time spent at Camp Anza was taken up in filling supply shortages, listening to security lectures, doing abandon ship drills, and watching films on various topics. On the morning of November 8 the men again boarded trains for the 140-mile trip to the Los Angeles Port of Embarkation where they boarded the USS *General John Pope*. Filled to overflowing with men of the 2nd ACG and other units, the big transport sailed on November 10, heading west for India. The voyage was generally calm, though many of the landlubbers suffered for a few days before gaining their sea legs.

The ship crossed the equator (twice!), at which time King Neptune came aboard to initiate the USAAF men into the Order of Shellbacks. Because there were so many pollywogs, or uninitiated soldiers and airmen, on board, officers from each squadron volunteered to undergo the painful initiation on behalf of their units. The *General John Pope* made a brief stop at Melbourne, Australia, but no one could go ashore. The crew and passengers had to be content with staring longingly at the land. India was finally sighted on December 10, and the transport docked at Bombay the following day.

The group entrained on December 13 for the eighty-mile trip to Kalaikunda. It took three days to cover that distance. Upon their arrival the men of the 2nd ACG were surprised to find DeBolt on hand to greet them. The surprise wore off quickly, though, and they set about preparing quarters and other facilities in anticipation of receiving their fighters and liaison aircraft.

As 1944 ended, only the 317th TCS was involved in combat operations, but the rest of the 2nd ACG was eager to show the doubters in the CBI what the Air Commandos could do.[39]

Chapter 11

A Far-Ranging War

T he novelty of being in a foreign country, with its exotic people, animals, and scenery, soon wore off the Air Commandos sitting at Kalaikunda. They had too much to do than admire the sights, anyway. When the group's equipment that had also come over on the USS *Pope* finally arrived via the inimitable Indian railway system, all units began setting up their supply sections and orderly rooms. Tents began to display more individuality, as the men made frequent midnight requisitioning forays on nearby salvage dumps and abandoned buildings. Packing crates, bamboo, and bits of Indian fabric were turned into all kinds of furniture, from ashtrays to beds. With considerable ingenuity and skill, the men of the 1st Fighter Squadron constructed a veritable nightclub in the rice paddies of India as their alert room. It was so comfortable and nicely appointed that DeBolt wondered that the squadron had its "rest house, but where was the work room?"[1]

Some of this labor had to be redone when a strong storm hit Kalaikunda on January 6. The wind pulled tent stakes out of the mud and collapsed a number of tents, forcing the occupants to seek firmer and higher ground. The storm passed quickly, though, and the Air Commandos soon had their quarters reconstructed. While the storm dampened the men physically, it did not dampen their spirits, which rose spectacularly the following day with the delivery of the group's first Mustang. The plane was a brand-new bubble-top P-51D, sparkling in the sun in its silver finish. To the men of the fighter squadrons the P-51D was a work of art far superior to the weary P-51Bs and Cs they had flown in the States. By the end of the month each squadron had received most of their P-51Ds, plus several F-6Ds, photo–reconnaissance versions of the Mustang. The fighters were swiftly adorned with the group's spectacular markings of black lightning bolts on wings and fuselage, plus black theater identification bands on the wings and tail surfaces. Having seen the question mark emblem carried on the tails of the 1st ACG's C-47s, the 2nd ACG decided to place an exclamation point on the tails of its aircraft. Meanwhile, the new group was officially assigned to operate under the Combat Cargo Task Force.[2]

Even as they were receiving their aircraft, the 2nd ACG's fighter pilots began logging combat time, albeit on ferry flights. On January 13 ten pilots from each squadron ferried new P-51Ds across the Hump to Chengkung, a field near Kunming, China.[3]

As the fighter squadrons settled in, the 317th TCS had already seen action, as mentioned above. The transport squadron made brief visits to Kalaikunda as it moved here and there in India and Burma to supply troops in the field and to train British glider troops. This constant movement put a great strain on the 317th, as it seldom remained in one spot long enough to do proper maintenance on its aircraft or let its men get adequate rest. Nonetheless, the 317th continued to operate with great efficiency, receiving numerous congratulatory messages from the units it supported.[4]

The liaison squadrons also received new aircraft in the form of L-5Bs capable of carrying a litter. In a theater always facing shortages of almost everything, but particularly of transports and liaison aircraft, the arrival of the 2nd ACG and its three liaison squadrons was greeted warmly. It did not take long for the light planes to be pried away from the group's direct control and to operate semiautonomously away from the rest of the Air Commandos. To acclimate them to conditions in the theater, a few planes and pilots were sent forward to operate with frontline units. The 156th LS sent six L-5s to the Shwebo area to work with the British XXXIII Corps, which was preparing to attack toward Mandalay. The fliers spent eight days flying high-ranking officers around the front lines and making mail deliveries to the troops before returning to Kalaikunda. Caught later in a tornado that destroyed many of its aircraft, the 156th would not be sent back to the front until April 8, when it reinforced the 155th LS at Myitchea.

In the meantime the 127th LS was the first 2nd ACG unit other than the 317th TCS to be committed in full strength, when it was dispatched to Cox's Bazar on January 19 to support the XV Indian Corps. The 155th LS spent time at Lalitpur practicing with the Chindits' 23rd Brigade before being assigned to the IV Corps at Sinthe on February 21.[5]

The liaison airmen quickly discovered that flying over the jungle was quite different from what they had experienced while training over Florida's relatively open terrain. Navigation was much more difficult while flying over the featureless jungle canopy. Also, turbulence could be dangerous to the low-flying aircraft, as could mechanical problems, which pilots could have little time to fix. The 127th LS lost three planes in February in just such situations. Fortunately, the pilots and the wounded they were transporting survived the crash landings.[6]

The 2nd Fighter Squadron was not as lucky as the liaison squadrons. Shortly after arriving in India the 2nd ACG's fighter squadrons received a shipment of rockets for their Mustangs. The 4.5-inch rockets could be mounted in triple tubes under each wing. While not the most accurate projectiles, the rockets still packed a potent punch. The airmen were sent to the Ranchi gunnery range for instruction by RAF Beaufighter pilots, who had been using rockets for some time. One of the old China hands, Captain Tempest, was practicing his rocket firing on February 6. Although his approach to the target looked fine to observers on the ground, he may have carried his pass too low. Just after firing his rockets, it appeared that Tempest was attempting an abrupt pull-up, but his plane snapped to the left and plunged into the ground.[7]

That same day Colonel Chase was made commander of the 1st Provisional Fighter Group that was made up of the fighter squadrons of both the ACGs and the 1st ACG's B-25 section. Although both groups' squadrons flew missions together, some 2nd ACG fliers claimed later that they never saw a P-47 from the 1st ACG.[8]

Early in February the 317th TCS flew members of the 327th ADS and the 236th Medical Dispensary to Cox's Bazar to prepare the field for the arrival of the fighter squadrons. The squadrons operated from there for much of their stay in the CBI. Additionally, the C-47s flew in stocks of bombs and other equipment for the fighters. Cox's Bazar lay just a few miles from the Burmese border and was situated on a narrow strip of land jutting into the Bay of Bengal. Space was at a premium, so some units already there were moved to other fields to accommodate the Air Commandos' P-51s.

Cox's Bazar was basically one large sand dune, which made dust and erosion a serious problem. Its runway and taxiways were tarred, but the hardstands were covered with a unique pattern of bamboo weaving overlaid with pierced steel plank. This worked surprisingly well in keeping both dust and erosion in check.[9]

As soon as the 317th finished transporting the advanced party to Cox's Bazar, it moved to Palel to join the 319th TCS. There, the two Air Commando squadrons were combined into the 1st Provisional Troop Carrier Group which was under the direct command of Major Holm and came under the operational control of the Combat Cargo Task Force. At Palel, the 317th ran the control tower, while the 319th handled the field lighting. The field became a major staging point of both troops and supplies for Operation Multivite, the 14th Army's offensive toward Mandalay and Meiktila that had begun in mid-January.[10] Throughout the fighting for Mandalay the 317th had its planes in the air twelve hours a day or longer, supplying the frontline troops with ammunition, rations, gasoline, and clothing.

Meanwhile, in anticipation of the planes' use when one of the Meiktila airstrips was captured, the 317th had towed sixteen gliders loaded with engineering equipment from Kalaikunda to Sinthe, which was about twenty-five miles northwest of Nyaungu. As it turned out, however, when the field at Thabutkon, twenty-five miles northwest of Meiktila, was captured in good condition on February 26, only one CG-4 was needed, and the rest of the glider operation was canceled.

A fly-in of the 99th Indian Infantry Brigade from Palel to Thabutkon codenamed Crossbow began on the 27th, when the glider carrying radar and signal equipment and runway lighting was towed from Sinthe in midmorning. An hour and one-half later a 317th TCS C-47 landed the first combat troops. During the day the planes of the 1st Provisional Troop Carrier Group flew some sixty-three sorties into Thabutkon. The airfield's capture did not mean that the enemy had been driven far from it. Both Air Commando TCSs found it to be quite a hot spot. Enemy mortar and artillery fire continued to fall within yards of the strip for some time. Japanese snipers also made nuisances of themselves by holing several planes, although with little damage.

On the first day of the operation the 317th did lose one plane when it landed downwind and ran off the end of the runway. Fortunately, there were no injuries to the crew or passengers. As the British and Indian infantrymen pushed the Japanese back and the fields at Meiktila became available, Thabutkon became less essential, and it was closed on the evening of March 3. The 317th's C-47s had been very busy during the operation, transporting more than one thousand troops of the 99th Indian Infantry Brigade and delivering 330 tons of supplies.[11]

General Slim was especially pleased with the efforts of the troop carriers, writing Stratemeyer, "Particularly I am impressed with the record of the transport squadrons which lifted 99 Brigade into Thabutkon. Their five days of practically continuous flying without losing a single sortie because of maintenance difficulties is outstanding."[12]

The 2nd ACG's fighters flew their first offensive combat sorties in support of the 7th Division. The fighters, which had been under the operational control of the 224 Group but were then under IV Corps' control, had arrived at Cox's Bazar on February 13. The fighter squadrons had hardly settled in before they were being briefed for a mission to be flown the next day. Their targets were in front of the 7th Division near Pakokku.

On the afternoon of February 14 forty P-51s, twenty from each ACG fighter squadron, took off for Pakokku. Each plane carried a pair of 500-pound bombs. Chase led the 1st Fighter Squadron, and Pryor led the 2nd Fighter Squadron.

Coached onto their targets by RAF ground parties operating as visual control parties (VCPs), a British version of U.S. forward air controllers, the Americans made accurate attacks on the enemy. Many fires and heavy smoke attested to this accuracy. Over the next several days the Air Commando units continued their support of the 7th Division as it expanded its bridgehead.[13]

Communications difficulties occasionally hampered the fighter squadrons on these missions. Arduous conditions on the ground knocked out most of the ground VHF radios, so they had to switch to HF radios. However, the 2nd ACG aircraft lacked the HF radios used by the VCPs. As a result instructions from the ground parties had to be relayed to the group's intelligence officer, Major Mallen, at IV Corps headquarters, who then radioed the fliers. It was an imperfect and time-consuming process, but it worked. In contrast the P-47s of the 1st ACG carried both HF and VHF radios, and when they were on joint missions, the P-47 flight leaders would pass instructions from the VCPs on to the P-51D pilots.[14]

From February 14 until March 1 the Air Commando fighters were up almost daily supporting IV Corps units. During that period the 2nd Fighter Squadron flew 277 combat sorties. Villages in the Meiktila area that were believed to be harboring Japanese troops were hit using bombs, rockets, and napalm. The latter often became the weapon of choice on these missions. Its flames not only killed the enemy, but also helped clear the dense foliage covering enemy positions.[15]

The British offensive brought out the JAAF in force. On February 17 eight Oscars from the 64th Sentai strafed British and Indian troops near Nyaungu and also shot down an L-5. Two days later the enemy planes appeared again, at one point bouncing three 5th Fighter Squadron P-47s. The Thunderbolts escaped, and RAF Spitfires claimed several victories when they were able to intercept the enemy planes. Worried about this enemy activity, the 224 Group directed the 2nd ACG to hit Japanese airfields at Toungoo, Magwe, and Pyinmana. It was believed these fields were being used by the Japanese as advanced bases. The ACG fighter squadrons struck the fields on February 17, strafing and dropping napalm, but no enemy aircraft were seen. Meiktila was attacked on February 23 but, again, no aircraft appeared to be present.[16]

Concerned about the enemy air attacks, IV Corps requested that the Air Commandos station some aircraft at Sinthe, which lay a few miles south of corps headquarters. The 1st Fighter Squadron sent six Mustangs, and the 2nd Fighter Squadron sent another four aircraft to Sinthe on February 22. The Air Comman-dos remained at Sinthe for the next ten days. Nothing untoward happened for the first couple of days as the Mustangs covered the bridgehead and patrolled over Meiktila. That these missions could be dangerous, though, was underscored on February 25, when a couple of 2nd Fighter Squadron pilots had to bail out of their stricken planes.

First Lt. Robert A. Beck and Capt. Edward E. Atha had taken off from Sinthe in hopes of intercepting a group of enemy fighters that had been reported to be in the area. Near Ledawyo, Beck's plane was hit by 20-mm antiaircraft fire. Pieces of cowling flew off, and his engine seized. Beck prepared to bail out, releasing his canopy and unbuckling his harness. Expecting to have to pull his ripcord immediately, he grabbed it and stood up to jump. The howling wind caught his arm and flung it back against the seat's armor plate, causing him to pull the ripcord. His chute began to blossom in the cockpit! Beck hardly had time to curse when he was suddenly yanked from the cockpit.

There was another tremendous shock as his chute snagged on his plane's tail and then tore loose, leaving a big hole in the chute. As Beck drifted down he noticed he was descending toward the burning remains of his P-51. Not wishing to burn to death, Beck chanced slipping his torn parachute to avoid the flames. It worked, but he fell like a stone toward the ground. He hit hard and sprained an arm and a leg, but fortunately did not suffer more serious injuries. Well behind enemy lines, Beck hobbled to nearby cover while Atha headed back to base to report the shootdown. Upon hearing of Beck's plight, Maj. Charles M. Gordon rushed over to the other side of the field to grab an L-5 for a rescue attempt.

With Atha leading an escort of several other P-51s, Gordon headed for the spot where Beck had bailed out. Gordon landed in a rice paddy about half a mile from where Beck was hiding. The downed pilot saw the L-5 land and hobbled toward it. Gordon never shut off his engine, and as soon as Beck climbed in, he took off. Gordon's takeoff from the tiny clearing almost led to two people being behind enemy lines, for he clipped the top of a tree. Luckily, it was just a glancing blow, and Gordon had Beck home just three hours after he had been shot down. Back at Sinthe Beck swiftly drained the quarter-full bottle of whiskey supplied him.[17]

Neither Gordon's nor Atha's day was over yet. Later in the day Atha went out again and found himself having to leave his Mustang when its engine seized. Gordon again comandeered an L-5 for a rescue attempt. Misfortune befell him this time. As he attempted to land in the growing darkness, he overshot a rice paddy and smashed into a grove of trees. His jaw, nose, and one leg were broken, but he had landed near some British troops, who soon pulled him from the wreckage. Gordon's combat days were over, however. His valor was noted by the award of the Silver Star. As for Atha, he spent the next fifteen hours behind enemy lines, until he was rescued by British troops.[18]

Following the capture of Thabutkon, IV Corps drove toward Meiktila, which fell on March 4. That would not be the end of the fighting. His eyes still focused on Mandalay, although he considered the only reason for defending it was for its prestige value, Lt. Gen. Kimura Hyotaro, commander of the Burma Area Army, was slow to react to the danger developing at Meiktila. When he finally realized his vulnerability Kimura dispatched two divisions (less one regiment each) and the remnants of a third division, plus smaller units, to the aid of the 3,500 defenders of the town. As it turned out, the decisive battle for central Burma was fought not at legendary Mandalay, but at the little-known town of Meiktila.

Instead of the pervasive jungle that covered so much of northern and central Burma, a broad plain covered by scattered trees and cacti surrounded Meiktila. A few hillocks dotted the plain, and two lakes lay north and south of town. The two main airfields were about three miles east of Meiktila. These would prove critical in the coming days because although the town had fallen, the Japanese were not about to allow the British to keep it. Newly arriving enemy units cut the IV Corps' land route back to its Irrawaddy bridgehead, and the corps found itself under siege and fighting a desperate battle. Control of the airfields was essential if the British were to retain Meiktila.[19]

The fight for the airfields was particularly fierce, as first one side and then the other gained control. Into this maelstrom flew the Air Commando C-47s. The first transports left Palel for Meiktila on the morning of March 15 carrying men of the 9th Brigade. Enemy artillery fire was seen bursting on the field as the aircraft came in to land. Luckily, only one 1st ACG plane suffered minor damage. After quickly unloading their passengers the C-47s returned to Palel to pick up more troops. These afternoon missions would be much more eventful.

After leaving Palel around 2:00 PM, the aircraft were directed by IV Corps to divert to Nyaungu because of heavy shelling of the field at Meiktila. Six of the 317th's planes did not receive this message and proceeded on to their destination. Upon their arrival they found nothing much going on and unloaded their troops and supplies without difficulty. The remaining aircraft, which had landed at Nyaungu and then took off again for Meiktila, had a far more interesting time.

As the C-47s approached the airfield, artillery fire could be seen bursting all around the field and in the unloading area. The Air Commandos landed, nevertheless, but heeded the tower's urgent instructions, "Land, taxi to the south end! Kick 'em out and get the hell out of here! Do not cut engines!"

When 1st Lt. Wayne Bishop began to land, he saw a shell hit midway down the runway. Pouring the coal to his plane, Bishop buzzed the runway to check its condition and then came around to land. More shells landed nearby as he taxied rapidly to the unloading area. Suddenly, an explosion under the tail threw everyone in the rear of the plane to the floor. Dust and smoke obscured the plane, and the tower called to see if they were okay. A quick inspection found nothing wrong, and everyone was speedily unloaded. Bishop took off as soon as possible, becoming airborne before reaching a huge shell hole in the runway. Further inspection of his plane back at Palel revealed several dents in its right elevator.

First Lt. Bert Russell also had some exciting moments. Russell had no problem landing and unloading even though the Japanese were shelling the airstrip. Takeoff was a different case. A shell hit fifty feet behind his plane as he taxied out, severely shaking the aircraft. As the crew chief checked out the tail section for damage, another shell burst seventy-five feet back, throwing the crew chief to his knees. Then, as Russell began to take off and had raised his tail, a shell struck in front of him. He jammed on the brakes and swerved left to miss the hole. Bennett stopped briefly to have his crew chief check again for damage and then took off down the middle of the runway. Standing in the C-47's astrodome, the radio operator saw an explosion at the spot where they had stopped. It had been a very close call.[20]

Flights into Meiktila the next day were just as exciting and more costly for the 317th. Because of enemy activity the morning missions were diverted to Nyaungu, where their equipment was unloaded before the planes returned to Palel. The transports returned to Meiktila that afternoon to find the field still under fire. Despite the shelling the Air Commando C-47s landed. Unloading was a chore because as soon as an aircraft stopped, the soldiers on board leaped off to head for foxholes, leaving the crews to unload the equipment.

First Lt. Roy Burger had just landed and was taxiing to the unloading area when a shell struck his aircraft's tail and collapsed it. Expecting another shell, Burger almost bent his throttles as he slammed them forward to gain speed. The drag of the ruptured tail kept him motoring at but ten miles per hour, however. Just as he reached the parking area, his plane received a direct hit on its right wing, which then burst into flames. Five Indian soldiers, the crew chief, and the radio operator managed to escape through the cargo door, but only after removing its hinges.

Meanwhile, the rapidly spreading blaze had trapped Burger, his copilot, and three other Indians in the front. Burger did not want to leave by the top escape hatch because he feared the right gas tank would explode. Instead, he kept trying to batter his way through a jammed escape hatch behind his seat. When he noticed everyone else going out the top, he decided to follow. Just as he left the airplane the cockpit was enveloped in flames. Luckily, those aboard suffered only minor injuries. The C-47 was a total loss, however.[21]

The 317th TCS continued to fly in reinforcements on March 17 and March 18. After the furor of the previous two days, these were remarkably peaceful. The lull was only temporary, though. On the 19th, the Air Commandos began delivering ammunition to Meiktila, and the enemy resumed bombardment of the field. Japanese snipers also crept close to fire on the transports. One airplane was hit by rifle fire on successive days, resulting in a "pretty breezy ship." Another C-47 came perilously close to crashing when a shell exploded just below it as the plane was landing. It rocked violently and the pilot almost lost control. Coupled with a strong crosswind, the rocking caused the landing to be in a crab and hard. The C-47's strong landing gear held up, though, and plane came to a safe stop.[22]

Another crew who also had a close call was that of Lt. Charles Brook and Lt. Glen Matousek. They had flown in the last supplies of the day before the British closed the strip for the night. Shellfire was sprinkling the strip when Brook and Matousek stopped to unload. The Indian troops they had brought in were so eager to get off the plane and into a foxhole that most left their duffel bags on the plane. The two pilots and the crew chief had to pitch the bags out onto the ground.

As soon as the last bag had been thrown out, Brook went back to the cockpit to prepare for a quick takeoff. In the meantime and unknown to either Brook or the crew chief, Matousek had jumped off the C-47 to kick away some of the bags that had fallen in front of the tail wheel. The crew chief closed the cargo door, and upon hearing the door slam shut, Brook advanced the throttles and began to taxi.

Suddenly, Brook heard a loud banging from the rear of the plane and the crew chief yelling to stop. Looking back to see what the problem was, Brook saw that the crew chief had opened the door and that Matousek was hanging onto it for dear life. Brook stopped just long enough for the crew chief to haul the copilot aboard and close the door.

He did not wait for Matousek to reach the cockpit to resume takeoff. Enemy shells were falling on the strip in increasing numbers, so Brook went to full power and headed down the runway. One shell hit the plane midway down the fuselage opposite the cargo door, leaving a big hole on that side of the C-47 and completely taking out the plane's latrine. The explosion shoved the transport 45 degrees to the right. Brook stood hard on the left rudder pedal and was able to straighten out his plane, although with only one wheel on the runway. After a couple of bounces over the hard ground, he eased his plane back on the runway and managed to take off. Meiktila had been a very hot spot.[23]

While the battle for Mandalay had been important, it was the fighting around Meiktila that had doomed the Japanese. The attack there had split the enemy forces, placing them in danger of being defeated in detail. The Burma Area Army commander, General Kimura, rushed many troops to the defense of the town. They came close to pushing back the British and Indian troops several times, but they did not succeed and suffered horrendous losses in the process. Coupled with the severe casualties sustained by the Mandalay defenders, these losses could not be endured. Although Slim and his subordinates did not know it yet, the Burma Area Army was no longer an effective fighting force. Still, even a wounded animal can remain a danger and inflict serious injury if not treated with caution.

The land corridor was finally reopened, and the services of the 317th TCS and 319th TCS were no longer needed at Meiktila. This did not mean the Air Commandos would get a rest. For the remainder of the month the 317th was kept very busy hauling gasoline, rations, ammunition, and troops to both XXXIII Corps and IV Corps at various fields throughout central Burma.

It was not only the Japanese with which the Air Commandos had to contend, but the elements, as well. As the battle raged around Meiktila the men back at Kalaikunda discovered that Mother Nature packed a pretty good punch herself. March 12 began as just another warm, sunny day at the 2nd ACG's home base. Parked around the field were numerous aircraft of the 2nd ACG and other units. Most of the L-5s of the 156th LS had been checked out, and the squadron was awaiting its first real combat missions. Maintenance was being done on other aircraft before sending them to the group's forward fields.

Clouds started building in late afternoon, and the sky darkened. This was nothing new, but things would be different this time. Lightning began to play about the field. Thunder roiled the air. Within a few minutes the light breeze kicked up to tornado velocity. Maintenance crews scrambled to tie down planes and set brakes. Their efforts came to naught. Shortly before 8:00 PM the howling wind brought with it sheets of rain, followed by hailstones the size of billiard balls.

The storm bellowed for 15 minutes, picking up planes like they were toys. Four C-46s belonging to the 1st Air Transport Squadron (Mobile) of the XX Bomber Command became airborne before crashing back to earth.[24] L-5s were mashed together in stacks of four. Gliders became kindling. Tents blew away, and other structures collapsed. Lights failed, and communications were knocked out. Men were flung through the air. At last, the storm passed.

When they could crawl from under the debris that littered the field, the

Air Commandos were appalled at the destruction. The 2nd ACG lost twelve F-6Ds, forty-five L-5s, seven UC-64s, and forty-three gliders to the storm. The 1st Air Transport Squadron (ATS) had five C-46s destroyed and had another eleven C-46s and C-47s damaged. Twelve of the 93rd Fighter Squadron's P-47s were damaged. A hangar was demolished, and many other buildings had various degrees of damage. Some two hundred men had been injured (most from the non-ACG units), and eight men of the 1st ATS had been killed when their quarters collapsed.

The ACG's dispensary performed yeoman service following the storm, receiving and caring for personnel as they were brought in and administering first aid to men all over the field. For all the damage Kalaikunda experienced, though, operations continued, albeit at a reduced pace. This was a testament to the ingenuity and perseverance of the Air Commandos. Unluckily for the 156th LS, which had been just days from being committed to action, the loss of so many aircraft delayed their entrance into combat for several more weeks.[25]

The activities of the liaison squadrons were very important to the ground campaign in Burma. While the fighters and transports may have been more glamorous or generated more press, the operations of the light planes brought more praise from the ground troops. While the 156th was digging out at Kalaikunda, the other squadrons had already been seeing action. Much of the 155th LS's activities in February included courier flights and reconnaissance missions for the 2nd ACG's intelligence section. Air Commando aircraft were also sent to Pauk to work with the 7th Division and the 17th Division as they drove toward Meiktila.

The 127th LS was very busy supporting the British offensive in Arakan. Missions for this squadron ran the gamut from evacuating wounded to dropping supplies and couriering men and matériel and almost anything else an L-5 or UC-64 could do. High-ranking officers were often carried on inspection trips, but one special personage the 127th carried was Lady Mountbatten. The wife of the SEAC commander held the rank of a general officer in the Queen's Ambulance Corps and was on an inspection visit to forward hospitals and casualty clearing stations for which 127th pilots took her from place to place.[26] The 127th kept a detachment at Akyab throughout March and regularly rotated flights between there and Kalaikunda.

The 155th saw action at Meiktila. Perhaps the most valuable service the light planes provided at Meiktila was the evacuation of wounded. During March the 155th evacuated 1,201 patients. In addition, the unit continued to fly other missions, including artillery spotting and, on a couple of occasions, the transport of Japanese prisoners to the rear for interrogation. It was hard, demanding duty that had the pilots flying from dawn to dusk and the mechanics performing maintenance whenever they could in the most primitive of conditions. And it was dangerous duty. Several planes were holed by enemy gunfire, but fortunately without injury or loss.[27]

While the battle raged at Meiktila the 2nd ACG's fighter squadrons entered a new phase of operations. Although Meiktila remained a hot spot for the next couple of weeks, support of the ground forces could be handled by other air units, and the Air Commandos were released from that support. They were then set to undertake the type of mission fighter pilots trained for and sought— counterair operations.

Chapter 12

Filling the Game Bag

J apanese airpower in Southeast Asia was a shell of its former self by early 1945. Many irreplaceable aircraft, not to say pilots, had been lost to the growing number of Allied aircraft and skilled pilots. Then, too, following the invasion of the Philippines in October 1944, the Japanese had begun transferring their aircraft from Southeast Asia to other theaters where they saw more imminent danger. From a Japanese force of 525 combat aircraft in southeast Asia in June 1944, the number had dwindled to only 258 in January 1945.[1] These few aircraft were still capable of inflicting serious pain on unsuspecting targets, however.

On Christmas Day 1944, three Lilys from the 8th Sentai managed to reach Calcutta, where they excited the populace but created little damage. Two of the three attackers were brought down by defending Beaufighters. Much more vulnerable were the USAAF and RAF transports. Japanese fighters downed five C-47s in November, destroyed two USAAF C-47s on the ground at Onbauk on January 12, and shot down two RAF DC-3 Dakotas near Shwebo on January 12. Hit-and-run raids on General Slim's troops were seldom very successful, but an inordinate number of Allied aircraft had to be diverted from ground support missions to combat the threat.[2]

With the Japanese finally being pushed away from Meiktila, IV Corps did not require as much close support, and the 2nd ACG's fighter squadrons could be utilized in counterair operations. On March 6 the fighter squadrons returned to the operational control of the 224 Group. The following day the fighters escorted B-24s to Moulmein and Martaban, southeast of Rangoon. No enemy aircraft attempted to intercept the bombers, and the fighter pilots returned to Cox's Bazar with nothing more than some sore rear ends from the flight.

A visit to air bases at Rangoon on March 8 proved more profitable. Chase led thirty-one Mustangs from both 2nd ACG fighter squadrons against the fields at Mingaladon and Hmawbi that afternoon. Not many enemy aircraft were found, but those that were discovered were caught flatfooted. As he led the 1st Fighter Squadron over Mingaladon, Chase saw an Oscar on the ground and burned it. Another parked Oscar caught his eye, and Chase slammed more shells into it. Although he claimed one aircraft destroyed and a second probably destroyed, a Tenth Air Force review changed that to just one aircraft probably destroyed. Capt. Walter R. Eason also claimed an Oscar destroyed during his pass, but the claims review changed that to damaged.

The enemy was slow to react but did shatter the canopy of one Mustang without causing injury to the pilot and holed another plane. That was the extent of the damage to the Air Commandos.

For its part the 2nd Fighter Squadron found no planes at Hwambi and took out their frustrations on the ground installations there. The Air Commandos could put only one probable and one damaged enemy plane into their "game bag," as they called their record of victories, for this mission, but they were just warming up. Something more exciting was in the offing.[3]

Another escort mission to Rangoon on March 9 should have alerted the Japanese that Allied fighters were out in force offensively and might press farther south, but it appears that they remained unconvinced that the Allies could or wanted to press farther south. They did not realize how far P-51s could fly or just what the Allied air planners had in store. Levi Chase had been studying the problem of bringing the JAAF out into the open and destroying it for some time. It was not enough to nibble at the edges of the enemy's airpower in Burma. The Japanese were holding back their main forces in Thailand and French Indochina (now Vietnam) and were only sending aircraft to forward bases in Burma to conduct quick forays against the Allies. It was necessary to strike at the heart of Japanese airpower to inflict the greatest damage.

Don Muang Airfield, located 12 miles north of Bangkok, had been a major base for the Japanese 5th Air Division since early in the war. It had become even more important as the central staging base for operations into Burma as JAAF units were pulled out of that country. The field was about 780 miles from the nearest Allied airfield, Cox's Bazar, and this meant that it was normally vulnerable only to attacks by long-range bombers. Though such attacks could put Don Muang out of action temporarily, they seldom caught aircraft on the ground because the Allied bombers usually were detected far enough distant that the Japanese planes could be flown to safety.

Thanks to aerial reconnaissance and agents on the ground, Allied intelligence on JAAF activities at Don Muang were generally reliable. Chase believed the Japanese would not expect supposedly short-ranged fighters to appear and would thus be more likely to be caught by surprise if P-51s were sent in attack. He calculated fuel management over and over using data collected from the hours of training the 2nd ACG fighter squadrons had flown in the United States. He figured the maximum weights a Mustang could carry, and he chose the routes out and back with care. The mission would require precision flying and navigation; there was no room for error. Still, Chase knew his pilots could do it.

With the data under his arm, Chase flew to Calcutta to discuss his plans with Stratemeyer. The EAC commander was doubtful about Chase's plans, but the Air Commando was persuasive, and Stratemeyer finally gave his approval.[4]

The moment for the Don Muang attack was not long in coming. On March 12 aerial reconnaissance spotted more than fifty aircraft parked around the Japanese airfield. Among these aircraft were Sallys, Helens, Lilys, and many Oscars. Ground reports confirmed the number of aircraft, and the EAC quickly passed the reports on to the 2nd ACG. This would be the longest fighter mission of the war, corresponding to a flight from England to Vienna and back. While the shuttle missions flown by Eighth Air Force fighters from England to Russia were longer from takeoff to target, some 1,440 miles, they were one-way missions.

The Don Muang mission was set for March 15. Upon receipt of the orders authorizing the mission, Chase told the fighter squadron operations and engineering officers to ready forty aircraft. On the evening of the 14th Chase and Mallen briefed the pilots on the target. There were audible intakes of breath as the pilots saw how far they were going to fly, but when they were told what targets awaited them, smiles of anticipation of good hunting broke out. Maps with courses plotted, and photos of Don Muang were given to the element leaders.

At 8:00 AM the following morning, the final briefing was given. Chase, who would lead the attack, gave the operational details of the mission. The two squadrons would proceed on a course to an initial point (IP) about thirty-five miles north of Bangkok. From there, the 1st Fighter Squadrons would turn south toward Don Muang. The 2nd Fighter Squadron, led by Pryor, was to turn to a heading of 210 degrees and then attack from the west about two minutes after the 1st had. The fliers were told to make only one pass over the field. They would not have enough fuel to stick around, so they were to make their lone pass a good one. Further briefings were given on what the enemy still had at Don Muang, the antiaircraft artillery situation, escape and evasion procedures, and the weather. The pilots went over their call signs and other information, and then it was time to head for their planes.

They were met by their ground crews who had been attending meticulously to their charges throughout the night and early morning. A quick walk-around of their planes, and the airmen climbed into their cockpits and, with the help of their crew chiefs, strapped in. Takeoff had been set for 10:15 AM, and the signal came from the ramshackle structure they called the control tower, "Start engines!" A propeller flicked over on one plane, followed by another and another. There was a slight delay as Chase had a problem with his carburetor air intake filter system fixed. Soon, the Air Commando ramp throbbed to the sound of forty Merlin engines idling. Another signal, and Chase led a parade of fighters weaving to the runway. One final signal, and he roared down the runway, followed closely by the rest of the force. By 10:29, the last Mustang was off the ground, and the Air Commandos had begun a three hour and fifteen minute flight for Don Muang.[5]

The outbound flight at 15,000 feet was generally quiet. There was no need to talk; the pilots had been well-briefed, and they knew what to do. So they watched their engine instruments while keeping their heads on a swivel to catch a glint in the sky that would reveal an enemy plane. But nothing was seen until they reached the target.

Near the IP, the Air Commandos descended to two thousand feet. Chase led his men over the IP right on schedule and turned south toward Don Muang, descending farther to a couple of hundred feet off the ground. About ten miles from the field the 1st Fighter Squadron dropped their tanks. At this point Pryor called to say his men were ready to attack. Although he thought Pryor was early, Chase told him to go ahead. Pryor had identified the wrong airfield and radioed to admit his mistake seconds later. He told Chase that the 2nd Fighter Squadron would attack later.

Moments after this exchange Chase spotted an Oscar flying about one thousand feet above him. As he pulled up for a pass on the fighter, a second Oscar joined the first one Chase had seen. Neither pilot seemed to know the Americans were there. Chase fired a long burst at the right-hand plane, which began to smoke and then rolled over and crashed. Switching to the other plane, Chase poured more shells into it. The Oscar began a left turn in front of the colonel's wingman, 1st Lt. Hadley M. Dixon, who nailed him. By this time the rest of the 1st Fighter Squadron was raking the airfield while flying in line abreast, and Chase saw numerous fires scattered around the enemy base.

Meanwhile, Maj. Bill Buxton and 2nd Lt. William D. Holman shared the kill of a twin-engine bomber identified as a Sally after the plane had evidently just taken off. Actually, a third member of the flight, 1st Lt. Bobby J. Spann, probably got in the first shots at the fleeing bomber. After making his run on the airfield, Spann saw the Sally desperately attempting to escape. When he could not gain on the enemy plane, Spann suddenly realized he had pulled back on his throttle while making his strafing run. Advancing his throttle, he began to gain on his quarry. He fired a few ranging shots as he closed in, and when he got within three hundred yards, he began firing in earnest. Twinkles of light spreading over the bomber's fuselage showed his shells were hitting. Another Mustang (Buxton) suddenly crossed in front of him, and Spann had to stop firing for fear of hitting it. Irritation over a poacher stealing his kill faded as the other fighter swung away after a few seconds. Spann resumed firing only to stop again when another P-51 (Holman) cut him off. When that plane was clear, Spann was only about one hundred yards behind the Sally. The bomber exploded and tumbled out of the sky Spann passed over it.

Spann decided later not to claim a one-third share of the enemy plane, so half credits for its demise were given Buxton and Holman. Despite losing this victory Spann had a big day at Don Muang. The evening before the mission, as he studied the reconnaissance photos, Spann noticed a line of attack that led over several bombers. As luck would have it, when he made his run on the field it was almost exactly on the same line he noted in the photos. He made the best of the opportunity and was credited with destroying two twin-engine aircraft on the ground and damaging five more.[6]

Don Muang was thrown into utter chaos as the Mustangs crisscrossed the field. Enemy personnel running to man guns or just ducking for cover were scythed down by the six .50-cal. machine guns on each P-51. Aircraft supposedly safe in hangars were not immune to the destruction. A number of Japanese planes were destroyed or damaged as the Air Commandos dropped down to just feet off the deck to fire through open doors straight into the hangars. Most of the ground fire was inaccurate as the antiaircraft gunners could not follow the attackers as they zipped by at close to eye level. But they did score a fatal hit on Capt. Warren Modine's fighter. Chase reported seeing Modine's P-51 pass him in a "strange attitude," its cockpit full of flames. Others saw Modine crash near the airfield. He would be the Air Commando's only loss over Don Muang.

Although he had directed his men to make only one pass on the field, the lack of significant opposition on the ground or in the air heartened Chase to order one more pass. Those who did not hear him headed for home, but those who did returned to beat up the field once more. Soon, burning aircraft, buildings, and fuel trucks and dumps were sending towering columns of smoke into the air to dirty the sky. It would be some time before Don Muang was fully operational again.

Chase landed at Cox's Bazar at 4:40 PM, followed by the remaining thirty-eight fighters. The average duration of the mission was six hours and forty-five minutes, and the fliers were worn out by the time they returned. But they were jubilant over the amount of damage they had caused. Their attack was one of the most successful such raid in any theater during the war. They left behind one Sally and two Oscars shot out of the sky, thirteen twin-engine and four single-engine aircraft destroyed on the ground, another four twin-engine planes probably destroyed on the ground, and twelve twin-engine and six single-engine aircraft damaged.[7]

Following his return Pryor had put in a claim for a twin-engine plane destroyed on the ground. Examination of his gun camera film showed that the aircraft was single-engine. His men would not let Pryor forget his error, promptly dubbing him "Weak Eyes Yokum," after a character in the comic strip *Li'l Abner*. Ever game, Pryor issued a memorandum to his squadron the day following the raid directing them (in his words, "I has spoken") to paint each squadron aircraft with the name of a character from the comic strip. Every plane soon sported names such as "Earthquake McGoon," "Available Jones," "Moonbeam McSwine," and the like.[8]

Praise for the Don Muang strike was quick in coming from the senior leaders in SEAC, including Stratemeyer, ACSEA commander (since February 24, 1945) Air Chief Marshal Sir Keith Park, and, particularly, Mountbatten.[9] The SEAC leader wrote, "Please convey my heartiest congratulations to Nos. 1 and 2 U.S. Squadrons of 2nd Air Commandos on their magnificent attack on Don Muang Airfield Bangkok. Apart from highly successful results which were achieved, the round trip from Cox's Bazar to Bangkok involved some 1600 miles representing some 8 or 9 flying hours. This remarkable achievement carried out by single-seater aircraft reflects most favourable on 2nd Air Commandos as a whole and in particular, on high standard of training and determination of pilots concerned."[10]

Don Muang would see the Air Commandos again, but for the time being the 2nd ACG was occupied with other places. On the morning of March 18 the 1st Fighter Squadron sent twelve P-51s to Mingaladon and Zayatkwin while the 2nd Fighter Squadron had sixteen more Mustangs over the Hmawbi and Hlegu fields. Pickings were slim this day, but the pilots took advantage of every opportunity given them. Eason got a clear shot at a pair of Oscars parked in a revetment at Mingaladon and hammered them with several long bursts. Second Lt. James R. Fishburn and 2nd Lt. Dean E. Wimer were able to put in telling blows on two more Oscars. Although three of the enemy fighters were claimed destroyed and the fourth was claimed as probably destroyed, the Tenth Air Force later reduced all the claims to damaged.[11]

The pilots of the 2nd Fighter Squadron, except for Atha, found little of importance at their fields. After making one pass at Hmawbi the squadron headed for Hlegu. As he neared the field, Atha saw a twin-engine plane approaching from the direction of Rangoon. At first he though it might be either a Mosquito or a Beaufighter, but as he closed the distance he could see that it was a Dinah, the JAAF's premier reconnaissance aircraft. He opened fire at four hundred yards and quickly got strikes on the enemy's left engine and wing. The Dinah shuddered as fire broke out. Atha made a sharp chandelle and dove in again to put a burst into the plane's other engine. By this time other pilots were firing at the hapless Dinah, and it exploded and crashed in a ball of fire. This time there was no doubt about the damage, and Atha was credited with the kill.[12]

Airfields in northern Thailand received the attention of the two fighter squadrons on March 20. Near Khun Yuam, Capt. William C. Marshall spotted a small plane he identified as a Stinson. The unarmed plane had no chance. Marshall made a rear quarter attack and sent the little aircraft into the ground burning. The "Stinson" was actually a Fairchild 24 belonging to the Aerial Transport Company of Thailand. It had unknowingly blundered into the path of the attackers.[13]

Pryor found himself caught between a rock and a hard place when he landed back at Cox's Bazar. Just as he was approaching the runway, his engine cut out, the result of a fuel line vapor lock. With a suddenly dead engine and a gusty thirty miles per hour crosswind, Pryor had little chance to recover. He landed short, wiped out his landing gear, and almost caught fire when his left wing tank dragged across the ground, causing a sheet of flame to trail behind. Pryor exited his plane swiftly with just a few bruises, but his Mustang was a washout.[14]

The Air Commandos lost another plane the following day. The fighters were out again on March 21, going after airfields in southern Burma. Thirteen 1st First Squadron Mustangs went to Tavoy, Burma, which is near the coast and in line with Bangkok, but came up empty when no enemy aircraft were found. The 2nd Fighter Squadron had better luck at Moulmein. First Lt. Julian Gilliam saw a twin-engine bomber parked in a hangar and poured one thousand rounds into it, causing it to burst into flames. The hangar was burning fiercely when he joined up for the return flight. Second Lt. Paul C. Kent saw an Oscar parked off the north end of the field's ramp. He proceeded to beat it up with very accurate fire, so accurate in fact that he lost sight of it in the dust and smoke his guns had raised.

On the return flight the men decided to take a quick look at the Zayatkwin airfield. Nothing was found there, but the Japanese defenders got their antiaircraft guns in action quickly and hit Gilliam's plane in its tail section. When Gilliam arrived back over Cox's Bazar and flight-checked the damage, he spun from 10,000 feet to 4,000 feet when he attempted to lower the landing gear and flaps. He tried unsuccessfully to bail out, but he eventually managed to get his fighter under control and made a belly landing. Gilliam walked away from the crash, but his plane would not fly again.[15]

The two squadrons went to the Bassein area west of Rangoon on the next two days and destroyed a couple of radar stations. On March 24 they returned to the Rangoon area with little success and lost a plane anyway when 2nd Lt. R. L. Galloway's engine cut out on takeoff. Galloway was not injured in the ensuing crash, but his aircraft's prop was demolished, both landing gear were sheared off, and the right wing suffered major damage.[16]

To show that they had not yet been rendered ineffective, the Japanese raided Akyab on the night of March 25. The four Sallys from the 58th Sentai, four Lilys from the 8th Sentai, and seven Oscars of the 64th Sentai did not inflict much damage. The British, however, were listening in on the Japanese as they returned and determined that the Oscars had landed at Hmawbi. This information was passed on to Chase.

Fearing that the Japanese fighters would get refueled and be off again for safer territory, Chase decided to catch them early on the 26th. He swiftly planned a sweep of the Hmawbi, Mingaladon, and Moulmein airfields just in case the intelligence people were a bit off on where the Japanese were. The Air Commando pilots were briefed at 3:00 AM, and takeoffs began at 4:30 AM. With the runway lined with dimly burning flare pots, it was a tricky takeoff, but no one had any problems. The 1st Fighter Squadron took off first, followed immediately by the 2nd Fighter Squadron.

At 6:25 AM the Air Commandos were a few miles north of Hmawbi. Suddenly, Chase saw a trio of Oscars taking off from the field and heading right for him. The Japanese pilots evidently saw the Americans at the same time, for they suddenly pulled up sharply and turned to the south. It was too late. The faster American planes were quickly upon the Oscars. Chase took the plane in the middle of the Japanese flight, his wingman, Spann, took the Oscar on the right, and 1st Lt. Harold Hettema Jr. took the fighter on the right. Hettema's wingman, Dixon, was left to watch. All three Air Commandos fired together. The lightweight Oscars could not stand up to this devastating fire, and all three plowed into the ground at the same time, still in a vee formation.[17]

The Japanese on the ground saw what had happened and were aggressively manning their guns when the Mustangs swept over the field. Chase's coolant system, a very vulnerable spot on a Mustang, was hit. A stream of liquid began pouring from his plane. Eason saw this and warned Chase. By that time Chase was also aware of his situation, as he saw his coolant temperature rise and his oil pressure drop. He decided it was time to leave his aircraft, but he also saw that he was only a few hundred feet off the ground. A rice paddy looked good to him, and he bellied in to it.

Chase was about twenty miles west of Hmawbi when he ditched. His men circling overhead saw him climb out of his cockpit and sprint toward the trees. Spann then strafed the wreck, setting it afire. The Japanese would not glean any information from that wreckage.

Chase was not the only Air Commando to go down. Antiaircraft fire at Mingaladon holed Pryor's P-51 in the same vulnerable spot as on Chase's plane. Coolant gushed from his stricken fighter as Pryor climbed away from the enemy airfield. In matter-of-fact tones Pryor radioed his flight, "Willie (1st Lt. William Wilson), you and Charlie (2nd Lt. Charles H. LeFan) go on and finish the mission, and Bonnie (1st Lt. Boniface J. Meyer), you come with me."[18] Pryor finally bailed out about twenty-five miles from where Chase had landed.

The rest of the squadron headed for Moulmein, where LeFan and 2nd Lt. Edwin W. Pearle caught a couple of Sallys on the ground and claimed them as destroyed. A review of their gun camera films later reduced their claims to damaged. During his attacks LeFan took a hit in his plane's prop reduction gear housing, which sent oil spraying not only over his windshield and canopy, but into his cockpit, as well. He had to open his canopy a few inches so he could see anything.[19]

LeFan was escorted back to Akyab by his flight leader, Capt. Al Abraham. As LeFan came in to land at the RAF field, he was told by Abraham to move a little to the left. Only when a row of Spitfires lined up alongside the runway flashed by did LeFan realize how close he had come to a disaster. LeFan's travails were not quite over. As he hopped off the wing of his plane, he stepped on a patch of oil and found himself staring at the sky from a prone position. Luckily, he was more irritated than hurt.[20]

After Chase bellied in, Eason and his wingman, Fishburn, raced for Kyauk-pyu on Ramree Island south of Akyab. Kyaukpyu was the closest Allied base, and perhaps someone or something could be found there to rescue Chase. Not far behind Eason and Fishburn were Spann and Hettema, who were considering a rescue attempt also. Luckily, the 127th LS had a detachment of L-5s based at Kyaukpyu, and Eason and Spann talked their light plane colleagues into loaning them a couple of the puddle jumpers to look for Chase and Pryor. The flight would be well beyond the usual range of the liaison aircraft, so the two men loaded the back seats of the planes with extra five-gallon cans of gasoline.

With Hettema and Fishburn providing escort in their P-51s, Eason and Spann headed east to locate their crashed leaders. Chase's Mustang was found, and Eason put down in a rice paddy about a mile away, unfortunately becoming stuck in the process. In the meantime, Chase, who had gone to a nearby village, had seen the Mustangs flying overhead and then had seen Eason approaching to land. He immediately took leave of the villagers, who had apparently been deciding whether or not to turn Chase over to the local police, and began running toward Eason.

Immediately after landing, Eason had begun refueling his plane from the five-gallon cans. He was just finishing when Chase came up. Overhead, Spann saw that Eason's plane appeared to be stuck, so he landed, fortunately on firmer ground, to lend a hand. The three men could not free the mired L-5, however, and a number of Burmese had gathered to watch the proceedings. Eason offered them some silver rupees from the escape kit the pilots always carried on their flights, and the villagers soon had the plane out of the mud.

With the L-5 free Eason and Chase hopped in to attempt a takeoff. The takeoff was across several rutted rice paddies separated by earthen dikes. It was a teeth-rattling takeoff, and the plane's tail skid was pushed up into the fuselage after encountering one of the dikes, but the L-5 finally staggered into the air. With Hettema and Fishburn weaving overhead, Eason headed back to Kyaukpyu. He landed with just half a gallon of fuel remaining. It was a successful ending to a remarkable rescue attempt.

While Eason headed back west Spann refueled his plane and took off to search for Pryor. The 2nd Fighter Squadron leader had gone down several miles farther east, and Spann hoped his search would be as successful as the first. But it was not to be.

The area where Pryor had gone down was photographed, and two L-1s from the Tenth Air Force moved to Cox's Bazar to participate in any rescue attempt. In addition, a YR-4 helicopter was crated and transported from Asansol to Cox's Bazar on March 29. There it was assembled and placed in readiness in case Pryor was located. Finally, the Air Commandos modified a pair of L-5s with long-range fuel tanks. This gave the little planes a range of five hundred miles. Both were flown to Akyab and assigned to the 127th LS for use in the search and rescue role.[21]

Sadly, all this effort came to naught. Pryor had landed safely, but he was captured by the Japanese before Spann could find him. His captors tied him to a tree and apparently had thoughts of executing him on the spot. A firing squad was lined up before him, but someone decided to let him live. Instead, Pryor would be held prisoner in Rangoon until the city fell in May. In Pryor's absence Grosvenor took command of the 2nd Fighter Squadron. For their remarkable actions in these rescue attempts, Eason and Spann received Silver Stars.[22]

Meanwhile, the rest of the two squadrons also headed for Akyab. Not aware of Eason's and Spann's efforts, they, too, hoped to rescue their leaders. Instead of a rescue attempt, though, more tragedy awaited them. The Dabaing No. 1 strip on Akyab was a very dusty field, and as the planes landed, they raised roiling clouds of dust which obscured vision. Capt. Sherard A. Sorenson landed safely, but his engine quit before he could clear the runway. Another pilot landed close behind and could not see Sorenson's plane still on the runway. He smashed into the first plane, killing Sorenson instantly. The second pilot escaped with minor burns to his face, but both planes caught fire and were destroyed.[23]

Not one to let such things as belly landing behind enemy lines and being picked up by a small L-5 bother him, Chase was flying the next day. He led the fighters on an escort mission for B-24s bombing enemy installations near Bangkok. That was a milk run, as enemy fighters did not put in an appearance. But on the way home Fishburn, flying wing on Hawkins, spotted a twin-engine plane parked in front of a revetment on the Pegu strip. Both men took turns strafing the plane, which they identified as a Lily. Hawkins was later given credit for the probable destruction of the aircraft.[24]

The mission ended badly, however. As the Mustangs neared Ramree, 2nd Lt. Robert H. Morris dropped out of formation. Flames could be seen behind his head. His flight leader called him several times to tell him to bail out, and he was seen to open his canopy, but then he rolled to the left and dove straight into the ground.[25]

March had been a spectacular month for the 2nd ACG's fighter squadrons. Seven Japanese aircraft were claimed destroyed in the air and another eighteen were claimed destroyed on the ground. Thirty-four were claimed as probables or as damaged. These victories added up to 82 percent of all claims by Allied units during the month.[26]

It had been evident to the Allies for some time, however, that the Japanese were pulling their air units out of Burma. With the deteriorating situation in the Philippines and the home islands under attack by B-29s, Burma had lost what little strategic value it had left. Many of the JAAF units were pulled back to Sumatra, French Indochina, and Thailand. A few aircraft remained in Burma to make hit-and-run raids on the advancing Allied forces, but for all intents and purposes, the Burmese airfields were useful to the Japanese only as forward staging bases.

The Air Commandos, though, were not yet finished with the enemy in Burma. April 1 was both Easter Sunday and April Fools' Day, and the Air Commandos celebrated the day by dropping their own Easter eggs on the enemy bases at Mingaladon and Hmawbi. The Americans were not seeking aircraft this time, but enemy installations. Of the forty Mustangs making the attack, twenty-four carried 500-pound bombs and sixteen carried 110-gallon tanks of napalm. As was usual with the fighter pilots, their drops were made with precision, and the enemy lost more badly needed machinery shops, barracks, and other facilities.[27]

The danger from Japanese aircraft in Thailand remained a concern of the Allied air leaders, however, and they directed the Air Commandos to put more emphasis on attacks there. Nakhon Sawan, a base in central Thailand, was hit on April 2. Twelve 1st Fighter Squadron Mustangs strafed hangars and other buildings, setting most on fire. Second Lt. Herman G. "Doc" Lyons caught the only aircraft found and destroyed it in three strafing runs. Later identified as a Betty (actually a Japanese Navy plane) or a Helen, it was most likely a Sally. While Nakhon Sawan was being beaten up, six other 1st Fighter Squadron planes joined six 2nd Fighter Squadron P-51s in pounding the fields at Koke Kathiem and Takhli. No aircraft were found, but many buildings went up in flames to the strafings.[28]

Don Muang continued to exert its pull on the Air Commandos, and when information was received that the enemy was again moving aircraft there, the Americans were eager to make a return visit. Careful planning was done again, but this time Chase decided to make one full-blooded attack instead of splitting his force into two. April 9 saw Chase lead thirty-two Mustangs from both ACG fighter squadrons against the enemy base. Another eight fighters of the 2nd would attack Nakhon Pathom, which lay about twenty miles west of Don Muang, at the same time.

The fighters hit the IP right on time, whereupon the Nakhon Pathom attackers turned for their target. The other pilots spread out in line abreast and poured the coal to their planes. In this formation the Air Commandos swept over Don Muang. Although there were not quite as many enemy aircraft on the field as had been present during the previous raid, there were enough to provide good hunting.

Chase bagged a single-engine fighter on his pass, while his wingman, 1st Lt. Malcolm MacKenzie, set a couple of JAAF fighters and a bomber ablaze. The Japanese reacted more quickly than they had earlier, and as MacKenzie began a pass on another aircraft, he was buffeted by a loud explosion. He immediately headed west and looked for some altitude as he opened his canopy to clear the smoke pouring into his cockpit.

MacKenzie made it across the Chao Phraya River, several miles west from Don Muang, but his plane was not going much farther, so he bellied into a rice paddy. First Lt. Benjamin F. Lundberg, who had also fired a couple of bombers, watched as MacKenzie leaped from his plane carrying his escape kit and an M1 carbine, which was not the usual personal weapon of a fighter pilot. As MacKenzie headed into the jungle, Lundberg made sure the Japanese could not gain any useful information from the P-51 by strafing it.

MacKenzie headed west and soon came upon a creek. Having stashed several packs of cigarettes in the lower pockets of his flight suit, he did not want to wade across. Instead, he turned north and quickly met some natives. Attempts to communicate with them were fruitless, so he decided to cross the creek anyway. Not many minutes later, he heard a large group shouting barely one hundred yards behind him. MacKenzie dropped to the ground and rolled behind a rice paddy embankment. The Thais—they were not Japanese—began firing. The shooting was not too close, but it did get MacKenzie's attention. He decided to return fire with his carbine, apparently killing one and wounding two others in the group. His firing did not last long, as a bullet hit his carbine and knocked it out of his hands.

He jumped up and ran for the middle of the rice paddy. This did not offer much cover, and when the Thais approached, they began throwing clumps of dirt at him. Using hand motions, they ordered him to throw away his pistol, which he did. Still unable to communicate with anyone, even by using the translation book from his escape kit, MacKenzie was unsure of what was going to happen next. Fortunately, the Thais were not interested in killing him and took him to the local police station. There, he was transferred to a small boat with an inboard engine. His captors motioned MacKenzie to lie down, then covered him with a rug. MacKenzie suddenly realized that they were hiding him from the Japanese.

The boat took him to Bangkok, where he was furtively taken to another police station. Inside, a policeman who spoke English talked to him briefly and told MacKenzie that a couple of other pilots had been shot down. He informed MacKenzie that he was being taken to an internment camp where he would probably be interrogated by the Japanese. Despite the circumstances, it appeared to MacKenzie that his problems could have been a lot worse.[29]

Meanwhile, the Air Commandos found the Japanese at Don Muang thoroughly riled. Antiaircraft fire had been quick in coming, and it was intense. Captain Marshall took several hits in his engine area. This did not stop him from destroying a couple of fighters. Fortunately, the hits were not fatal, and Marshall got home.

Not as lucky were Abraham and Wimer. Both had their coolant systems taken out by the ground fire, and they had to leave their planes. Both were injured when they bailed out. Abraham sprained his ankle when he landed heavily, and he hobbled about for the next few days. Wimer hit the tail of his plane when he bailed out, breaking several ribs. Like MacKenzie, they, too, were swiftly rounded up by the Thai police. The two men were taken to Bangkok, where their injuries were treated. At one point the Thai doctor treating Wimer told him that he would try to get him out of Thailand, but when word was received that the Japanese were looking for the Americans, Abraham and Wimer were turned over to the Japanese.

They were taken to the same internment camp to which MacKenzie had been sent. In the abandoned college a few miles outside of Bangkok, POWs and civilian internees were separated by just a strand of barbed wire. It was not long before the three Air Commandos were reunited. The Thais told the trio that they would be interrogated by the Japanese within a few days, so the Americans got together to concoct stories that would seem plausible and would also be similar. The interrogations did not take long, and the Japanese were relatively reserved in their handling of the prisoners. MacKenzie was threatened with beheading at one point, and Abraham was slapped with a rolled-up newspaper, but that was the extent of any physical abuse.

Returned to the camp Abraham, MacKenzie, and Wimer sat out the rest of the war in some comfort, if one can be comfortable in a POW camp. Through the Swiss Consulate, they were able to obtain Thai money. This enabled them to buy some shirts and shorts and tobacco and cigarette paper. Boredom was the big problem for the captives, but they did learn to play cricket and, at times, were able to listen to BBC broadcasts over a hidden radio.[30]

Despite the loss of three men and aircraft, the second raid on Don Muang was nearly as successful as the first. The attackers destroyed nine bombers and seventeen fighters and damaged another bomber. The eight fighters sent to Nakhon Pathom had good success, also. When no aerial or ground opposition was encountered, the Air Commandos took their time in plastering the field and left behind four enemy fighters reduced to scrap.[31]

Although more costly, the second Don Muang raid had been another well-planned and well-executed attack. Three days later Stratemeyer visited Cox's Bazar to honor the men of the 1st and 2nd fighter squadrons. A bit under the weather from a bad cold, Stratemeyer still took obvious delight in presenting Chase with the Oak Leaf Cluster to the Silver Star. He then told the assembled men that they were now "nationally known" in the United States and that they had compiled an outstanding record.[32]

Chase called a general assembly in the base theater that evening. He talked about receiving the award but stressed that he did not regard it as a personal decoration. Rather, he viewed it as the high command's appreciation of the excellent work done by all members of the group.[33]

Much of the 2nd ACG fighter squadrons' work for the remainder of the month was in support of IV Corps as it pushed toward Rangoon. It was on one of these cover missions on April 22 that the 1st Fighter Squadron came close to losing another pilot. Second Lt. John R. Hanna's engine began running rough, and when he turned to return to base, it cut out on him completely. Hanna bailed out and was picked up by some natives. Although not entirely trusting them, he was able to talk them into taking him toward the front lines. They ran into a Gurkha patrol as night fell, and Hanna was turned over to them. The next morning he was taken to a nearby village that had an L-5 strip for the evacuation of wounded. An L-5 flight to Myitcha followed and after a short wait there, Buxton picked up Hanna in a B-25.

The last counterair mission of the month was flown April 29 against Japanese airfields in central Thailand. Chase sent sixteen P-51s from both squadrons against Koke Kathiem, and he dispatched another eight Mustangs to Nakhon Sawan. Nothing was found at the latter field, but three enemy fighters were caught and destroyed on the ground at Koke Kathiem. These aircraft had probably been part of a group that had attacked a British convoy near Toungoo earlier in the day.

The 2nd ACG's very last counterair mission took place on May 2, when twelve 1st Fighter Squadron aircraft made a sweep of the Moulmein airfield. Little of interest was found except for one aircraft parked in the open. It was most likely a wreck that had been set out to serve as a decoy, for although it was heavily strafed, it did not burn.[34]

The work of the 2nd ACG's fighter squadrons throughout their combat operations had been outstanding. The first Don Muang raid, in particular, had drawn much praise. On April 30 the two fighter squadrons and the 327th ADS were recognized for their efforts in planning, preparing, and executing that raid when Stratemeyer awarded them a unit citation. This award was rescinded and replaced on June 23 with a new unit citation covering operations between February 12 and May 10.[35]

But the fighter squadrons had not been the only pistons in the engine driving the 2nd ACG. The men of the liaison squadrons and the TCS had been extremely active, as well.

Chapter 13

Mandalay Was in the Other Direction

W hen Rudyard Kipling wrote his poem "Mandalay" in 1892, the flotilla's paddles were "a-chunking from Rangoon to Mandalay," and the route to that fabled city was generally by water. The Irrawaddy River was the preferred route north.[1] Fifty-three years later, in 1945, Mandalay had been just a way station along the road to the Allies' primary target in Burma, Rangoon. And waterways were just one method of travel. Mechanized warfare had made movement through the jungle, if still arduous, at least less difficult. Perhaps the most important component of modern war, particularly in the jungles of Burma, however, was air. American and British aircraft supplied Slim's advancing troops even where roads were poor or nonexistent and approach by water was impossible. The Japanese were never able to do the same. As a result, the enemy could launch pinprick raids that could hurt, but never stop, the British and Indian troops. On the other hand, the Allies had both a qualitative and quantitative edge over their adversaries. Eventually, the USAAF and RAF obtained air superiority over the enemy and with that, the Japanese lost any chance to regain the initiative. The men of the 2nd ACG played important roles in securing that air superiority and helping ensure that the Fourteenth Army would take Rangoon.

For Mountbatten, however, Rangoon was not an end in itself. Nor did the British chiefs of staff view it that way. Several other operations were planned to follow Rangoon's capture. Operation Roger, the capture of the Thai island of Phuket off the Kra Isthmus, would be next. Unsurprisingly, the island's name gave rise to a number of waggish interpretations by the planners. Next would be Zipper, a four- or five-division landing on Malaysia's west coast near Port Swettenham/Port Dickson. This was to take place in October 1945. Finally, as soon as possible after Zipper, Operation Mailfist, the capture of Singapore, was to occur. This was a pretty tight timetable.

Dracula was the operation to capture Rangoon. In it, an amphibious force would land at the mouth of the Rangoon River while an infantry division would drive south overland to the city and a parachute battalion would drop on Elephant Point to take out the enemy defenses overlooking the river. Weather was a significant factor in planning the operation. The Allies had to be in Rangoon before the monsoon set in. Otherwise, offensive operations would come to a sodden halt as roads and tracks turned into impassable mud holes or lakes.

Air transport was a big concern, too. The Fourteenth Army was very dependent on air supply to continue its forward movement. The airlift of Chinese troops back to China and Chiang Kai-Shek's demand on February 23 that U.S. troops and his remaining troops in northern Burma leave for China to undertake an offensive there against the Japanese were worrisome problems for Mountbatten and Slim. On top of these demands Chiang wanted the Fourteenth Army to halt its advance well north of Mandalay.

Mountbatten received assurances from General Marshall that the United States was not about to remove the invaluable transports from Burma just then. These assurances came with a caveat, however, that the aircraft would stay until June 1 or Rangoon's capture, whichever came first. After that time the United States planned on removing most of its forces from Burma and sending them to China, which had always been the more important country to the Americans. So Mountbatten and Slim had a great impetus placed upon them to take Rangoon as quickly as possible.

The success of Dracula depended greatly on the capture of Toungoo, which lay almost 190 miles north of Rangoon, because of its pair of all-weather airfields. Mountbatten stressed to Slim that Toungoo had to be taken by April 25 so that the airfields could be used for the close air support of the attack on Rangoon, which had now been set for May 2. While Slim had great confidence that his men would capture Rangoon in due course, the fierce fighting at Meiktila showed that the cities en route would not be walkovers.

The transports were not the only aircraft proving their worth in Burma. The liaison squadrons, not only from both Air Commando groups but others assigned to Tenth Air Force, received little publicity but were very popular with the ground forces. The L-1s and L-5s were requested constantly for the pickup and transport of wounded, for flying senior officers to their units, and for the seemingly more mundane, though important to the troops, tasks of delivering mail and fresh fruits, vegetables, and bread.

At the start of April the 2nd ACG's three liaison squadrons were widely separated. Most of the 127th LS was down at Akyab supporting XV Corps in its

Arakan operations. During the month the squadron flew more than 1,600 missions, including a rescue mission of a 2nd ACG fighter pilot near Rangoon. The 155th LS was based at Myitche, southwest of Pakokku on the Irrawaddy. From there, they supported units of the Fourteenth Army. Their missions included the usual evacuation (the little L-5s flew out some 1,110 wounded in April), courier, air supply, passenger, and reconnaissance flights, and even some artillery spotting. The 156th LS, which had been hit hard by the tornado at Kalaikunda, finally moved most of its planes to Myitche on April 8. Not wishing to be outdone by the pilots of the other squadrons who had seen most of the action so far, the 156th's pilots flew 4,232 sorties in 2,815 hours of flying in April while supporting XXXIII Corps. The 2nd ACG's historian described the liaison squadrons as like "ants building mountains" for their efforts.[2]

The work of the 317th TCS had been as important as that of the liaison squadrons. Following Meiktila's capture, the 317th remained at Palel until April 12. During this period the TCS continued to supply Fourteenth Army units at numerous forward airfields. On April 9 the squadron was alerted for a move to Meiktila. From there, the 317th and its partner in the 1st ACG, the 319th TCS, would supply the ground forces attacking southward. The following day the TCSs began ferrying gasoline to Meiktila for a fuel dump. They would also bring gliders forward to the newly captured field.

As some C-47s continued to fly in gasoline, others ferried gliders from Lalaghat to Palel. Ten of the gliders were then towed to Meiktila on April 12, followed by another eight the next day. In the meantime the rest of the 317th flew back to Kalaikunda for training in formation flying and dropping paratroopers. Joined by the 319th and a detachment of CCG C-47s, the 317th practiced from April 14 to April 26 on night formation missions, dropping supply parapacks, and doing parachute drops with men of the 2nd Gurkha Parachute Battalion. Because the Gurkhas were trained in the British method of jumping, which differed greatly from the American style, the U.S. crews had to pick up this new method quickly. In addition, the planes had to be fitted with parapacks to hold supply bundles and with British static lines.[3]

While this training was going on eight of the gliders at Meiktila were loaded with engineering equipment in preparation for movement forward in an operation code-named Gumption I. This commenced on April 21. The 317th's C-47 and glider pilots were briefed on a mission to Lewe, about eighty-five miles south of Meiktila, at 8:00 AM, and the first glider was airborne an hour later. Lewe had been taken on April 20, and British engineers, always located at the head of the advancing columns so they could begin rebuilding bridges and airfields as quickly as possible, set about refurbishing the airfield there using a couple of bulldozers they brought with them. They soon had a glider strip leveled and ready for use, as well as a shorter, narrower L-5 strip laid out on one of the taxiways.

The Air Commandos had been briefed that the airstrip they were to land on would be outlined. When they arrived over Lewe they found that both strips had been outlined. Not seeing smoke pots and green flares that normally marked a glider strip, the lead glider pilot picked the wrong field. Four other gliders followed him in. The chosen strip had a number of camouflaged ditches, and one of the gliders was lost when it struck one of them. Fortunately, no one was injured. The last three pilots landed on the correct strip, where their supplies were swiftly unloaded and put to work by the engineers.

With no job now, the glider pilots began digging foxholes at the edge of the airstrip. Their digging was hastened by the fire of Japanese snipers still in the area. Enemy artillery and machine-gun fire during the night also served to keep the men tense. Rain, which began in the late afternoon and kept falling through the night, turned the foxholes into muddy bathtubs, and the pilots were glad to return to "shore" when dawn broke. Several of the pilots went back to their gliders to see how personal equipment that had been left inside had fared.

While inventorying this equipment, the Air Commandos noticed eight fighter planes cavorting about the sky. The glidermen did not pay much attention to the planes aloft because enemy aircraft were no longer considered a threat. Shortly, the men saw the planes making what they thought was going to be a buzz job of the field. Work on prepping the gliders stopped as crews gazed curiously at the planes. This curiosity suddenly turned to panic when the lead fighter's engine "appeared to be on fire."[4] Sprays of dirt and grass flew into the air as shells from the enemy fighters dug into the ground. The Americans hit the ground as Japanese bullets tore into the gliders, just missing the men. As quickly as it began, the attack ended. The Japanese headed for home, and the Air Commandos dusted themselves off. One of the gliders that was carrying gas and had not yet been unloaded was hit and exploded. The resulting fire spread and destroyed several other gliders. It had been a close thing, but fortunately, no one had been killed or injured.[5]

While the 317th TCS had been readying itself for a drop on Rangoon, the 1st Fighter Squadron and the 2nd Fighter Squadron had not been resting. The Fourteenth Army needed photos of the invasion area, and the fighters of the 2nd ACG were given the tasks of covering the photo planes as they made their low-level runs and of taking out gun positions that might cause trouble for landing craft. On April 20 sixteen planes from the 1st Fighter Squadron and twenty-two from the 2nd Fighter Squadron hit antiaircraft and artillery positions with bombs and rockets and enabled the photo planes to complete their mission without loss. This was not the case for the Air Commandos, however.

Enemy flak hit Lyons' P-51. He got as far as Bassein, ninety miles west, before he had to bail out. Japanese troops captured him shortly afterwards. Tragically, unlike the other Air Commandos who had been captured, Lyons would not return home. Unwilling to take their prisoner with them when they retreated, the Japanese soldiers beheaded Lyons.[6]

Earlier, for three days beginning April 12, the 2nd ACG fighter squadrons had plastered the Kyauktainggan area east of Pegu with bombs and napalm. The area was covered thoroughly, but not one Japanese was seen. Nevertheless, reconnaissance units claimed that the Air Commandos had killed nearly two thousand Japanese in these attacks.[7]

Pegu itself, which lay about fifty-five miles northeast of Rangoon, was the site of several supply dumps and a major railroad junction. The American fighters spent several days pounding these installations and the roads surrounding the area. On the afternoon of April 23 Captain Marshall was leading a flight searching for vehicles. Several trucks were spotted, and the Air Commandos dove after them. Lt. McGinnis Clark went after a truck speeding down the road. As he roared along at fifty feet or less, Clark began walking his shells up toward the truck, which suddenly veered off into a field. Intent on bagging his quarry, Clark did not see a telegraph pole until it was too late. His Mustang slammed into the pole and broke it in two. The impact almost flipped his P-51 over, but Clark was able to regain control. When he looked to his left Clark saw bits of wire, some wooden cross arms, and other remnants of the pole hanging from a huge gash in this wing just outboard of the machine guns. These fragments soon fell away.

His plane seemed to be flying reasonably well considering what had just happened, but Clark knew this might not continue for long. He had to get it down soon. Lewe had just been captured days earlier, so Clark and his element leader, Lt. Edward Harkins, headed there. Clark was running low on fuel when he and Harkins arrived, and Clark could make but one approach. C-47s were taking off in the opposite direction as Clark lined up to land. Harkins led the way, waggling his wings to warn a pair of transports preparing to take off. One of the transport pilots got the message and pulled off the runway. The other pilot did not and barreled down the runway, fortunately to one side of the strip. Clark landed on the other side as the C-47 swept by, each plane passing less than 50 feet from the other.

The Air Commandos flew in materials and mechanics to attempt repairs on Clark's plane. Their efforts were successful, and Clark flew his fighter out the following day, carrying only enough fuel to get him back to Cox's Bazar and with his landing gear down in case some damage had gone undetected. The flight home was uneventful, and Clark was able to relate to a rapt audience how he had tangled with a telegraph pole.[8]

A similar attack with similar results on April 28 was not quite as lucky for Captain Marshall. He spotted a big staff car motoring along a road and came down to strafe it. Although he succeeded in destroying the car, in his excitement, he failed to see a grove of trees ahead and flew right through them, which did his Mustang no good. Marshall was able to coax a few miles and a few hundred feet out of his plane before he had to bail out.

Marshall's wingman, Clark (back in the air again after his meeting with the telegraph pole), noted where Marshall landed and then sped back to Cox's Bazar to report. There, it was decided that Clark would fly to Akyab, where he and a 127th LS pilot would team up to attempt to rescue Marshall. Clark and MSgt. Stanley G. Morris loaded two L-5s with five-gallon cans of gasoline and took off for the rescue attempt. When the pair arrived over the spot where Marshall had gone down, some 170 miles from Akyab, he could not be found. Actually, Marshall had found a village where the residents had taken him in.

After some time in fruitless searching, Morris signaled Clark that he would have to land and refuel if he was going to get back to Akyab. The two men landed and refueled. They took off once more only after having to spend some time in dislodging Morris' tail wheel, which had become stuck in mud. By the time they returned to Akyab, it was dark. Clark, a P-51 pilot not an L-5 pilot, could not find the landing light switch, so he and Morris landed simultaneously using Morris' lights. Disappointed that he had been unable to find Marshall, Clark talked his superiors into allowing him to resume the search the next day.

Marshall's benefactors were taking him to another village on April 30 when Marshall saw a couple of Mustangs passing overhead. Whipping out his signal mirror, he caught the fighter pilots' attention, and they dropped down to take a look. The Mustangs were from the 2nd Fighter Squadron, and the pilots recognized Marshall. They radioed Akyab, and Clark and Morris were on their way, led by one of the Mustangs.

Within a few hours, Morris saw the captain on the road and landed while Clark circled overhead. Marshall introduced Morris to the natives, and Marshall gave them the contents of his jungle pack while Morris chipped in a couple of empty gas cans. The natives waved goodbye as Morris took off for Akyab, where they stopped only to be refueled on their way to Cox's Bazar. Marshall received a tremendous welcome, and the little liaison planes had once again proved their value.[9]

While Marshall's luck held, that of another Air Commando ran out. A group of enemy motor torpedo boats had been patrolling the waters of the Gulf of Martaban south of Rangoon. These had to be neutralized for the protection of the invasion fleet, but they had proved elusive. On April 29 two flights of 2nd Fighter Squadron Mustangs came upon the Japanese boats at anchor near Amherst, about twenty miles south of Moulmein. The pilots immediately went after these choice targets with rockets and gunfire. Two of the boats began to sink, and six others were heavily damaged. Return fire was not heavy, but it was very accurate. Lt. Roy H. Long Jr. was just above the water when his plane was hit. Unable to recover, he plowed into the water. Long's plane disintegrated, and he was killed immediately. His death was the group's last combat loss.[10]

In the meantime Slim's forces drove toward Rangoon. Toungoo, with its all-important airfields, fell on April 22. It was in the nick of time, for the monsoons arrived ahead of schedule. The final assault on Rangoon began under scudding clouds and increasing showers, and the Japanese defenses swiftly crumbled. Some stout resistance was met, notably around Pegu, but for all intents and purposes, the Japanese were spent. This became evident on April 30 when reconnaissance aircraft flying over Rangoon reported seeing words painted on the roof of the city jail. One message read, "Japs Gone." The other boldly stated, "Extract Digit." While the first one might have been Japanese trickery, the second was RAF slang for "get your tails moving." By this time, however, Operation Dracula could not be called off, and the three-pronged assault on Rangoon went ahead as planned.[11]

The last day of April also saw the 2nd ACG receive great news when a telephone call revealed that Pryor was a prisoner in Rangoon. Plans were initiated to fly there as soon as possible to retrieve him and bring him home. First, though, Rangoon had to be taken.

Leading the way to Rangoon were the Air Commandos. Mustangs from both of the group's fighter squadrons, along with planes from another squadron, provided air cover for the invaders. Also participating were the TCSs, which had moved to Akyab on April 29 to make final preparations for the drop of the men of the 50th Indian Parachute Brigade. The drop zone was located five miles southwest of Elephant Point, which extended into the Gulf of Martaban. There, several guns overlooking the sea approaches to Rangoon had to be neutralized.

At 2:30 AM on May 1 a 317th TCS C-47 containing a twenty-man pathfinder team took off for Rangoon, followed by a CCG plane carrying a pair of VCP teams. Half an hour later the main force of thirty-nine planes followed. The weather was poor, with an overcast continually lowering until it was at just 1,500 feet over the drop zone. The transports slogged through intermittent rain to reach the drop zone on schedule at 6:35 AM. The inclement weather forced most of the fighters that were to escort the transports to abort, but six P-51s from the group were able to break through to complete the mission. Little opposition was noted over the drop zone, and the seven hundred Ghurka paratroopers and their supplies were dropped right on target. A second mission in the afternoon brought more supplies to the paratroopers.[12]

Because most of the defenders had fled south or moved into the hills northeast of the city, fighting was not heavy, and Slim's troops occupied Rangoon on May 3. That same day, DeBolt and Ball, the deputy group commander, flew a borrowed B-25 to the city to pick up Pryor. Before this, however, Pryor and many other prisoners had been marched north toward Pegu by their captors, who had panicked and set all the prisoners free before fleeing. Nevertheless, DeBolt and Hall finally found Pryor after commandeering a jeep. The 2nd Fighter Squadron commander had lost considerable weight while being imprisoned, but he had not lost his spirit. A joyous reception awaited him when he returned to Cox's Bazar before he headed to the rear for medical attention.[13]

It took a bit longer for the other three Air Commando prisoners—MacKenzie, Abraham, and Wimer—to reach home. Imprisoned in Bangkok, it was not until August 25 that they were released by the Thais. The three were taken on that day to Don Muang, where they boarded a Japanese bomber flown by a Thai pilot. They were flown to a field in northern Thailand, where medical personnel were waiting to check them over before sending them back to Calcutta for hospitalization. They spent a couple of weeks in the hospital, and then it was back to the United States. Imprisonment had not been too harsh for these men. While boredom had been their main problem, they did lose weight, and both Wimer and MacKenzie contracted malaria, which afflicted them for several years afterward.[14]

Following the Rangoon missions the 2nd ACG's C-47s returned to Kalaikunda and then moved on to Comilla. The TCS crews spent the next two weeks supplying XV Corps troops fighting in the hills northeast of Rangoon. This mission proved difficult because the monsoon had settled in, and the rains and turbulence had made flying extremely hazardous and flooded many of the forward airfields. Nonetheless, the 317th TCS was able to complete most of its missions in support of XV Corps. The squadron finished this job on May 19 and returned to Kalaikunda the following day. Its stay there was relatively brief, as orders were received to move to Ledo on June 1.[15]

Meanwhile, in spite of the terrible weather that had descended on the area, the 2nd ACG's fighter squadrons continued to provide air cover over Rangoon. With no enemy air opposition, the task was completed on May 9, so they, too, returned to Kalaikunda. At this time the 1st Provisional Fighter Group was dissolved, and its component units returned to the control of their groups.

By May 21 all of the 2nd ACG's squadrons except the 156th LS, which remained in Burma until June 3, were back at their home field. Earlier, however, the 2nd ACG bid farewell to two men who had been with the group from almost the beginning. On May 15, as men of the group gathered to wish them well, DeBolt and Chase boarded a B-25 that would take them on the first leg of their trip back to the United States. Colonel Ball replaced DeBolt as commanding officer, and Major Hawkins took over as group operations officer. More Air Commando veterans soon followed as a few replacements trickled in.[16]

For most of the men of the 2nd ACG, the war was essentially over. Training occupied much of their time after their reunion at Kalaikunda, but passes to see the sights of India became easier to get. The 317th TCS, however, labored on. Transports, ever the rare commodity in the CBI, were still needed. Operating from Ledo, the Air Commando transports flew supplies and men throughout northern Burma and into China. It was hard, demanding work, flying over some of the worst terrain imaginable and in weather that could obliterate any signs of the ground in an instant. Losses were inevitable. Two C-47s crashed during landings, fortunately without injury to their crews. Second Lt. Herbert H. Gumble's plane with three other crewmen aboard, however, disappeared without a trace. Yet in spite of the poor weather throughout most of the summer, the 317th logged more flying hours per month and carried more tons in that period than it had since it arrived in the theater.[17]

The 2nd ACG began losing aircraft and men at an increasing rate during the summer of 1945. One of the most interesting transfers of men and planes began on June 13, when Hawkins left his normal fighter pilot role to climb into the cockpit of an L-5 to lead thirty of the light planes (ten from each liaison squadron) over the Hump to Kunming. Hawkins was chosen to lead this mission because of his previous experience in the theater.

He led ten L-5s from the 127th LS from Kalaikunda on June 13 bound for Myitkyina. Heavy rain forced this group to land on a road a few miles from Tezpur, which is on the Indian side of the Himalayas and was scheduled as an intermediate stop. A few L-5s hit trees crowding the road, but the planes were not rendered unflyable. After some gas was begged off a nearby engineer unit, the planes reached Tezpur, where they spent the night.

The 127th's crews flew to Chabua the next morning, where the damaged wingtips were repaired. Then they were off for Myitkyina, but heavy rains forced the pilots to land their little planes on an abandoned strip alongside the Ledo Road. While the Air Commandos waited for the weather to clear, some Army engineers appeared, this time with C rations for the hungry fliers. The planes took off again in the afternoon and finally reached Myitkyina, where they would rendezvous with the rest of the group.

The second element of ten ACG liaison planes left Kalaikunda on June 14, led by 1st Lt. Benedict Lukacs from the 155th LS. They stayed overnight at Lalmanhir Hat, India (now Rajshadi, Bangladesh) before proceeding to Tezpur for another overnight stay. These aircraft reached Myitkyina on June 16.

Meanwhile, the last ten liaison aircraft left Kalaikunda on June 15. Led by 2nd Lt. John F. Nevins of the 156th LS, they encountered little of the weather that had plagued the other two groups and reached Myitkyina shortly after the planes of the 155th arrived.

For the final leg from Myitkyina across the Hump to Kunming, Hawkins led the twenty aircraft of the 127th LS and the 156th LS, while Lukacs led the remaining L-5s of the 155th LS. All three squadrons took off on the morning of June 17. Horrendous weather met them as they battled their way over the Hump. Hawkins decided to detour a bit to the south to get around thunderstorms, and his planes finally broke out into the clear. The fliers were greeted by jagged peaks sticking up out of the clouds. Some of the peaks soared well above the altitude of the planes. Now in the clear, the twenty L-5s reached Yunnanyi, China, after about three hours of flying. The final 140-mile leg to Kunming was routine.

The flight by the planes of the 155th LS was anything but routine. The group initially headed for Paoshan, China, east of Myitkyina, but the planes became separated when the passed through a line of thunderstorms. Seven fliers were able to return to Myitkyina, but the other three were reported missing. SSgt. Lee E. East was last heard reporting that he was out of control in the heavy weather, and nothing was heard from MSgt. William Oldaker or TSgt. John Raynak Jr.

Attempts to reach Bhamo over the next couple of days were thwarted by the weather, but on June 20 the seven remaining ACG L-5s finally reached Paoshan. There, the Air Commandos met a pilot from the 5th LS who was on a run to pick up eggs. He agreed to lead them to Kunming, and on June 22 the last of the L-5s arrived in that city. Waiting for them were Oldaker and Raynak. The pair had kept going through the thunderstorms to reach Kunming. Even better news reached the Air Commandos a few days later: East was alive and well. He had survived the crash of his aircraft and then walked fifty miles before meeting some Chinese engineers who delivered him to American forces.

Along with the delivery of the aircraft, fifteen pilots, five from each liaison squadron, were transferred to the Fourteenth Air Force. This had been a remarkable journey for such small planes over such a forbidding landscape. But twenty-nine of the thirty planes had made it, and, in the end, there had been no casualties. It was just one more indication of the skill and determination of the Air Commandos.[18]

August 10 should have been a day of celebration for the men of the 2nd ACG. Word came that the Japanese had agreed to surrender terms. Sadly, any excitement was swiftly dampened. Gordon, who had exhibited such courage in rescuing Beck and attempting to do the same for Atha, had finally recovered from the terrible injuries he had suffered when he crashed while searching for Atha. But the ebullient Gordon, who so much wanted to see combat, never got the chance. On the 10th, he was out on a night training flight when the news came that the war was over.

The men on the ground were still celebrating when they were informed that radio contact with Gordon had been lost. It was too dark to look for him then, but a search set out early the next morning. It was not long before the crash site was found three miles north of the field. What happened was never ascertained. Gordon's plane had plowed almost vertically into the ground, and the pilot's body was found buried nearly ten feet into the soft earth. Instead of elation over the war being over, gloom over Gordon's loss settled over the group.[19]

There was gloom, too, on what the future held for the men. It was already apparent to many in the group that the unit's days were numbered, but they soldiered on. Earlier, on August 3 and 4, the first squadrons left the 2nd ACG. The three liaison squadrons were relieved from their assignment to the group and embarked by train for Calcutta, where they boarded the USS *General John T. Collins* for transport to an unknown destination. Most of the men were hoping that it was the United States, and when they received word about the atomic bomb, they were sure that was where they were heading. It would be a few more months, however, before most would see "Uncle Sugar."

The transport stopped in Fremantle, Australia, for a couple of days, and the men took full advantage of the opportunities to visit a modern city, drink good beer, see women, and be able to converse in English. Fremantle was just a stopover, though, and the *General John T. Collins* sailed again northward, stopping at Hollandia on New Guinea, and Leyte and Lingayen Gulf in the Philippines before arriving at Okinawa on September 15.[20]

Thus, war's end found the 2nd ACG's elements widely scattered. The liaison squadrons were en route to Okinawa and were no longer assigned to the group. The 318th ADS and the 342nd ADS were at Ledo and would soon be sent to China. For the rest of the Air Commandos, they could only wonder and wait.

PART THREE

...Anywhere
3rd Air Commando Group

Chapter 14

Across the Broad Pacific

After Alison arrived back in Washington, D.C., Arnold asked him for a report on Operation Thursday and advice on what to do with the two new ACGs being formed. Alison said that the CBI could use another group and that perhaps the other group could be sent to the Pacific theater for use in the invasion of the Philippines. Liking the idea, Arnold ordered Alison to go to Australia and make a pitch to FEAF commander General Kenney to take an Air Commando group.

Alison made a quick trip out to the southwest Pacific in late June carrying a letter from Arnold describing the Air Commandos.[1] Arnold wrote about "the broad field which exists for operations involving the movement by air of large ground forces (airborne and ground infantry) and the maintenance and supply of these forces for an extended period from the air. The Air Forces will not be able to play their full part in major campaigns until they are able to move and supply troops without dependence on surface transportation."[2] The new ACGs and CCGs being formed were tailor-made for this activity, Arnold believed. He also felt that the CBI was not the best place to send them, saying that "circumstances" in that theater would deny them the bold and imaginative employment needed. "We are willing to go a long way on this project provided the expenditure is justified," Arnold concluded.[3] Kenney, who was MacArthur's air leader, was requested to give his opinion on the subject as soon as possible.

It did not take long for Kenney to become enthusiastic about the Air Commandos. Perhaps recalling his own proposal back in 1942 for an Air Blitz Unit and always eager to get his hands on men and planes for his undermanned Fifth Air Force and Thirteenth Air Force, Kenney was ready to take the new units now. "It did not require any argument from you or Alison to sell us on this idea," he replied on July 5. "My immediate reaction is to ask you to send all or any of these units as soon as possible. . . . These types of operations are right down our alley. The organization, the equipment, the method of employment, and, in fact, the whole idea fits in perfectly with the tools, necessities and experience of this theater."[4]

Kenney requested that if the Air Commando and Combat Cargo units could reach him not later than October, they would be employed in an "eye-opener" of a tactical role. This was most likely at the upcoming assault of Sarangani Bay on Mindanao. He also wanted both Alison and Cochran to come over. "These two men are cracker-jacks and I will need them to operate these expeditions," he explained.[5] Kenney finished, "I think it is vital that we switch to airborne operations and air supply. Boats are alright in their place but the Navy fights a different war and the Air Force here would like nothing better than to rely solely on air transportation."[6]

Kenney did not get Cochran, but he did receive Alison. Not long after returning to the United States, Alison was ordered back to Kenney's headquarters, where he was to assist in drawing up plans for the use of the Air Commando and Combat Cargo units during the invasion of the Philippines.[7]

It should be noted that although Kenney was eager to exploit Alison's and Cochran's expertise on Air Commando operations, the tenor of his letter suggests that he was really interested in the air transportation and cargo supply side of those operations. And indeed, the early enthusiasm for the concept of self-sustained and self-contained airborne operations behind enemy lines had begun to wane in Washington and in the CBI as the Allied offensives in the Pacific and Burma had begun to accelerate. Such airborne operations were no longer viewed as necessary. Rather, the matter of air transport had assumed a much larger role in the minds of planners. Thus, though the 3rd ACG would be active in Mac-Arthur's Southwest Pacific Area (SWPA) command, it would be in an entirely different manner than that of the 1st ACG in Burma.

The last of the World War II Air Commando groups, the 3rd ACG, was activated at Lakeland AAF on May 1, 1944. Pending the arrival of Colonel Olson, Maj. Klem F. Kalberer was the acting group commander. The 3rd ACG was organized similarly to the 2nd ACG—two fighter squadrons with twenty-five P-51s each, a TCS with sixteen C-47s and thirty-two gliders assigned, three liaison squadrons of thirty-two L-5s and four UC-64s each, four ADSs, and a medical dispensary.[8] At the time of its activation, the 3rd ACG consisted of only the 3rd Fighter–Reconnaissance Squadron, the 4th Fighter–Reconnaissance Squadron (both of which were soon redesignated fighter squadrons), the 334th ADS, and the 335th ADS.

Many of the group's original cadre of fighter pilots came from the 2nd ACG's 1st Fighter Squadron, to which they been reassigned from the 23rd Tactical Reconnaissance Squadron, the 97th Tactical Reconnaissance Squadron, and the 76th Tactical Reconnaissance Group, which had all been disbanded in April. Many of these fliers, though, were soon transferred again and replaced by pilots with "reputations for exceptional gunnery ability."[9] Since no aircraft were yet assigned to the 3rd ACG's fighter squadrons, most of the fighter pilot personnel were granted leave in May. Men in the ADSs, on the other hand, underwent intensive training, as befits newly organized units.[10]

Over the next couple of months the remainder of the group's units were activated. Most of these were stationed far from Lakeland, which was a precursor of how the group would actually be used in combat. On May 1 both the 318th Troop Carrier Squadron, Commando, and the 343rd Airdrome Squadron, Commando, were activated at Camp MacKall. For the time being they remained at that station working with gliders and paratroopers from nearby Fort Bragg. Only in mid-August, when the two units moved to Dunnellon AAF, did they work jointly with the rest of the 3rd ACG. Their members did not meet Olson until September 5, when he gave a talk on what their mission was and what he expected of them. His talk was received favorably, and the men returned to their training with renewed vigor.[11]

Three liaison squadrons were assigned to the 3rd ACG—the 157th LS, 159th LS, and 160th LS. Both the 157th and 160th were activated at Brownwood AAF, Texas; the former was activated on February 10, and the latter was activated on April 1. The 159th came into being at Cox AAF, in Paris, Texas, on March 1. All three squadrons were redesignated as Liaison Squadrons, Commando on May 4 and assigned to the 3rd ACG. They began moving to Statesboro AAF in late May and were up and operating from their new field by the middle of June.

Upon their arrival at Statesboro, the squadrons found the 341st Airdrome Squadron, Commando awaiting them. The 341st had just been activated on May 18, and it would serve as the service organization for all three liaison squadrons. These units remained at Statesboro until mid-August, when they moved to Cross City AAF, Florida. A sense of urgency permeated the squadrons throughout the period. The men believed that movement overseas was imminent, and training was conducted with a high level of energy and purpose.[12]

The final piece that completed the 3rd ACG's puzzle was the 237th Medical Dispensary, Aviation. Activated at Robins Field, Georgia, on March 15, 1944, it finally joined the group at Lakeland on July 6. Like its sister unit, the 236th with the 2nd ACG, the 237th would prove a valuable asset to the Air Commandos.[13]

When Olson arrived in June to assume command of the group, he quickly cleared up any uncertainty among his men concerning their mission and how he expected them to perform it. He described what the 1st ACG had done in Burma and explained that his group would probably be employed in a similar manner. Olson inherited a smoothly running group staff and made few changes. By mid-July, his staff comprised (among others) Lt. Col. Elmer W. Richardson, operations officer; Kalberer, executive officer; Maj. John H. Easley, flight surgeon; Capt. Clarence W. Thomas, intelligence; and Capt. Ulysses S. Aswell, chaplain. All the squadron commanders are listed in the accompanying table.[14]

Olson was blessed with a number of veterans, including Richardson, an eight-plane ace in China, and 1st Lt. Louis E. Curdes, an eight-plane ace in Europe

---

3rd Air Commando Group August 1944
> Lt. Col. Arvid E. Olson Jr.

3rd Fighter–Reconnaissance Squadron/3rd Fighter Squadron, Commando
> Maj. Walker M. Mahurin

4th Fighter–Reconnaissance Squadron/4th Fighter Squadron, Commando
> Maj. Steven H. Wilkerson

318th Troop Carrier Squadron, Commando
> Capt. Charles C. Carter Jr.

157th Liaison Squadron, Commando
> Capt. Clarence L. Odum

159th Liaison Squadron, Commando
> Capt. Rush H. Limbaugh Jr.
> 1st. Lt. William G. Price III (October 25, 1944)

160th Liaison Squadron, Commando
> Maj. John E. Satterstrom

334th Airdrome Squadron
> Capt. Harmon V. Howe

335th Airdrome Squadron
> Capt. Woodson S. Herring

341st Airdrome Squadron
> Capt. Bertram E. Solomon
> Capt. Floyd W. Fuller (September 21, 1944)

343rd Airdrome Squadron
> Maj. Charles L. Foster

237th Medical Dispensary, Aviation
> Maj. Milford N. Childs

Note: The dates in parentheses indicate when the officer began serving with the 3rd ACG.

and the Mediterranean. Another individual of note assigned to the group was one "Rush" Russhon, the same man who took the critical pictures of Broadway for the 1st Air Commandos. He now was the 3rd ACG's photographic officer and would later be its public relations officer. But the group's best-known individual was probably the 3rd Fighter Squadron's leader, Maj. Walker M. "Bud" Mahurin. Mahurin had flown with the famed 56th Fighter Group in Europe, where he had downed twenty-one German aircraft. When his twenty-first kill also fatally damaged his Thunderbolt on March 27, 1944, Mahurin had to take to the silk. Fortunately, he was able to contact members of the French Resistance, who got him back to England on May 7.[15]

Although Mahurin knew D-day was imminent and wanted to be in on that show, he was ordered back to the United States to make a few speeches for the War Bond drive and then to take a thirty-day leave. The speeches were excruciating to him, and though leave was pleasant when dealing with the public, he was itching to get back into combat. He heard that Alison was recruiting for some new ACGs, so he contacted his old friend to see if he could be of use. Regulations, however, prohibited fliers returned to the United States from going back into combat for one year. Alison said he would see about a job and also about getting Mahurin a waiver to return to combat if he wanted it. Mahurin soon received a telegram from USAAF Headquarters stating that if he waived the regulations for return to combat, a position as commanding officer of the 3rd ACG's 3rd Fighter Squadron, Commando, was available. Within five minutes Mahurin had the waiver speeding back to Washington.[16]

Mahurin was a very aggressive fighter pilot, and he made quite an impression on the mostly young fliers. Lieutenant Vincent Krout, a pilot in the 4th Fighter Squadron, recalled Mahurin coming over occasionally in the Philippines to lead a flight from the 4th. "When he did," Krout said, "I usually got assigned to fly his wing. And he was a maniac. When he got in the airplane, I think he shoved the throttle all the way to the firewall and left it there. He just flew like a crazy man, in my opinion. It was all you could do to keep up with him. Extremely difficult to fly with. I don't know how he flew with his own squadron, but he could wear you out."[17]

When the 3rd ACG's fighter squadrons finally received their planes, it was a mixed bag of weary P-40s and P-51B/Cs that were well worn from many hours of use by countless fliers. Nonetheless, the pilots were happy to get anything to fly. Unfortunately, accidents happened during this period. Accidents were not uncommon throughout the USAAF in World War II because training was conducted at a hectic pace. There were midair collisions and landing accidents and mechanical failures of various sorts. Some of the pilots were able to get out of their crippled planes, some did not. There would be brief periods of mourning for fallen friends, and then the fliers returned to the job at hand. For time was running short.

In mid-August 3rd ACG headquarters and the fighter squadrons and their ADSs moved from Lakeland to Alachua AAF outside of Gainesville, Florida, to begin a series of important exercises involving the entire group. The liaison squadrons and their ADSs were located forty-five miles west of Gainesville at Cross City, while the 318th TCS and the 343rd ADS operated from Dunnellon, about fifty miles southwest of Gainesville. It was in the triangle formed by these airfields that the group generally held its exercises. The high point of this training was a combined field maneuver involving all the units. Group aircraft reconnoitered and photographed an "enemy" airfield, conducted simulated bombing and strafing attacks, and carried out a night glider assault. The assault troops had to hold out against an "enemy" force for a couple of days before being pulled out by night glider snatches. The exercise was deemed successful by the exercise umpires, and the men felt they were ready to take the next step—movement overseas and entry into combat.[18]

Observers from III Fighter Command, the 3rd ACGs parent organization, and USAAF Headquarters concurred with the Air Commandos' assessment and, at long last, the group underwent its Preparation for Overseas Movement (POM) inspections. Even as these inspections were being made, the plans and timing on how to use the 3rd ACG were undergoing drastic changes. For months the Joint Chiefs of Staff (JCS) had been debating whether the next advance across the Pacific should be aimed at the Philippines (specifically Luzon), at Formosa (a then-commonly used name for Taiwan) and the China coast, or at both targets. MacArthur pressed for the Philippines, while Admiral King, the chief of naval operations and commander of the U.S. fleet, argued just as forcefully for Formosa. In June, as the Marianas invasion was unfolding, the JCS were even considering bypassing both the Philippines and Formosa. Such a thought appalled MacArthur, who had pledged to return to the Philippines. He presented the JCS his latest plan—Reno V. In this plan, Sarangani Bay on Mindanao would be assaulted on October 25, 1944, followed by landings on Leyte about November 15, on southeastern Luzon in mid-January 1945, and in Lingayen Gulf, Luzon, on April 1, 1945.

If Reno V was accepted, however, the Formosa operation would have to be postponed until October 1945, and this King would never accept. MacArthur met with Adm. Chester W. Nimitz, CinC for Pacific Ocean Areas, and President Roosevelt at Pearl Harbor in late July to press his case. Following the conference MacArthur believed he had won support for going into the Philippines first, but

Roosevelt (cagey politician that he was) never said that the Formosa operation was canceled, nor had he said which of the two options would come first.

Wrangling over the strategy for the forthcoming Pacific operations continued for the next couple of months. Then, in early September, the JCS approved MacArthur's plan for landings at Sarangani Bay and set a target date of September 15. Further advances in the Philippines were set for December 20, with landings on Leyte in the Surigao area. Whether Luzon or Formosa would follow was left unspecified.

When Alison returned to the southwest Pacific, he was placed in charge of planning an airborne assault on Mindanao using gliders from both the 3rd ACG and other troop carrier units. This plan was scratched with spectacular suddenness in mid-September. Adm. William F. Halsey, whose Third Fleet was operating off the Philippines in support of the Peleliu and Morotai operations, came to the conclusion (based on the reports of his fliers) that the Japanese were weak in the Philippines. He recommended canceling the above two operations and, instead, striking directly at Leyte.

Although it was too late to call off the Peleliu and Morotai landings, Nimitz was willing to forego landings at Yap that were scheduled to occur at about the same time as the other invasions, and he offered MacArthur the use of the Army corps scheduled for Yap. As it turned out, Halsey was wrong; the Japanese were very strong in the Philippines, and fighting would be bloody before the islands were retaken. Nonetheless, a radical decision was made to invade the Philippines at Leyte on October 20 rather than at Mindanao on November 15. The Air Commandos would have been hard pressed to have been available by November 15. Now there was no way they could be used in the invasion of the Philippines.

The men of the 3rd ACG, naturally, knew nothing about such high-level planning. They just knew they were getting ready to go overseas, and the sooner the better. Following the POM inspections, most of the group proceeded to Drew Field in Tampa to begin processing for the overseas movement. The 318th TCS and the 343rd ADS returned to Camp MacKall for some brief training before going to Baer Air Field in Fort Wayne, Indiana, on their next step what seemed to be an interminable journey overseas. Deliverance from ennui and the anxiety of not knowing if they were heading into combat was finally at hand for the men of the group, however.

The 3rd ACG's air echelons were the first to leave. The fighter pilots were flown by transports to Nadzab, New Guinea, where they picked up new P-51D Mustangs. The squadrons also picked up some replacement pilots. Most of these airmen had been in the southwest Pacific for a couple of months and had been ferrying P-40s between bases. None had any Mustang experience, but their checkout was simple. Given an airplane, they were told to fly it! The P-51 had a little quirk that caught many by surprise on their first flights. It was customary in the P-40 to slide its canopy back for landing. When the fliers did this in the P-51, dust and debris flew everywhere, momentarily blinding them. Even goggles could be ripped off. The windstorms caused no injuries, but pilots always landed with canopies closed afterward.[19]

The 318th TCS flew its own aircraft to New Guinea, leaving Baer on October 10. Their final stop in the United States was Fairfield AAF, near San Francisco. Final processing and the making up of some equipment shortages took three days, and then it was out over the Golden Gate to Hawaii. From Hawaii the C-47s headed for Christmas Island and then to Canton Island. The sixteen transports were split into two sections at Canton, one going by way of Tarawa and Guadalcanal, and the second going via Fiji, New Caledonia, and Guadalcanal. The last leg was to Nadzab, where the squadron touched down on October 26.

Upon their arrival, the men discovered that they had not been expected and that the local commander had decided, over the protests of the Air Commandos, to place the men and planes in a replacement pool. It was only the intervention of Olson, who appeared seemingly out of nowhere, that set matters straight. The 318th TCS was an integral part of the 3rd ACG, Olson told the other man, and it would be treated as a functioning unit.

Shortly afterwards the men and planes of the 318th began carrying cargo and passengers all over New Guinea and evacuating wounded to Australia. It was tough, demanding work, particularly since the squadron had few supplies and no maintenance men. The 3rd ACG ground crews were just then beginning their own trip to the combat zone. Nevertheless, in typical Air Commando spirit, the 318th's pilots and crew chiefs kept their planes flying with remarkable efficiency.[20]

Meanwhile, back in the United States, Olson and Richardson and several other staff officers had disappeared from Florida on October 18. They would not be seen again by the Air Commandos, except for by pilots of the 318th, until they rejoined the group on Leyte. The group commanders were swiftly followed by the ground echelons. The units at Drew began leaving by train on October 24, while those at Baer left on the 27th. Both trains were headed for Camp Stoneman, which was north of Oakland on San Francisco Bay's east side.

The group's stay at Stoneman lasted only about a week, but the brief period was packed with last-minute activities, including drawing new uniforms and equipment, listening to more lectures, getting more shots, and filling out form after form. Most sobering of the latter were the insurance papers for next of kin and the wills, as those served to remind the men that where they were going would not be a picnic.

On the afternoon of November 6 the men boarded ferries for the short trip down the bay to their home for the next three weeks, the USS *General M. L. Hersey*. The transport was big and new, some 38,000 tons and making just her second voyage to the war zone. As big as she was, the Pacific was bigger, and for at least the first few days after their departure on the 7th, the Air Commandos noted that their ship rolled a lot. Attendance at meals was low for a time as many decided hanging over the rails was a better choice than being in a hot, crowded mess.

On November 16 the transport crossed the equator, and King Neptune came aboard to initiate the pollywogs into his realm. While outnumbered by the nautical neophytes, the shellbacks aboard the *General M. L. Hersey* more than held their own to administer the usual punishments to the pollywogs. Although many of the Air Commandos were aching the next day, they were full-fledged shellbacks and could look back on the previous day's ceremonies with a certain amount of rueful grace. At least the beatings and such had broken the voyage's monotony.

A brief stop was made at Guadalcanal, which had become a major logistics base. Then it was on to Finschafen and Hollandia on New Guinea. There was no time for the troops to disembark at any of these harbors, but they could get a close look at land after days of seeing nothing but water. On November 26 the *General M. L. Hersey* left Hollandia bound for her final destination, Leyte. The transport ship anchored off Leyte near the village of Palo on the 30th. Most of the night was spent preparing to go ashore, and finally around 8:00 AM, DUKWs (pronounced "ducks") and landing craft began shuttling the Air Commandos to shore. The reception they received was not what they had anticipated. Apparently, their arrival, like that of the 318th TCS in New Guinea, had not been foreseen. "The group found itself orphans; unexpected, uninvited, and unwanted," wrote the 159th LS's historian.[21] The 3rd Fighter Squadron's historian concurred, noting, "It was hard to believe that the Commandos were unheard of. . . . We came to help but nobody seemed to give a particular damn."[22] To add insult to injury, a WAC detachment had landed a day earlier to much greater enthusiasm.

The men of the 3rd ACG also discovered that rain would be a constant companion over the next few weeks. Pup tents were pitched on the muddy ground but provided scant protection, as they just seemed to sink into the water-logged ground as torrential rains pounded Leyte. Moving to a different spot and repitching the tents did no good. The group continued its semisubmerged existence for three days before someone higher up, out of pity or just wanting them off the crowded beachhead, directed a move a few miles down the beach to San Roque. Conditions were only slightly better there, but the group's equipment, including cots, had begun to arrive, finally enabling the men to stay above the floods that gushed through the tents each night.

San Roque was a reasonably pleasant interlude, with some fine swimming offshore. The group was just getting established when a near disaster struck. A portion of the 3rd ACG's bivouac was occupied by a fuel dump. A fire started in the dump on the evening of December 10, and barrels of gasoline began exploding and flying through the air. Little firefighting equipment was available, so the fire was allowed to burn itself out. Unfortunately, much of the group's personal equipment was lost in the fire, and its men had to rely on the good-heartedness of others for some time before their equipment was replaced.[23]

December 15 saw the group receive surprise visitors in the persons of Olson and several of his staff. Olson was just as surprised as his men because the first he knew of their presence on Leyte was when he was on his way to V Fighter Command Headquarters and saw a sign proclaiming that one of the areas he passed belonged to the 3rd ACG. All concerned were happy to see each other again, and Olson assured his men that they would soon see action. Even as the reunion was taking place, the fighter pilots were getting acquainted with their new P-51Ds down in New Guinea, and they would soon arrive on Leyte.

In the meantime, the 3rd ACG's status in Fifth Air Force was formalized. The Air Commandos were assigned to the V Fighter Command on December 13, and five days later they were further assigned to the 86th Fighter Wing.[24]

A few day after Olson's arrival at Leyte, the group made yet another move, this time a couple of miles north of San Roque to the vicinity of Tanauan. There, an airfield paralleling the coast had been under construction since November 21, and it had just opened to traffic on December 16. The field had a 5,300-foot-long pierced steel plank runway, another 3,500 feet of taxiways, and ten hardstands. Further construction lasting into January lengthened the strip another 700 feet and added more taxiways and another forty-three hardstands.

Tanauan, however, had an interesting obstruction at its south end. Immediately to the south rose a rocky hill that was three hundred feet high. Naturally, this limited approaches from that direction. Approaches from the north, on the other hand, were over water, and there were no problems landing from that direction. No accidents were ever reported due to the hill.

It was at Tanauan that the 3rd ACG's fighters would begin operations. This site was much nicer (and somewhat drier) than any so far. A lot of work other than airfield construction remained to turn the place into a fully functioning facility, though, and much of the rest of December was involved in those activi-

The 3rd ACG's commander, Col. Arvid Olson, at his headquarters, which had been established in a school in San Nicolas, Luzon. Note the dispatcher working in the open. (U.S. Army Air Forces archives)

Col. Walker M. "Bud" Mahurin poses with his suitably decorated fighter showing the twenty-one kills he had amassed in Europe and the one Japanese victory he obtained with the Air Commandos. (U.S. Army Air Forces archives)

A typical light plane strip bulldozed out of rice paddies: At least one of the parked L-5s is from the 3rd ACG's 159th Liaison Squadron. (U.S. Army Air Forces archives)

First Lt. Louis E. Curdes' Mustang sports a new victory symbol to go with his German and Italian kills. (U.S. Army Air Forces archives)

TSgt Vincent T. McNally chalks up another enemy aircraft on the group's scoreboard at the 3rd ACG's headquarters. (U.S. Army Air Forces archives)

Swamp Angel II taxies at Laoag for another mission. (Courtesy of the World War II Air Commando Association via Edward Young)

A wounded soldier is loaded into a 157th Liaison Squadron aircraft for evacuation to a hospital in the rear. (U.S. Army Air Forces archives)

A landing accident claimed this Mustang at Gabu. (Courtesy of the World War II Air Commando Association via Edward Young)

ties. Tanauan was not the only airfield available to the 3rd ACG. While waiting for the arrival of their planes, the men of the liaison squadrons and their ADSs built an airstrip using their hands and a single bulldozer. After it opened in January, the strip was dubbed "Mitchell Field," after the 157th LS's 2nd Lt. William Mitchell, who had led the construction effort.

The liaison pilots, who had not flown in several months, visited the nearby 25th LS to see about borrowing some of their planes. The 25th was happy to see the Air Commandos and loaned them a couple of L-5s to keep up their flying proficiency and also to fly a variety of missions for the 25th LS.[25]

As 1944 ended and 1945 began, the men of the 3rd ACG were ready to assume their station among the combat-hardened units of the Fifth Air Force. That time was about to come.

Chapter 15

The Zebras Are Loose

January 7, 1945, found most of the 3rd ACG's ground personnel and members of the liaison squadrons lining the runway at Tanauan. The Mustangs of the group's 3rd Fighter Squadron were scheduled to arrive that day, and all were eagerly anticipating the moment. Their expectations were met in "spectacular" fashion, as the V Fighter Command history stated later.[1] When the sixteen P-51Ds arrived over Tanauan following the long flight from Biak Island in New Guinea, they were grouped in a tight "show" formation. They then broke into flights of four and buzzed the airstrip before making sharp breaks into the landing pattern. The tower officer had obviously never seen such airmanship, for he began yelling over the radio, "Zebras! Zebras! You are landing too close! Pull up and go around!"[2]

Mahurin, who was leading his men, calmly radioed the panicky tower officer, "Leave the Zebras alone, Tower. These pilots have been flying like this for a long time. They know what they are doing!"[3] The fighters landed two at a time, one on each side of the runway, and all sixteen fighters were on the ground in less than three minutes. To the Air Commandos this technique was old hat; they had been practicing it for months. To the Fifth Air Force, however, it was something new, but it did not take long for the other fighter groups to adopt the technique. They also began taking off in pairs, a procedure that shortened the time needed for rendezvous and added to time use over the target.

The arrival of his fighters was bittersweet to Olson. He was delighted that his group could now take an active part in the war, but his happiness was tinged with sorrow because just four days earlier he had lost a friend from his days with the 1st ACG. Grant Mahony had returned to the United States from Burma in late May 1944 as a lieutenant colonel. Like Mahurin, Mahony was a fighter. Driven by a deep hatred for the Japanese, he could not stand being out of combat. After numerous entreaties to return to combat, he was finally assigned to the 8th Fighter Group as a staff officer in group headquarters. He joined the group at Noemfoor Island in Indonesia in November and soon after began flying missions in P-38s as often as he could. In late December the group moved to Mindoro in the Philippines, where it quickly saw heavy action.

On January 3, 1945, Mahony joined 1st Lt. George Lynch on a strafing mission to Puerta Princesa on the island of Palawan. The pair spotted a floatplane in the bay near the airfield. Lynch warned Mahony that it could be a flak trap, but Mahony decided to attack anyway. It was a trap. Lynch saw flashes on the ground and red balls of tracer fire arcing into the air. Although he silenced some of this fire with strafing, it was too late. Mahony's P-38 was hit, went straight in, and exploded. At the time of his death Mahony was only 26 years old.[4]

Meanwhile, the 3rd Fighter Squadron's Mustangs had hardly been parked when orders were received for their first missions the following day. Eight fighters were sent to bomb and strafe the enemy airfields at Surigao and Del Monte on Mindanao, while the remainder of the squadron flew patrol missions. The mission on the morning of the January 8 was uneventful, but a return visit in the afternoon by eight Mustangs proved disastrous. Although the Japanese airfields were put out of action temporarily and two enemy planes were destroyed on the ground, when 1st Lt. Earl J. Thibodeau and 2nd Lt. William T. Tudor pulled up from their strafing runs, they collided and crashed. It happened so quickly that neither man could escape from their tumbling aircraft. It had been Thibodeau's first combat mission, but Tudor had already chalked up fifty missions in the Mediterranean. The flight back to Tanauan was considerably more subdued than the flight out had been.[5]

For the next couple of weeks the 3rd Fighter Squadron, joined by the 4th Fighter Squadron on January 16, kept busy with missions all over the Philippines. Poor weather hampered operations at times, but the two squadrons remained active. Also quite busy were the 318th TCS's C-47s, as they flew sorely needed supplies in from Nadzab to Tanauan. Much of the 3rd ACG's supplies had disappeared somewhere in transit, and it was mainly the efforts of the 318th that kept the Air Commandos operating.

By January 10 the transport unit completed its own movement to Leyte. Its stay there was short, though, because orders were received five days later for the 318th to move to Mindoro, which had been assaulted on December 15. Kamikaze attacks on the invasion convoys and regular aerial attacks on the beachhead, though inflicting damage, were unavailing, and Mindoro rapidly became an important air garrison in support of MacArthur's upcoming invasion of Luzon. The 318th flew supply missions from Mindoro not only for the 3rd ACG, but for many other Fifth Air Force units.

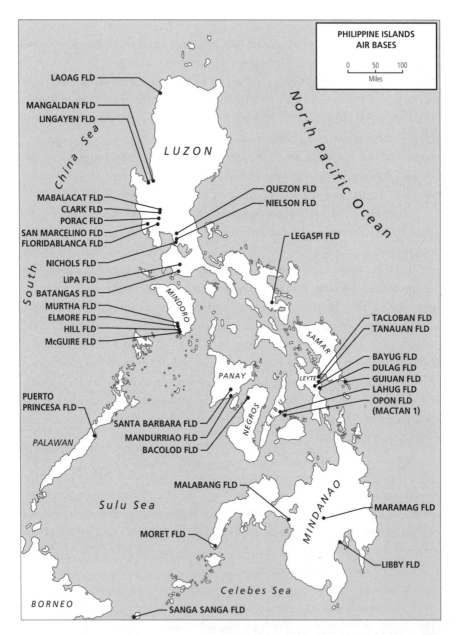

PHILIPPINE ISLANDS
AIR BASES

0   50   100
Miles

LAOAG FLD

MANGALDAN FLD
LINGAYEN FLD

China Sea

LUZON

North Pacific Ocean

MABALACAT FLD
CLARK FLD
PORAC FLD
SAN MARCELINO FLD
FLORIDABLANCA FLD

QUEZON FLD
NIELSON FLD

LEGASPI FLD

NICHOLS FLD
LIPA FLD
BATANGAS FLD
MURTHA FLD
ELMORE FLD
HILL FLD
McGUIRE FLD

South

MINDORO

TACLOBAN FLD
TANAUAN FLD

SAMAR

BAYUG FLD
DULAG FLD
GUIUAN FLD
LAHUG FLD
OPON FLD
(MACTAN 1)

PANAY

LEYTE

CEBU

PUERTO
PRINCESA FLD

SANTA BARBARA FLD
MANDURRIAO FLD
BACOLOD FLD

NEGROS

PALAWAN

MALABANG FLD

Sulu Sea

MINDANAO

MARAMAG FLD

MORET FLD

LIBBY FLD

Celebes Sea

BORNEO

SANGA SANGA FLD

The stay at Mindoro also saw the 318th lose its first plane. A C-47 crashed on takeoff on January 21, killing two men on the ground when it cartwheeled into the tent in which they were sleeping. All aboard the transport—a crew of four and fifteen enlisted men from the 343rd ADS—survived despite being singed and bruised. It was believed the copilot, who was inexperienced, lost control of his heavily laden aircraft.[6]

The pace of operations from Mindoro was heavy, placing an even greater strain on the pilots, who had each been flying well over one hundred hours per month. This stress was reduced considerably when the squadron's glider pilots began to fly as copilots. The tale of the 318th's glider pilots was a sad one. Although the squadron had a glider section, it never received its own gliders, thus the glidermen were unemployed. Only during a short period in January and February, when they were used as copilots, did they feel like they were useful, but when more C-47 crews arrived, they went back to being jobless. It was pretty much the same situation for the glider mechanics. Too often they were used for menial tasks far below their training. The 318th's historian stated their situation bluntly:

> From the very first day in the Glider Program they have been showered with promises and better things to come, but with each new promise they were shifted to another pool or school for someone else to keep. They have been through the worst camps in the United States, lived in tents kept warm by their own efforts, while others lived in barracks, they have had their pride dented a hundred times but nowhere in the Army where men are segregated into units, can there be found a group with the sense of humor and willingness to put forth superior effort as these men.
>
> Then overseas, the realization of all their work, but still they were on the outside as usual sitting, waiting to do their job with no encouragement from any quarters. The Army has failed them, efficient, capable Officers and Enlisted Men doing nothing.[7]

Unfortunately, several more months elapsed before the glider pilots and mechanics finally received duties that utilized their abilities.

Leyte and Mindoro were just preludes to the main attack on Luzon. That island had been MacArthur's primary focus for some time. It was the enemy's main bastion in the Philippines, and even though many Japanese troops had been shunted off to Leyte, where most died, approximately 275,000 troops of General Yamashita Tomoyuki's Fourteenth Area Army were still on Luzon. Three major Japanese forces were emplaced from Manila northward: The 80,000-man Shimbu Group covered the Manila area; 30,000 men of the Kembu Group, of which about half were sailors, defended the Bataan Peninsula and the Clark Field complex northwest of Manila; and approximately 152,000 soldiers of the Shobu Group were under Yamashita's direct command. This latter group was nearest to MacArthur's planned landing beaches, and it controlled operations north of Manila and up through the fertile Cagayan Valley.

On January 9 two U.S. corps landed on the shores of Lingayen Gulf, just a few miles south of where the Japanese had landed on December 22, 1941. From Lingayen, the two U.S. corps were to drive south to Manila while maintaining a strong defensive line to the north. Within a week of the landings, a firm beachhead almost thirty miles deep and thirty miles wide was established. Two major airfields plus smaller liaison strips sprang up inside the beachhead. An old Japanese strip on the shore of the gulf became the site of Lingayen Airdrome. Drainage was poor at this place, and rains could render its surface unusable. To check erosion, the strip was covered with palm fronds and bamboo mats overlaid with pierced steel planking. Lingayen became the home for several fighter and reconnaissance squadrons.

A second strip was begun near Dagupan, but the ground there proved unsuitable for airfield construction, so another site near Mangaldan was chosen. The area picked for the airfield was in the middle of rice paddies, and the water table was very high. Aviation engineers bulldozed the tops off the paddies and filled in low spots until a reasonably level surface of compacted earth formed a single 7,500-foot runway. The sun baked the earth until it was almost as hard as concrete, but the high water table and heavy rains often combined to shut down operations at the field. Until better airfields were seized near Manila, Mangaldan remained a primary airfield, with several groups and squadrons, including the Air Commandos, based there.[8]

In the meantime about the only units of the 3rd ACG that remained concerned about their role in the fighting were the liaison squadrons. They had yet to receive their planes, but this did not mean they were idle. The pilots continued to help the 25th LS with missions and the 343rd ADS kept Mitchell Field in tip-top shape in expectation of the arrival of their planes. Their planes would finally arrive just in time to move to Luzon.[9]

Spectacular results were obtained by the 3rd Fighter Squadron on January 13 during a reconnaissance of southeast Luzon. The pilots discovered a concentration of enemy troops and vehicles attempting to cross a river using a cable-drawn ferry. Repeated strafing runs destroyed the ferry and caused several trucks to blow up with tremendous force, leveling a village at the ferry site. The Mustangs then continued moving up and down the road while firing at any truck that could be seen. When the strafing runs were over, an estimated twelve to fifteen trucks had been destroyed, and an undetermined number had been damaged. To cap off this successful mission, a Zeke was found in a revetment at Bulan and destroyed.[10]

Further sweeps followed the next morning. Ten Mustangs led by Mahurin escorted B-25s in a strike on the town of Aparri. After the town was plastered by the B-25s, the P-51s came down to strafe the neighboring airfield. A Tony, a Betty, a Ki-45 Nick, and one other unidentified aircraft were destroyed by the strafing, and a pair of camouflaged luggers hidden in a nearby cove also received a .50-caliber treatment. As the P-51s returned south down the verdant Cagayan Valley, a pair of twin-engine enemy planes were spotted heading north. They were flying about five thousand feet below the Americans and evidently had not seen the Mustangs. Capt. Charles B. Adams, the operations officer for the 3rd Fighter Squadron, and his wingman dove on the nearest plane, a Sally. The enemy pilot took no evasive action other than increasing his speed as Adams closed to almost pointblank range. Adams' six .50-calibers made quick work of the bomber, which crashed into the hills. Meanwhile, Mahurin went after the second plane, a Dinah.

The Dinah was one of the JAAF's premier reconnaissance aircraft. Sleek and elegant looking, it was very fast but not fast enough that day. When the enemy pilot saw the fate of his friend, he immediately reversed course and poured the coal to his aircraft. Mahurin dropped his wing tanks so he could go faster, but it took ten minutes for him to get close enough to begin firing. A few short bursts were all that were needed. Its pilot probably dead, the Dinah rolled slowly onto its back and crashed.[11]

For the next couple of weeks both of the 3rd ACG's fighter squadrons kept busy strafing and bombing locomotives and rolling stock, trucks, and other vehicles. They generally made themselves extremely dangerous nuisances to the Japanese. Four 3rd Fighter Squadron fighters found lucrative targets on January 16 when they attacked the Clark Field complex. Clark had been the USAAF's major installation in the Philippines prior to the war, and it had remained the primary air base for the Japanese. That afternoon the four Air Commando fliers discovered a fighter pilot's dream, a group of unsuspecting enemy aircraft caught on the ground. At Angeles South, located a few miles southeast of the main Clark complex, a quartet of Ki-44 Tojos were lined up at the end of the runway with their propellers ticking over slowly. Their pilots were apparently concentrating on checking their engine magnetos prior to takeoff.

First Lt. Glenn E. Larimore toggled off a 500-pound bomb that struck one of the Tojos squarely. The blast set off an explosion in an adjacent fighter, which, in turn, set the remaining two planes aflame. Five more enemy fighters were destroyed, and three more were damaged before the Air Commandos were through. None of the American planes received a scratch.[12]

The same day, other 3rd Fighter Squadron fighters conducted a barge sweep of Iloilo Bay on Negros Island. No barges were found, but several aircraft were discovered camouflaged on an airstrip. Adams burned one of these, but enemy

20-mm antiaircraft fire holed his plane and he had to bail out over the sea. Under the watchful eyes of his comrades, friendly natives rescued Adams and took him to a nearby island. An OA-10A, the USAAF's version of the Navy's PBY-3 Catalina seaplane, picked up Adams the following day and returned him to Leyte.[13]

With their numbers dwindling, the Japanese resorted to hiding their remaining aircraft, and few enemy planes were caught in the open. One unlucky victim, however, was found by 3rd ACG Capt. Ray Lahmeyer on the 18th as he made a late afternoon sweep of Del Monte airfield on Mindanao. The Japanese had been making things uncomfortable for the men on Leyte with nocturnal nuisance raids, and the 4th Fighter Squadron was directed to end "Washing Machine Charlie's" harassment. The sun was on the horizon, and dusk was beginning to creep across the land when Lahmeyer and his wingman reached Del Monte. A flickering caught Lahmeyer's eye as he neared the field. An airplane, he thought, but then he noticed puddles of water on the ground and decided he had just seen reflections from the puddles.

The flickering continued, however, and then Lahmeyer spotted a Betty with its engines running. Light from the dying sun was hitting the bomber's propellers and causing the pulsation that had caught Lahmeyer's attention. Racking his fighter around in a tight turn, Lahmeyer made a run on the Betty. He could see several Japanese running away from the plane as his .50-caliber shells walked up to and through it. There was a flash, and the bomber exploded. Washing Machine Charlie made no further flights over Leyte.[14]

The 3rd ACG's stay on Leyte turned out to be rather short. On the same day as Lahmeyer's victory, the Air Commandos found themselves on the move again. This time, their destination was Luzon. Most of the ground personnel and a few pilots of the three liaison squadrons and all of the members of the 341st ADS, plus those men's and units' vehicles, baggage, and supplies, loaded onto LST 919 for the trip to Lingayen Gulf. LSTs were not nicknamed "large, slow targets" for no reason. It was a long way from Leyte to Luzon, and the trip seemed to take forever.

Not until around midnight of January 30 did LST 919 beach near San Fabian on the northern edge of the landing beaches. The Air Commandos unloaded the following morning and proceeded by convoy to Calasiao, where a light plane field was in use by the artillery spotters of the 168th Field Artillery Group. It was nicknamed "Stinson Field," after the L-5's original manufacturer. Two strips, a northern one and a southern one, running generally north–south, made up Stinson Field. The 3rd ACG's liaison squadrons were split between the two strips. After enduring the rain and relatively primitive living conditions on Leyte, the men were overjoyed to see paved roads, railroad tracks, and what seemed to be a higher standard of living enjoyed by the Luzon residents.[15]

As LST 919 meandered toward Lingayen Gulf, the remaining 3rd ACG liaison pilots and some ground personnel were assembling new L-5Bs that were just arriving at Leyte. Also remaining behind temporarily were the fighter squadrons, which continued flying missions until they, too, pulled up roots to move to Luzon. Sadly, these final missions out of Leyte were not without cost. During a fighter sweep of Mindanao on January 20, 2nd Lt. William N. Isgrigg pressed his attack on a truck too low and snagged a tree. His plane cartwheeled and exploded, killing Isgrigg instantly.[16]

The 3rd Fighter Squadron's final mission from Tanauan was impressive. Baguio, in the hills northeast of Lingayen Gulf, had been the prewar summer capital of the Filipino government. It was noted for its cooling breezes and relative lack of humidity, and it was considered a delightful spot to escape to when the summer heat became too oppressive in Manila. The Americans also esteemed Baguio and had established Camp John Hay there early in the century. Now another army occupied the area, and it had become General Yamashita's Fourteenth Area Army headquarters.

Sixteen ACG Mustangs, each carrying two 1,000-lb. bombs, followed B-24s of the 22nd Bombardment Group in attacking Yamashita's headquarters on January 23. Shortly after the Liberators pulled off the target, the P-51s darted in to dive-bomb Camp John Hay. Their bombs were right on target, with direct hits being scored on the administration building, the message center, the quartermaster stores, a barracks, and the "luxurious" staff officers quarters.[17]

Following this mission, the 3rd Fighter Squadron's aircraft returned to Tanauan, refueled, then flew to their new base at Mangaldan, which had received the code name "Honey Strip." Three days later, the 4th Fighter Squadron also moved to the new field. The 318th TCS, which the Fifth Air Force had also directed to move to Luzon, was not far behind. By February 18 the entire transport squadron and its accompanying ADS had settled in at Mangaldan. The liaison squadrons soon followed.

After slow-timing the newly arrived L-5Bs and installing bomb shackles for the carrying and dropping of supplies, the small planes were ready for the move to Luzon. One further addition had to be made before the flight. Auxiliary gas tanks were installed in the rear of the cockpit to give the L-5s greater range and to provide some fuel reserve in case of bad weather. On February 6, Kalberer led twenty-eight aircraft of the 159th LS from Tanauan for Calasiao via Mindoro. A pair of Marine F4U Corsairs and a Navy Catalina provided the navigation and fighter escort for the trip, which was uneventful. The 159th was joined presently by the other two 3rd ACG liaison squadrons, which followed the same route.

The pilots and ground crews of the liaison squadrons and their ADS had little time for rest following their arrival. They flew courier missions the day after landing at Calasiao, and they began evacuating wounded from forward strips a few days later. The pace was intense; in just a day's work, one pilot could log almost eight hours of flying time and thirty-seven landings while evacuating 17 patients and delivering 840 pounds of supplies. In its first three weeks of operations from Luzon, the 159th LS, for example, evacuated 1,553 patients, flew seventy supply missions, and delivered 14,650 pounds of supplies. The other two liaison squadrons recorded similar figures.

The importance of the liaison squadrons was also underscored by the fact that one of the 159th's pilots, 2nd Lt. Volie A. Williams, along with Cpl. Paul E. Richards as crew chief, was attached to the Sixth Army to serve as personal pilot to the army's commander, Lt. Gen. Walter Krueger.[18]

The 3rd ACG had hardly settled in before its services were being coveted by units elsewhere. In early February Maj. Gen. Ennis Whitehead, the Fifth Air Force commander, wrote General Kenney about Kenney's staff requesting that the Air Commandos and another fighter squadron be sent south for use in the Mindanao campaign, which started on March 10. Whitehead opposed this idea strongly. He mentioned in his letter that the P-51 was the longest-ranged fighter in the Fifth Air Force and that it was needed for use against Formosa. The "very highly trained" Air Commandos would be invaluable against Formosa, he noted.

Whitehead also pointed out that although Kenney's staff seemingly believed that the 3rd ACG, because of its organic transport squadron, could be moved more easily by air than a standard fighter group, this was not the case. He stated that it would require nearly three hundred plane loads just to move the Air Commando fighter squadrons. Instead of using the Air Commandos, Whitehead thought that the short-legged SBDs of the Marines, which were also at Mangaldan, and Marine Corsairs would be a better choice for the Mindanao campaign. The Fifth Air Force leader's letter apparently had an effect, for the Air Commandos did not move, and the Marines were sent south.[19]

While the Air Commandos settled in at Mangaldan and Calasaio, the Sixth Army drove toward Manila. Despite heavy resistance in the Bamban area, about midway between Lingayen and Manila, Sixth Army soldiers captured Clark Field on January 26. As Krueger's forced pushed south toward Manila, troops from Lt. Gen. Robert L. Eichhelberger's Eighth Army made a combined amphibious–airborne assault south of Manila. Men of two of the 11th Airborne glider infantry regiments, the 188th and the 187th, landed without opposition at Nasugbu, southwest of Manila, on January 31.

On February 3 troopers of the division's 511th Parachute Infantry Regiment dropped on Tagaytay Ridge, again with little opposition, and quickly joined up with the glidermen. From there, the 11th Airborne Division pressed northward toward Manila. The Japanese in Manila were caught between the pincers of the Sixth Army and the Eighth Army, but like so many of their countrymen in other battles, the men of the Shimbu Group fought tenaciously. Some escaped to the east, where they remained serious threats to the security of Manila. Those who stayed made the capture of Manila a hard, slogging, bloody struggle. MacArthur announced on February 5 that the assault phase of the Luzon campaign was completed, but it took another month of terrible house-to-house fighting before Manila was considered clear of the enemy. In the process, the "Pearl of the Orient" was virtually destroyed, and some 100,000 Filipino civilians were killed. Actually, the Luzon campaign itself was not termed officially over until midnight of June 30/July 1, and even then fighting continued for some weeks afterward.

Throughout this period the Air Commandos' light planes were active in support of the Sixth Army. Because the 3rd ACG's liaison squadrons were based several miles from the rest of the group at Mangaldan, Olson decided to restructure his group temporarily. A Light Plane Section composed of the three liaison squadrons and their ADS was established under the command of Kalberer, the group's former executive officer. With "everyone on Luzon (wanting) our L-5s," according Olson, this arrangement proved the most efficient way to meet all the requests for their services. About the same time, the other flying squadrons and their ADSs were also restructured into fighter and transport sections. Although Calasaio remained the liaison squadrons primary field, detachments numbering from two to seven aircraft were soon scattered all over Luzon, Mindoro, Panay, and Negros. These detachments usually had one or two pilots and a mechanic assigned per aircraft. Much of the work performed by these detachments involved the evacuation of wounded soldiers, courier flights, and supply missions.[20]

With such a heavy schedule of flights, it was not long before the liaison squadrons suffered losses. The first light plane lost in combat came from the 159th LS. SSgt. Donald P. McDonell was flying a courier mission on February 10 with an engineer officer in the back seat. As he flew over Nichols Field, southeast of Manila, enemy ground fire riddled his aircraft. Both of his plane's wingtips were blown off, and McDonell suffered wounds to a knee and wrist. In spite of his painful injuries, McDonell coaxed his plane back to the recently captured

Grace Park Field in Manila's northern suburbs. McDonell recovered from his wounds, but his L-5 was declared a total loss.[21]

A much more serious loss was suffered by the 318th TCS four days later. Since their arrival on Luzon, the squadron's C-47s had been flying constantly, carrying cargo and passengers, evacuating wounded, and making supply drops to ground forces. These latter drops became known as the "Biscuit Bomber" missions. Weather, turbulence, mountains that often surrounded the drop zones, and enemy ground fire made these flights very dangerous. First Lt. Thomas P. Snecker and his crew of five were dropping supplies to guerillas supporting the advance of the 1st Cavalry Division. The drop zone was near Antipolo, in the hills east of Manila.

There was some concern when the C-47 did not return to Mangaldan at its scheduled time, but aircraft could be delayed for all sorts of reasons. As the afternoon lengthened, however, it was apparent that something was wrong. Fighters were dispatched to search for the missing C-47, but weather precluded a systematic search. The next day, when the weather lifted, another search took off, and a sad discovery was made. The burned-out hulk of a C-47 was spotted lying on the side of a mountain. Guerillas in the area radioed that no one on the plane had survived. About all that could be found in the charred wreckage were ID bracelets and dog tags.

Yes, biscuit bombing was a dangerous undertaking, but the pilots and crews knew that. They also knew that it was absolutely necessary if the Allied infantrymen were going to prevail over the stubborn enemy.[22]

For the fighter pilots, the move to Mangaldan meant new tasks and new hunting grounds. Much of their time would be spent flying close support missions for infantrymen. Manila had been the prize since the invasion of Luzon began, and, thus, the drive toward the capital had been on a rather narrow front. Both of the Sixth Army's flanks were often hanging out in the open as the GIs fought south. The time would come soon enough when the Sixth Army turned back north to assault Yamashita's stronghold, and the Air Commandos would help in that endeavor. But for the time being they were needed to protect the Sixth's open flanks.

The 4th Fighter Squadron started this part of the Air Commando's tasks on January 28, when they attacked possible enemy positions northeast of Manila. From then until even after the campaign was declared over, the 3rd ACG kept busy providing much-appreciated close air support to the infantry.[23]

Two more ground support missions were flown the following day. The late-morning mission by sixteen aircraft of the 4th Fighter Squadron produced excellent results. The Mustangs attacked several villages east of Plaridel that were thought to be harboring the enemy. Except for a couple of near misses, all of the 500-pounders dropped by the Air Commandos landed on target. One bomb hit on a school building produced a spectacular cloud of yellow-brown smoke that shot up over seven hundred feet. Group intelligence officers thought the color of the smoke indicated that chemicals of some sort had been stored in the school.[24]

The month of February opened with an unusual mission for the Air Commandos. A pair of enemy ships, identified as a *Terutsuki*-class destroyer and a destroyer escort, had been sighted heading south in the Luzon Strait between Formosa and Luzon. The 3rd ACG was directed to get them.

Twenty-two Mustangs gathered from both fighter squadrons were loaded with 500-pound bombs and took off in the afternoon. The planes found the ships just before 6:00 PM. In a wild melee the fighters scored two direct hits and five near misses on the larger vessel and two hits on the smaller one. Strafing runs added to the enemy sailors' misery. Fires broke out on both ships, but the enemy's damage control was good, and the fires were quickly extinguished.

When the P-51s left, the destroyer was proceeding slowly toward Luzon, while her escort raced ahead. It had not been a one-sided battle. The Japanese gunners were good, and they holed several of the attackers. Two fighters went down following the action, but both pilots were recovered. After the war, when checking enemy records, American intelligence officers discovered that the "destroyer" and "destroyer escort" were actually the landing ship T.115, which eventually sank, and the submarine chaser Ch 28, which escaped, though damaged.[25]

Meanwhile, the new hunting grounds for the group lay about 230 miles north of Luzon, on the island of Formosa. This enemy bastion was dotted with numerous airfields, and several harbors provided excellent anchorages for Japanese naval units and merchant vessels. There would be no close air support missions over Formosa. Instead, the 3rd ACG's fighters flew fighter sweeps and antishipping strikes and escorted the bombers pounding away at the island. Formosa was no picnic. "The A/A over Formosa is the real McCoy," the group historian stated. "The Japs on Formosa are no amateurs at using this as our planes encountered it every time they went there."[26] Four Air Commandos would be lost to the flak, and four more would be shot down but recovered. Yes, Formosa was a dangerous place.

February 7 was the day the Air Commandos first became acquainted with Formosa. That day the 3rd ACG's two fighter squadrons escorted B-25s making a shipping strike off the island's southwest coast. When no enemy planes put in an appearance, the Mustangs went after targets of opportunity. The bombers and fighters joined to destroy a small submarine in Takao Harbor and then

damaged several merchant vessels.[27] The Takao airfield was also visited by the
Air Commandos. Of interest on the airfield were fifteen new Japanese fighters,
possibly Ki-84 Franks, adorned with bright white noses. Several enemy aircraft
were claimed damaged, and a number of vehicles were destroyed. Unfortunately,
the mission also revealed that the enemy could hit back.[28]

As 2nd Lt. Clifford Huntington and 2nd Lt. Marvin Menter made their
runs on the airfield, antiaircraft fire holed their planes. At first it appeared that
Huntington's Mustang had received the worst of it. A shell had burst directly
under his seat, leaving a gaping hole underneath and disabling his landing gear.
Menter, on the other hand, seemed to have suffered nothing more than minor
damage to one wing. On the way back to the rendezvous point, however, Menter
radioed Huntington that his oil pressure was dropping and that he was going to
bail out. About seventeen miles offshore, Menter jumped and was seen climbing
into his life raft. The water was very choppy, and by the time a Catalina could
reach him, it was dark. A search the next morning did not turn up any trace of
the young flier.[29]

Some retribution for Menter's loss was attained by Lieutenant Curdes, of
the 4th Squadron. Thirty miles from Formosa Curdes spotted a twin-engine
Dinah at about his own altitude. The enemy pilot evidently saw the Americans at
the same time, for he suddenly dove for the deck and went to full throttle. A tail
chase ensued and lasted for several minutes before Curdes could open fire. A few
bursts was all it took; the Dinah became a smear of flame coating the water.[30]

Planes from both of the 3rd ACG's fighter squadrons were out the following day, again escorting B-25s to a shipping strike at Formosa. Poor weather,
however, forced the cancellation of the mission, and all aircraft returned to
Luzon to attack secondary targets. The twelve P-51s of the 4th Fighter Squadron strafed enemy installations on the Philippine island of Fuga on their way
home, noting that the Japanese trenches looked like "spider webs" extending
over the ground.

Meanwhile, some Mustangs of the 3rd Fighter Squadron ran across a Sally
also heading for Luzon. A flight led by Lieutenant Lairmore had been late in
getting off the ground and never joined the rest of the squadron. When the
recall was broadcast Lairmore led his flight back toward home. Soon, the enemy
bomber was sighted some distance ahead making a slow climb toward an overcast layer at about nine hundred feet. Dropping their wing tanks, Lairmore and
his wingman slowly overtook the Sally. The pair boxed in the bomber, one on
each side, and Lairmore made a 20-degree deflection shot from two hundred
yards. His shells went completely through the Sally, shattering its cockpit and set-

ting the opposite engine on fire. The bomber burst into flames, nosed over, and went into the sea. Lairmore had fired just one hundred rounds for his victory.[31]

On the morning of the February 10 Curdes led three other pilots on a search mission for some missing pilots. A run along the west coast of Formosa turned up nothing except a lone Dinah. Like so many of his comrades, the enemy pilot made little effort to evade his attackers. Second Lt. Robert Scalley made quick work of the Dinah. A 20-degree deflection shot set the plane's right engine on fire; a second pass set the other engine aflame, and the Dinah crashed into the water.

With no luck so far finding the missing fliers, Curdes split his flight so as to cover a wider area. While Curdes and his wingman went one way, Scalley and 2nd Lt. Robert LaCroix checked out Bataan Island, one of a string of smaller islands between Luzon and Formosa. As the pair neared Bataan they ran across yet another Dinah. It was LaCroix's turn this time. A couple of bursts, and the enemy plane joined its sister aircraft at the bottom of the sea. The two fliers were not finished. Several aircraft, including some apparently new Tonys, were seen parked on Bataan's airstrip, and Scalley and LaCroix went down to strafe them. Three of the Tonys were claimed destroyed, but the Japanese had their revenge. Accurate flak pummeled LaCroix's fighter. Hot coolant and smoke filled his cockpit, and the Air Commando decided it was time to leave.

It proved more difficult getting out of his plane than he had anticipated, though. LaCroix had forgotten to roll in enough trim, so when he rolled over to drop from his fighter, it stayed with him, and he became wedged between the seat back's armor plate and the rear of his cockpit. The ocean was coming up fast, and a desperate kick on his control stick popped him out and away from the plane. When he pulled the ripcord of his parachute, it seemed to him that it took forever for the chute to open. But open it did, and he plopped into the water, where he was able to scramble out of his chute and inflate his life raft. LaCroix then discovered that, one, he had a bullet hole in his ankle, and, two, the Japanese on Bataan were firing at him. Scalley, in the meantime, had called for help.

Curdes and his wingman were quickly on the scene and proceeded to beat up the Japanese guns while Scalley kept an eye on LaCroix. What happened next was one of the more bizarre and, in hindsight, amusing, incidents of the war. As the Americans were finishing their strafing runs, a wandering C-47 suddenly appeared. The transport was from the 39th TCS and had been en route to Clark Field from Leyte. Up until reaching the south end of Manila Bay, the weather had been clear and the flight uneventful. Clouds then began building, and the transport pilots were soon flying on instruments. They realized they were lost shortly before noon; all they could see in the breaks in the clouds was water. Turning east, they let down slowly until some small islands were sighted. They could see an airstrip on one of the islands. Not realizing that the Japanese held the island and, if they did see the P-51s, perhaps thinking they were just "beating up" the strip, the transport pilots decided to land before running out of gas. Lowering the landing gear, they prepared to land.

About this time Curdes noticed the strange C-47 approaching the airfield. He tried to contact it but received no reply. Unsure that the C-47 was American but unwilling to chance a mistake, Curdes fired a warning burst across the transport's nose. This caught the attention of the crew, who made a sharp left turn but then headed back toward the island. Curdes next made a head-on firing pass, striking the C-47's right engine. A second pass from the rear knocked out the plane's other engine. The C-47 crew made a remarkably smooth ditching about three hundred yards offshore, and all twelve people on board, including two nurses, scrambled into three rafts.

As soon as they got into the rafts, the Americans were fired on by the Japanese. The enemy's gunfire was wild, though, and the crew stayed well away from the island throughout the remainder of the day. Curdes circled the survivors for about an hour before he and the other Air Commandos headed back to Mangaldan. Air–Sea Rescue was notified of the C-47's ditching, but because of approaching darkness, it would be the next day before they could be on the scene. In the meantime, the 39th TCS crew and passengers put up sails on the rafts and, by oar and wind power, were able to put about six miles between them and Bataan.

Rough seas kicked up in the morning, and the survivors decided the waters near the island would be calmer. A short time later they pulled LaCroix from the water, and he explained what had happened. Just a few minutes later a Catalina rescue plane touched down and recovered everyone. A short investigation followed, and Curdes was absolved of any blame. Actually, his quick thinking and accurate shooting prevented a disaster, and he was rewarded with a Distinguished Flying Cross. Too, his Mustang soon sported a new victory symbol to go with the German, Italian, and Japanese flags that recorded his victories—an American flag![32]

While Formosa continued to be visited regularly by the Air Commandos, air support of the ground troops was flown just as steadily. The airmen became very familiar with places carrying names like Baguio, Antipolo, Balete Pass, Tuguerarao, and the Villa Verde Trail. Invariably, the bombing of enemy positions brought high praise from the infantrymen. Such activities, though, were not usually satisfying to the fliers. Seldom did they get clear looks at their targets. It was only after a forward air controller reported "bombs on target" or some like phrase that the Air Commandos felt like they were accomplishing something.

Results from missions to Formosa, conversely, were more clear-cut. Buildings could be seen destroyed, locomotives could be spotted exploding, and vehicles and aircraft could be seen blazing on the ground. For example, on February 18 six "Hell-raising Fighters" of the 3rd ACG, as the Fifth Air Force's historian colorfully stated, swept over rail yards on Formosa's east coast. When they were finished they left behind nine locomotives, a railway station, a water tower, a railway crane, and a streetcar destroyed. Another eleven locomotives, many boxcars, and several warehouses were damaged. Although the flak was plentiful, none came near the attackers.[33]

Usually, the flak encountered over Formosa was far more deadly than that met over Luzon. But it was not always so. On February 22 sixteen Mustangs of the 4th Fighter Squadron bombed and strafed the village of Angin. As one pilot made his strafing run, ground fire could be seen erupting from the trees, and the pilot was apparently hit, for he made no attempt to pull up. His aircraft plowed into the ground, and he was killed instantly.[34] Three days later the antiaircraft guns on Formosa made a strong statement, reminding the Air Commandos that they were not to be taken for granted.

Sixteen P-51s of the 3rd Fighter Squadron made a fighter sweep of Formosa's east coast on February 25. At Garan-Bi on the island's southern tip, a radar station and several gun emplacements were strafed. The enemy defenders were very good, holing three aircraft and knocking down another pair. Flight Officer Sylvester Everhart made it only about one-half mile offshore before he bailed out. After he entered the water, it appeared that he was having trouble getting loose from his parachute shroud lines. It also looked as though his life raft fell apart when he attempted to inflate it. The circling planes lost sight of Everhart in the tossing seas, and when an Air–Sea Rescue Catalina landed to pick him up, all that was found was a glove and a piece of life raft.

Meanwhile, 1st Lt. Scott M. Alexander had nursed his fighter about thirty miles out before he, too, had to bail out. His exit from his doomed aircraft was nerve-wracking. First, his foot caught under his seat, and he had several frantic seconds before he was able to extricate himself. Then, as he fell free, his leg struck the horizontal stabilizer, which broke his leg. Despite the intense pain Alexander was able to inflate his Mae West. Like Sylvester's, Alexander's raft also failed to inflate. This time, though, the outcome was more successful. The Catalina soon picked Alexander up, beginning the first leg of a trip back to the United States.

Upon their return to Mangaldan, one of the damaged 3rd Fighter Squadron's planes cracked up on landing, fortunately without injury to the pilot. With two planes shot down, one crashing on landing, and two more suffering minor damage, February 25 had not been a good day.[35]

March saw a number of personnel changes in the 3rd ACG, as Olson reorganized the group, and individuals were promoted or left for assignments elsewhere. In addition to forming a Light Planes Section, Olson merged the other ADSs with their respective flying squadrons. The 3rd Fighter Squadron and the 334th ADS became the 3rd Fighter Section. The 4th Fighter Squadron and the 335th ADS were combined into the 4th Fighter Section, and the 318th TCS and the 343rd ADS became the Troop Carrier Section. Among the more significant personnel moves were the transfer of group operations officer Richardson to the 308th Bombardment Wing, where he replaced Alison as wing operations officer when Alison moved up to the Fifth Air Force, and Mahurin becoming the new group operations officer and being replaced as 3rd Fighter Section commander by Captain Adams. Also, Kalberer was officially appointed commanding officer of the Light Planes Section, which was a position he had already been holding for several weeks.

The liaison squadrons also saw command changes. The 160th's commander, Maj. John E. Satterstrom, was named group air inspector. His place was taken by Capt. Richard R. Lawton, formerly the 157th's operations officer. The 157th also underwent a changeover as Capt. Michael Tomaro assumed command, and the former commander, Capt. Clarence L. Odum, moved to group headquarters as assistant operations officer. Additionally, Capt. George Nallou moved from the 4th Fighter Squadron to the 335th ADS to become its commander, while the 335th's former commander, Capt. Samuel O. Sartor, switched over to lead the 343rd ADS.[36]

The month also saw nearly 95 percent of the 3rd ACG's activities focused on close air support. That the front lines were still not that far from Mangaldan was underscored on March 1, when the Mustangs attacked enemy positions on the Villa Verde Trail. The trail ran from the vicinity of San Nicolas (about twenty-five miles from Mangaldan) to the village of Santa Fe on Route 5 north of Balete Pass. The trail crossed some of the roughest terrain on Luzon, and the GIs were always grateful for the air support they received from the Air Commandos. This day, sixteen P-51s planted 500-pound bombs squarely on target and started a large grass fire whose smoke could be seen back at Mangaldan.[37]

Although enemy planes had snooped over Mangaldan several times in the last two months, they usually caused little more than sleepless nights. This was not the case on March 2. Shortly before 1:00 AM a red alert was sounded, followed by an all clear a few minutes later. Most everyone at the field settled back down to sleep. Then, about two hours later, four Japanese bombers swept in over the field and dropped both fragmentation and demolition bombs throughout the camp areas and on the taxiway. An ammunition dump went up with a roar, one Marine SBD was destroyed, another SBD was damaged, four men were killed, and seventy-eight more men were wounded, none Air Commandos. Up to this time, because enemy air activity had become rare, the men had become somewhat lax in digging foxholes and slit trenches. The attack reawakened their burrowing instincts, however, and numerous deep holes quickly appeared over the next couple of days.[38]

The bombs did only minor damage to the taxiway, and Mangaldan's runway was untouched, so the full schedules all units had for March 2 were followed as planned. For the Air Commandos this meant sending thirty-two mustangs, sixteen from each section, to escort B-24s to Formosa. There was no aerial inter-ference, so the fighters went low to strafe rail lines and installations. Even this activity failed to arouse much interest from the Japanese, and all ACG planes returned unscathed.[39]

The 3rd ACG had pioneered two-ship takeoffs in the Philippines. Now they led the way again. Mangaldan was a crowded field. In addition to the Air Commandos, the Marine Aircraft Group 24, the Marine Aircraft Group 32, the 38th BG, and the 312th BG were shoehorned in. Normal one-ship takeoffs were excruciatingly long affairs. The field's runway was one hundred feet wide, which the Air Commandos decided was more than wide enough for four-ship takeoffs. After some wrangling with the field commander, a Marine colonel, permission was given to make the four-ship takeoffs. It was evident that the ACG's take-offs were the most efficient way of conducting these operations, and the other groups on the field soon followed suit. Not long after, other units throughout the Philippines also adopted the procedure.[40]

A new vista, if it could be described as such, opened up to the Air Com-mandos in March. The fighter sections flew several missions to the China coast. Other than allowing the pilots to see new sights, these missions were uneventful. Close support missions, on the other hand, always provided some excitement, as the 4th Fighter Section's Lahmeyer discovered on March 17.

Normally when bombing, the Mustang pilots liked to drop down from about 10,000 feet in a steep dive. This altitude gave them plenty of room to pull up. A cloud deck at six thousand feet this day, however, meant coming in lower and flatter. Not wanting to haul their bombs back home, the fliers decided to attack anyway. As Lahmeyer pulled up after dropping his bombs, he felt a bump and heard a popping noise. Something was not right, but other than the popping sound, his engine kept ticking over. Then he noticed a puff of smoke come over his wing in unison with the popping. Flames suddenly shot back past the wing. "That was bad," he recalled.

Pushing back his canopy, he rolled his plane over and dropped out. When he saw the tail section flash by, he pulled his ripcord. As he did, his P-51 exploded. Lahmeyer landed backwards in an open field. He did a somersault, bounced onto his feet, and spilled the air out of his parachute. Not knowing where he was, Lahmeyer ran to the top of a hill to get his bearings. There, he found an Army personnel carrier with men from an artillery unit. They took him to their outfit, gave him a beer, and sent him on to division headquarters. Lahmeyer asked the division commander if he could spare an L-5 to take him back to Mangaldan. The general said sure, and within an hour, Lahmeyer was back home.[41]

The group lost another pair of fighters on March 29 during an attack on enemy troops along the Villa Verde Trail. As the two P-51s pulled out of their runs, they collided. Both pilots were able to get out of their fatally damaged planes, however, and were picked up later by friendly troops.[42]

As March came to a close Fifth Air Force headquarters was busy planning a major move for the Air Commandos and, for that matter, all of the units based at Mangaldan. The monsoon season was approaching, and the rains would make Mangaldan, with its high water table, unsuitable for operations. What the high brass planned for the 3rd ACG was a move more fitting with the group's originally planned mission.

Chapter 16

Behind Enemy Lines

T he town of Laoag, located about 150 miles north of Mangaldan, was one of the largest in northern Luzon. It had been one of the first Filipino towns to fall to the Japanese in December 1941, being captured on December 11. The Japanese maintained an airfield near Laoag throughout the war.

When the Americans returned to the Philippines, some eight thousand troops defended northwest Luzon, most in the vicinity of Laoag and Vigan, which lay about forty-five miles south of Laoag. Most of these men, however, were not combat troops; rather, they were mainly garrison soldiers manning service units. The long occupation had softened them, and they were ripe for picking. In their midst and ready to exploit this softness was a U.S. Army Forces in the Philippines (Northern Luzon), or USAFIP(NL), guerilla regiment. This regiment was led by Army officers who had not surrendered when the Philippines had fallen to the Japanese. While not armed as well as their adversaries, the guerillas were better led and had a deeper desire to fight.

Just days after the Lingayen landings, the guerillas struck in force. By mid-February the Japanese had been pushed back in several areas, and the guerillas had entered Laoag. The Japanese retreated south to Vigan and inland into the mountains. Seeking to exploit the situation the Fifth Air Force directed the 318th TCS's C-47s to fly supplies in to the guerillas. The airfield the Air Commandos were to use, known either as Gabu or the Laoag Airdrome, was located between the mouths of the Laoag River and Gabu River. It was in pretty shabby shape. The Japanese had not maintained it properly for some time, and filled-in shell holes pockmarked the runway. These holes had not been tamped down well and remained soft. This caused the loss of one of the C-47s when its tail wheel dug into a soft spot, and the plane ground looped. Beyond repair, the aircraft was salvaged by the 318th, and its parts were used as replacements for items not in stock.[1]

Enemy ordnance also littered the area. One of the 318th's pilots found out that much of this ordnance was still live. As he took off for return to Mangaldan, he discovered enemy land mines exploding just behind his transport. This served to make his takeoff much faster, but the guerillas had to comb the airstrip much more carefully for land mines.[2]

Utilizing Gabu enabled the Fifth Air Force to extend its reach toward Formosa and the Chinese mainland. One of the first units sent to Gabu was a communications detachment from the 334th ADS. The eight enlisted men and one officer who were dispatched flew in to the field on March 5. There they set up VHF and HF radio facilities, as well as a direction finder station. In late March officers representing each of the 3rd ACG sections flew to Gabu to stake out bivouac and operations areas for their men.

Because the airstrip was still not in good shape, the group's C-47s flew in an aviation engineer unit to rehabilitate the runway. The ground at Gabu was more suitable for construction than what existed at Mangaldan, but dust was always a problem, and a 5,100-foot asphalt and gravel runway, a parallel taxiway, and extensive hardstands were built. Meanwhile, the problem of keeping Mangaldan operational during rainy periods was driven home on April 4. A heavy rain fell, which shut down the field for several days because the water would not drain. Thus, there was some urgency about completing the construction at Gabu; Mangaldan would be of little use when the rainy season began in earnest.[3]

Runway construction moved ahead rapidly, and the 3rd ACG began packing for its move in early April. It took about twelve days to move all of the units, less the liaison squadrons, with most of their equipment and personnel to Gabu. As had become typical with so many Air Commando operations, the liaison squadrons operated separately from the rest of the group. Most of the light planes, which had been flying from Calasiao, moved to Mabalacat Field near Clark Field on the last day of April. Small liaison detachments also operated from other fields on Luzon, as well as from Mindoro, Negros, and Panay.

The 318th TCS's C-47s did most of the lifting for the move, although aircraft of the 39th TCS provided additional help. Except for one serious incident, the move went off without a hitch. The incident, however, came close to being a disaster. A C-47 of the 39th TCS was taking off from Mangaldan when its right engine cut out. The sudden loss of power caused the airplane to swerve, and its wing caught the ground. The transport crashed and burst into flames, but fast action by men on the ground saved all aboard, mainly pilots from the 4th Fighter Section.[4]

Group headquarters was established in San Nicolas, a small town about six miles from the Gabu field. The headquarters offices were on the ground floor of a school, and while plans for combat were made on that floor, children still attended classes on the building's second floor. Most of the section housing areas, consisting mainly of bamboo shacks with tent coverings, were located about three miles from Gabu. Olson, promoted to a full bird colonel on April 8, was the field commander for Gabu, which soon became the home of numerous other units in addition to the Air Commandos.

Not long after the 3rd ACG finished flying its aircraft, personnel, and light equipment in to Gabu, an overland route was established between Lingayen and Laoag. The first road convoy between the two points in three years left Lingayen on April 27. Protection for the convoy, which was hauling heavy equipment, was provided by the guerillas. No Japanese put in an appearance, for they were more interested in heading east toward the main Japanese positions. Still, because of many destroyed bridges, the 175-mile journey lasted almost two days. This trip, however, showed there was now little danger from the enemy and, indeed, the entire west coast of Luzon was now in friendly hands. For that matter, the trip resembled something more like a victory parade. As the convoy passed through various towns, provincial governors turned out in their finery to meet their "liberators." Laughing children chased the trucks, and young women waved shyly at the Americans. Other Filipinos wept openly, realizing that they were finally free of their oppressors. The group's time "behind enemy lines" had lasted less than a month.[5]

The move to Gabu did not mean that the Air Commandos' aerial activities had halted. Missions continued to be flown from Mangaldan, and the switch to operations from Gabu proceeded flawlessly. In fact, when the 3rd Fighter Section moved, sixteen of its Mustangs were loaded with bombs and ammunition at Mangaldan, flew a strike on Baguio, then landed at their new field. The following day the section escorted B-24s to Formosa. The switch in fields had not cost a day of operations.

Fighter sweeps continued to be flown to Formosa, as well, with missions on April 1, April 22, and April 26 being particularly productive. On these three days the Mustangs destroyed twenty-three trucks, eight locomotives, and many enemy facilities.[6] For the fighter pilots, however, aerial combat was their *raison d'être*, and on April 2 they showed they had not lost their touch despite not having encountered an enemy plane in the air for three months.

Twelve 3rd Fighter Section Mustangs escorted B-24s on a shipping strike to Hong Kong that day. Shortly after rendezvousing with the bombers near the target, two Zekes were spotted. These began a head-on pass on the P-51s, which were lined up in three flights in trail. Seeing the Zekes trying to bounce them, the first Air Commando flight dove away, leaving the second flight to handle the enemy. Unable to continue their pass on the first Mustangs, the Japanese pilots shifted their attention to the second flight. Led by Lairmore, the Americans traded shots with the enemy before one of the Zekes broke off its attack. The other enemy pilot, however, whipped his agile fighter around and got on 2nd Lt. Joseph Singletary's tail. Unable to drop his external fuel tanks, Singletary was in a vulnerable position and screamed for help.

When the enemy planes zoomed past, 2nd Lt. Barrett D. Wagner broke left, then whipped his Mustang back behind Singletary's pursuer. Now the prey, not the hunter, the Zeke pilot tried to dive away. Wagner closed swiftly and began firing as the two aircraft passed through three thousand feet. He noticed his tracers sparkling on the enemy fighter's fuselage and wing root. Expecting his adversary to pull out, Wagner stayed high. He watched as the Zeke pilot belatedly realized how close he was to the water. The Zeke banked slightly, then made a sharp turn. Its wing caught the water, and suddenly there was a welter of spray, foam, and debris as the Zeke disintegrated.

Meanwhile, Lairmore, who had reformed the rest of his flight at 12,000 feet, saw two more Zekes heading away from him. Just as he began to chase them, they turned back in a head-on pass. Lairmore began firing at about six hundred yards and saw pieces of one of the Zeke's cowling break off. The Zeke rolled over and spiraled downward. Lairmore lost sight of his victim when he noticed his wingman was no longer with him.

As he searched the sky for his missing mate, Lairmore sighted the other Zeke below him making a run on a flight of Mustangs. He dove on this plane, opening fire at eight hundred yards and continuing until he was just twenty-five yards distant. The Zeke rolled over on its back, then began spinning earthward. The spin continued from eight thousand feet until Lairmore lost sight of the second Zeke in the haze and smoke at one thousand feet. With no more enemy fighters present and the B-24s finished with their job, the Air Commandos reformed and headed back to Mangaldan.

Wagner, who had only nineteen hours of combat time, received credit for one Zeke destroyed, while Lairmore got two probables. The only damage suffered by the Air Commandos in this fight was a single bullet hole through the spinner of one Mustang.[7]

Except for an uneventful trip to Hong Kong on April 13 and a few equally boring missions to Formosa, the Air Commando fighters spent the remainder of their stay at Gabu flying close support missions for the 32nd Infantry Division and working its way painfully over very difficult terrain along the Villa Verde Trail. Often, the infantrymen were just yards from enemy positions, which was too close to be supported according to conventional wisdom for air attacks.

Knowing that his men already had a good working relationship with the GIs, however, Olson was confident his fliers could make such strikes. To test this trust Olson sent his flight leaders to the front lines to work with the ground commanders of the 32nd. After examining the terrain and consulting with the infantrymen, the pilots convinced the soldiers that the Air Commandos could do the job. They then returned to the airfield, carefully briefed the other pilots, and proceeded to fly a highly successful mission. To the delight of the men of the 32nd Division, such cooperation soon became standard operating procedure.[8]

The work of the 3rd ACG was greatly appreciated by the 32nd's commander, Maj. Gen. William H. Gill, who wrote a letter of commendation to Olson. In it he stated:

> The close support strikes accomplished by the men of your command have been most gratifying to me. These attacks have materially aided the advance of the 32nd Infantry Division troops along the Villa Verde Trail and other fields of battle in northern Luzon. . . . The bombings have been precise and accurate; their strafing runs have been to my mind perfection itself. . . . It is my belief that this is the first time that pilots of the supporting air arm have visited the forward ground units in the combat zone to view the terrain and study the tactical situation in the area they are to be employed. To my knowledge it is the first time that such action has been undertaken by the pilots own volition.
>
> The daring and aggressiveness displayed by the Third Air Commando Group is indeed gratifying to myself and the men of my command. I am proud to say I have had them as a supporting arm to my offensive in the northern Luzon campaign.[9]

The Japanese were not the only enemy the Air Commandos faced on Luzon. On April 21, Captain George Nallou, the 335th ADS's commander, contracted polio. Initially confined to his quarters and then moved to the hospital at Lingayen, he died just five days later. Nallou was just the first of several Air Commando and Fifth Air Force personnel to come down with polio during a mini-epidemic of the disease. The 318th TCS and its ADS, the 343rd, was hardest hit by the epidemic. Four cases were diagnosed in the two units in early May, with one Air Commando, Cpl. Robert Davis, dying. Fortunately, just as quickly as the polio had appeared, it disappeared.[10]

Meanwhile, as the fighter sections and the 318th TCS continued working from Gabu, the liaison sections were operating in somewhat of an organizational limbo, virtually isolated from the rest of the group. Throughout the spring the

L-5s evacuated the wounded and the sick (for the 157th LS this totaled 2,104 individuals for April alone), dropped food and medical supplies to the infantry, directed artillery fire and air strikes, ferried officers from place to place, and performed all manner of other tasks. Not typical, but indicative of what the light planes were called upon to do, were missions flown by 157th aircraft to lay a telephone line between two mountaintops and to broadcast propaganda to Japanese troops.

In the first instance, an officer sat in the backseat of the L-5 reeling out the line through an inspection hole in the belly of the aircraft while the pilot successfully flew through turbulent air at just above stalling speed. In the second, loudspeakers were mounted on the wings of an L-5 and a record player was carried by a passenger in its back seat. Then, while the pilot slowly circled over Japanese strongpoints, well within gunfire range, the passenger played surrender propaganda to the Japanese on the ground. These missions were successful; not all ended as happily.[11]

On April 11 MSgt. Oliver M. Edwards, a pilot with the 159th LS, was carrying an infantry officer on a mission to drop supplies to an isolated patrol on Negros when their plane was shot down. Although their L-5 was spotted from the air and cries for help were heard by the patrol, neither man was seen again. In the 160th LS SSgt. Earl Y. Edmonds disappeared in bad weather on April 4 while on a supply mission from Legaspi, Luzon, to San Jose, Mindoro. Several other liaison pilots were also killed or disappeared while on missions.[12]

With the intense workload they were under, the liaison sections were very grateful for additional help. It came in the guise of the little-used and frustrated glider pilots and mechanics of the 318th TCS. Apart from their temporary use earlier as C-47 copilots, these fliers had seen little employment. Attempts by the Fifth Air Force to find positions generally failed, so Olson sought other avenues in which to use these men.

Following Nallou's death one of the 318th's glider pilots, 1st Lt. Earle Hyatt, was made commander of the 335th ADS, and he served with distinction. Others were placed in various ground jobs at group headquarters and with the other squadrons.

However, it was at the insistence of Kalberer, commander of the Light Plane Section, that many of the glider pilots and mechanics really got the opportunity to show what they could do. In mid-April the liaison sections received a few glider pilots and mechanics on detached service from the 318th. They did so well that Kalberer requested more. Although their primary duties would be on the ground, the pilots would also be checked out on the L-5s, thus enabling the light plane pilots to get some much needed rest from their grueling schedules.

The mechanics, meanwhile, would help the overworked liaison mechanics maintain their aircraft, which by May now included UC-64s. It had taken longer than expected for these bigger aircraft to arrive, but the two UC-64s each squadron received were swiftly put to good use.[13]

The hectic pace at which the liaison sections were operating, along with their isolation from the rest of the 3rd ACG, created administrative headaches that were only overcome when the Fifth Air Force assumed control of the liaison section and the 341st ADS on May 3. On that date the 5th Air Liaison Group Commando (Provisional) was formed and assigned to V Fighter Command. The group was placed under the operational control of the 308th Bombardment Wing, but it was returned to the administrative control of the 3rd ACG on June 29. Kalberer remained in command of the new group, which was really just an extension of the old Light Plane Section. The result of these moves was that the new group had the authority to perform all administrative and operational functions of a group, which produced noticeable savings of time and paperwork.[14]

The 3rd ACG also underwent a change in administrative control when it was removed from under the 86th Fighter Wing and assigned directly to V Fighter Command on May 16. Nearly two weeks later it ended its longtime association with the 308th Bombardment Wing and was placed under the operational control of the 309th Bombardment Wing. These changes made little difference in the group's daily operations, which continued at a breakneck pace. Close support for the infantry remained a high priority, but missions to Formosa continued to be flown.[15]

May proved especially deadly to the 3rd ACG fighter pilots. During a fighter sweep by the 4th Fighter Section along Formosa's east coast on the first day of the month, 2nd Lt. Robert M. McNeill apparently carried his attack on a bus too low, and his plane crashed into the bus, careened into a telegraph pole, then plowed into the ground in a ball of fire. No pilots were lost on the next few missions, but 1st Lt. Kenneth Ogden was seriously injured during an attack on an airfield near Okayama, Japan on May 11. As he and Curdes flashed past a truck convoy they had been strafing, an enemy shell slammed into Ogden's cockpit and ripped into his leg. Despite the intense pain of his wound, Ogden nursed his plane back to Gabu and a safe landing.[16]

On May 19 thirty Air Commando Mustangs attacked the Heito Airdrome on Formosa. Although none of the planes appeared to have been hit, 1st Lt. Durward J. Fortier had to bail out of his fighter because of a coolant leak. He landed in the water a few miles southwest of the small island of Ryukyu Sho and was picked up by a rescue sub within thirty minutes. Because the sub remained on station, it took two weeks before Fortier was put ashore. During his enforced stay on the sub, however, its captain let him speak to the Air Commandos as they flew back and forth between Formosa and Luzon.[17]

Several other pilots were not as lucky. On a fighter sweep along Formosa's west coast on May 30, 2nd Lt. Joseph T. Bulack and his element leader had great success busting locomotives near Hokuwan. After making a second pass on a bus, the pair turned back out to sea. During the turn the element leader lost sight of Bulack, who was never seen again despite a long search.[18]

The next day was even more costly, when the 4th Fighter Section sent sixteen Mustangs on another fighter sweep of Formosa. The Air Commandos enjoyed good hunting, destroying nine trucks and five locomotives and damaging several more vehicles. Enemy ground fire was not heavy, but it was very accurate. Four P-51s of A Flight had flown up the island's eastern shore at low level with little trouble, but almost as soon as they turned inland to head back south, enemy small arms fire erupted and 1st Lt. Fergus Mead Jr.'s plane was hit. The plane began to spiral earthward. Being only a couple of hundred feet above the ground, Mead had no chance to bail out before he crashed. A Flight's ordeal was not over yet, however.

The remaining fliers continued south and were about to turn out to sea when Flight Officer Bernard H. Moncrief felt a burning sensation in his right leg as his cockpit filled with acrid smoke. He had been hit by an antiaircraft gun firing from almost directly underneath his plane. Moncrief immediately released his canopy and yanked his stick back in a desperate attempt to gain altitude. As he tried to climb out of his cockpit, his parachute (a replacement for his usual one, which was being repacked) snagged on something. Moncrief suddenly found himself flying through the air. His plane had apparently stalled and flipped Moncrief away. Moncrief blacked out and did not remember pulling his ripcord, but his chute blossomed, and he swung three times before hitting the ground with a jolt. He was dragged some distance before he was finally able to slip his chute.

Moncrief suffered a dislocated shoulder, a wrenched left leg, and huge blisters on his right leg that were probably caused by the hot coolant. Any thought he might have had of escape was quickly dispelled by the appearance of a large party of Japanese soldiers and civilians. His wounds were treated only superficially in prison camp, and his shoulder remained dislocated while his burns festered. When Moncrief was shot down, he weighed 135 pounds; when he was liberated at the end of the war (just two and a half months later), the lack of food and medical treatment in camp had driven his weight down to just 89 pounds. Yet he survived to return home.[19]

But it was not all moments of terror and hours of hard work for the Air Commandos. Softball games were held between the sections and other forms of physical activity were encouraged. An occasional movie was shown, but the highlight for many was the visit of comedian Joe E. Brown. He put on a great show, according to those who saw it, and a capacity crowd responded with a tremendous ovation. Brown had shoehorned in his appearance at Gabu at the urging of Rush Russhon and could spend little time with the Air Commandos, but he made every moment count.

Following his show Olson and Mahurin flew Brown back to Fifth Air Force Headquarters in a C-47 borrowed from the 318th. Olson had not flown a C-47 since before the 3rd ACG left the United States, and Mahurin had only a couple of hours of copilot time in one. After they were seated in the cockpit they discovered they did not know how to start the plane. As they pondered which switches to turn on, Brown appeared at the cockpit door to ask if they knew how to start a C-47. Before they could answer "no," he leaned over, turned on the battery and ignition switches, and soon had both engines purring. He then looked Olson and Mahurin up and down, shook his head, and returned to his seat.

Chagrined and embarrassed, the two officers plotted a practical joke to play on Brown. About an hour into the flight they sent the crew chief back through the cabin. After setting the plane on autopilot they went back themselves. While Olson leaned by the open cargo door and watched the ground slide by, Mahurin sat down by Brown, who was playing gin rummy, and asked to be dealt in. It took a couple of minutes for Brown to react, but when he did, he jumped up and began yelling about who was flying the plane. He then rushed to the cockpit, where a fantastic sight greeted him. The two airmen had tied a glove on top of one of the control wheels and had inserted into it a flexible hose attached to an outside air vent. When they opened the vent, the air inflated the glove making it seem as though a disembodied hand was controlling the plane. Olson and Mahurin finally calmed Brown down and confessed to their joke, but he remained in the cockpit for the rest of the flight, keeping an eagle eye on the two the entire time.[20]

As much as the men of the 3rd ACG enjoyed Brown's show, they had a much more interesting topic to hold their attention. Almost as soon as Germany had surrendered on May 7, the Army began to demobilize. A points system, the Adjusted Service Rating System, was instituted in which length of service, overseas service, decorations and battle stars, and number of dependent children were computed to establish a priority for discharging individuals. The higher the number, the sooner the discharge. The critical number was 85, and it soon seemed as though everyone in the group was counting and recounting the number of points to their credit. Each man also wanted to know how many points his buddy had. In at least one section those who tired of being asked the same question over and over pinned signs on their caps showing their totals.

Although the 3rd ACG had a number of old-timers in its midst, most were in for the long haul. Nevertheless, the counting of points continued unabated, and a few men soon began their journey home. They were not many—not yet—but their departures served to keep alive the hopes of many others who longed to make that trip back to Uncle Sugar as early as possible.[21]

Flying was not the only activity the group was involved in heavily. The group communications section established four radio stations to coordinate efforts with guerilla and U.S. infantry units. The stations were normally operated by one or two ACG men who lived with the troops. It was tough duty, and the living conditions were primitive. On several occasions the stations came under enemy fire and had to be pulled back temporarily. Nonetheless, the radio operators work was highly praised by the ground troops.[22]

Gabu became even busier in June than it had been. Its location as the northernmost field on Luzon meant it became a popular stopping point for shot-up planes returning from Formosa. During the month thirty-seven aircraft carrying 209 people made emergency landings at Gabu. The 3rd ACG's 327th Medical Dispensary was kept busy treating the injured and could proudly state that no lives were lost in these emergencies during June. But it was as a staging field for aircraft moving to Okinawa in preparation of the invasion of Japan proper that Gabu saw its greatest activity. Large quantities of gas, oil, spare parts, and all other types of supplies were flown in to meet the demand, and a transient camp was swiftly built to handle all the personnel also on the move.

Olson oversaw this frantic activity in his capacity as field commander. Some 253 aircraft staged through Gabu in June, and even more followed in July. Seeing the other fighter squadrons heading for Okinawa, where they would more likely be involved in aerial combat, was hard to take for the Air Commandos. Not having seen a Japanese plane in the air since the Hong Kong mission of April 3, the 3rd ACG fighter pilots were eager to show that they, too, could hold their own against the enemy. Instead, it seemed, they were being relegated to the backwaters.[23]

Actually, they now were operating in a rear area, for MacArthur declared the Luzon campaign over at midnight of June 30/July 1. This pronouncement was somewhat misleading because the Japanese remained active in the Cagayan Valley, where Yamashita had gathered the remnants of his forces on Luzon. During July the Air Commando fighter sections flew numerous missions in support of the infantrymen closing in on Yamashita. Their final mission was flown on July 25, almost one month after MacArthur declared the Luzon campaign over.

Before then, however, the Air Commandos suffered the loss of five pilots in June. Captain Adams was one of the most popular pilots in the group, and his promotion to commander of the 3rd Fighter Squadron when Mahurin moved up to group operations officer had been well received by all. Leading a ground support mission near Mankayan on June 5, he decided to press on when clouds began to gather in the target area. Adams reported to his flight that to be safe, he would make a glide-bombing attack rather than dive-bombing.

As his flight watched, Adams made his pass. He apparently realized the clouds were lower than he thought, for he suddenly dropped his bombs and began a sharp pull-up. His Mustang stalled and whipped into a vicious spin from which he could not recover. The fighter smashed into a mountainside, killing Adams instantly. Tragically, orders promoting Adams to major had been received at Gabu while he was out on this mission. An eager crowd had been awaiting his return to pin on his oak leaves as soon as he climbed from his cockpit. The excitement quickly turned to gloom when the dispirited pilots landed to report what had happened. Taking Adams' place as commanding officer was his good friend Capt. Thomas J. Williams.[24]

With the Japanese beginning to retreat toward the interior and into the Cagayan Valley, targets for the Air Commandos became more scarce and planes often returned to base with their bombs. When they did find targets, their bombs were usually dropped accurately, to the pleasure of the GIs, who then moved in to mop up. Missions to Formosa continued to be flown regularly, although many of these were just to cover rescue submarines and Catalinas or to escort B-24s bombing the island. Nevertheless, ACG fighter sweeps continued to have a devastating effect on the enemy. In June alone Air Commando fighters destroyed (among other things) five locomotives and fifty-two box cars, twenty-five trucks, ten bridges, and numerous buildings and other structures.[25]

The Japanese defending Formosa continued to exact a toll on the attackers, however. On June 26, as eight 4th Fighter Section aircraft made a fighter sweep of the island, clouds began to build over the mountains. The fliers turned to head for home. Capt. John C. Bleecker Jr., 1st Lt. John B. Tillou, and 2nd Lt. Raymond E. Wingo were last seen entering the clouds. One pilot later reported seeing a flash, followed by fire, in the clouds. The three men had evidently flown into a mountain as they attempted to maintain formation. The 4th's hard luck A Flight had lost three more men.[26]

June drew to a close with more tragedy for the fighter pilots. On the 29th newly commissioned 2nd Lt. Paul G. Krikoroff was killed while ferrying a P-51 from Tacloban on Leyte to Gabu. It was never definitely determined what happened to the former flight officer, but his plane crashed into San Pablo Bay just after taking off from Tacloban. Probably stunned from the impact, Krikoroff went down with his Mustang.[27]

Meanwhile, the 157th LS, now commanded by 1st Lt. Walter M. Coble, was preparing to make a historic move. The squadron was ordered to move to Okinawa, and the ground echelon left Mabalacat on June 15 for Subic Bay on Bataan's west coast. There, they boarded an LST for a ten-day trip to Okinawa. For the time being the pilots left behind were attached to the 160th LS. The ground echelon set up initially at Yontan, Okinawa, where the main airfield was located. After a few days they moved to an area just north of the village of Bise on the Motobu Peninsula. This was to be the site of the airstrip for the 3rd ACG's light planes, but the engineers discovered that it had too steep a grade so another site in Bise itself was found.

Back at Mabalacat the 157th's pilots, under the supervision of Alison, were busy installing seventy-five–gallon belly tanks in the rear seats of their planes and checking their navigation charts. The squadron's twenty-four L-5s and two UC-64s were going to make a 748-mile flight from Gabu to Okinawa, all of it over water. The little planes gathered at Gabu, where they were topped off with fuel and given a thorough inspection by their pilots. Many of them were skeptical that the L-5s were up to the trip, but that did not stop them from making the attempt.

Early on July 5 the first of the planes lifted heavily off Gabu's strip. Soon, all of the aircraft, shepherded by a pair of Air–Sea Rescue OA-10s, were in loose formation and heading north. The hazardous journey, flown generally at about 1,500 feet, took nearly seven hours, and gas was very low in most of the planes when they touched down at Yontan. It had been a remarkable journey. While on Okinawa the 157th LS again came under the operational control of the 5th Air Liaison Group. For all intents and purposes, both organizations were the same because most of the group's personnel were 157th people on temporary duty with the provisional organization.[28]

Meanwhile, though despairing that they would ever see aerial combat again, the 3rd ACG's fighter pilots continued flying to Formosa. Most of these missions, however, were just to cover Air–Sea Rescue Catalinas and lifeguard submarines. Their perseverance was at last rewarded on July 11 while they were on such a mission. That morning four 3rd Fighter Section Mustangs were assigned to cover a Catalina and submarine operating off Formosa's northwestern coast near Shinchiku. For the first hour it was another boring flight, making circle after lazy circle over their wards. Then 1st Lt. Herbert R. French spotted a bogey at his 10 o'clock position and out to sea. French and his wingman, 2nd Lt. George W. Mooney, were flying high cover, while the flight leader and his wingman were the low cover.

Upon hearing French report his sighting, the flight leader told French and Mooney to go after it while the other Mustangs kept watch on the rescue team. The pair immediately set off toward the unknown aircraft. As they neared the plane, which had been heading toward Formosa at about eight thousand feet, it suddenly reversed course and dove for the water. The Americans dropped their belly tanks, fire walled their throttles, and began to chase the plane, which they identified as a B5N Kate. The enemy plane was fast, perhaps indicating that it was a newer, faster aircraft like a B6N Jill, and it took the pair some fifteen minutes to catch it. French and Mooney came up on both sides of the enemy plane, preventing it from breaking one way or the other.

In desperation the enemy pilot tried a bank to the right, but Mooney was ready and sent a burst of .50-caliber shells into the Kate's wing root. Pieces flew off the plane, and orange flame streaked back as it headed for the sea. Suddenly, a wing ripped off, and the Kate began to tumble wildly. Just feet above the water, its pilot tried to bail out. His parachute did not open, and he and his plane smashed into the water almost simultaneously. Mooney's victory was the 3rd ACG's last in the air or on the ground.[29]

July 12 also saw one of the 3 Fighter Section pilots go beyond the call of duty when a B-24 crew had to leave their bomber after it had been hit by flak over Formosa. In his excitement the bomber pilot forgot the Catalina's call sign and had to ask what it was from the Air Commandos escorting him. The sea was very rough, however, and the OA-10 could not land. The fighter pilots located the lifeguard sub and guided it toward the stricken bomber. Instead of dropping his men close to the submarine, though, the B-24 pilot scattered them across fifteen miles of choppy water. None of the other bombers stayed around to keep an eye on their comrades, and it was left to the four fighter pilots that had escorted the B-24 to keep an eye on the men in the water.

As they circled low over the men they tossed out sea markers in order to keep track of the downed airmen. It appeared to 2nd Lt. Charles E. House that one man was floundering in the water with no life raft. House decided that the only way to save the man was to drop his own dinghy, which was attached to the seat part of his parachute. He trimmed his plane for a slight climbing turn so that it would continue to circle over the downed flier. Next, he unfastened all of his parachute straps and seat belt and pushed his feet against the rudder pedals, raising himself off his seat. In his plane's cramped cockpit, it was a struggle to pull the dinghy from its pack, but House finally succeeded. Descending to just a few feet over the bomber crewman, he tossed the man the dinghy. House watched as the man inflated the dinghy, climbed in, and waved. The sub eventually picked up the waterlogged airman, saved thanks to the tremendous effort on House's part.[30]

In mid-July, the group received orders to move to Ie Shima, a small island off Okinawa's west coast. An advanced party of personnel from all of the ground echelons was directed to move by boat and set up camp on the island. While this group was preparing to leave Laoag, new orders instructed the air echelon to leave first. This party was composed primarily of mechanics, not pilots or planes, and so when they arrived on Ie Shima, they had nothing to work with. The 3rd ACG's own 318th TCS handled the move, making one-day round trips between Laoag and Ie Shima. Thunderstorms and thick clouds were encountered often on these flights, which could last twelve hours or more. Yet the crews kept flying day and night, not only moving the group forward, but continuing also to drop supplies to guerilla units and American troops in the mountains of Luzon.[31]

August began with the Air Commandos scattered from the Philippines to Okinawa and Ie Shima. Most of the ground personnel had already moved north or were en route. The fighter pilots remained at Laoag, flying little (their last support mission was flown on July 25) but being fed well and getting in a lot of sack time. Then, on August 6, the Enola Gay dropped an atomic bomb on Hiroshima. Three days later, another atomic bomb devastated Nagasaki. Heated arguments erupted throughout the Japanese government as some advocated surrender, while others wanted to continue the fight. Emperor Hirohito broke the impasse on August 14 when he went to a secret location and recorded a cease-fire announcement to be broadcast the following day. It was well he took precautions, because a group of Japanese army officers attempted to capture the emperor, overthrow the government, and continue the war. Their mutiny failed, and the Japanese people accepted Hirohito's edict.

The Air Commandos on Ie Shima witnessed a bit of history of the ending of the war on August 19 when a pair of Bettys, now painted an overall white and carrying large green crosses on their wings and fuselages, touched down on the island. The aircraft were carrying a surrender delegation to meet MacArthur for preliminary negotiations. The envoys transferred to a C-54 for the final leg to Manila while their crews stayed behind to tend their planes and be observed by curious onlookers on the island. On September 2, as U.S. Navy ships filled Tokyo Bay and formation after formation of U.S. Navy and USAAF aircraft flew overhead, MacArthur and the formal Japanese surrender party led by Foreign Minister Shigemitsu Mamoru and Japanese Imperial Army Chief of Staff General Umezu Yoshijiro signed the surrender document aboard the battleship USS *Missouri*. The war was over.

Epilogue

With the war over, the clamor of the American public and politicians to bring the boys home rose to a deafening roar. The resulting implosion of America's armed services had a devastating impact on the country's military capabilities that was revealed just five years later with the outbreak of the Korean War. But that was in the future, and in the fall of 1945, the joy of ending a bloody and costly conflict overrode anyone's contemplations of other wars.

Certainly not immune to these cutbacks were the Air Commandos. The end of the war found most of the Air Commando squadrons widely separated, particularly the liaison units. The 1st ACG's fighters were at Asansol, while the 2nd's were at Kalaikunda. For these men, much of their time was spent sightseeing, as flying time was slashed and men began returning home. The 1st ACG's liaison squadrons were at Asansol also, but the 2nd ACG's had left the group earlier to move to Okinawa, where they had been farmed out to various commands. The 127th LS was initially attached to the Thirteenth Air Force and then was with the Seventh Air Force. Both the 155th LS and 156th LS had been attached to the Fifth Air Force and then went to Pacific Air Command, U.S. Army. The 127th LS was inactivated in November 1945, and the other two squadrons were inactivated in January 1946. Finally, in a paper transaction, the 1st ACG and the 2nd ACGs, their fighter squadrons, and the 1st ACG's three liaison squadrons were inactivated at Camp Kilmer, New Jersey, in November 1945.[1]

Prior to this, the two group's C-47 squadrons had remained active, both moving to China in September to transport men and equipment around the country. After turning over its planes to other units in China, the 319th TCS returned to India in early November, followed shortly thereafter by the 317th TCS, which also left its aircraft behind. Other than take part in the usual military formations, there was little for the men to do in India except relax and sightsee as their numbers quickly dwindled. On December 27, 1945, the 319th

1

TCS was inactivated in India. The 317th TCS followed into the history books on February 28, 1946.[2]

The squadrons of the 3rd ACG hung on a bit longer. When the cease-fire was announced, the group's fighter pilots were still on Luzon. They did not arrive on Ie Shima until August 28, but they did get in a few missions over Japan before V-J Day. The 318th TCS also did not move to the island until late in the month. The 5th Air Liaison Group (Provisional) was discontinued on September 10, and the 157th LS was assigned to the Fifth Air Force, while the 159th LS went to the Thirteenth Air Force. Only the 160th LS survived the immediate demobilization, although it went to Korea, where it operated apart from the rest of the 3rd ACG. The 157th was inactivated on October 25, 1946, and the 159th was inactivated on May 31, 1946.[3]

Olson received orders to proceed home on September 2, and Mahurin replaced him as group commander. Mahurin returned to the United States on November 20 and was succeeded by Col. Charles H. Terhune Jr. Meanwhile, the group's stay on Ie Shima was relatively short. A few days following the official surrender ceremonies, the 318th TCS moved to Atsugi just outside Tokyo. There, it was heavily involved in transporting occupation troops into Japan and flying ex-POWs back to Okinawa for further movement home. By September 15 most of the 318th and the 343rd ADS were stationed at Atsugi.

The 3rd ACG fighter squadrons made the move to Japan on September 20, when the Mustangs and a few ground personnel flew to Atsugi on the first leg of a trip that eventually led to Chitose on the northern Japanese island of Hokkaido. The fighters settled in there to perform air defense missions and other occupation chores. Then, on March 25, 1946, the 3rd ACG and all its remaining squadrons were inactivated at Chitose.[4]

The history of the World War II Air Commandos was thus relatively short, not much more than two years for the oldest group, the 1st ACG. And their times in combat were even more brief. Yet they accomplished much in that time. Operation Thursday had been remarkable, demonstrating that a large ground force could be flown in behind enemy lines and completely supplied and supported by air. That Thursday was not a complete success was not the fault of the Air Commandos or the Chindits. It was supposed to be part of a larger Allied offensive, and when that overarching effort was not made, the Chindits were left exposed. Nonetheless, Operation Thursday showed that with strong leadership, innovative tactics, and full commitment, much could be achieved.

Likewise, the 2nd ACG's spectacular Don Muang raid showcased the flexibility and capability of the Air Commandos. Perhaps not surprisingly, the mission (the longest fighter mission on record to the time) was not mentioned in either the official history of the USAAF in World War II or in the official USAAF chronology of the war.

Primarily because it arrived late in the war and involved a command, the FEAF, that already had a number of groups committed to action, the 3rd ACG was unable to fully display its flexibility. It still performed all the tasks it was given admirably.

The most-respected Air Commando units were perhaps the light plane squadrons. They flew everyone and everywhere, carrying senior ground officers, delivering messages, dropping supplies, and the like. The evacuation of sick and wounded troops from the front lines drew the loudest praise from the troops, though. This one mission provided the infantry with confidence and faith that they would be taken care of and not left to suffer in the jungles of Burma and the Philippines.

Following the end of the war Arnold issued his *Third Report of the Commanding General of the Army Air Forces to the Secretary of War*, in which he discussed USAAF activities during the last year of the war and looked to the future of the service he had led. One of the "new concepts" he mentioned in this report was of fully equipped airborne task forces that were able to strike far distant points and could be totally supplied by air. In other words, it was an extension of the Air Commando concept.[5]

But this idea was not to be. For some, the Air Commando concept had been too exotic. The groups never quite fit into a "proper" USAAF organizational structure, so no tears were shed at the dissolution of the Air Commandos by the skeptics who had never conceived the enormous possibilities of unconventional warfare afforded by these units. As the noted military theorist Liddell Hart wrote, "The only thing harder than getting a new idea into the military mind, is to get the old one out."[6]

Alison put it another way. In an April 1944 report to General Giles, Alison stated, "Air Commando is a way of thinking and not a branch of the Air Force."[7] This way of thinking escaped many in the USAAF and, later, the USAF, but not all.

Cochran had his own ideas on why the World War II Air Commandos did not survive. In a 1975 interview he said,

> The first one . . . was a task force, and it was a single-purpose organization that was to run about six months and just work itself out and go away. But as we kept building, and building, and building, we realized that this could be another form of combat unit. . . . The closest organizational unit to what we had was a group in the [Army] Air Force[s]. So they made up

a provisional group . . . because after we got over there, we had to have
a number. . . . This was an attempt to make order out of this completely
different kind of unit that was floating around, the task force. So they
formalized it and made it a group. Well, then they said, "Well, now we
can make more groups of Air Commandos, and it will be like a bomber
group, or a fighter group, or whatever, and then it will build itself into
wings. You will have three and a headquarters and a wing, or something
of that nature, three groups."

Now, it started to take that form. . . . One was already out there. The
one that was the task force became now a group. Then there was another
group sent out, the 2nd Air Commando, and that was sent to India for
the next season. Then the other two [actually, one] went to the South
Pacific. They were diverted. Evidently, the structure, or the animal, was
not healthy, because it didn't last. It didn't, in fact, become another kind
of air unit. It never jelled, because here you've got transports, fighters,
bombers, gliders, liaison aircraft, and you put that together, and you say,
"Now, that's a group." Well, it wasn't, and there was always the tendency
to split it off. There was always the thing there that if it got in position
it had to be supported by other people, and it would start to draw from
other units. "Bring in that fighter squadron; bring in those transports over
there, and attach them to this thing." So the concept just did not lend
itself to order, and it died.[8]

Cochran was perceptive. It became too much of a temptation for senior
air leaders to grab various pieces of the Air Commandos to shore up shortcom-
ings (real or imagined) in their own organizations. The Air Commando concept
worked well in Operation Thursday when all components were employed to the
same end of supporting Chindit operations behind enemy lines. But with Wingate's death and the Chindits being used more as regular infantry, the Air Commando concept lost much of its relevance. And with the war finally turning in
the Allies' favor, the need for such specialized units became less important.

Yet, the new idea of unconventional units organized to carry out special
operations that was lit by the World War II Air Commando groups did not die.
Its flames flickered and ebbed over the years, but they kept burning. Others
took up Alison's "way of thinking" and sustained and refined it. Today, although
the concept has changed in form, the Air Force Special Operations Command
carries on the proud tradition of the Air Commandos—Any Place, Any Time,
Anywhere.

Note on Sources

Most of the sources used in this work are official documents that are in the files of the Air Force Historical Research Agency (AFHRA), which is located at Maxwell AFB, Alabama. These documents are in both paper and microfilm formats. Documents are classified under two systems, Mood and Decimal. The Mood System is generally used for documents of Air Force units at the division level or below. Units are identified by their numerical designations and alphabetical symbols representing organizational echelons or functions. Thus, GP-A-CMDO-1 identifies the 1st Air Commando Group. A designation of GP-A-CMDO-1-HI indicates that it is a unit history of that organization; GP-A-CMDO-1-SU indicates supporting documents for the unit. Some other symbols used include "CO" for correspondence, "OP" for operations, and "OR" for orders.

The Decimal System employed by AFHRA is similar to the Dewey Decimal System found in many libraries, and it is generally used to classify documents of organizations above the division level. Blocks of three-digit numbers are allocated to organizations grouped by general functions or geographical location. Thus, records of the China–Burma–India theater can be found under the classification number 800; southwest Pacific area records can be located under the classification number 700. These three-digit numbers are further divided to identify organizations in a theater (e.g., 820 for Eastern Air Command, 830 for Tenth Air Force, 862 for Fourteenth Air Force). Finally, numerous subdivisions of the decimal numbers indicate functional areas such as histories, operations, intelligence, and personnel. For example, 830.01 indicates Tenth Air Force histories. Finding aids listing the various classifications and subclassifications are held at both the AFHRA and in the library of the Air Force Historical Studies Office (AFHSO) at Bolling AFB, D.C.

Microfilm copies of many of the agency's holdings are also kept in the AFHSO library. The author would have preferred to use the original paper documents, but the sheer amount of documentation was daunting. Also, the indexes to the various files are brief and do not always indicate just what is in each file. Documents—not just for this book, but for research throughout the AFHRA files—occasionally appear in places that seeming to have nothing to do with the subject being studied. For example, several documents on Air Commando operations were discovered under an index heading of "Tactical Reconnaissance." Only the first document in this rather large file pertained to that heading, while the remainder concerned not only Air Commando operations, but many other topics as well. The titles of the official documents in the following notes and bibliography are as they are listed in the indexes to the microfilm reels.

Ease of use and the ability to move through files much more quickly led the author to use the microfilm format. Thus, in the notes, reference is made to the frame number(s) of the appropriate microfilm reel, along with its file and reel numbers (Memorandum, Forces of Long-Range Penetration . . ., 10 Aug 1943, AFHRA No. 145.81-170, Reel No. A1378, fr. 575). For anyone wishing to check a specific document, this method of identifying the document will make it easier and quicker for the researcher. Those wishing to use these microfilms should be aware, however, that it is not uncommon to find unreadable sections on the microfilm, the result of poor original documents or poor microfilming.

Mention should be made of the internal, as compared to the external or photographed, quality of the documents. Record keeping was not always a priority for military units. Some units kept voluminous records, including narrative histories. Others were content with statistical summaries. Still others, fortunately few in number, kept hardly any records. This hodgepodge of documentation occasionally results in situations in which a unit is barely mentioned only because it had few useful records.

The secondary sources vary widely in quality, ranging from the journalistic, such as *Back to Mandalay*, to the more scholarly, such as the famed U.S. Army World War II "Green Book" series of histories. Nonetheless, each provided another piece of the puzzle that eventually formed a complete picture of the Air Commandos.

Notes

Preface

1. R. D. Van Wagner, *1st Air Commando Group: Any Place, Any Time, Anywhere*, Military History Series 86-1 (Maxwell AFB, Ala.: Air Command and Staff College, Air University, 1986).
2. H. H. Arnold, "The Aerial Invasion of Burma," *National Geographic* 86 (August 1944): 130.
3. Van Wagner, *1st Air Commando Group*, 76.

Chapter 1

1. Unless otherwise noted, this material on Wingate has been obtained primarily from Christopher Sykes, *Orde Wingate* (Cleveland: The World Publishing Co., 1959); Trevor Royle, *Orde Wingate: Irregular Soldier* (London: Weidenfeld and Nicolson, 1994); John Bierman and Colin Smith, *Fire in the Night* (New York: Random House, 1999); and Lowell Thomas, *Back to Mandalay* (New York: The Greystone Press, 1951), 57–70.
2. Sheldon Bidwell, *The Chindit War* (New York: Macmillan Publishing Co., 1979), 135.
3. See Bidwell, *Chindit War*, 37–9, for a discussion on Wingate's mental stability.
4. Sykes, *Orde Wingate*, 132–3.
5. Leonard Mosley, *Gideon Goes to War* (New York: Charles Scribner's Sons, 1955), 94.
6. Derek Tulloch, *Wingate in Peace and War* (London: History Book Club, 1972), 51–2; Royle, *Orde Wingate*, 216–9; Col. Philip G. Cochran, interview by Dr. James C. Hasdorff, Rochester, N.Y., and Washington, D.C., October 20–21, 1975, and November 11, 1975, AFHRA No. K243.0512-876, 215–7 (hereafter cited as Cochran Interview).
7. Louis Allen, *Burma: The Longest War, 1941–1945* (New York: St. Martin's Press, 1984), 123–4. Sykes, on pages 378 and 380 of his *Orde Wingate*, has a different version of how the name came about.
8. S. Woodburn Kirby, et al., *The War against Japan,* vol. 2, *India's Most Dangerous Hour* (London: Her Majesty's Stationery Office, 1958), 309–29; Royle, *Orde Wingate*, 248–55.
9. Tulloch, *Wingate in Peace*, 116.
10. For the American viewpoint, see Grace Person Hayes, *The History of the Joint Chiefs of Staff in World War II: The War against Japan* (Annapolis: Naval Institute Press, 1982),

253

413–71. For the British side, see John Ehrman, *Grand Strategy*, vol. 5, *August 1943–September 1944* (London: Her Majesty's Stationery Office, 1956), 1–15.

11. Hayes, *History of the Joint Chiefs*, 429, 434.
12. Eric Larrabee, *Commander in Chief* (New York: Harper & Row, 1987), 550.
13. It should be noted that throughout Quadrant, Wingate, realizing this was a tremendous opportunity for him, was on his best behavior. His presentations were concise and well thought-out, and he did not fall into his usual habits of lecturing his listeners or digressing into long-winded monologues on topics far removed from the subject at hand.
14. Memorandum, Brig. Orde Wingate to War Cabinet, Chiefs of Staff Committee, C.O.S.(Q) Subj: Forces of Long-Range Penetration: Future Development and Employment in Burma, 10 Aug 1943, AFHRA No. 145.81-170, Reel No. A1378, fr. 573 (hereafter cited as Wingate War Cabinet Memo).
15. Ibid.
16. Wingate War Cabinet Memo, fr. 574.
17. Ibid.
18. Wingate War Cabinet Memo, fr. 575.
19. Wingate War Cabinet Memo, fr. 579.
20. Wingate War Cabinet Memo, frs. 573–9.
21. Minutes of 110th Meeting, Combined Chiefs of Staff, 17 Aug 1943, Papers and Minutes of Quadrant Conference, August 1943, 449–50, National Archives Record Group 165; Hayes, *History of the Joint Chiefs*, 451.
22. Maj. Gen. George C. Kenney to Lt. Gen. H. H. Arnold, May 18, 1942, Gen. H. H. Arnold Papers, Box 84/1, Library of Congress.
23. Lt. Gen. H. H. Arnold to Maj. Gen. George C. Kenney, June 10, 1942, Gen. H. H. Arnold Papers, Box 84/1, Library of Congress.
24. Memorandum by Brig. Gen. L. S. Kuter to Commanding General, 8th Air Force, Subj: Air Force Offensive–Defensive Basic Unit, June 16, 1942, Gen. H. H. Arnold Papers, Box 84/1, Library of Congress.
25. Memorandum, Forces of Long-Range Penetration . . ., 10 Aug 1943, AFHRA No. 145.81-170, Reel No. A1378, fr. 575.
26. In the second draft of his *Supreme Allied Commander's Despatch on SEAC Southeast Asia Operations*, Mountbatten claimed that it was he who brought up the need for aircraft, including gliders, and that it was only at his insistence that Arnold decided to form the Air Commandos (see AFHRA No. 805.04A, Reel No. A8015, frs. 521–2). Mountbatten did not repeat this assertion in his final *Report to the Combined Chiefs of Staff.*
27. Hayes, *History of the Joint Chiefs*, 293.
28. Hayes, *History of the Joint Chiefs*, 199.
29. Hayes, *History of the Joint Chiefs*, 437.
30. Hayes, *History of the Joint Chiefs*, 437–8.
31. Hayes, *History of the Joint Chiefs*, 439.
32. CCS No. 308/3, Southeast Asia Command, 21 August 1943, Papers and Minutes of Quadrant Conference, Aug 1943, 125–6, National Archives Record Group 165.
33. See Philip Ziegler, *Mountbatten* (New York: Alfred A. Knopf, 1985), for a full biography. Chapter 16 of Ziegler's book, particularly pages 216–26, covers the Quebec Conference.

34. Gen. H. H. Arnold Papers, Murray Green Collection, File No. 8.48, Air Force Academy, Colorado Springs, Colo. (hereafter cited as Green Collection).

35. Thomas, *Back to Mandalay*, 91.

36. Cochran Interview, 17–23; John Bainbridge, "'Flip Corkin,'" *Life*, August 9, 1943, 42–8; Merle Miller, "The Real Flip Corkin," *Yank*, August 4, 1944, 10–11.

37. Maj. Gen. John R. Alison, interview by Maj. Scottie S. Thompson. April 22–28, 1979, Washington, D.C., AFHRA No. K239.0512-1121, 55–9 (hereafter cited as Alison Interview); John R. Alison, interview by Kenneth Leish, July 1960, AFHRA No. K146.34.2, Reel No. K1213 (hereafter cited as Alison 1960 Interview). Despite a nineteen-year time span, these two interviews are very similar. Unless the earlier interview has substantially different information, the 1979 session is the one referenced. Maj. Gen. Claire L. Chennault, *Way of a Fighter* (New York: G. P. Putnam's Sons, 1949), 101–2.

38. Zemke made a name for himself later in the war as commander of the 56th and 479th Fighter Groups and as a 17.75-plane ace.

39. The following information on Alison's service in the Soviet Union and Iran is from pages 61 through 140 of the transcription of the Alison Interview and from Interview with Lt. Col. John Allison [*sic*], 3 July 1943, AFHRA No. 142.052, Reel No. A1272, frs. 94–6 (hereafter cited as Alison Air Room Interview).

40. Alison Interview, 77.

41. Ibid., 79.

42. Ibid., 80.

43. Ibid., 88, 94.

44. Griffiss AFB, New York, was later named in the colonel's honor.

45. The following information on Alison's service in China is from the Alison Interview, 197–219, 227–343, and from Alison Air Room Interview, frs. 96–100.

46. Alison Interview, 250–8; Wanda Cornelius and Thayne Short, *Ding Hao* (Gretna, La.: Pelican Publishing Co., 1980), 202–6; Carl Molesworth, *Sharks over China* (Washington, D.C.: Brassey's, 1994), 30–3.

47. Alison Interview, 302–5; 75th FS History, AFHRA No. SQ-FI-75-HI, Reel No. A0755, fr. 547.

48. Alison Interview, 306–8, 336–7; Alison 1960 Interview, fr. 592; Cornelius and Short, *Ding Hao*, 271–2.

49. Olson, an ex–Flying Tiger, became the 1st Air Commando Group's operations officer, and he later commanded the 3rd Air Commando Group.

50. Maj. Gen. John R. Alison, USAF (Ret.), interview by William T. Y'Blood, July 23, 1996 (hereafter cited as Alison Y'Blood Interview); Alison 1960 Interview, frs. 605–6.

51. Miller, "The Real Flip Corkin," 11.

52. Unless otherwise noted, the following section on Cochran's tour in North Africa is from the Cochran Interview, 46–129, 402–35.

53. 33rd FG History: The Medical History of the Thirty-Third Fighter Group, 7 Jan 1945, AFHRA No. GP-33-HI, Reel No. B0111A, fr. 226.

54. Thomas J. Mayock, *The Twelfth Air Force in the North African Winter Campaign, 11 November 1942 to the Reorganization of 18 February 1943*, USAF Historical Study No. 114 (Washington, D.C.: AAF Historical Division, 1946), 73.

55. Cochran Interview, 56.
56. Ibid., 61.
57. The 33rd FG history states that Cochran did hit the hotel; the 58th FS history says that he missed it (see 33rd FG History, AFHRA No. GP-33-HI, Reel No. B0111A, fr. 193; 58th FS History, AFHRA No. SQ-58-HI, Reel No. A0744, fr. 1322).
58. See pages 118 through 127 of the transcription of the Cochran Interview for his comments on these airmen.
59. Cochran Interview, 142,

Chapter 2

1. Cochran Interview, 145.
2. Ibid., 146.
3. Ibid.
4. Ibid., 146–7.
5. Alison 1960 Interview, fr. 607. Oddly, in Arnold's Visitor Log, Cochran is not listed as being at this meeting (see Visitor Log, 18 Jul 1943–45 May 1944, Murray Green Collection, Series 5, Box 90, Envelope 10).
6. Unless otherwise noted, all quotations from this meeting are from the 1960 Alison Interview, frs. 607–10.
7. Alison interview with, 23 July 1996.
8. Alison Interview, 347. See also, Interview with Col. John R. Allison [sic], 25 April 1944, AFHRA No. 810.6091A, Reel No. A8042, fr. 2091 (hereafter cited as Alison Air Room Interview II).
9. Thomas, *Back to Mandalay*, 55.
10. Alison Interview, 347.
11. For some reason, numerous official documents (both American and British) continually referred to the unit as the "Allison [sic] Task Force," even after it was widely known that Cochran was the commander and that the unit had an official designation. Also, the spelling of both Cochran's and Alison's last names has bedeviled writers from the beginning. British writers, especially, consistently refer to *Cochrane* and Alison's name is invariably spelled with two *k*s.
12. Arnold, "Aerial Invasion," 130.
13. Ibid.
14. Joint Intelligence Collection Agency/CBI Report No. 1448, 29 Mar 1944, Burma—First Air Commando Invasion of, AFHRA No. 810.6091A, Reel No. A8042, fr. 2071 (hereafter cited as JICA No. 1448).
15. Memorandum, Gen. H. H. Arnold to Gen. George C. Marshall, Subj: Air Task Force Windgate [sic], 13 Sep 1943, AFHRA No. 145.81-170, Reel No. A1378, fr. 633.
16. There appear to be no official documents on Cochran's visit and his talks with Wingate. The account described is from Thomas, *Back to Mandalay*, 14–9, 71–80. Thomas does not mention his sources, although it was probably Cochran in this instance, and Thomas may have taken some journalistic license in his description of these talks.
17. Thomas, *Back to Mandalay*, 19.
18. Cochran Interview, 152.

19. Ibid., 156.

20. Green Collection, Box 47, File No. 8.48.

21. Cochran Interview, 155. The following quotations in this section are from this interview.

22. Ibid., 158–9.

23. Memorandum, Col. John Alison to Gen. Giles, Subj: Summary of Operations of First Commando Group, 10 Apr 1944, AFHRA No. 145.81-171, Reel No. A1378, fr. 1080.

24. Data on the 1st ACG's aircraft were drawn from specific references throughout David Donald, ed., *American Warplanes of World War II* (London: Aerospace Publishing Ltd, 1995).

25. Unit History of the First Air Commando Force, AFHRA No. GP-A-CMDO-1-HI, Reel No. B0680, fr. 1405 (hereafter cited as Unit History of the First Air Commando Force).

26. Thomas, *Back to Mandalay*, 93–4.

27. Ibid., 95.

28. Memorandum, Arnold to Marshall, 13 Sep 1943, AFHRA No. 145.81-170, Reel No. A1378, fr. 634; Visitor Log, 18 Jul 43–5 May 44, Green Collection, Series 5, Box 90, Envelope 10.

29. Memorandum, Arnold to Marshall, 13 Sep 1943, AFHRA No. 145.81-170, Reel No. A1378, fr. 634; Thomas, *Back to Mandalay*, 89–90.

30. Office of the Adjutant General to Commanding Generals, Army Air Forces, Army Service Forces, and U.S. Army Forces in China–Burma–India: Rear Echelon, Subj: Allotment of Personnel for Provisional Air Commando Force, 4 Oct 1943, AFHRA No. 168.492, Reel No. A1674, frs. 1262–6.

31. Office of the Adjutant General to Commanding Generals, Army Air Forces, Army Service Forces, and USAAF in China–Burma–India: Rear Echelon, Subj: Allotment of Personnel for Provisional Air Commando Force, 20 Dec 1943, AFHRA No. 168.492, Reel No. A1676, frs. 904–5.

32. Memorandum, John Alison to Gen. H. H. Arnold, Subj: History, Status and Immediate Requirements for First Air Commando Force, 21 Jan 1944, Enclosure, AFHRA No. 145.81-170, Reel No. A1378, fr. 609. The author of JICA No. 1448 stated that these one thousand men were doing the work normally assigned to five thousand (see JICA No. 1448, Reel No. A8042, fr. 2072).

33. Col. P. G. Cochran to Commanding General, Eastern Air Command, Subj: First Air Commando Force, United States Army Air Forces, 22 Jan 1944, Tab 17 of SEAC Information Book, 1943–1944, AFHRA No. 805.011, Reel No. A8015, fr. 324.

34. Information on personnel is from R. D. Van Wagner, *Any Place, Any Time, Anywhere: The 1st Air Commandos in World War II*. (Atglen, Pa.: Schiffer Publishing, 1998), 24–5; JICA No. 1448, Reel No. A8042, frs. 2072–3; Maj. Robert C. Page, The Medical History of Project # 9, AFHRA No. GP-A-CMDO-1-HI, Reel No. B0680, frs. 1575–7 (hereafter cited as Medical History of Project #9).

35. Thomas, *Back to Mandalay*, 274, 276; Van Wagner, *Any Place*, 25–6.

36. Alison 1960 Interview, fr. 610.

37. Unless otherwise noted, the following quotations are from the Alison 1960 Interview, fr. 611.

38. Alison Interview, 360.

39. Requirements Division Daily Diary, 20 Oct 1943, AFHRA No. 123.309, Reel No. A1046A, fr. 429.

40. Requirements Division Daily Diary, 22 Oct 1943, AFHRA No. 123.309, Reel No. A1046A, fr. 440; Allocations and Programs Division Daily Diary, 25 Oct 1943, AFHRA No. 123.309, Reel No. A1046A, fr. 455.

41. Alison 1960 Interview, fr. 612.

42. Ibid., frs. 613–4. Although Cochran always believed that Harry Hopkins had been instrumental in obtaining the helicopters, Alison claimed this was not true (see Cochran Interview, 166–8, and Alison Interview, 364). Diary of the Assistant Chief of Air Staff, Operations, Commitments and Requirements, 14–15 Nov 1943, AFHRA No. 123.2, Reel No. A1039, fr. 1848; Requirements Division Daily Diary, 14 Nov 1943, AFHRA No. 123.309, Reel No. A1046A, fr. 541. The first four helicopters delivered were the fourteenth through seventeenth YR-4s constructed.

43. Medical History of Project #9, fr. 1575.

44. Unit History of the First Air Commando Force, fr. 1404.

45. Medical History of Project #9, fr. 1576; Ed Cunningham, "Twelve Thousand Miles from Griffith Stadium," *Yank*, July 28, 1944, 23.

46. JICA No. 1448, Reel No. A8042, fr. 2071.

47. JICA/CBI Report No. 1449, 1 Apr 1944, Burma—Glider Operations in, AFHRA No. 810.6091A-1, Reel No. A8042, fr. 2297 (hereafter cited as JICA No. 1449).

48. Alison Y'Blood Interview.

49. JICA No. 1449, fr. 2302; Gerard M. Devlin, *Silent Wings* (New York: St. Martin's Press, 1985), 139.

50. Medical History of Project #9, fr. 1578.

51. AAFSAT Special Intelligence Report No. 54, Sept 1944, Maj. William H. Taylor, Glider Operations on Two Fronts, AFHRA No. 248.532-63B, Reel No. A2891, frs. 531–2 (hereafter cited as Glider Operations); Medical History of Project #9, fr. 1578; Chronological History of Project 9 (Cochran), AFHRA No. 145.81-170, Reel No. A1378, fr. 618 (hereafter cited as Project 9 Chronology).

52. Van Wagner, *Any Place*, 29.

53. JICA/CBI Report No. 3138, 5 Jun 1944, Burma—Light Plane Operations of the First Air Commando Group in, AFHRA No. 810.6091A, Reel No. A8042, fr. 2283 (hereafter cited as JICA No. 3138). JICA No. 1448, Reel No. A8042, fr. 2074.

54. Glider Operations, fr. 532.

55. Van Wagner, *Any Place*, 28; JICA No. 1449, frs. 2299–2300.

56. Glider Operations, frs. 532–3.

57. Thomas, *Back to Mandalay*, 100.

58. Gen. H. H. Arnold to Maj. Gen. G. S. [*sic*] Stratemeyer, 17 Sep 1943, AFHRA No. 145.81-170, Reel No. A1378, frs. 638–9.

59. Project 9 Chronology, frs. 612–3.

60. Memorandum, Brig. Gen. S. C. Godfrey to Maj. Gen. George E. Stratemeyer, Subj: Glider Borne Engineers, A New Technique of Building Airfields Behind Enemy Lines, 28 Mar 1944, AFHRA No. 825.935-1, Reel No. A8220, fr. 47; Project 9 Chronology, fr. 613.

61. Unit History of the First Air Commando Force, fr. 1405.
62. JICA No. 1449, fr. 2300; R. D. Van Wagner, *1st Air Commando Group*, 46.
63. Medical History of Project #9, fr. 1580.

Chapter 3

1. Message, WAR to AMMISCA, 26 Aug 1943, in Riley Sunderland and Charles F. Romanus, eds., *Stilwell's Personal File: China–Burma–India, 1942–1944*, vol. 2 (Wilmington, Del.: Scholarly Resources, 1976), 833 (hereafter cited as Stilwell Files).
2. Earl Mountbatten of Burma, *Report to the Combined Chiefs of Staff by the Supreme Allied Commander South-East Asia, 1943–1945* (London: His Majesty's Stationery Office, 1951), 7 (hereafter cited as Mountbatten Report).
3. Mountbatten Report, 7–8.
4. Ibid., 11.
5. Green Collection, Box 47, File No. 8.48.
6. Oral Histories, Lt. Gen. Charles B. Stone with Murray Green, San Antonio, Tex., May 8, 1970, Green Collection, Box 76, Folder 7; Maj. Gen. Howard C. Davidson with Murray Green, Washington, D.C., Feb 17, 1970, Green Collection, Box 62, Folder 8.
7. Henry Probert, *The Forgotten Air Force* (London: Brassey's, 1995), 221–2.
8. Gen. H. H. Arnold to Maj. Gen. George E. Stratemeyer, 28 Aug 1943, AFHRA No. 820.161A, Reel No. A8072, fr. 1166; Wesley Frank Craven and James Lea Cate, eds., *The Army Air Forces in World War II*, vol. 4, *The Pacific: Guadalcanal to Saipan, August 1942 to July 1944* (Washington, D.C.: Office of Air Force History, 1983), 452.
9. Gen. H. H. Arnold to Maj. Gen. George E. Stratemeyer, 28 Aug 1943, AFHRA No. 820.161A, Reel No. A8072, fr. 1166.
10. HQs Eastern Air Command, General Orders No. 1, 15 Dec 1943, AFHRA No. 820.193, Reel No. A8090, frs. 986–7.
11. Ibid.; Craven and Cate, *Army Air Forces*, vol. 4, 455, 457–8.
12. CCS No. 305, "Effect of Indian Floods on Burma Campaign," 14 Aug 1943, Enclosure: Message, Armindia [Auchinleck] to Air Ministry Special Cypher Section, Subj: Program of Planning for Operations from India, 13 Aug 1943, Papers and Minutes of Quadrant Conference, Aug 1943, 108–12 National Archives, Record Group 165 (hereafter cited as CCS No. 305).
13. CCS No. 305, 112.
14. Hayes, *History of the Joint Chiefs*, 450.
15. CCS No. 327, Operations From India, 23 Aug 1943, Papers and Minutes of Quadrant Conference, Aug 1943, 318–9, National Archives Record Group 165 (hereafter cited as CCS No. 327); Luigi Rossetto, *Major General Orde Charles Wingate and the Development of Long-Range Penetration* (Manhattan, Kans.: MA/AH Publishing, 1982), 226–30.
16. CCS No. 327, 319.
17. CCS 115th Meeting, 23 Aug 1943, Item 5, Operations From India, Papers and Minutes of Quadrant Conference, Aug 1943, 482, National Archives Record Group 165.
18. CCS No. 319/5, Final Report to the President and Prime Minister, 24 Aug 1943, Papers and Minutes of Quadrant Conference, Aug 1943, 256, National Archives Record Group 165 (hereafter cited as CCS No. 319/5).

19. CCS No. 319/5, 257; Hayes, *History of the Joint Chiefs*, 467–8.

20. CCS 329/2, Implementation of Assumed Basic Undertakings and Specific Operations for the Conduct of the War, 1943–1944, 26 Aug 1943, Annex I, Papers and Minutes of Quadrant Conference, Aug 1943, 331, National Archives Record Group 165; Hayes, *History of the Joint Chiefs*, 471; Tulloch, *Wingate in Peace*, 122: Rossetto, *Major General Orde Charles Wingate*, 229–30.

21. Message, AMMDEL to AMMISCA, 29 Aug 1943, in Stilwell Files, vol. 2, 846.

22. Stilwell Files, vol. 2, 870; Message, AMMDEL to AMMISCA, 2 Sep 1943, in Stilwell Files, vol. 3, 881.

23. Report by the Joint Planning Staff, India Command: Operations in Northern Burma —1944, Course B, JPS Paper No. 107, 25 Sep 1943, Annex 1, AFHRA No. 805.322-6, Reel No. A8019, fr. 1070.

24. Indaw is approximately forty miles southeast of Mansi. Because it lay along a railroad track, this Indaw was often called Rail Indaw to differentiate it from another Indaw to the southwest that received the name Oil Indaw.

25. JPS Paper No. 107, Annex 1, Reel No. A8019, fr. 1070; S. Woodburn Kirby, *The War against Japan*, vol. 3, *The Decisive Battles* (London: Her Majesty's Stationery Office, 1961), 8–9.

26. JPS Paper No. 107, Annex 1, Reel No. A8019, frs. 1072–3, 1076, 1082.

27. Telegram, No. 73873/COS, from Armindia to Air Ministry (Special Cipher Section), Sep 1943, AFHRA No. 822.452.B, Reel No. A8144, fr. 131.

28. Ibid.

29. JPS Paper No. 107, Reel No. A8019, frs. 1068–9; Kirby, *War against Japan*, vol. 3, 10.

30. JPS Paper No. 107, Reel No. A8019, Annex 1, fr. 1077, and Appendix E, fr. 1094.

31. Report by the Joint Planning Staff: Examination of JPS Paper No. 107—Plan B, JPS Paper No. 109, 2 Oct 1943, AFHRA No. 805.322-6, Reel No. A8019, frs. 1099–1100 (hereafter cited as JPS Paper No. 109).

32. JPS Paper No. 109, frs. 1100–1.

33. Ibid., fr. 1101.

34. Ibid., frs. 1103–4.

35. Message, Col. F. D. Merrill to AGWAR, 2 Oct 1943, AFHRA No. 805.322-6, Reel No. A8019, fr. 1063.

36. Sykes, *Orde Wingate*, 469, 476; Royle, *Orde Wingate*, 274.

37. Sykes, *Orde Wingate*, 471–2; Royle, *Orde Wingate*, 274, 277.

38. Sykes, *Orde Wingate*, 471, 473.

39. Allen, *Burma*, 319–20.

40. Harkening back to his service in Palestine and Abyssinia, Wingate wanted to call his organization "Gideon Force." India Command would not agree to this and instead gave his unit the undistinguished name of "Special Force" (see Sykes, *Orde Wingate*, 473).

41. Report on Operations Carried Out by the Special Force Oct 1943 to Sept 1944, AFHRA No. 808.04A, Reel No. A8036, frs. 595–6, 598 (hereafter cited as Special Force).

42. Bidwell, *Chindit War*, 55–7; Special Force, fr. 595.

43. Sykes, *Orde Wingate*, 475–81; Royle, *Orde Wingate*, 279.

44. Cochran Interview, 261.
45. Thomas, *Back to Mandalay*, 109–11.
46. Cochran Interview, 206.
47. Alison Air Room Interview II, Reel No. A8042, fr. 2092; Thomas, *Back to Mandalay*, 117–9; Cochran Interview, 375–7.
48. Kirby, *War against Japan*, vol. 3, 5.
49. JPS Paper No. 107, Reel No. A8019, fr. 1067.

Chapter 4

1. Unit History of the First Air Commando Force, fr. 1406.
2. JICA No. 1449, fr. 2302.
3. Ibid., frs. 2302–3, 2305; Glider Operations, fr. 534. Although the TG-5s were apparently considered for use behind enemy lines in a communications and air warning role, lack of the necessary equipment forced the cancellation of this idea (see Glider Operations, fr. 547).
4. JICA No. 1449, fr. 2305.
5. Project 9 Chronology, fr. 616.
6. HQ AAF, IBT/CBI, General Orders No. 20, 27 Nov 1943, AFHRA No. GP-A-CMDO-1-SU-OR-G, 1943–1945, Reel No. B0681, fr. 597.
7. JICA No. 1833, 12 Apr 1944, Burma—Wingate Report on Airborne Invasion of, AFHRA No. 810.6091-A, Reel No. A8042, fr. 2209 (hereafter cited as JICA No. 1833); Thomas, *Back to Mandalay*, 143; JICA No. 1449, fr. 2305; Medical History of Project #9, fr. 1688.
8. Thomas, *Back to Mandalay*, 140; Unit History of the First Air Commando Force, fr. 1406.
9. JICA No. 1449, fr. 2305.
10. JICA No. 1449, fr. 2306.
11. Memorandum, John Alison to Gen. H. H. Arnold, Subj: History, Status and Immediate Requirements for First Air Commando Force, 21 Jan 1944, AFHRA No. 145.81-170, Reel No. A1378, fr. 606 (hereafter cited as Alison Memo).
12. JICA No. 1448, fr. 2072.
13. Probert, *Forgotten Air Force*, 173. See also, John Masters, *The Road Past Mandalay* (New York: Bantam Books, 1979), 146; and Richard Rhodes James, *Chindit* (London: John Murray, 1980), 32.
14. William Slim, *Defeat into Victory* (New York: David McKay Company, 1961), 188.
15. Brig. Gen. William D. Old Command Diary, 4 Jan 1944, AFHRA No. 833.13-1, Reel No. A8263, fr. 13 (hereafter cited as Old Diary).
16. Old Diary, 5 Jan 1944, fr. 13; JICA No. 1579, 16 Mar 1944, Report of Troop Carrier Command Participation in "Thursday Operation," AFHRA No. 810.6091A, Reel No. A8042, fr. 2288 (hereafter cited as JICA No. 1579).
17. Old Diary, 8 and 15 Jan 1944, frs. 14 and 20.
18. JICA No. 1449, fr. 2306.
19. Ibid., fr. 2307.
20. Ibid., frs. 2306–7; Project 9 Chronology, fr. 616; Thomas, *Back to Mandalay*, 128.
21. Thomas, *Back to Mandalay*, 128; Special Force, frs. 595–6.

22. Troop Carrier Command aircraft also participated in exercises with Special Force. Serious night training for the TCC crews did not begin until late January, however (see Old Diary, 28 Jan 1944, fr. 40).

23. Bernard Fergusson, *The Wild Green Earth* (London: Collins, 1952), 218.

24. Nonetheless, the Air Commando's brashness and uninhibited demeanor soon led the Chindits to call their American comrades "Cochran's Glamour Girls" or "Cochran's Young Ladies." This tongue-in-cheek cognomen alluded to a British impresario by the name of Cochran, whose specialty was shows featuring scantily clad showgirls (see Masters, *Road Past Mandalay*, 146, and Hilary St. George Saunders, *The Fight Is Won* [London: Her Majesty's Stationery Office, 1954], 332).

25. Ibid.; James, *Chindit*, 33.

26. Maisters, *Road Past Mandalay*, 147–8.

27. JICA No. 1448, fr. 2084; British Air Ministry, *Wings of the Phoenix* (London: His Maesty's Stationery Office, 1949), 64–5.

28. Terence O'Brien, *Out of the Blue* (London: Collins, 1984), 23–4, 48.

29. Fergusson, *Wild Green Earth*, 219.

30. Unit History of the First Air Commando Force, fr. 1406; Memorandum, Capt. Charley T. Embree, Subj: Project 9 Training, 14 Mar 1944, AFHRA No. 822.452B, Reel No. A8144, frs. 59–60.

31. Maj. Gen. George E. Stratemeyer to Gen. H. H. Arnold, Subj: Resume of "Thursday" Operations, 22 Mar 1944, AFHRA No. 815.452, Reel No. A8056, fr. 1596.

32. Unit History of the First Air Commando Force, fr. 1406; Van Wagner, *Any Place*, 36.

33. Masters, *Road Past Mandalay*, 148; Fergusson, *Wild Green Earth*, 219–22.

34. Message, Maj. Gen. George E. Stratemeyer to Gen. H. H. Arnold, 7 Jan 44, AFHRA No. 822.452B, Reel No. A8144, fr. 66; Lt. Gen. George E. Stratemeyer, Personal Diary, 1943–1947, 16 December 1943, Thomas Overlander Collection, Air Force Academy, Colorado Springs, Colo. (hereafter cited as Stratemeyer Personal Diary).

35. The Medical History of Project #9, fr. 1641; Message, CG, AAF, IBS, CBI to CG 10th AAF, Calcutta, 13 Jan 44, AFHRA No. 825.16231, Reel No. A8183, fr. 927. One source wrote that the Air Commandos had eleven B-25Hs and one B-25J. The J model reverted to the earlier glazed "bombardier" nose, but it kept the four blister guns of the H. It also went back to two pilots, increasing the crew to six (see Chuck Baisden, *Flying Tiger to Air Commando* [Santa Fe, N. Mex.: Mustang International Publishers, 1994], 93).

36. Thomas, *Back to Mandalay*, 179–80.

37. Ibid., 131.

38. Ibid., 134.

39. Ibid., 129–34.

40. Glider Operations, fr. 535.

41. Ibid.; Cochran Interview, 238; JICA No. 1449, fr. 2308.

42. Thomas, *Back to Mandalay*, 135–6; Alison Interview, 371.

43. JICA No. 1449, fr. 2308.

44. Glider Operations, fr. 536; Thomas, *Back to Mandalay*, 138, 140.

45. Alison Memo, fr. 605.

46. Ibid.

47. Medical History of Project #9, Reel no. B0680 fr. 1597.

48. Thomas, *Back to Mandalay*, 141.

49. Glider Operations, fr. 537.

50. Thomas, *Back to Mandalay*, 141–2.

51. Adm. Louis Mountbatten to Col. P. Cochran, 18 Jan 1944, AFHRA No. GP-A-CMDO-1-SU-CO, Jan 1944–Aug 1945, Reel No. B0681, fr. 581.

52. Alison Memo, fr. 607.

53. Rear Echelon, HQ USAF, CBI, General Orders No. 28, 28 Mar 1944, AFHRA No. GP-A-CMDO-SU-OR-G, 1943–1945, Reel No. B0681, fr. 596.

54. Ibid.

55. Old Diary, 1 Feb 1944, frs. 49–50.

56. Old Diary, 2 Feb 1944, fr. 51.

57. Brig. Gen. Charles B. Stone III to Air Commander, 3rd Tactical Air Force, 13 Jan 1944, Subj: Integration, AFHRA No. 822.311, Reel No. A8143, fr. 461; Fourteenth Army and Eastern Air Command Combined Operation Instruction No. 4, 4 Feb 1944, AFHRA No. 815.452, Reel No. A8056, frs. 1531–5.

58. Old Diary, 16 Jan 1944, fr. 21.

59. Old Diary, 17 Jan 1944, fr. 22; Minutes of Conference Held between Brig. Touloch [*sic*] and Brig. General Old and Their Staffs, at HQs, Troop Carrier Command, 17 Jan 1944, AFHRA No. 822.151, Reel No. A8142, fr. 454.

60. Old Diary, 18 and 20 Jan 1944, frs. 23–4, 26.

61. Old Diary, 5 Feb 1944, fr. 55; Old Diary, 17 and 20 Jan 1944, frs. 23 and 26; Message, Air Cdr. Eastern Air Command (India) to Air Cdr. Troop Carrier Command, 22 Jan 1944, AFHRA No. 820.16231, Reel No. A8086, fr. 1763; Brig. Gen. William D. Old to Maj. Burwell, Subj: Directive, 27 Jan 1944, with handwritten note, "I cancelled this. Lyons," AFHRA No. 833.452A, Reel No. A8263, fr. 254.

62. Message, HQ Air Cdr. SEA to Eastern Air Command, 10 Jan 1944, AFHRA No. 820.312, Reel No. A8104, fr. 1211; Message, Eastern Air Command to A.C. Strategic Air Force, et al., 11 Jan 1944, AFHRA No. 820.16231, Reel No. A8086, fr. 1799; Old Diary, 8, 15, and 22 Jan and 7 Feb 1944, frs. 14, 20, 29, 58; Col. Samuel T. Moore, "Tactical Employment in the U.S. Army of Transport Aircraft and Gliders in World War II," n.d., AFHRA No. 546.04, Reel No. C5017, frs. 448–9 (hereafter cited as Moore, "Tactical Employment").

63. Old Diary, 20, 25, 26, 27 Jan 1944, frs. 27, 33, 35, 37.

64. Thomas, *Back to Mandalay*, 144; The Medical History of Project #9, fr. 1598.

65. Message, Ledo to Hqs AAF, 28 Jan 1944, AFHRA No. 825.16222-21, Reel No. A8180, fr. 1725; Medical History of Project #9, fr. 1640; Message, AC, Eastern Air Command (India) to Davidson, 25 Jan 1944, AFHRA No. 820.1623, Reel No. A8086, fr. 1752.

66. To Commanding General, Tenth Air Force, Subj: Company History, 10 May 1944, AFHRA No. ENGR-900-HI, Reel No. A0267, fr. 1308.

67. Old Diary, 6 Mar 1944, fr. 116. Major Page, the flight surgeon, makes no mention of this incident in his medical history of Project #9, although he does discuss this episode and of meeting Old in his postwar memoir *Air Commando Doc* (see Robert Collier Page, Air Commando Doc, as told to Alfred Aiken [New York: Bernard Ackerman, 1945], 121–5). Page mistakenly believed Old was fresh from the States

and was extremely disparaging of Old in his book. Stratemeyer's chief of staff, Brig. Gen. Charles B. Stone III, also noted the unit's appearance, saying after the war, "They were well-disciplined for doing the job, but they were very unsoldierly like" (see Lt. Gen. Charles B. Stone III, interview by Capt. Mark C. Cleary, 26–28 April 1984, 112, AFHRA No. K239.0512-1585).

68. Thomas, *Back to Mandalay*, 149.

69. Moore, "Tactical Employment," fr. 446.

70. "Burma Operations Record. 15th Army Operations in Imphal Area and Withdrawal to Northern Burma," Japanese Monograph No. 134, in *War in Asia and the Pacific*, vol. 6 (New York: Garland Publishing, Inc., 1980), 9–10, 27 (hereafter cited as "Burma Operations Record").

71. Allen, *Burma*, 150–88; Patrick Turnbull, *Battle of the Box* (London: Ian Allan Ltd., 1979), 35.

72. Old Diary, 25 Feb 1944, fr. 97.

73. Old Diary, 8 and 21 Feb 1944, frs. 60, 89.

74. Historical Reports, Tenth AAF Combat Camera Unit, 1 Feb 1944 and 1 Mar 1944, AFHRA No. UNIT-CC-10-HI, Reel No. A0487, frs. 1671–2, 1686.

75. Historical Reports, Tenth AAF Combat Camera Unit, 1 Feb 1944 and 1 Mar 1944, AFHRA No. UNIT-CC-10-HI, Reel No. A0487, fr. 1681; Thomas, *Back to Mandalay*, 198–9.

76. Thomas, *Back to Mandalay*, 152.

Chapter 5

1. JICA No. 1834, 15 Apr 1944, Burma—Supplemental Report on First Air Commando, AFHRA No. 810.6091A, Reel No. A8042, fr. 2158 (hereafter cited as JICA No. 1834); Message, Comilla to HQ AAF CBI, et al., 8 Feb 1944, AFHRA No. 825.16222-10, Reel No. A8174.

2. Thomas, *Back to Mandalay*, 182.

3. JICA No. 1834, fr. 2159; Van Wagner, *Any Place*, 39.

4. Ibid.; Thomas, *Back to Mandalay*, 183; Medical History of Project #9, fr. 1641; Edward Young, *The Air Commando Fighters of World War II* (North Branch, Minn.: Voyageur Press, 2000), 15–6.

5. JICA No. 1834, fr. 2159; Thomas, *Back to Mandalay*, 183.

6. Ibid., frs. 2158–64; Unit History of the First Air Commando Force, fr. 1408.

7. JICA No. 1448, fr. 2074; JICA No. 3138, fr. 2281.

8. Charles F. Romanus and Riley Sunderland, *Stilwell's Command Problems* (Washington, D.C.: Office of the Chief of Military History, 1956), 136–8; JICA No. 1448, fr. 2074; Unit History of the First Air Commando Force, fr. 1408; JICA No. 1338, fr. 2282.

9. Fergusson, *Wild Green Earth*, 54.

10. Medical History of Project #9, fr. 1641.

11. Headquarters, Troop Carrier Command Operations Order No. 7, 2 Feb 1944, AFHRA No. 833.327-1, Reel No. A8263, fr. 217; Memorandum, Headquarters, Troop Carrier Command to Commanding General, Tenth U.S. Air Force, Subj: History of Organization, 1 Mar 1944, AFHRA No. 833.01, Reel No. A8262, frs. 1072–4.

12. There is some confusion in the records as to when this squadron went to Tamu. The Medical History of Project #9 indicates the squadron was there prior to February 21 (see fr. 1641). The Unit History of the First Air Commando Force states that the light plane base was established on March 2 (see Unit History of the First Air Commando Force, fr. 1409).

13. Unit History of the First Air Commando Force, fr. 1409.

14. Allen, *Burma*, 175–88. The term "box" went back many years to when British forces, under pressure from the enemy, formed squares and boxes so as to repel attacks from any direction.

15. Turnbull, *Battle of the Box*, 51, 69, 133–4.

16. Report, "Air Support to 15 Corps in Arakan," n.d., AFHRA No. 818.4501-1, Reel No. A8067, frs. 1384–5.

17. JICA No. 1448, fr. 2075; Medical History of Project #9, frs. 1645–9.

18. JICA No. 1449, fr. 2311; Thomas, *Back to Mandalay*, 155.

19. Thomas, *Back to Mandalay*, 155.

20. Philip D. Chinnery, *Any Time, Any Place* (Annapolis: Naval Institute Press, 1994), 18. "Any Time, Any Place," is today the motto of the USAF's 16th Special Operations Wing.

21. Thomas, *Back to Mandalay*, 184; JICA No. 1448, fr. 2075; JICA No. 1449, fr. 2311.

22. Fergusson, *Wild Green Earth*, 60–5; Thomas, *Back to Mandalay*, 186; JICA No. 1448, frs. 2075–76; JICA No. 1449, fr. 2312.

23. Fergusson, *Wild Green Earth*, 67–9.

24. Ibid., 68–9.

25. Unit History of the First Air Commando Force, fr. 1408.

26. Old Diary, 20 Feb 1944, fr. 87.

27. Old Diary, 23 Feb and 6 Mar 1944, frs. 92, 116.

28. Moore, "Tactical Employment," fr. 450.

29. Brig. Gen. William D. Old to Commanding General, Eastern Air Command, 16 Mar 1944, Subj: Report of Troop Carrier Command Participation in Thursday Operation, AFHRA No. 815.452, Reel No. A805, fr. 1577. JICA No. 1579 is a sanitized version of this letter. Also see Old Diary, 6 Mar 1944, fr. 117.

30. Old Diary, 23 Feb 1944, fr. 92.

31. Old Diary, fr. 93; Old Diary, 6 Mar 1944, fr. 117; JICA No. 1579, 1 Apr 1944, Report of Troop Carrier Command Participation in "Thursday Operation," AFHRA No. 810.6091A, Reel No. A8042, fr. 2289 (hereafter cited as JICA No. 1579).

32. Headquarters, Troop Carrier Command Operations Order No. 14, 29 Feb 1944, AFHRA No. 833.327-1, Reel No. A8263, frs. 208–12.

33. JICA No. 1579, fr. 2289.

34. Medical History of Project #9, frs. 1642–3.

Chapter 6

1. Thomas, *Back to Mandalay*, 192–3.

2. Unless otherwise noted, Russhon's account is from Thomas, *Back to Mandalay*, 198–204.

3. Historical Report, Tenth AAF Combat Camera Unit, 31 Mar 1944, AFHRA No. UNIT-CC-10-HI, Reel No. A0487, frs. 1680–1.

4. JICA No. 1833, fr. 2195; Slim, *Defeat into Victory*, 278; Michael Calvert, *Chindit—Long Range Penetration* (New York: Ballantine Books, 1973), 21–3. Interestingly, retired USAF chief of staff Gen. John P. McConnell claimed in a 1971 interview that it was he who was in charge of the entire operation, that he sent Russhon to take the photos, and that he made the decision to put everything into Broadway. Actually, in March 1944, though he was 3rd TAF deputy commander, McConnell was then just a colonel and hardly in position to do any of the things he claimed (see Gen. John P. McConnell Interview, 24 Sep 1971, 13–5, AFHRA No. K239.0512-611).

5. JICA No. 1833, fr. 2195; Slim, *Defeat into Victory*, 227–8; Tulloch, *Wingate in Peace*, 198–200; Bidwell, *Chindit War*, 105–6.

6. Slim, *Defeat into Victory*, 228.

7. Barbara P. King and Edward M. Leete, *The 1st Air Commando Group of World War II: An Historical Perspective* (Maxwell AFB, Ala.: Air Command and Staff College, 1977), 120–1; Moore, "Tactical Employment," fr. 451.

8. General Old recorded in his diary that Olson and CWO Bruce Evans were picked up on March 9 off a sandbar onto which a TG-5 glider was landed. The small glider was then snatched by an L-5. No other Air Commando records mention this event, but if it is true (and it is doubtful the general made it up), it marked the only use of the training glider in combat operations (see Old Diary, 9 Mar 1944, fr. 129).

9. Thomas, *Back to Mandalay*, 233–45; Medical History of Project #9, fr. 1670.

10. Ibid., 233; Allen, *Burma*, 326; JICA No. 1833, fr. 2196; Glider Operations, fr. 541; Medical History of Project #9, frs. 1662–4. Another Air Commando glider pilot, Flight Officer Martin J. McTigue, was also captured. His captors executed him soon after (see Philip D. Chinnery, *March or Die* [Shrewsbury, England: Airlife, 1997], 114).

11. "Burma Operations Record," 94–5; Allen, *Burma*, 327–8.

12. "Burma Operations Record," 95–6; Kirby, *War against Japan*, vol. 3, 185–6; Rossetto, *Major General Orde Charles Wingate*, 311–2.

13. Unless otherwise noted, the details of the Broadway operations are derived from JICA No. 1833, frs. 2199–204; JICA No. 1448, frs. 2077–83; and Thomas, *Back to Mandalay*, 207–30.

14. JICA No. 1833, fr. 2201.

15. Old Diary, 6 Mar 1944, fr. 119.

16. Alison Interview, 403.

17. Ed Cunningham, "Burma Air Invasion," *Yank*, May 5, 1944, 3.

18. JICA No. 1834, fr. 2140.

19. Alison Interview, 405.

20. JICA No. 1448, fr. 2080.

21. Old Diary, 7 Mar 1944, fr. 123.

22. Old Diary, 8 Mar 1944, fr. 126; JICA No. 1833, frs. 2202–3, 2220–1. Old's distress about the Air Commandos did not just concern their combat operations. On March 14, he requested an inspector general investigation into the conduct of one individual who he alleged had destroyed telephone communications to the rear by shooting out insulators on telephone poles while Operation Thursday was under way (see Old Diary, 14 Mar 1944, fr. 138).

23. Special Force, frs. 600–1.

24. JICA No. 1833, frs. 2196–7, 2202–3, 2222–7.
25. JICA No. 1448, fr. 2082.
26. JICA No. 1834, fr. 2166.
27. Alison Interview, 411–3; Old Diary, 10 Mar 1944, fr. 131.
28. Alison Interview, 413.
29. JICA No. 1448, fr. 2082; JICA No. 1833, frs. 2228, 2237.
30. Message, Combined Headquarters, 3rd Indian Division to No. 1 Air Commando, n.d. ca. 9 Mar 1944; Unit History of the First Air Commando Force, fr. 580.
31. Message, Headquarters Air Command SEA to Eastern Air Command, 18 Mar 1944, AFHRA No. 820.2981, Reel No. A8096, fr. 964.
32. Hubert Krug, interview by Edward Young, Sept. 18–21, 1996 (hereafter cited as Krug Interview); Young, *Air Commando Fighters*, 27.
33. JICA No. 468, 22 Jun 1944, Radar Operations at Air Commando Field ("Broadway") in Burma, AFHRA No. 810.6091T, Reel No. A8044, frs. 846–8; Young, *Air Commando Fighters*, 27.
34. JICA No. 1834, fr. 2147; Old Diary, 14 Mar 1944, fr. 138.
35. Maurer Maurer, ed., *Air Force Combat Units of World War II* (Washington, D.C.: Office of Air Force History, 1983), 19; Message, Washington to HQ Army Air Forces and Headquarters USAF CBI, 26 Mar 1944, AFHRA No. 825.16222-32, Reel No. A 8182, fr. 716.
36. JICA No. 3138, 5 Jun 1944, Light Plane Operations of the First Air Commando Group in Burma, AFHRA No. 810.6091A, Reel No. A8042, fr. 2282; Van Wagner, *Any Place*, 67; Message, Hailakandi to Delhi, 2 Apr 1944, AFHRA No. 825.16221, Reel No. A8161, fr. 1494; Message, CG AAF IBS CBI to CO, 5318th Air Unit (Prov), 4 Apr 1944, AFHRA No. 825.16231, Reel No. A8184, fr. 201.
37. Special Force, frs. 603, 611.
38. JICA No. 1448, fr. 2084; Special Force, fr. 601; Glider Operations, frs. 542–3.
39. Special Force, frs. 601–2.
40. Ibid., fr. 602.
41. The B-25 crew was 1st Lt. Brian F. Hodges, pilot; 2nd Lt. Stephen A. Wanderer, navigator; TSgt. Frank Sadoski, gunner; TSgt. James W. Hickey, radioman; and SSgt. Vernon A. McIninch, flight engineer. In addition to Wingate, the passengers were Captain George Borrow, Wingate's aide, and war correspondents Stanley Wills and Stuart Emeny.
42. JICA No. 1834, fr. 2170.
43. Special Force, fr. 623.
44. Unit History of the First Air Commando Force, fr. 1414.
45. JICA No. 3137, 20 May 1944, Final Operations of First Air Commando Group in Burma, AFHRA No. 810.6091A, Reel No. A8042, fr. 2120 (hereafter cited as JICA No. 3137); Young, *Air Commando Fighters*, 31.
46. JICA No. 3137, fr. 2125.
47. Unit History of the First Air Commando Force, fr. 1415.
48. U.S. Navy Air Combat Information Report No. 1, Direct Air Support to Long Range Penetration Groups of the Third Indian Division in North Burma, Provided by the First Air Commando Group, USAAF. Unit History of the First Air Commando Force, frs. 1970–1; JICA No. 1834, fr. 2171.

Chapter 7

1. Young, *Air Commando Fighters*, 23.
2. JICA No. 1834, fr. 2168.
3. Young, *Air Commando Fighters*, 31.
4. Ibid., 31–2; Lt. Col. Grant Mahony to Commanding General, USAAF, 27 Apr 1944. Subj: Report on Rocket Installation on P-51 Type Aircraft, AFHRA No. GP-A-CMDO-1-SU-RE, Reel No. B0681, frs. 694–5.
5. Young, *Air Commando Fighters*, 32.
6. JICA No. 1834, fr. 2165.
7. JICA No. 1834; Young, *Air Commando Fighters*, 24.
8. Young, *Air Commando Fighters*, 30.
9. Ibid., 24.
10. Krug Interview. Krug initially identified the bombers as Bettys. The twin-engine Betty was probably the most famous Japanese bomber of the war, and Allied pilots invariably described any twin-engine bomber they attacked as a "Betty." The Betty was, however, an Imperial Japanese Navy aircraft, and, more often than not, it was not even based in regions such as the CBI, which was Japanese Army Air Force territory.
11. JICA No. 1834, fr. 2166; Young, *Air Commando Fighters*, 24–5; Olin B. Carter, interview by Edward Young, Sept. 18–21, 1996.
12. JICA No. 1834, fr. 2166.
13. Message, CG, AAF, IBS, CBI to 5318th Air Unit (P), 9 Mar 1944, AFHRA No. 825.16231, Reel No. A8183, fr. 602.
14. JICA No. 1834, fr. 2167.
15. Ibid., frs. 2167–8; Olin B. Carter, interview by Edward Young, Sept 18–21, 1996; Young, *Air Commando Fighters*, 25–6.
16. JICA No. 1834, fr. 2171.
17. Ibid., fr. 2178.
18. Young, *Air Commando Fighters*, 28.
19. Ibid.
20. JICA No. 1834, frs. 2155–7, 2178–9; Young, *Air Commando Fighters*, 27–8.
21. JICA No. 1834, fr. 2131; Craven and Cate, *Army Air Forces*, vol. 4, 490–1.
22. Craven and Cate, *Army Air Forces*, vol. 4, 491.
23. JICA No. 3137, fr. 2125; Young, *Air Commando Fighters*, 31.
24. Craven and Cate, *Army Air Forces*, vol. 4, 490; JICA No. 3137, fr. 2126.
25. JICA No. 2330, 3 May 1944, First Combat Use of Helicopter in Burma, AFHRA No. 810.609.1, Reel No. A8041, frs. 1238–41; JICA No. 3137, fr. 2116
26. JICA No. 3137, frs. 2123, 2126–7.
27. Ibid., fr. 2123.
28. Ibid., frs. 2123–4; Young, *Air Commando Fighters*, 29.
29. JICA No. 3137, fr. 2129.
30. Ibid., fr. 2131; Young, *Air Commando Fighters*, 33.
31. Jack Klarr, interview by Edward Young, May 20, 1996.
32. JICA No. 3137, fr. 2132; Young, *Air Commando Fighters*, 30.
33. JICA No. 3137, fr. 2132.

34. Ibid., frs. 2112–5.
35. Unit History of the First Air Commando Force, fr. 1418.

Chapter 8

1. Air Marshal James Baldwin to Maj. Gen. George E. Stratemeyer, 24 Mar 1944, Subj: Absorption of No. 1 Air Commando Force, AFHRA No. 815.452, Reel No. A8056, fr. 1429.
2. Ibid.
3. Message, Air Ministry to Headquarters Air Command, SEA, 12 Apr 1944, AFHRA No. 815.452, Reel No. A8056, fr. 1431.
4. Message, CG AAF, IBS, CBI to CG AAF, 18 Mar 1944, AFHRA No. 825.16231, Reel No. A8183, frs. 526–8; Maj. Gen. George E. Stratemeyer to Air Commander-in-Chief, Air Command, South East Asia, 26 Mar 1944, Subj: 5318th Air Unit (Provisional), AFHRA No. 820.161, Reel No. A8070, frs. 1785–7; Maj. Gen. George E. Stratemeyer to AM Sir James Baldwin, 29 Mar 1944, AFHRA No. 815.452, Reel No. A8056, frs. 1426–7; Memorandum, Lt. Col. J. T. Kenny for Col. Halverson, Subj: CBI Activities—17 thru 22 Mar, 1944, AFHRA No. 145.81-170, Reel No. A1378, fr. 1141.
5. Message, CG AAF, IBS, CBI to CG AAF, 13 Apr 1944, AFHRA No. 825.16231, Reel No. A8184, fr. 122; Memorandum, Maj. Gen. H.A. Craig to AC/AS Plans, Subj: Personnel for CBI Theatre, 21 Mar 1944, AFHRA No. 145.81-170, Reel No. A1378, fr. 1141.
6. Gen. H. H. Arnold to Adm. Louis Mountbatten, 24 Mar 1944, AFHRA No. 145.81-170, Reel No. A1378, frs. 556–7.
7. Message, Washington to Hqrs, Army Air Forces, 28 Mar 1944, AFHRA No. 145.81-170, Reel No. A1378, fr. 707.
8. Alison Interview, 422–3.
9. Ibid., 425. For examples of the messages directing Cochran's return, see Message, Washington to Hqrs Army Air Forces, 14 Apr 1944, AFHRA No. 825.16222-32, Reel No. A8182, fr. 629; Message, CG AAF, IBS, CBI Theater to CO, 5318th Air Unit (P), et al., 17 Apr 1944, AFHRA No. 825.16231, Reel No. A8184, fr. 94; Message, WAR to CG AAF, CBI, IBS, 4 May 1944, AFHRA No. 825.16222-32, Reel No. A8182, fr. 564.
10. See summaries of messages to and from SEAC in Agenda for Meeting: Air Commando and Combat Cargo Groups, n.d., AFHRA No. 145.81-170, Reel No. A1378, frs. 497–502.
11. Memorandum, AC/AS Operations, Commitments and Requirements to AC/AS Plans, 22 Apr 1944, Subj: Plans for Utilization of Air Commandos in CBI, AFHRA No. 145.81-170, Reel No. A1378, fr. 536.
12. Ibid.
13. Administrative History, Army Air Forces, India–Burma Sector, China–Burma–India, May–June 1944, AFHRA No. 825.02, Reel No. A8155, frs. 553–63.
14. Message, New Delhi to CG AAF CBI IBS, 11 Apr 1944, AFHRA No. 825.16222-11, Reel No. A8174, fr. 304.
15. Message, CG AAF IBS CBI to CG AAF, 16 Aug 1944, AFHRA No. 825.16231, Reel No. A8185, frs. 589–90. See also, Message, CG AAF IBS CBI to CG AAF

Washington, 12 Aug 1944, AFHRA No. 825.16231, Reel No. A8185, fr. 655; Message, CG AAF IBS CBI Theater to CG AAF Washington, 13 Aug 1944, AFHRA No. 825.16231, Reel No. A8185, fr. 638; and Message, Washington to CG AAF, 15 Aug 1944, AFHRA No. 825.16222-32, Reel No. A8182, fr. 186.

16. Message, Washington to CG AAF CBI IBS, et al, 19 Aug 1944, AFHRA No. 825.16222-32, Reel No. A8182, fr. 160.

17. HQ AAF, India–Burma Sector, CBI Theater General Orders No. 144, 26 Aug 1944, AFHRA No. GP-A-CMDO-1-HI, Reel No. B0681, frs. 594–95; HQ AAF, India–Burma Sector, CBI Theater General Orders No. 170, 30 Sep 1944 and No. 175, 5 Oct 1944, AFHRA No. SQ-FI-CMDO-6-HI, Reel No. A0828, frs. 1373–5; Headquarters AAF–CBI History, Jul–Dec 1944, AFHRA No. 825.02, Reel No. A8155, frs. 729–30.

18. Minutes of Meeting Held in B.G.S. Office on 3 Sep 1944 to Discuss Provision of Aircraft for Training of Special Force, HQ Special Force, 3 Sep 1944, AFHRA No. 815.142, Reel No. A8047, frs. 1838–9. See Bidwell, *Chindit War*, 256–80, for graphic descriptions of the Chindit's last battles.

19. Unit History of the First Air Commando Force, frs. 1506, 2005–6.

20. Wedemeyer had been the SEAC deputy chief of staff from November 16, 1943 to August 27, 1944.

21. Hayes, *History of the Joint Chiefs*, 645–52; Mountbatten Report, 68.

22. A longer strip, suitable for C-47s, opened on November 16, and a second strip for L-5s and gliders became operational two days later (see 165 LS Intell Report, 20 Nov 1944, AFHRA No. 820.301, Reel No. A8097, fr. 172).

23. 165 LS Intell Report, 20 Nov 1944, AFHRA No. 820.301, Reel No. A8097, frs. 1506–8; 165 LS Intelligence Report, 10 Nov 1944, AFHRA No. GP-A-CMDO-1-SU, Reel No. B0681, frs. 470–2.

24. Unit History of the First Air Commando Force, frs. 1507–8.

25. 165 LS Intelligence Report, 10 Nov 1944, Reel No. B0681, fr. 472.

26. 165 LS Intell Report, 20 Nov 1944, AFHRA No. 820.301, Reel No. A8097, frs. 1264, 1267.

27. 166 LS History, AFHRA No. SQ-LIA-166-HI, Reel No. 0849, frs. 44–5 (hereafter cited as 166 LS History); Message, Asansol to CG AAF, 7 Nov 1944, AFHRA No. 825.16221, Reel No. A8162, fr. 123.

28. Message, Air Commander, EAC to Air Commander, 3 TAF, 10 Oct 1944, AFHRA No. 820.322-1, Reel No. A8109, fr. 68.

29. Message, AC, EAC to CG, Tenth Air Force, et al, AFHRA No. 820.322-1, Reel No. A8109, fr. 69; Message, CG, EAC to CO, 1st ACG, 10 Oct 1944, AFHRA No. 820.322-1, Reel No. A8109, fr. 70.

30. EAC Weekly Intelligence Summary No. 14, 1 Dec 1944, AFHRA No. 820.607, Reel No. A8119, fr. 423 (hereafter cited as EAC Weekly Intelligence Summary No. 14); 5th Fighter Squadron, Commando, No. SQ-FI-CMDO-5-HI, Reel A0828, fr. 1916 (hereafter cited as 5 FS History).

31. EAC Weekly Intelligence Summary No. 14, fr. 423; 6th Fighter Squadron, Commando. No. SQ-FI-CMDO-6-HI, Reel No. A0828, fr. 1947 (hereafter cited as 6 FS History).

32. HQ AAF, IBS, CBI Theater, A Study of Operation "L," 24 Oct 1944, AFHRA No. 820.423-1, Reel No. A8112, frs. 1275–6 (hereafter cited as A Study of Operation "L"); HQ EAC, Results of Fighter Attacks on Japanese Airfields in the Rangoon Area, 18–20 October, AFHRA No. 820.3121, Reel No. A8106, frs. 386–8 (hereafter cited as Results of Fighter Attacks).

33. Results of Fighter Attacks., frs. 386–8; A Study of Operation "L," fr. 1276; EAC Weekly Intelligence Summary No. 14, fr. 424; 6 FS History, fr. 1947.

34. 1st Air Commando Fighter Pilots, group interview by Edward Young, Sep 18–21, 1996.

35. A Study of Operation "L," fr. 1278.

36. Ibid., fr. 1280.

37. Ibid., fr. 1279.

38. Young, *Air Commando Fighters*, 39.

39. JICA No. 489, 8 Nov 1944, Air Attacks 3-4 November on Rangoon, Burma, AFHRA No. 810.6091Q-1, Reel No. A8043, frs. 1296–304; Special Report on Operation "Eruption," AFHRA No. 820.306, Reel No. 8097, frs. 190–6.

40. 5 FS History, frs. 1917–9; Young, *Air Commando Fighters*, 41.

41. EAC Intelligence Summary, 23 Feb 1945, "Air Commando Pilot Escapes From Hostile Territory," AFHRA No. 820.607, Reel No. A8120, frs. 736–7; Message, 221 Grp to 5 Sqdn, 041756 Jan 1945.

42. 165 LS Intell Report, 20 Nov 1944, AFHRA No. 820.301, Reel No. A8097, fr. 1272; First Air Commando Group Light Plane and Glider Operations, "Boston" Detachment, 23 Nov 1944, Reel No. A8097, fr. 171 (hereafter cited as Boston Detachment).

43. 165 LS Intell Report, 20 Nov 1944, AFHRA No. 820.301, Reel No. A8097, fr. 1277; 166 LS History, fr. 103; Boston Detachment, 3 Dec 1944, frs. 154–5.

44. King and Leete, *1st Air Commando Group*, 184–5.

45. General Orders No. 11, Headquarters Eastern Air Command (SEA), 1 Dec 1944, AFHRA No. 830.1623, Reel No. A8233, frs. 1094–5; G.O. No. 13, HQ EAC (SEA), 4 Dec 1944, AFHRA No. 820.193, Reel No. A8090, frs. 895–6.

46. Charles F. Romanus and Riley Sunderland, *Time Runs Out in CBI*, United States Army in World War II: The China–Burma–India Theater (Washington, D.C.: Office of the Chief of Military History, 1959), 142–7.

47. Ibid., 147.

48. JICA No. R15-C-45, 12 Mar 1945; Operation "Grubworm," The Airlift of Two Chinese Divisions from Burma to China, AFHRA No. 810.6091F-2, Reel No. A8043, fr. 366 (hereafter cited as Operation Grubworm Airlift).

49. Operation Grubworm Airlift, frs. 364–72; HQ 10AF Diary of Operation "Grubworm," 2 Dec 1944 thru 5 Jan 1945, AFHRA No. 830.04-2, Reel No. A8229, frs. 1042–66 (hereafter cited as Diary of Operation Grubworm); Col. Thomas H. Davies to Commanding General, Northern Combat Area Command, 12 Jan 1945, Subj: Air Lifts, New Sixth Army Units, AFHRA No. 830.04-2, Reel No. A8229, frs. 1101–11.

50. Van Wagner, *Any Place*, 101.

51. Unit History of the First Air Commando Force, fr. 2045; B-25h Night Intruder

Missions from the Period of the 23rd Dec 1944 to the 3rd Jan 1945, 9 Jan 1945, AFHRA No. GP-A-CMDO-HI, Reel No. B0681, frs. 21–3; B-25H Night Intruder Missions from the Period of 21 Jan through 31 Jan 1945, 7 Feb 1945, AFHRA No. 820.306, Reel No. A8097, frs. 604–5; Van Wagner, *Any Place*, 104.

52. EAC Intelligence Summary, 2 February 1945, "B-25 Crew Bails Out Safely After Jap LMG Fire K.O.s Engine," AFHRA No. 820.607, Reel No. A8120, frs. 430–3.

53. 5 FS History, fr. 1917; 6 FS History, fr. 1952.

54. 6 FS History, fr. 1953.

55. Ibid., fr. 1954.

56. Jack Klarr, interview by Edward Young, May 20, 1996.

Chapter 9

1. 5 FS History, fr. 1922; EAC Intelligence Summary, 26 Jan 1945, "Experiment with Three 1,000-lb. Bombs on P-47D23," AFHRA No. 820.607, Reel No. A8120, fr. 286; Roland Lynn, interview by Edward Young, Sept. 18–21, 1996; Young, *Air Commando Fighters*, 43–4.

2. Message, 404 Area to L of C Command, 151715 Jan 45, AFHRA No. 820.16221, Reel No. A8075, fr. 1674; Young, *Air Commando Fighters*, 44.

3. 5 FS History, Reel A0828, frs. 1237–8.

4. Ibid., frs. 1239–40; Young, *Air Commando Fighters*, 45.

5. JICA No. R-21-C-45, 28 Mar 1945, Burma—Joint Air/Ground Operations in Capture of Meiktila, AFHRA No. 810.6091M, Reel No. A8043, frs. 689–90 (hereafter cited as JICA R-21-C-45).

6. Allen, *Burma*, 398.

7. Minutes of Conference held at Combined Headquarters 14th Army/221 Group on 26th January, 1945 at 1130 hours, AFHRA No. 820.151, Reel No. A8069, frs. 1556–8; Joint Army/Air Plan for 4 Corps' Coming Operations, 31 Jan 1945, AFHRA No. 824.452-2, Reel No. A8151, frs. 54–6, 58–9, 66–7.

8. Col. L. S. Moseley to Air Officer, Commanding, No. 224 Group, RAF, 6 Feb 1945, Subj: Fighter Squadrons of First and Second Air Commando Groups, AFHRA No. 825.01, Reel No. A8153, frs. 1441–2; Message, CGCCTF to CG Eastern Air Command, 8 Feb 1945, AFHRA No. 820.1622-7, Reel No. A8078, fr. 61; Van Wagner, *Any Place*, 119.

9. Maj. Gen. George E. Stratemeyer to AOC, 224 Group, RAF, et al., 1 Mar 1945, Subj: Fighter Squadrons of 1st and 2nd Air Commando Groups, AFHRA No. 820.201-4, Reel No. A8091, frs. 319–20; HQ USAAF. AAF Evaluation Board, Aug 1944– Jul 1945, Nos. 138.7-5/-6/-8, 138.7A, Reel No. A1179; India–Burma and China Theaters Report No. 6, 15 Mar 1945, Effectiveness of Air Attack in Battle Areas in the India–Burma Theater, AFHRA No. 138.7-6, Reel No. A1179, fr. 996; Van Wagner, *Any Place*, 119.

10. Romanus and Sunderland, *Time Runs Out in CBI*, 220–1.

Chapter 10

1. Memorandum for the Record, Col. S. F. Giffin, Subj: Air Commando—Combat Cargo Groups for CBI, 3 Apr 1944, AFHRA No. 815.452, Reel No. A8056, fr. 1413.

2. Gen. H. H. Arnold to Adm. Louis Mountbatten, 24 Mar 1944, Gen. H. H. Arnold Papers, Container 199: CBI, 1941–44, Library of Congress.

3. Ibid.

4. Agenda for Meeting, Air Commando and Combat Cargo Groups, n.d., AFHRA No. 145.81-170, Reel No. A1378, fr. 498.

5. Memorandum, Maj. Gen. Thomas T. Handy for Chief of Staff [Gen. Marshall], Subj: Air Commando and Combat Cargo Groups for the CBI Theater, 9 Apr 1944, AFHRA No. 143.04J, Reel No. A1329, frs. 1852–5; Memorandum, Maj. Gen. Thomas T. Handy for Commanding General, Army Air Forces, Subj: Air Commando and Combat Cargo Groups for the CBI Theater, 9 Apr 1944, AFHRA No. 143.04J, Reel No. A1329, fr. 1856.

6. The inclusion of a second fighter, instead of a medium bomber, squadron was done at the recommendation of Alison (see Daily Activity Report of the Assistant Chief of Air Staff, Operations, Commitments & Requirements, 11 Apr 1944, AFHRA No. 123-2, Reel No. A1040, fr. 392).

7. Memo for Gen. Marshall, Subj: Air Commando and Combat Cargo Groups for the CBI Theater, 1 Apr 1944, AFHRA No. 145.81-170, Reel No. A1378, frs. 584–7.

8. Memorandum, Col. S. F. Giffin to Col. Wetzel, 27 Mar 1944, AFHRA No. 143.04J, Reel No. A1329, fr. 1729.

9. Daily Activity Reports to the Assistant Chief of Staff, Operations, Commitments & Requirements, 11 and 18 Apr 1944, AFHRA No. 123-2, Reel No. A1040, frs. 357, 389; Memo for the Assistant Chief of Staff, Operations Division, War Department General Staff, Subj: Air Commando Project, 11 Apr 1944, AFHRA No. 143.04J, Reel No. A1329, frs. 1593–95.

10. Daily Activity Reports, Assistant Chief of Staff, Operations, Commitments & Requirements, 21 and 22 May 1944, AFHRA No. 123-2, Reel No. A1040, fr. 652; Routing and Record Sheet, Asst C/AS, OCR (Requirements Division) to Asst C/AS, Personnel, Subj: Air Commando—Combat Cargo Project, 17 Apr 1944, AFHRA No. 143.04J, Reel No. A1329, fr. 1587.

11. Memorandum, AC/AS, OC&R to AC/AS, Personnel, Subj: Air Commando—Combat Cargo Groups, 11 Apr 1944, AFHRA No. 143.04J, Reel No. A1329, fr. 1770; Gen. Giles to Commanding General, Air Transport Command, Subj: Air Commando—Combat Cargo Groups, 15 Apr 1944, AFHRA No. 143.04J, Reel No. A1329, fr. 1848; Memorandum, Col. Lloyd P. Hopwood to Gen. Bevans, Subj: Procurement of First Pilot Requirements for Air Commando—Cargo Supply, 2 May 1944, AFHRA No. 143.04J, Reel No. A1329, fr. 1788.

12. Memorandum, Col. Lloyd P. Hopwood to Gen. Bevans, Subj: Procurement of First Pilot Requirements for Air Commando—-Cargo Supply, 2 May 1944, AFHRA No. 143.04J, Reel No. A1329, frs. 1788–9; Memorandum, Lt. Col. Roy H. Clarke to the Executive, Office of Assistant Chief of Air Staff, Personnel, Subj: Historical Report for Week Ending 29 April 1944, 2 May 1944, AFHRA No. 121.40, Reel No. A1022, fr. 703; Memorandum, Lt. Roy H. Clarke to Officers Branch, Subj: Manning of Flight Echelon Requirements for Air Commando—Combat Cargo Groups, 3 May 1944, AFHRA No. 143.04J, Reel No. A1329, fr. 1780; Memorandum, Lt. Col. Roy H. Clarke to (1) Officers Branch, (2) Enlisted Branch, Subj: Manning of Flight

Echelon Requirements for Air Commando—Cargo Supply, 3 May 1944, AFHRA No. 143.04J, Reel No. A1329, frs. 1782–3.

13. History of Headquarters, 2nd Air Commando Group, 1 May–31 May 1944, AFHRA No. GP-A-CMDO-2-HI, Reel No. B0681, frs. 701–2 (hereafter cited as 2 ACG History).

14. General Orders No. 163, Headquarters Third Air Force, 6 June 1944, AFHRA No. GP-A-CMDO-2-HI, Reel No. B0681, fr. 842; 2 FS History, fr. 853.

15. To many in the squadron Grosvenor was "the best pilot in the world," one who consistently beat Alison in friendly dogfights (see W. Robert Eason, Dale L. Grastorf, and Charles LeFan, interview by Edward Young, Oct. 13, 1995 [hereafter cited as Eason et al. Interview]; 2nd Air Commando Group, AFHRA GP-A-CMDO-2-HI, Reel No. B0681, fr. 852 [hereafter cited as 2 ACG]).

16. Maurer, *Air Force Combat Units*, 387; 318th Troop Carrier Squadron, AFHRA No. SQ-TR-CARR-318-HI, Reel No. B0004, frs. 251–2.

17. Maurer, *Air Force Combat Units*, 351.

18. Ibid., 354; 155 Liaison Sqdn Historical Reports, Feb–Apr 1944, AFHRA No. SQ-LIA-155-HI, Reel No. A0846, frs. 351–84; 155 Liaison Sqdn History, 1 May to 1 June 1944, AFHRA No. GP-A-CMDO-2-HI, Reel No. B0681, fr. 808 (hereafter cited as 155 LS History).

19. 156 Liaison Sqdn Historical Reports, Feb–Apr 1944, AFHRA No. SQ-LIA-156-HI, Reel No. A0846, frs. 554–76 (hereafter cited as 156 LS History); 2 ACG, frs. 760–3.

20. 236th Med Disp Avn Historical Report, Jun 1944, AFHRA No. GP-A-CMDO-2-HI, Reel No. B0681, fr. 881.

21. 327 ADS History, AFHRA No. GP-A-CMDO-2-HI, Reel No. B0681, fr. 772 (hereafter cited as 327 ADS History).

22. Histories, 327th, 328th, and 340th ADSs, May 1944, AFHRA No. GP-A-CMDO-2-HI, Reel No. B0681, frs. 769–73, 788–92, 802–4; History 342nd ADS, May 1944, AFHRA No. SQ-ADRM-342-HI, Reel No. A0519, fr. 1118.

23. Meeting Notes, ca. 27 Apr 1944, AFHRA No. 143.04J, Reel No. A1329, frs. 1604–5; Air Commando—Combat Cargo Project Status Report, 22 Jun 1944, AFHRA No. 143.04J, Reel No. A1329, frs. 1546, 1556.

24. Field Visitation Report, 14 Dec 44, AFHRA No. 830.935, Reel No. A261, frs. 1536–41.

25. Gen. H. H. Arnold to Adm. Lord Louis Mountbatten, 7 Jun 44, AFHRA No. 145.81-171, Reel No. A1378, frs. 881–2; Gen. H. H. Arnold to Maj. Gen. George E. Stratemeyer, 9 Jun 1944, AFHRA No. 145.81-171, Reel No. A1378, frs. 878–9.

26. Lt. Gen. Joseph W. Stilwell to Gen. H. H. Arnold, 26 Jun 1944, AFHRA No. 145.81-171, Reel No A1378, frs. 765–7.

27. Lt. Gen. J. W. Stilwell to Gen. H. H. Arnold, 5 Aug 1944, AFHRA No. 145.81-171, Reel No. A1378, frs. 1730–2.

28. 2 ACG History, frs. 707, 709; 2 FS History, frs. 868–70, 932; 155 LS History, frs. 743, 745.

29. 2 ACG History, fr. 720; 1 FS History, fr. 925; 2 FS History, frs. 854, 868–9; 155 LS History, fr. 954; 317 Troop Carrier Squadron History, AFHRA No. SQ-TR-CARR-317-HI, Reel No. B0004, frs. 282–5 (hereafter cited as 317 TCS History).

30. Message, Marshall to Sultan, 19 Sep 1944, AFHRA No. 824.164, Reel No. A8148, fr.

242; Memo for Operational Plans Division, Subj: Allocation of the Two Remaining Combat Groups and the Two Remaining Air Commando Groups. Col. W. E. Whitson, AFHRA No. 145.81-170, Reel No. A1378, fr. 1631; Daily Activity Report AC/AS, OC&R, 19 Sep 1944, AFHRA No. 123-2, Reel No. A1040, frs. 997–8; Message, Sultan to CG AAF CBI IBS, 24 Sep 1944, AFHRA No. 825.16222-11, Reel No. A8174, fr. 1093.

31. 2 ACG History, fr. 1269.
32. Ibid., frs. 1269–70, 1278.
33. Operation Grubworm Airlift, frs. 368–9; HQ 10AF Diary of Operation Grubworm, frs. 1044, 1046–7. Sadly, Maj. Wirt E. Thompson would become a bizarre footnote in the story of the Cold War. An author would write a book many years later claiming that the Russians had kept in captivity thousands of U.S. prisoners who had been held by the Germans and Japanese. One of these prisoners was supposedly Thompson, who, the author asserted, had been in Russian hands at least until the mid-1950s, long after his remains had been found and identified. See "United States Prisoners of War and the Red Army, 1944–45: Myths and Realities," by Timothy K. Nenninger in the July 2002 *Journal of Military History* for a debunking of this fanciful contention.
34. 317 TCS History, frs. 296–7.
35. Diary of Operation Grubworm, fr. 1050.
36. Ibid., fr. 1051.
37. HQ 10AF, Animal Haul of Operation "Grubworm" (10 Dec 1944 thru 2 Jan 1945), AFHRA No. 830.04-2, Reel No. A8229, frs. 1071, 1073.
38. Diary of Operation Grubworm, frs. 1061–6.
39. 2 ACG History, frs. 1279, 1300; 127 Liaison Sqdn History, No. SQ-LIA-127-HI, Reel No. A0846, frs. 1391–3 (hereafter cited as 127 LS History); 327 ADS History, frs. 1352, 1355.

Chapter 11

1. 1 FS History, fr. 1695.
2. Ibid.
3. The 2 FS History says it was January 11 (see fr. 1624); 1 FS History, fr. 1699.
4. 317 TCS History, frs. 341–3.
5. 156 LS History, fr. 1767; 127 LS History, fr. 1748; 155 LS History, frs. 1759–60.
6. 127 LS History, frs. 1752–4.
7. 2 FS History, frs. 1625, 1639; Aircraft Accident Report, 6 Feb 1945, AFHRA No. 825.16221, Reel No. A8165, fr. 610.
8. Eason et al. Interview.
9. 2 ACG History, frs. 1662–4; 317 TCS History, fr. 364.
10. 317 TCS History, frs. 364, 367.
11. 317 TCS History, frs. 367–8, 394–5; CCTF Report on Operation "Crossbow," AFHRA No. 824.02, Reel No. A8147, frs. 355–7; JICA No. R-21-C-45, frs. 696–7.
12. Maj. Gen. George E. Stratemeyer to Commanding General, Combat Cargo Task Force, 7 Mar 1945, Subj: Commendation, in 2 ACG History, fr. 1896.
13. 1 FS History, frs. 1701–2; 2 FS History, fr. 1640; Young, *Air Commando Fighters*, 65–6.

14. Young, *Air Commando Fighters*, 65.
15. 2 FS History, fr. 1640.
16. Young, *Air Commando Fighters*, 66.
17. 1 FS History, frs. 1702–3; 2 FS History, fr. 1641; World War II Air Commandos, *History of the World War II Air Commandos*, vol. 2 (Dallas, Tex.: Taylor Publishing Company), 21–2.
18. 1 FS History, fr. 1703; 2 FS History, fr. 1641; Young, *Air Commando Fighters*, 67.
19. Allen, *Burma*, 425–42.
20. 317 TCS History, frs. 395–7.
21. Ibid., frs. 397–8.
22. Ibid., frs. 399–401.
23. World War II Air Commandos, *History*, vol. 2, 46–7.
24. This was a unit of the XX Bomber Command.
25. Message, [Brig. Gen. Roger M.] Ramey to CG AAF, 131001Z Mar 1945, AFHRA No. 825.16221, Reel No. A8167, frs. 875–6; Message, Ramey to CG AAF IBS, 151206Z Mar 1945, Reel No. A8167, frs. 787–90; 2 ACG History, frs. 1787–8.
26. 155 LS History, frs. 1763–4; 127 LS History, frs. 1756–7.
27. 127 LS History, frs. 1902–4; 155 LS History, frs. 1917–9.

Chapter 12
1. Probert, *Forgotten Air Force*, 242, 244; Young gave different figures on page 68 of his *Air Commando Fighters*, noting a total of about 300 aircraft in southeast Asia, with less than 100 in Burma.
2. Probert, *Forgotten Air Force*, 244; Edward M. Young, "Counter-Air," *AIR Enthusiast*, no. 53 (Spring 1994).
3. 2 ACG History, AFHRA No. GP-A-CMDO-2-SU, Reel No. B0681, frs. 2182–3; Young, *Air Commando Fighters*, 69–70.
4. Young, *Air Commando Fighters*, 70.
5. Don Muang was in a different time zone, thus making it appear in the reports that the flying time was an hour shorter than it actually was.
6. Young, *Air Commando Fighters*, 73–4; Young, "Counter-Air."
7. 2 ACG History, AFHRA No. GP-A-CMDO-2-SU, Reel No. B0681, frs. 2184–207, 2227, 2280–3.
8. 2 FS History, fr. 1853; Eason et al. Interview.
9. Air Chief Marshal Sir Keith Park had commanded the 11 Group during the Battle of Britain. It was this group that was most responsible for the RAF's success in the battle. However, he was removed from that command shortly afterward because his tactics in the battle were considered inferior to those espoused by Air Vice Marshal Sir Trafford Leigh-Mallory with his "big wings." Ironically, Park replaced Leigh-Mallory when the latter was killed in a plane crash while en route to India to assume command of ACSEA.
10. Message, AOC, Headquarters, No. 224 Group RAF to 2nd ACG, 22 Mar 1945, in 2 ACG History, fr. 1802.
11. 2 ACG History, AFHRA No. GP-A-CMDO-2-SU, Reel No. B0681, frs. 2208–10; Young, *Air Commando Fighters*, 76.

12. 2 ACG History, AFHRA No. GP-A-CMDO-2-SU, Reel No. B0681, fr. 2211.
13. Ibid., fr. 2212.
14. Message, Cox Bazaar [*sic*] to CG AAF, 200900Z Mar 1944, AFHRA No. 825.16221, Reel No. A8165, fr. 387.
15. 2 ACG History, AFHRA No. GP-A-CMDO-2-SU, Reel No. B0681, frs. 2212–3; Message, Cox Bazaar [*sic*] to CG AAF, 210015Z Mar 1944, AFHRA No. 825.16221, Reel No. A8165, fr. 385; Young, *Air Commando Fighters*, 76.
16. Message, Cox Bazaar [*sic*] to CG AAF, 240700Z Mar 1944, AFHRA No. 825.16221, Reel No. A8165, fr. 370.
17. 2 ACG History, AFHRA No. GP-A-CMDO-2-SU, Reel No. B0681, frs. 2215–7; Young, *Air Commando Fighters*, 76–7.
18. Eason et al. Interview.
19. 2 ACG History, AFHRA No. GP-A-CMDO-2-SU, Reel No. B0681, frs. 2218–9; Young, *Air Commando Fighters*, 77.
20. Eason et al. Interview; Young, *Air Commando Fighters*, 77.
21. Field Visitation Report, Maj. R. L. Walker, 4 Apr 1945, AFHRA No. 820.153, Reel No. A8070, frs. 1313–4.
22. 1 FS History, fr. 1827; 2 ACG History, fr. 1791; Young, *Air Commando Fighters*, 77–8; AAF IBT General Orders No. 125, 3 Jun 1945, AFHRA No. SQ-TR-CARR-317-HI, Reel No. B0004, fr. 481.
23. Message, Cox Bazaar [*sic*] to CG AAF, 281500Z Mar 1944, AFHRA No. 825.16221, Reel No. A8165, fr. 351; 1 FS History, frs. 1827–8; Young, *Air Commando Fighters*, 78.
24. 2 ACG History, AFHRA No. GP-A-CMDO-2-SU, Reel No. B0681, fr. 2230; 1 FS History, fr. 1828.
25. 2 FS History, fr. 1836.
26. Young, *Air Commando Fighters*, 78.
27. Ibid., 80; 1 FS History, fr. 1959.
28. 1 FS History, fr. 1959; Young, *Air Commando Fighters*, 80.
29. World War II Air Commandos, *History*, vol. 2, 32–3.
30. Ibid.
31. Young, *Air Commando Fighters*, 80–1; Headquarters AAF IBT, Adjudication-Class 289, n.d., AFHRA No. 820.375, Reel No. A8112, fr. 322.
32. Stratemeyer Personal Diary, 12 April 1945.
33. 2 ACG History, fr. 1938.
34. Young, *Air Commando Fighters*, 83–4.
35. AAF IBT General Orders No. 103, 30 Apr 1945, and No. 145, 23 Jun 1945, AFHRA No. 825.193, Reel No. A8196, frs. 54, 431.

Chapter 13

1. Kipling got his geography a bit mixed up in that poem when he placed the Moulmein pagoda looking east across the bay. Since Moulmein is on the east side of the bay, the pagoda could hardly be facing east toward the water.
2. 2 ACG History, fr. 1939; 127 LS History, frs. 1990–3; 155 LS History, frs. 1993–5; 156 LS History, frs. 2008–9.
3. 317 TCS History, frs. 1973, 1975.

4. 317 TCS History, fr. 1974.

5. Ibid.; Combat Cargo Task Force Intelligence Extract No. 16, AFHRA No. 824.606-1, Reel No. A 8152, fr. 1097; World War II Air Commandos, *History*, vol. 2, 44.

6. Young, *Air Commando Fighters*, 82; 1 FS History, fr. 1961.

7. 1 FS History, fr. 1961.

8. World War II Air Commandos, *History*, vol. 2, 28–9.

9. 1 FS History, frs. 1961–2, 2004–8; 127 LS History, fr. 1990; World War II Air Commandos, *History*, vol. 2, 30–1; Young, *Air Commando Fighters*, 83.

10. 2 FS History, fr. 2053; Young, *Air Commando Fighters*, 84.

11. Allen, *Burma*, 477–80.

12. 317 TCS History, fr. 1974; 2 ACG History, AFHRA No. GP-A-CMDO-2-SU, Reel No. B0681, fr. 2090.

13. 2 FS History, fr. 2062; Young, *Air Commando Fighters*, 84.

14. 2 ACG History, AFHRA No. GP-A-CMDO-2-SU, Reel No. B0681 fr. 2103; World War II Air Commandos, *History*, vol. 2, 33.

15. 317 TCS History, fr. 2068.

16. 2 ACG History, AFHRA No. GP-A-CMDO-2-SU, Reel No. B0681, frs. 2090–1; 156 LS History, Reel B0681, fr. 2049, Reel A0846, fr. 721. DeBolt later made brigadier general. Chase went on to command a fighter–bomber group in the Korean War and a tactical fighter wing in Vietnam, and he retired as a major general in command of the Ninth Air Force.

17. 317 TCS History, frs. 538–9.

18. 155 LS History, frs. 494–5; World War II Air Commandos, *History*, vol. 2, 55–7.

19. 2 ACG History, AFHRA No. GP-A-CMDO-2-SU, Reel No. B0681, fr. 2125.

20. Message, New Delhi to CG AAF IBS, 180716Z 2 Jul 1945; 127 LS History, frs. 142–3; 155 LS History, frs. 508–9.

Chapter 14

1. The letter was actually written by Lt. Gen. Barney M. Giles, the deputy commander of Army Air Forces, in Arnold's absence, but it contained the information the USAAF leader wished to convey to Kenney.

2. Lt. Gen. Barney M. Giles to Lt. Gen. George C. Kenney, 18 Jun 1944, AFHRA No. 145.81-171, Reel No. A1378, fr. 852.

3. Ibid., fr. 854.

4. Lt. Gen. George C. Kenney to Lt. Gen. Barney M. Giles, 5 Jul 1944, AFHRA No. 720.161-3, Reel No. A7247, fr. 791.

5. Ibid., fr. 792.

6. Ibid., fr. 793.

7. Alison Interview, 425–7.

8. Air Commando—Combat Cargo Project Status Report, 22 June 1944, AFHRA No. 143.04J, Reel No. A1329, frs. 1546, 1556.

9. History of Headquarters, 3rd Air Commando Group, May 1944, AFHRA No. GP-A-CMDO-3-HI, Reel No. B0682, fr. 51 (hereafter cited as 3 ACG History).

10. 3 ACG History, frs. 6, 17, 22.

11. Historical Record, 318th TCS, Cmdo, May–Dec 1944, AFHRA No. SQ-TR-CARR-

318-HI, Reel No. B0004, frs. 756–60, 780–84, 810–11 (hereafter cited as 318 TCS History); History, 343rd Airdrome Sqdn, AFHRA No. SQ-ADRM-343-HI, Reel No. A0519, frs. 1167, 1179 (hereafter cited as 343 ADS History).

12. History, 157th Liaison Squadron, AFHRA No. SQ-LIA-157-HI, Reel No. A0846, frs. 808, 874–5; History, 159th Liaison Squadron, AFHRA No. SQ-LIA-159-HI, Reel No. A0847, frs. 238, 267 (hereafter cited as 159 LS History); History 160th Liaison Squadrons, AFHRA No. SQ-LIA-160-HI, Reel No. A0847, frs. 455, 462 (hereafter cited as 160 LS History); History, 341st ADS, AFHRA No. SQ-ADRM-341-HI, Reel No. A0519, frs. 1030–3 (hereafter cited as 341 ADS History).

13. 3 ACG History, frs. 95, 98.

14. Ibid., frs. 33, 71.

15. Walker M. Mahurin, *Honest John* (New York: G. P. Putnam's Sons, 1962), 139–54.

16. Ibid., 155–6.

17. Vincent Krout, interview by Edward Young, Oct. 14, 1995.

18. 3 ACG History, frs. 242–3.

19. Ray Lahmeyer and Jacques Young, interview by Edward Young, Oct. 14, 1995.

20. Tommy Thompson, ed., *Highlights—The 318th Troop Carrier Squadron, Commando, October 1943 to October 1945* (Privately printed, n.d.).

21. 159 LS History, fr. 329.

22. 3rd Fighter Squadron, Commando, History, AFHRA Nos. SQ-FI-CMDO-3-HI, Reel No. A0828, No. A0828, fr. 397 (hereafter cited as 3 FS History).

23. 3 FS History, frs. 397–8; 318 TCS History, fr. 821.

24. 3 ACG History, frs. 287, 295–6.

25. Ibid., fr. 319; 157 LS History, frs. 912, 914, 924; 159 LS History, fr. 331; 160 LS History, fr. 504; 341 ADS History, fr. 1051.

Chapter 15

1. History, V Fighter Command, Jan–Dec 1945, AFHRA No. 731.01, Reel No. A7498, fr. 156.

2. The call sign "Zebra" was the Fifth Air Force's generic name for its P-51s.

3. 3 ACG History, fr. 309.

4. John C. Stanaway and Lawrence Hickey, *Attack and Conquer: The 8th Fighter Group in World War II* (Atglen, Pa.: Schiffer Publishing, 1995), 316.

5. 3 ACG History, fr. 320; 3 FS History, frs. 430–1.

6. 318 TCS History, frs. 892–3; 343 ADS History, frs. 1217–8.

7. 343 ADS History, fr. 1110.

8. Wesley Frank Craven and James Lee Cate, eds., *The Army Air Forces in World War II*, vol. 5, *The Pacific: Matterhorn to Nagasaki, June 1944 to August 1945* (Washington, D.C.: Office of Air Force History, 1983), 418.

9. 3 ACG History, frs. 320–1.

10. 5 AF Situation Summary No. 14, 14 Jan 1945, AFHRA No. 730.606, Reel No. A7476, fr. 256.

11. 5 AF Situation Summary No. 15, 15 Jan 1945, AFHRA No. 730.606, Reel No. A7476, fr. 244; 3 FS Unit Narrative Combat Report, 16 Jan 1945, AFHRA No. SQ-FI-CMDO-3-SU-OPS, Reel No. A0828, frs. 649–50; Young, *Air Commando Fighters*, 90–1.

12. 5 AF Situation Summary No. 17, 17 Jan 1945, AFHRA No. 730.606, Reel No. A7476, fr. 507; 3 FS History, fr. 432.

13. 3 FS History, frs. 431–2; 5 AF Situation Summary No. 17, fr. 509.

14. Ray Lahmeyer and Jacques Young, interview by Edward Young, Oct. 15, 1995.

15. 157 LS History, fr. 925; 341 ADS History, fr. 1052.

16. 3 FS History, fr. 432; 5AF Situation Summary No. 21, 21 Jan 1945, AFHRA No. 730.606, Reel No. A7476, fr. 457.

17. 5 AF Situation Summary No. 24, 24 Jan 1945, AFHRA No. 730.606, Reel No. A7476, frs. 401, 404. Interestingly, because MacArthur's interest was south toward Manila, movement toward Baguio, which lay only about thirty-five miles from the 3rd ACG's new base, would not begin for a time, and the town would not be captured until April 27.

18. 159 LS History, frs. 355–6; 160 LS History, fr. 551.

19. Maj. Gen. Ennis Whitehead to Gen. Kenney, 7 Feb 1945, AFHRA No. 730.161-3, Reel No. A7403, frs. 1704–5.

20. 3 ACG History, frs. 331, 349; 157 LS History, frs. 938–9.

21. 159 LS History, fr. 355.

22. 318 TCS History, frs. 1111–2.

23. 5 AF Situation Summary No. 29, 29 Jan 1945, AFHRA No. 730.606, Reel No. A7476, frs. 330–1.

24. 5 AF Situation Summary No. 30, 30 Jan 1945, AFHRA No. 730.606, Reel No. A7476, frs. 315, 319.

25. 5 AF Situation Summary No. 33, 2 Feb 1945, AFHRA No. 730.606, Reel No. A7476, frs. 643, 648; 3 FS History, frs. 444–5.

26. 3 ACG History, fr. 333.

27. The submarine was never identified when a list of Japanese naval vessels lost was compiled following the war.

28. 5 AF Situation Summary No. 39, 8 Feb 1945, AFHRA No. 730.606, Reel No. A7476, frs. 560, 566.

29. 3 FS History, frs. 445–6.

30. 4 FS Unit Narrative Combat Report, 7 Feb 1945, Southwest Pacific Area Far East Air Forces. Narrative Mission Reports, 3 Jan–4 Mar 1945, AFHRA No. 720.333, Reel No. A7316, fr. 1698.

31. 3 FS Unit Narrative Combat Report, 10 Feb 1945, AFHRA No. SQ-FI-CMDO-3-SU-OP-S, Reel No. A0828, frs. 651–3; 5 AF Situation Summary No. 40, 9 Feb 1945, AFHRA No. 730.606, Reel No. A7476, frs. 545–6, 549, 551–2.

32. 4 FS Unit Narrative Combat Report, 10 Feb 1945, AFHRA No. 720.333, Reel No. A7316, fr. 1696; 3 ACG History, frs. 333–4; 5AF Situation Summary No. 42, 11 Feb 1945, AFHRA No. 730.606, Reel No. A7476, frs. 905–6; 39 TCS Narrative Combat Report, 12 Feb 1945, AFHRA No. 720.333, Reel No. A7314, frs. 773–5.

33. 5 AF Situation Summary No. 50, 19 Feb 1945, AFHRA No. 730.606, Reel No. A7476, fr. 797.

34. 5 AF Situation Summary No. 54, 23 Feb 1945, AFHRA No. 730.606, Reel No. A7476, fr. 753.

35. 3 FS History, frs. 447–8; 3 FS Final Mission Report, 25 Feb 1945, AFHRA No. SQ-FI-CMDO-3-SU-OPS, Reel No. A0828, fr. 664.

36. 3 ACG History, frs. 344–5, 350; 157 LS History, fr. 956; 160 LS History, frs. 548–9.
37. 5AF Situation Summary No. 61, 2 Mar 1945, AFHRA No. 730.606, Reel No. A7476, fr. 1051.
38. 5AF Situation Summary No. 62, 3 Mar 1945, AFHRA No. 730.606, Reel No. A7476, fr. 1031.
39. 5AF Situation Summary No. 62, 3 Mar 1945, AFHRA No. 730.606, Reel No. A7476, fr. 1035.
40. 3 FS History, frs. 458–9.
41. Ray Lahmeyer and Jacques Young, interview by Edward Young, Oct. 14, 1995.
42. 5 AF Situation Summary No. 89, 30 Mar 1945, 5AF Situation Summary No. 62, 3 Mar 1945, AFHRA No. 730.606, Reel No. A7476, fr. 1094.

Chapter 16

1. 318 TCS History, fr. 1156.
2. 3 ACG History, fr. 349.
3. History, 334th Airdrome Squadron, No. SQ-ADRM-334-HI, Reel No. A0518A, frs. 136–7, 147 (hereafter cited as 334 ADS History); 318 TCS History, frs. 1185–6.
4. 3 ACG History, frs. 370–1.
5. 3 ACG History, fr. 374; 334 ADS History, fr. 149.
6. 3 ACG History, fr. 376; 3 FS History, fr. 475.
7. 3 FS Final Mission Report, n.d., Reel No. A0828, fr. 730; 3 FS Unit Narrative Combat Report, 4 Apr 1945, frs. 733–4; 3 FS Individual Combat Reports of 2nd Lt. Barrett D. Wagner, 8 Apr 45, and 1st Lt. Glenn E. Lairmore, 14 Apr 1945, frs. 753, 755; Young, *Air Commando Fighters*, 106.
8. 3 ACG History, fr. 311.
9. 3 ACG History, frs. 383–4.
10. 335th Airdrome Squadron History, AFHRA No. SQ-ADRM-335-HI, Reel No. A0518A, fr. 280; 343 ADS History, fr. 1280.
11. 157 LS History, frs. 974–5.
12. 159 LS History, frs. 387–8; 160 LS History, fr. 568.
13. 318 TCS History, frs. 1219–21.
14. 3 ACG History, fr. 394; 160 LS History, fr. 583; 5 AF General Orders No. 87, 3 May 1945, AFHRA No. 730.193, Reel No. A7446, fr. 2066; 5 AF General Orders No. 32, 29 Jun 1945, AFHRA No. 731.01, Reel No. A7498, fr. 595.
15. 3 ACG History, frs. 394–5; V Ftr Cmd General Orders No. 22, 16 May 1945, AFHRA No. 731.01, Reel No. A7498, fr. 585.
16. 3 ACG History, fr. 397; 5 AF Situation Summary No. 122, 2 May 1945, AFHRA No. 730.606, Reel No. A7476, fr. 422; Young, *Air Commando Fighters*, 109.
17. 3 ACG History, fr. 399; 5 AF Situation Summary No. 140, 20 May 1945, AFHRA No. 730.606, Reel No. A7476, fr. 637.
18. 3 ACG History, fr. 398.
19. World War II Air Commandos, *History*, vol. 2, 105–6; 3 ACG History, frs. 397–8; 5 AF Situation Summary No. 152, 1 Jun 1945, AFHRA No. 730.606, Reel No. A7476, fr. 769.
20. Mahurin, *Honest John*, 166–8; 3 ACG History, fr. 396.

21. 3 FS History, fr. 494.
22. Ibid., frs. 401–3.
23. 3 ACG History, fr. 433–4; Young, *Air Commando Fighters*, 109–10.
24. 3 FS History, frs. 510–3.
25. 3 ACG History, frs. 438–9.
26. Ibid., fr. 436.
27. 3 FS History, fr. 515.
28. 157 LS History, frs. 1006–7, 1019–21, 1025; 5 AF A-3 Section History, 1 Jan 1945 to 2 Sept 1945, AFHRA No. 730.302, Reel No. A7452, fr. 1292.
29. 3 FS History, Final Mission Report, 11 Jan 1945, AFHRA SQ-FI-CMDO-3-SU-OP-S, Reel No. A0808, fr. 929; 5 AF Situation Summary No. 193, 12 Jul 1945, AFHRA No. 730.606, Reel No. A7476, fr. 1187.
30. 3 FS History, frs. 341–2; 3 FS History, AFHRA No. SQ-FI-CMDO-3-SU-OP-S, Reel No. A0828, fr. 934.
31. 3 ACG History, frs. 475, 480–1.

Epilogue

1. Maurer, *Air Force Combat Units*, 8, 15, 35, 40, 351, 354, 356.
2. Maurer, *Air Force Combat Units*, 387, 392; 317 TCS History, frs. 618–20, 635, 686, 704–12.
3. 3 ACG History, frs. 500–2; 5AF General Orders No. 150, 10 Sep 1945, AFHRA No. 730.193, Reel No. A7447, fr. 91; Maurer, *Air Force Combat Units*, 356, 358.
4. 3 ACG History, frs. 512–3, 535; 3 FS History, frs. 543–4, 559–60; Maurer, *Air Force Combat Units*. All three groups were finally disbanded on October 8, 1948. For this time period USAF lineage policy states that when a unit was inactivated, all personnel were withdrawn from that unit, and it was placed on the inactive Army list (for the period of the Air Commandos existence, but after 1947, on the USAF list). Such a unit could later be reestablished. However, when a unit was disbanded, it was completely removed from the inactive list.
5. *War Reports of General of the Army George C. Marshall, General of the Army H. H. Arnold, Fleet Admiral Ernest J. King* (Philadelphia: J. B. Lippincott Co., 1947), 462.
6. James Charlton, ed. *The Military Quotation Book* (New York: St. Martin's Press, 1990), 63.
7. Memorandum, Col. John Alison to Gen. Giles, 10 Apr 1944, Subj: Summary of Operations of First Commando Group, AFHRA No. 145.81-171, Reel No. A1378, fr. 1082.
8. Cochran Interview, 390–2.

Bibliography

Official Documents

All record numbers cited are Air Force Historical Research Agency (AFHRA) identification numbers unless otherwise noted.

1st Air Commando Group. Nos. GP-A-CMDO-1-HI and GP-A-CMDO-1-SU-RE. Reel Nos. B0680 and B0681.

2nd Air Commando Group. No. GP-A-CMDO-2-HI and GP-A-CMDO-2-SU. Reel No. B0681.

3rd Air Commando Group. No. GP-A-CMDO-3-HI. Reel No. B0682.

33rd Fighter Group. Nos. GP-33-HI and GP-33-SU-OPS-S. Reel Nos. B0111A and B0112 [the group is misidentified on the indexes to these reels as a bomb group].

1st Fighter Squadron, Commando. No. SQ-FI-CMDO-1-HI. Reel No. A0827.

2nd Fighter Squadron, Commando. No. SQ-FI-CMDO-2-HI. Reel No. A0828.

3rd Fighter Squadron, Commando. Nos. SQ-FI-CMDO-3-HI and SQ-FI-CMDO-3-SU-OP-S. Reel No. A0828.

4th Fighter Squadron, Commando. No. SQ-FI-CMDO-4-HI. Reel No. A0828.

5th Fighter Squadron, Commando. No. SQ-FI-CMDO-5-HI. Reel No. A0828.

6th Fighter Squadron, Commando. No. SQ-FI-CMDO-6-HI. Reel No. A0828.

58th Fighter Squadron. No. SQ-FI-58-HI. Reel No. A0744.

75th Fighter Squadron. No. SQ-FI-75-HI. Reel No. A0755.

127th Liaison Squadron. No. SQ-LIA-127-HI. Reel No. A0846.

155th Liaison Squadron. No. SQ-LIA-155-HI. Reel No. A0846.

156th Liaison Squadron. No. SQ-LIA-156-HI. Reel No. A0846.

157th Liaison Squadron. No. SQ-LIA-157-HI. Reel No. A0846.

159th Liaison Squadron. No. SQ-LIA-159-HI. Reel No. A0847.

160th Liaison Squadron. No. SQ-LIA-160-HI. Reel No. A0847.

164th Liaison Squadron. No. SQ-LIA-164-HI. Reel No. A0848.

165th Liaison Squadron. No. SQ-LIA-165-HI. Reel Nos. A0848 and A0849.

166th Liaison Squadron. No. SQ-LIA-166-HI. Reel No. A0849.

317th Troop Carrier Squadron. No. SQ-TR-CARR-317-HI. Reel No. B0004.

318th Troop Carrier Squadron. No. SQ-TR-CARR-318-HI. Reel No. B0004.

319th Troop Carrier Squadron. No. SQ-TR-CARR-319-HI. Reel No. B0004.

72nd Airdrome Squadron. No. SQ-ADRM-72-HI. Reel No. A0515A.

309th Airdrome Squadron. No. SQ-ADRM-309-HI. Reel No. A0518.

326th Airdrome Squadron. No. SQ-ADRM-326-HI. Reel No. A0518.

327th Airdrome Squadron. No. SQ-ADRM-327-HI. Reel No. A0518.

328th Airdrome Squadron. No. SQ-ADRM-328-HI. Reel No. A0518.

334th Airdrome Squadron. No. SQ-ADRM-334-HI. Reel No. A0518A.

335th Airdrome Squadron. No. SQ-ADRM-335-HI. Reel No. A0518A.

340th Airdrome Squadron. No. SQ-ADRM-340-HI. Reel No. A0519.

341st Airdrome Squadron. No. SQ-ADRM-341-HI. Reel No. A0519.

342nd Airdrome Squadron. No. SQ-ADRM-342-HI. Reel No. A0519.

343rd Airdrome Squadron. No. SQ-ADRM-343-HI. Reel No. A0519.

900th Airborne Engineer Company, Aviation. No. ENGR-900-HI. Reel No. A0267.

British Air Ministry. Campaigns in the Far East, 1942–1945. Vol. 5. No. 512.04G. Reel No. A5251.

China–Burma–India (CBI): U.S. Army Air Force (USAAF), India–Burma Theater (IBT). History of U.S. Army Air Force Operations in the India–Burma Theater, Jan 44–Sep 45. Vol. 1. No. 825.01. Reel No. A8153. [In the archives, the USAAF is often shortened to AAF. The longer abbreviation is used here for clarity.]

CBI: USAAF, India–Burma Theater. Documents for the Administrative History of USAAF IBS and IBT Headquarters, Army Air Force India–Burma Sector, China–Burma–India Theater, Jan 44–Sep 45. No. 825.01. Reel No. A8154.

CBI: USAAF, India–Burma Theater. CBI Theater History, 1941–1945. Vols. 3 and 4. No. 825.01C. Reel No. A8155.

CBI: USAAF, India–Burma Theater. Headquarters USAAF–CBI History, Jul–Dec 44. No. 825.02. Reel No. A8155.

CBI: USAAF, India–Burma Theater. Eastern Air Command, May–Jun 44. No. 825.02. Reel No. A8155.

CBI: USAAF, India–Burma Theater. Headquarters USAAF, Stratemeyer's Personal File, 28 Jul 43–Sep 44. No. 825.161-1. Reel No. A8157.

CBI: USAAF, India–Burma Theater. General Arnold Letters, Aug 44–Jun 45. No. 825.161-2. Reel No. A8158.

CBI: USAAF, India–Burma Theater. Miscellaneous Incoming Radios, Jan 44–Sep 45. No. 825.16221. Reel Nos. A8161-A8162, A8165-A8170.

CBI: USAAF, India–Burma Theater. Incoming Radios [Various Bases], Jan 44–Sep 45. Nos. 825.16222-10, -11, -15, -21, -25, -32. Reel Nos. A8174–A8175, A8180–A8182.

CBI: USAAF, India–Burma Theater. Outgoing Radios [Various Bases], Mar 44–Jul 45. Nos. 825.16231 and 825.16232-6, -8, -16. Reel Nos. A8183–A8188, A8190.

CBI: USAAF, India–Burma Theater. Headquarters USAAF, India–Burma Theater. General Orders No. 101–150. No. 825.193. Reel No. A8196.

CBI: USAAF, India–Burma Theater. Planned-for Deployment of USAAF Units to China, 17 Apr 45. No. 825.229-4. Reel No. A8199.

CBI: USAAF, India–Burma Theater. Personnel Strength Summary, Mar 45–10 May 45. No. 825.245. Reel No. A8199.

CBI: USAAF, India–Burma Theater. Eastern Air Command Statistical Summaries of Aircraft and Aircraft Crews, Apr 45–30 May 45. No. 825.245. Reel No. A8199.

CBI: USAAF, India–Burma Theater. Complete Report on Raid on Aungban, 4 Apr 44. No. 825.306A. Reel No. A8202.

CBI: USAAF, India–Burma Theater. USAAF–IBT Fighter Unit Statistics, Aug 44–Mar 45. No. 825.3083-1. Reel No. A8203.

CBI: USAAF, India–Burma Theater. Historical Data USAAF India–Burma Sector, 5–13 Mar 44. No. 825.452A. Reel No. A8212.

CBI: USAAF, India–Burma Theater. Observations and Data Concerning India, Burma and China Theater, 3 Dec 44–16 Feb 45. No. 825.609.1. Reel No. A8212.

CBI: USAAF, India–Burma Theater. Investigation of and Report on the Airplane Accident which Resulted in the Death of Gen Wingate. No. 825.7501-1. Reel No. A8216.

CBI: USAAF, India–Burma Theater. Report of Airdrome Engineer Operations in Burma, Mar 44. No. 825.935-1. Reel No. A8220.

CBI: USAAF, India–Burma Theater. Extracts of Weekly Diaries CBI, Dec 44–Jun 45. No. 835.13. Reel No. A8265.

CBI: USAAF, India–Burma Theater. IB–ASC History Office of the Air Engineer, May 42–Mar 45. No. 835.930. Reel No. A8279.

CBI: USAAF, China Theater. Headquarters USAAF, China Theater, 1 Jan 44–9 Oct 45. No. 860.161. Reel No. A8288.

CBI: Tenth Air Force. Historical Data 10th AF, Aug–Oct 45. No. 830.01. Reel No. A8225.

CBI: Tenth Air Force. Hqs, 10th AF Operation Grubworm, 5 Dec 44–5 Jan 45. No. 830.04-2. Reel No. A8229.

CBI: Tenth Air Force. Movement of 14th Division, 5 Dec 44–5 Jan 45. No. 830.057-1. Reel No. A8229.

CBI: Tenth Air Force. Outgoing Correspondence of Air Liaison Section—10th AF, Sep 43–May 44. No. 830.1611-1. Reel No. A8232.

CBI: Tenth Air Force. 10th AF Miscellaneous Incoming and Outgoing Messages, May 44–Mar 45. No. 830.1621. Reel No. A8232.

CBI: Tenth Air Force. Policy File 10th AF, 1942–1944. No. 830.164. Reel No. A8233.

CBI: Tenth Air Force. 10th AF Miscellaneous Correspondence, Mar 42–Apr 44. No. 830.168. Reel No. A8233.

CBI: Tenth Air Force. 10th AF Operations in China, Aug–Nov 45. No. 830.451A. Reel No. A8246.

CBI: Tenth Air Force. Tenth Air Force Myitkyina Invasion, 16 May 44–12 Jun 44. No. 830.919-1. Reel No. A8261.

CBI: Tenth Air Force. Headquarters USAAF–IBS–CBI Letter Re: Airdrome Construction, 1944–1945. No. 830.935. Reel No. A8261.

CBI: Tenth Air Force. 10th Air Force Troop Carrier Command History, Feb–Mar 44. No. 833.01. Reel No. A8262.

CBI: Tenth Air Force. 10th Air Force History of Air Supply in CBI, 1943–1944. No. 834.04-1. Reel No. A8263.

CBI: Tenth Air Force. CBI Dromes, July 44–July 45. No. 835.935-3. Reel No. A8281.

CBI: Tenth Air Force. 10th AF Combat Camera, Aug 43–May 44. No. UNIT-CC-10-HI. Reel No. A0487.

CBI: Combat Cargo Task Force. Combat Cargo Task Force, 14 Sep 44–31 May 45. No. 824.01. Reel No. A8146.

CBI: Combat Cargo Task Force. Combat Cargo Task Force Unit History, 15–30 Sep 44. No. 824.02. Reel No. A8146.

CBI: Combat Cargo Task Force. Combat Cargo Task Force Monthly History, Sep 44–May 45. No. 824.02. Reel No. A8146.

CBI: Combat Cargo Task Force. Hqs. Combat Cargo Task Force (Unit History), Dec 44–May 45. No. 824.02. Reel No. A8147.

CBI: Combat Cargo Task Force. Hqs. Combat Cargo Task Force Daily Journal, Nov 44–Jan 45. No. 824.1623. Reel No. A8147.

CBI: Combat Cargo Task Force. Hqs. Combat Cargo Task Force, Mar 44–May 45. No. 824.164. Reel No. A8148.

CBI: Combat Cargo Task Force. Hqs. Combat Cargo Task Force, Jan–Feb 45. No. 824.183. Reel No. A8148.

CBI: Combat Cargo Task Force. Hqs. Combat Cargo Task Force, 1944–1945. No. 824.309. Reel No. A8149.

CBI: Combat Cargo Task Force. Operation Dracula, Apr–May 45. No. 824.452-1. Reel No. A8149.

CBI: Combat Cargo Task Force. Combat Cargo Task Force Field Order, Jan–Feb 45. No. 824.452-2. Reel No. A8151.

CBI: Combat Cargo Task Force. Operation Multivite Target Situation Report, Feb–Mar 45. No. 824.452-2. Reel No. A8151.

CBI: Southeast Asia Command. Information Book, 1943–1944. No. 805.011. Reel No. A8015.

CBI: Southeast Asia Command. Southeast Asia Command, Supreme Allied Commander's Dispatch, Second Draft, Aug 1943–Jan 1944. No. 805.04A. Reel No. A8015.

CBI: Southeast Asia Command. Supreme Allied Commander Meeting Minutes, Oct 43–May 44. No. 805.151-1. Reel Nos. A8015 and A8016.

CBI: Southeast Asia Command. SACSEA, Jan 44. No. 805.1623. Reel No. A8016.

CBI: Southeast Asia Command. JPS Papers, Sep 44–May 45. No. 805.317. Reel No. A8017.

CBI: Southeast Asia Command. War Staff Papers—CPS and JCS Papers, 1944. No. 805.317. Reel No. A8018.

CBI: Southeast Asia Command. SEAC–SACSEA Secretary Plans, 1943–1945. No. 805.317. Reel No. A8018.

CBI: Southeast Asia Command. SEAC Operation Capital, Sep 44–Jan 45. No. 805.322-3. Reel No. A8019.

CBI: Southeast Asia Command. SEAC Operation Matador, Jan–Feb 45. No. 805.322-5. Reel No. A8019.

CBI: Southeast Asia Command. SEAC Plan Basin, Oct–Nov 43. No. 805.322-6. Reel No. A8019.

CBI: Southeast Asia Command. SEAC Operation Basin, Sep–Oct 43. No. 805.322-6. Reel No. A8019.

CBI: Southeast Asia Command. Southeast Asia Translation and Interrogation Center, Translation Report No. 14, 7 Jul 1944. No. 805.6252-14. Reel No. A8023.

CBI: Southeast Asia Command. Southeast Asia Translation and Interrogation Center, SEATIC Pictorial Bulletin. No. 805.6252-190. Reel No. A8027. [Although the title is applied to all SEATIC reports indexed on this reel, "Pictorial Bulletin" refers only to Report No. 175.]

CBI: Southeast Asia Command. Joint Intelligence India Burma China Reports, Apr–Dec 44. No. 810.6091D. Reel No. A8042.

CBI: Southeast Asia Air Command. Air Command SEA Air, Jan 44–Feb 45. No. 815.142. Reel No. A8047.

CBI: Southeast Asia Air Command. Air Commando Operations "Thursday," Mar–Apr 1944. No. 815.452. Reel No. A8056.

CBI: Southeast Asia Air Command. RAF Group Operation Order, Apr 45. No. 818.327-4. Reel No. A8066.

CBI: Southeast Asia Air Command. Second Arakan Campaign, Nov 43–May 44. No. 818.4501-1. Reel No. A8067.

CBI: Eastern Air Command. Activation of Headquarters EAC, Dec 43–Jan 44. No. 820.01. Reel No. A8069.

CBI: Eastern Air Command. RAF Historical, Dec 43–May 44. No. 820.04A. Reel No. A8069.

CBI: Eastern Air Command. RAF Despatch on Air Operations, Dec 43–May 44. No. 820.04B. Reel No. A8069.

CBI: Eastern Air Command. Air Conquest of Burma. No. 820.04C. Reel No. A8069.

CBI: Eastern Air Command. EAC Staff Conference Meetings, Aug–Dec 44. No. 820.181. Reel No. A8069.

CBI: Eastern Air Command. Report on Visits Headquarters EAC (SEA), Mar 45. No. 820.153. Reel No. A8070.

CBI: Eastern Air Command. Incoming Messages, Apr–May 44. No. 820.161. Reel No. A8070.

CBI: Eastern Air Command. Correspondence of Gen. Stratemeyer, Aug 43–May 45. No. 820.161A. Reel No. A8072.

CBI: Eastern Air Command. Correspondence of Gen. Stone, Jan–Aug 44. No. 820.161B. Reel No. A8072.

CBI: Eastern Air Command. Incoming and Outgoing Messages EAC, Mar–Dec 44. No. 820.162I. Reel No. A8072.

CBI: Eastern Air Command. Messages of the Troop Carrier Command, 1–9 44. No. 820.1621-4. Reel No. A8073.

CBI: Eastern Air Command. EAC Incoming Messages, 17 Jul 44–May 45. No. 820.16221. Reel Nos. A8074–A8075.

CBI: Eastern Air Command. EAC Incoming Messages, Oct 44–May 45. Nos. 820.16222-4, -19, -34, -35, -36, -48, -51, -149, -166, -192. Reel Nos. A8076, A8078–A8081, A8084–A8085.

CBI: Eastern Air Command. Eastern Air Command Outgoing Messages, Jan 44–Apr 45. No. 820.16231. Reel Nos. A8086–A8089. [These records are also indexed as Outgoing Radios.]

CBI: Eastern Air Command. EAC Miscellaneous Correspondence, Sep 44. No. 820.168. Reel No. A8090.

CBI: Eastern Air Command. Eastern Air Command G.O. and OP Dir. and OP Ins., Dec 43–May 45. No. 820.193. Reel No. A8090.

CBI: Eastern Air Command. General Orders of Eastern Air Command, Nov 43–Aug 44. No. 820.193-1. Reel No. A8090.

CBI: Eastern Air Command. Original Miscellaneous File of EAC, Jan 44–Jan 45. No. 820.201-2. Reel No. A8091.

CBI: Eastern Air Command. EAC Fighter Sq. of 1st and 2nd, Mar 45. No. 820.201-4. Reel No. A8091.

CBI: Eastern Air Command. Headquarters EAC Troop Movements, Mar–Jun, Dec 44. No. 820.229. Reel No. A8092.

CBI: Eastern Air Command. Eastern Air Command, Dec 43–May 45. No. 820.2981. Reel No. A8096.

CBI: Eastern Air Command. EAC Operation Report, Sep 44–Feb 45. No. 820.3011-1. Reel No. A8097.

CBI: Eastern Air Command. 373.2 Operation and Reports, Dec 43–Nov 44. No. 820.306. Reel No. A8097.

CBI: Eastern Air Command. 384-5 Aerial Attacks, Raids, Mar 44–May 45. No. 820.306. Reel No. A8097.

CBI: Eastern Air Command. Operational Reports, Oct 44–May 45. No. 820-306. Reel No. A8097.

CBI: Eastern Air Command. 1st Provisional Fighter Group, 15 Mar 45. No. 820.306-1. Reel No. A8097.

CBI: Eastern Air Command. Daily Operations and Intelligence Summary, Feb–Mar 44. No. 820.3071. Reel No. A8097.

CBI: Eastern Air Command. Eastern Air Command Correspondence, Oct 44–Jun 45. No. 820.311. Reel No. A8104.

CBI: Eastern Air Command. Fly OPTI Miscellaneous, Jan–Jun 44. No. 820.312. Reel No. A8104.

CBI: Eastern Air Command. Operation Fighter, Dec 43–Jan 45. No. 820.3121. Reel No. A8106.

CBI: Eastern Air Command. Operation Bomber, Dec 43–Feb 45. No. 820.3122. Reel No. A8107.

CBI: Eastern Air Command. Eastern Air Command, Mar 44–May 45. No. 820.317. Reel No. A8108.

CBI: Eastern Air Command. Eastern Air Command, Oct 44–May 45. No. 820.3171-1. Reel No. A8108.

CBI: Eastern Air Command. Headquarters Eastern Air Command, Jan–Aug 44. No. 820.321-1. Reel No. A8108.

CBI: Eastern Air Command. Headquarters Eastern Air Command, Sep–Oct 44. No. 820.322-1. Reel No. A8109.

CBI: Eastern Air Command. Incoming Messages, Dec 44–Mar 45. No. 820.322-3. Reel No. A8109.

CBI: Eastern Air Command. Headquarters Eastern Air Command (SEA), May 44–May 45. No. 820.323. Reel No. A8111.

CBI: Eastern Air Command. A Study of Operation "L," 16–20 Oct 44. No. 820.423.1. Reel No. A8112.

CBI: Eastern Air Command. Headquarters Eastern Air Command, Feb 44–Mar 45. No. 820.4501-1. Reel No. A8113.

CBI: Eastern Air Command. The Part of Air Support in Burma Fighting Against the Japs. No. 820.4501-2. Reel No. A8113.

CBI: Eastern Air Command. Air Commando Force, Jan 44–Apr 45. No. 820.452-1. Reel No. A8113.

CBI: Eastern Air Command. Air Commando File, Mar 44–Apr 45. No. 820.452-1. Reel No. A8113.

CBI: Eastern Air Command. Weekly Intelligence Summary, Sep 44–18 May 45. No. 820.607. Reel Nos. A8118–A8121. [On Reel A8118 these summaries are listed by volume number, not date, and are indexed under Headquarters Eastern Air Command (SEA).]

CBI: Eastern Air Command. Hqs. EAC Aircraft, Miscellaneous, Jan–Oct 44. No. 820.831. Reel No. A8131.

CBI: Eastern Air Command. Headquarters Troop Carrier Command. Command Diary of the Commanding General, 15 Dec 43–4 Jun 44. No. 833.13-1. Reel No. A8263.

CBI: Eastern Air Command. Troop Carrier Command Operations, 8 Jan 44–29 Feb 44. No. 833.327-1. Reel No. A8263.

CBI: Eastern Air Command. Troop Carrier Command EAC, SEA. Monthly Intelligence Survey, Apr 44. No. 833.608. Reel No. A8263.

CBI: Third Tactical Air Force. Dispatch Covering Operations, 15 Nov 43–1 Jun 44. No. 822.04A. Reel No. A8141.

CBI: Third Tactical Air Force. 3rd TAF, Dec 43–Jun 44. No. 822.151. Reel No. A8142.

CBI: Third Tactical Air Force. 3rd TAF Daily Synopsis of Operations, 1 Oct–3 Dec 44. No. 822.3061. Reel No. A8143.

CBI: Third Tactical Air Force. 3rd TAF, Jan 44–Feb 45. No. 822.311. Reel No. A8143.

CBI: Third Tactical Air Force. 3rd TAF Operation Directive, 19–21 Mar 44. No. 822.327-1. Reel No. A8143.

CBI: Third Tactical Air Force. 3rd TAF Operations, 9 Jan 44–12 Mar 44. No. 822.452A. Reel No. A8143.

CBI: Third Tactical Air Force. 3rd TAF Collected Reports, Sep 43–May 44. No. 822.452B. Reel No. A8144.

CBI: Third Tactical Air Force. Operation of 77th Brigade, 3rd TAF, 5 Mar 44–26 Jun 44. No. 822.452C. Reel No. A8144.

CBI: Special Forces. Operations Carried Out Special Forces. No. 808.04A. Reel No. A8036.

CBI: Joint Intelligence Collection Agency. Joint Intelligence India–Burma–China Reports, Jan 44–Mar 45. No. 810.6091 series. Reel Nos. A8041–A8044. [These reports are listed under various names in the indexes to these reels.]

ETO: IX Troop Carrier Command. Tactical Employment—Aircraft and Glider, 1941–1945. No. 546.04. Reel No. C5017.

HQ USAAF. Collected Interviews with General Officers of CBI in Connection with the Report on "A History of Air Operations in Continental Asia." No. 105.5-13. Reel No. K1019.

HQ USAAF. D.D. Requirement and Resources Branch, Sep 43–Jul 45. No. 121.40. Reel No. A1022.

HQ USAAF. Activity Report O.C. & R., Mar–Dec 43. No. 123.2. Reel No. A1039.

HQ USAAF. AC/AS Oper. Requirements, Nov 43–Jul 45. No. 123-2. Reel No. A1040.

HQ USAAF. Troop Carrier Branch, Mar–Jul 44. No. 123.2036. Reel No. A1044.

HQ USAAF. Oper. Division, Jun 43–Dec 45. No. 123.305. Reel No. A1045.

HQ USAAF. Org. Division, Dec 43–Dec 45. No. 123.306. Reel No. A1046.

HQ USAAF. Military Requirements/Requirements Division, Jun 43–Jun 45. No. 123.309. Reel Nos. A1046A-A1047.

HQ USAAF. USAAF Evaluation Board, Aug 44–Jul 45. Nos. 138.7-5, -6 -8, 138.7A. Reel No. A1179.

HQ USAAF. Air Staff Intelligence, Jun and Jul 1943. No. 142.052. Reel No. A1272.

HQ USAAF. Air Staff Intelligence [Various Subjects]. No. 142.053 series. Reel Nos. A1274–A1278.

HQ USAAF. Tactical Reconnaissance, 1944. No. 143.04J. Reel No. A1329.

HQ USAAF. Miscellaneous—Officers, 1944–1945. No. 145.81-80. Reel No. A1372.

HQ USAAF. Airborne Study for AC/AS Plan. No. 145.81-170. Reel No. A1378.

HQ USAAF. Reading Files, Feb–Dec 1944. No. 145.81-171. Reel No. A1378.

HQ USAAF. General Letters, Oct, Dec 1943. No. 168.492. Reel Nos. A1674 and A1676.

HQ USAAF. Troop Carrier. No. 248.271-12. Reel No. A2812.

HQ USAAF. Battle of Burma. No. 248.272-2. Reel No. A2812.

HQ USAAF. Glider Operations, Sep 1944. No. 248.532-63B. Reel No. A2891.

Papers and Minutes of Quadrant Conference, Aug 1943. National Archives, Records of the War Department General and Special Staffs: Record Group 165.

Papers and Minutes of Sextant and Eureka Conferences, Nov–Dec 1943. National Archives, Records of the War Department General and Special Staffs: Record Group 165.

Southwest Pacific Area (SWPA): Far East Air Forces. FEAF Conferences, Sep–Nov 44. No. 720.151. Reel No. A7247.

SWPA: Far East Air Forces. FEAF General Correspondence, Jun–Oct 44. No. 720.161-3. Reel No. A7247.

SWPA: Far East Air Forces. FEAF Journal/Conversational Journal, Aug 44–Jun 45. No. 720.13. Reel No. A7246.

SWPA: Far East Air Forces. Narrative Mission Reports, 3 Jan–4 Mar 45. No. 720.333. Reel Nos. A7314, A7316.

SWPA: Far East Air Forces. FEAF Aircraft Authorization, n.d. No. 720.53. Reel No. A7349.

SWPA: Far East Air Forces. Operation Blacklist, Aug–Nov 45. No. 720.97A. Reel No. A7352.

SWPA: Far East Air Forces. Troop Movement Directives, Aug and Nov 45. No. 720.97A. Reel No. A7352.

SWPA: Fifth Air Force. 5th AF History, Sep–Dec 45. No. 730.01. Reel No. A7388.

SWPA: Fifth Air Force. 5th AF Correspondence, Jul 44–Dec 45. No. 730.161. Reel No. A7403.

SWPA: Fifth Air Force. 5th AF Letters, Apr 43–Oct 45. No. 730.161-3. Reel No. A7403.

SWPA: Fifth Air Force. 5th AF General Orders, Jan–May 45. AFHRA No. 730.193. Reel No. A7446.

SWPA: Fifth Air Force. 5th AF Movement Orders, Jan–Dec 45. No. 730.226. Reel No. A7449.

SWPA: Fifth Air Force. 5th AF Commendations, Mar 43–Aug 45. No. 730.2981. Reel No. A7452.

SWPA: Fifth Air Force. 5th AF History A-3 Section, Jan–Sep 45. No. 730.302. Reel no. A7452.

SWPA: Fifth Air Force. 5th AF Operation X, Apr 45. No. 730.321-1. Reel No. A7467.

SWPA: Fifth Air Force. 5th AF Daily Intelligence Summary, 1 Jan 45–29 Jul 45. No. 730.606. Reel Nos. A7476 and A7477.

SWPA: V Fighter Command. History 5th Fighter Command, Jan–Dec 45. No. 731.01. Reel No. A7498.

SWPA: V Fighter Command. 5th Fighter Command Casualties, Apr–Sep 45. No. 731.288. Reel No. A7500.

SWPA: V Fighter Command. 5th Fighter Command Daily Journal, Jul 44–Dec 45. No. 731.305. Reel No. A7500.

SWPA: V Fighter Command. 5th Fighter Command Combat Evaluation Report, Apr 44–Aug 45. No. 731.310. Reel No. A7501.

SWPA: V Fighter Command. 5th Fighter Command Journal, Feb–May 45. No. 731.667. Reel No. A7503.

SWPA: 308th Bomb Wing. Nos. WG-308-HI, WG-308-SU, and WG-308-SU-MG. Reel Nos. C0118–C0119, C0125.

Official Publications

British Air Ministry. *Wings of the Phoenix*. London: His Majesty's Stationery Office, 1949.

Craven, Wesley F., and James L. Crate, eds. *The Army Air Forces in World War II*. Vol. 4, *The Pacific: Guadalcanal to Saipan, August 1942 to July 1944*. Washington, D.C.: Office of Air Force History, 1983. Reprint.

―――. *The Army Air Forces in World War II*. Vol. 5, *The Pacific: Matterhorn to Nagasaki, June 1944 to August 1945*. Washington, D.C.: Office of Air Force History, 1983. Reprint.

Ehrman, John. *Grand Strategy*. Vol. V, *August 1943–September 1944*. London: Her Majesty's Stationery Office, 1956.

Kirby, S. Woodlawn, et al. *The War against Japan*. Vol. 2, *India's Most Dangerous Hour*. London: Her Majesty's Stationery Office, 1958.

―――. *The War against Japan*. Vol. 3, *The Decisive Battles*. London: Her Majesty's Stationery Office, 1961.

―――. *The War against Japan*. Vol. 5, *The Reconquest of Burma*. London: Her Majesty's Stationery Office, 1965.

Link, Mae Mills, and Herbert A. Coleman. *Medical Support of the Army Air Forces in World War II*. Washington, D.C.: Office of the Surgeon General, USAF, 1955.

Mason, Herbert A., Jr., et al. *Operation Thursday: Birth of the Air Commandos*. Washington, D.C.: Air Force History and Museums Program, 1994.

Matloff, Maurice. *Strategic Planning for Coalition Warfare, 1943–1944*. United States Army in

World War II: The War Department. Washington, D.C.: Office of the Center for Military History, 1959.

Maurer Maurer, ed. *Air Force Combat Units of World War II*. Washington, D.C.: Office of Air Force History, 1983.

Mayock, Thomas J. *The Twelfth Air Force in the North African Winter Campaign, 11 November 1942 to the Reorganization of 18 February 1943*. USAF Historical Study No. 114 [ex-AAFRH No. 14]. Washington, D.C.: USAAF Historical Division, 1946.

Mountbatten of Burma, Vice Admiral the Earl. *Report to the Combined Chiefs of Staff by the Supreme Allied Commander, South-East Asia 1943–1945*. London: His Majesty's Stationery Office, 1951.

Romanus, Charles F., and Riley Sunderland. *Stilwell's Mission to China*. United States Army in World War II: The China–Burma–India Theater. Washington, D.C.: Office of the Center of Military History, 1953.

———. *Stilwell's Command Problems*. United States Army in World War II: The China–Burma–India Theater. Washington, D.C.: Office of the Chief of Military History, 1956.

———. *Time Runs Out in CBI*. United States Army in World War II: The China–Burma–India Theater. Washington, D.C.: Office of the Center for Military History, 1959.

Saunders, Hilary St. George. *The Fight Is Won*. Vol. 3, *Royal Air Force, 1939–1945*. London: Her Majesty's Stationery Office, 1954.

Taylor, Joe G. *Air Supply in the Burma Campaigns*. USAF Historical Study No. 75. Maxwell AFB, Ala.: April 1957.

Victory in Burma. New York: British Information Services, July 1945.

Books

Allen, Louis. *Burma: The Longest War*. New York: St. Martin's Press, 1984.

Baisden, Chuck. *Flying Tiger to Air Commando*. Santa Fe, N. Mex.: Mustang International Publishers, 1994.

Bidwell, Shelford. *The Chindit War*. New York: Macmillan Publishing Co., 1979.

Bierman, John, and Colin Smith. *Fire in the Night*. New York: Random House, 1999.

Bryant, Arthur. *The Turn of the Tide*. Garden City, N.Y.: Doubleday & Co., 1957.

Callahan, Raymond. *Burma, 1942–1945*. Newark, Del.: University of Delaware Press, 1979.

Calvert, Michael. *Prisoners of Hope*. London: Jonathan Cape, 1952.

———. *Chindit--Long Range Penetration*. New York: Ballantine Books, 1973.

Charlton, James, ed. *The Military Quotation Book*. New York: St. Martin's Press, 1990.

Chennault, Claire Lee. *Way of a Fighter*. New York: G. P. Putnam's Sons, 1949.

Chinnery, Philip D. *Any Time, Any Place*. Annapolis: Naval Institute Press, 1994.

———. *March or Die: The Story of Wingate's Chindits*. Shrewbury, UK: Airlife Publishing, 1997.

Cornelius, Wanda, and Thayne Short. *Ding Hao: America's Air War in China 1937–1945*. Gretna, La.: Pelican Publishing Co., 1980.

Detwiler, Donald S., and Charles B. Burdick, eds. *War in Asia and the Pacific*. Vol. 6, pt. 1, *The Southern Area*. New York: Garland Publishing, 1980.

Devlin, Gerard M. *Silent Wings*. New York: St. Martin's Press, 1985.

Donald, David. *American Warplanes of World War II*. London: Aerospace Publishing, 1995.

Fellowes-Gordon, Ian. *The Magic War*. New York: Charles Scribner's Sons, 1971.

Fergusson, Bernard. *The Wild Green Earth*. London: Collins, 1952.

Hawley, Dennis. *The Death of Wingate and Subsequent Events*. Braunton, UK: Merlin Books, 1994.

Hayes, Grace Person. *The History of the Joint Chiefs of Staff in World War II: The War against Japan*. Annapolis: Naval Institute Press, 1982.

Hickey, Michael. *The Unforgettable Army*. Tunbridge Wells, UK: Spellmont, 1992.

James, Richard Rhodes. *Chindit*. London: John Murray, 1980.

Larrabee, Eric. *Commander in Chief*. New York: Harper & Row, 1987.

Mahurin, Walker M. *Honest John*. New York: G. P. Putnam's Sons, 1962.

Masters, John. *The Road past Mandalay*. New York: Bantam Books, 1979.

Mead, Peter. *Orde Wingate and the Historians*. Braunton, UK: Merlin Books, 1987.

Molesworth, Carl. *Sharks over China*. Washington, D.C.: Brassey's, 1994.

Mosley, Leonard. *Gideon Goes to War*. New York: Charles Scribner's Sons, 1955.

O'Brien, Terence. *Out of the Blue*. London: Collins, 1984.

Page, Robert Collier. *Air Commando Doc*. As told to Alfred Aiken. New York: Bernard Ackerman, 1945.

Probert, Henry. *The Forgotten Air Force: The Royal Air Force in the War against Japan 1941– 1945*. London: Brassey's, 1995.

Rooney, David. *Burma Victory*. London: Arms and Armour Press, 1992.

———. *Wingate and the Chindits: Redressing the Balance*. London: Arms and Armour Press, 1994.

Royle, Trevor. *Orde Wingate: Irregular Soldier*. London: Weidenfeld & Nicolson, 1994.

Slim, William. *Defeat into Victory*. New York: David McKay Company, 1961.

Smith, E. D. *Battle for Burma*. New York: Holmes and Meier Publishers, 1979.

Stanaway, John C., and Lawrence Hickey. *Attack and Conquer: The 8th Fighter Group in World War II*. Atglen, Pa.: Schiffer Publishing, 1995.

Sunderland, Riley, and Charles F. Romanus. *Stilwell's Personal File: China–Burma–India, 1942–1944*. 5 vol. Wilmington, Del.: Scholarly Resources, 1976.

Sykes, Christopher. *Orde Wingate*. Cleveland, Ohio: The World Publishing Co., 1959.

Thomas, Lowell. *Back to Mandalay*. New York: The Greystone Press, 1951.

Tulloch, Derek. *Wingate in Peace and War*. Edited by Arthur Swinson. London: History Book Club, 1972.

Turnbull, Patrick. *Battle of the Box*. London: Ian Allan, 1979.

Van Wagner, R. D. *Any Place, Any Time, Anywhere: The 1st Air Commandos in World War II*. Atglen, Pa.: Schiffer Publishing, 1998.

War Reports of General of the Army George C. Marshall, General of the Army H. H. Arnold, Fleet Admiral Ernest J. King. Philadelphia; J. B. Lippincott Co., 1947.

Warner, Philip. *Auchinleck: The Lonely Soldier*. London: Buchan & Enright, 1981.

Young, Edward. *The Air Commando Fighters of World War II*. North Branch, Minn.: Voyageur Press, 2000.

Ziegler, Philip. *Mountbatten*. New York: Alfred A. Knopf, 1985.

Newspapers and Periodicals

Alison, John R. "Glider Invasion—A Jungle Epic." *New York Times Magazine*, May 1, 1944, 34–5.

Arnold, H. H. "The Aerial Invasion of Burma." *National Geographic* 86 (August 1944): 129–48.

Bachmann, L. P. "Burma RFD." *Air Force*, June 1945.

Bainbridge, John. "'Flip Corkin.'" *Life*, August 9, 1943, 42–8.

Bellah, James W. "Long Range Penetration Groups." *Infantry Journal* 55 (October 1944): 45–7.

Bellah, James Warner. "The Air Commando Tradition." *Air Force*, February 1963, 69–76.

Cunningham, Ed. "Burma Air Invasion." *Yank*, May 5, 1944, American edition, 2–5.

———. "Twelve Thousand Miles from Griffith Stadium." *Yank*, July 28, 1944, American edition, 23.

Dickson, H. B. "Our Troop Carriers in Burma." *Air Force*, June 1944, 4–5.

Hawley, Dennis. "The Death of Orde Wingate." *After the Battle*, no. 96 (May 1997): 1–13.

McCann, John A. "Air Power and 'The Man.'" *Air Power Historian* 6 (April 1959): 108–24.

Mead, P. W. "The Chindit Operations of 1944." *Journal of the Royal United Service Institution* 100 (May 1955): 250–62.

Miller, Merle. "The Real Flip Corkin." *Yank*, August 4, 1944, American edition, 10–11.

Nenninger, Timothy K. "United States Prisoners of War and the Red Army, 1944–45: Myths and Realities." *Journal of Military History* 66 (July 2002): 761–81.

Richardson, Dave. "Rangoon Jump." *Yank*, June 22, 1945, American edition, 8–9.

Rossetto, Luigi. "The First Air Commandos." *Aerospace Historian* 29 (Spring/March 1982): 2–12.

Sciutti, W. J. "The First Air Commando Group August 1943–May 1944." *American Aviation Historical Society Journal* 13 (Fall 1968): 178–85.

Young, Edward. "Counter-Air: The 2nd Air Commando Group in Burma and Thailand." *Air Enthusiast* 69 (Spring 1994).

Interviews

Alison, John R., interview by Kenneth Leish, July 1960. No. K146.34.2. Reel No. K1213.

Alison, Maj. Gen. John R., interview by Maj Scottie S. Thompson, April 22–28, 1979. USAF Oral History Collection, No. K239.0512-1121.

Alison, Maj. Gen. John R., USAF (Ret.), interview by William T. Y'Blood, July 23, 1996.

Carter, Olin B., interview by Edward M. Young, September 18–21, 1996. In author's possession.

Cochran, Col. Philip G., interview by Dr. James C. Hasdorff, October 20–21 and November 11, 1975. USAF Oral History Collection, No. K239.0512-876.

Eason, W. Robert, Dale L. Grastorf, and Charles Le Fan, interview by Edward M. Young, October 13, 1995. In author's possession.

Hall, Benton, Eugene Piester, O. B. Carter, Franklin Misfeldt, Rudy Melichar, Daniel Mitchell, Walter Radovich, and Aurele Van DeWeghe, group interview by Edward M. Young, September 18–21, 1996. In author's possession.

Klarr, Jack, interview by Edward M. Young, May 20, 1996. In author's possession.

Krout, Vincent, interview by Edward M. Young, October 14, 1995. In author's possession.

Krug, Hubert, interview by Edward M. Young, September 18–21, 1996. In author's possession.

Lahmeyer, Ray, and Jacques Young, interview by Edward M. Young, October 14, 1995. In author's possession.

Luedecke, Maj. Gen. Alvin R., interview by Dr. James C. Hasdorff, July 7–8, 1987. USAF Oral History Collection, No. K239.0512-1759.

Lynn, Roland, interview by Edward M. Young, September 18–21, 1996. In author's possession.

McConnell, Gen. John P., interview by unknown interviewer, September 24, 1971. USAF Oral History Collection, No. K239.0512-611.

Stone, Lt. Gen. Charles B., III, interview by Capt. Mark C. Cleary, April 26–28, 1984. USAF Oral History Collection, No. K239.0512-1585.

Other Works

Arnold, Gen. H. H. Papers. Washington, D.C.: Manuscript Division, Library of Congress.

Arnold, Gen H. H. Papers. Murray Green Collection. Colorado Springs, Colo.: U.S. Air Force Academy.

Cannon, Hardy D. *Box Seat over Hell.* Privately printed, 1985.

"Chindit Operations in Burma." In *Symposium on the Role of Airpower in Counterinsurgency and Unconventional Warfare,* ed. by A. H. Peterson, et al. RAND Memorandum RM-3654—PR. San Diego: RAND, July 1963.

Chindits Old Comrades' Association. *Major General O. C. Wingate, D.S.O.* Privately printed, 1982.

King, Barbara P., and Edward M. Leete. *The 1st Air Commando Group of World War II: An Historical Perspective.* Maxwell AFB, Ala.: Air Command and Staff College, Air University, May 1977.

Rossetto, Luigi. *Major-General Orde Charles Wingate and the Development of Long-Range Penetration.* Manhattan, Kans.: MA/AH Publishing, 1982.

Stratemeyer, Lt. Gen. George E. Personal Diary, 1943–1947. Thomas Overlander Collection. Colorado Springs, Colo: U.S. Air Force Academy.

Thompson, Tommy, ed. *Highlights—The 318th Troop Carrier Squadron, Commando, October 1943 to October 1945.* Privately printed, n.d.

Torres, John J. *Historical Analysis of the 1st Air Commando Group Operations in the CBI Theater, August 1943 to May 1944.* Maxwell AFB, Ala.: Air Command and Staff College, Air University, March 1997.

Van Wagner, R. D. *1st Air Commando Group: Any Place, Any Time, Anywhere.* Military History Series 86-1. Maxwell AFB, Ala.: Air Command and Staff College, Air University, 1986.

World War II Air Commando Association. Newsletters, January 1994–May 2002.

World War II Air Commandos. *History of the World War II Air Commandos.* Vols. 1 and 2. Dallas, Tex.: Taylor Publishing Company, 1989, 1994.

World War II Glider Pilots. Paducah, Ky.: Turner Publishing, 1991.

Index

way, 95; Joe Brown appearance, 241; Project 9 assignment, 34; reconnassiance flight and photos, 88–90; 3rd ACG assignment, 207

San Nicolas, Luzon, 234–35
Sarangani Bay, 208–9
Sartor, Samuel O., 230
Sartz, Jacob P., 33, 35
Satterstrom, John E., 206, 230
Scalley, Robert, 227
Schneider, Erle H., 110
Scott, Walter, 90–91, 95
2nd Air Commandos (2nd ACG): activation of, 152; CBI, movement to, 158–59, 160–61; command arrangements, 152–53, 154; control of, 150, 155, 163; creation of, ix; demand for, x; inactivation of, 247–48; markings for planes of, 162–63; Operation Grubworm, 159–60; organizational structure of, 125; performance of, 248–49; planes for, 124, 162–63; readiness dates, 155; return to U.S., 199; service groups to support, 150–51, 155; training of, 156–58; transfers from, 197–99; use of, 155–56
Seese, Donald E., 82, 95
Setnor, Joe, 135
77th Indian Brigade, viii, 5. *See also* Chindits
Shaw, Troy C., 82
Shenam Saddle, 75
Shwebo airfield, 77, 79, 107, 108, 109, 110–11, 117, 118
Shwebo–Myitkina railway, 9
Sikorsky, Igor, 31
Sikorsky XR-4 helicopters, 31. See also helicopters
Singkaling Hkamti, 83
Singletary, Joseph, 236
Sinzweya, 81
Skalin, Peter, 126
Slater, Frank J., 154
Slim, William J.: Box, Battle of the, 81; Broadway, decision to only use, 91; command arrangements, 42; 1st ACG as private air force for Wingate, 59; 1st ACG, control of, 70; HA-GO

(Z Operation), 75; Operation Multivite, 144; Operation Thursday, 71, 88; Rangoon, capture of, 190; reconnassiance flight and photos, 90; 2nd ACG, success of, 165
Slocumb, Tyler H., 154
Smith, Everett F., 34, 64
Smith, Robert T. "Tadpole", 33, 65, 67–68, 77, 78, 89, 118
Smith, Samson, 33
Snecker, Thomas P., 224
Solomon, Bertram E., 206
Somerville, James, 42
Sorenson, Sherard A., 184
Southeast Asia Command (SEAC), 12–13, 41–44, 133–34
Spaatz, Carl A., 23, 123
Spann, Bobby J., 177–78, 181, 182, 183–84
Special Forces (3rd Indian Division): command arrangements, 52, 53; 1st ACG as private air force for, 59–60; formation of, 55; gliders to transport, 54–56; headquarters of, 53; maneuvers, 65–70; Operation Thursday, 70, 71; supplies for, 56, 63, 72; training of, 52, 61; troop strength, 52; withdrawal of, 127
Special Night Squads, 4
Stewart, Ray E., 126
Stillwell, Joseph "Vinegar Joe": Air Commandos, use of, 156; air transport need requirements, 47, 54; character of, 42; Chiang, relationship with, 127–29; Chindits, use of, 127; command arrangements, 41, 42, 43, 52; evacuation of wounded, 79; 1st ACG assignment, 38; Operation Thursday, ix; removal of, 128, 129, 156
Stinson Field, 220
Stone, Charles B., III, 42
Strategic Force, 44
Stratemeyer, George: ACG, use of, 124, 156; bomber support for LRPGs, 64–65; bombing missions, success of, 111; Broadway, activity at, 100; C-47 replacement, 61; command arrangements, 43, 44; command headquarters, 125; Don Muang airfield

About the Author

William T. Y'Blood, a pilot in the U.S. Air Force and later in commercial aviation, served as a historian for the Air Force at Bolling Air Force Base. He was an avid student of military history, especially that of World War II and Korea, for over fifty years and published eight books, including three with the Naval Institute Press: *Red Sun Setting, Hunter-Killer: U.S. Escort Carriers in the Battle of the Atlantic*, and *The Little Giants: U.S. Escort Carriers against Japan*. He passed away in 2006, just after completing this book. He is survived by his wife, Carolyn; two children, Kent and Laura; and two granddaughters, Jenna and Kiera.